CONTENTS

ISBN 0 85147 637 6

First Edition 1976

839

Printed and bound in Brighton England for Autobooks Ltd by G. Beard & Son Ltd A

Datsun 140J, 160J, 710 1973-76 Autobook

By Kenneth Ball and John Plummer

Datsun 140J Violet 1973-76
Datsun 160J Violet 1976
Datsun 160J SSS Violet 1974-76
Datsun 710 1974-76

Autobooks Ltd. Golden Lane Brighton BN1 2QJ England

The AUTOBOOK series of Workshop Manuals is the largest in the world and covers the majority of British and Continental motor cars, as well as the majority of Japanese and Australian models.

ACKNOWLEDGEMENT

We wish to thank Datsun (UK) Ltd for their co-operation and also for supplying data and illustrations. Considerable assistance has also been given by owners, who have discussed their cars in detail, and we would like to express our gratitude for this invaluable advice and help.

INTRODUCTION

This do-it-yourself Workshop Manual has been specially written for the owner who wishes to maintain his vehicle in first class condition and to carry out the bulk of his own servicing and repairs. Considerable savings on garage charges can be made, and one can drive in safety and confidence knowing the work has been done properly.

Comprehensive step-by-step instructions and illustrations are given on most dismantling, overhauling and assembling operations. Certain assemblies require the use of expensive special tools, the purchase of which would be unjustified. In these cases information is included but the reader is recommended to hand the unit to the agent for attention.

Throughout the Manual hints and tips are included which will be found invaluable, and there is an easy to follow fault diagnosis at the end of each chapter.

Whilst every care has been taken to ensure correctness of information it is obviously not possible to guarantee complete freedom from errors or omissions or to accept liability arising from such errors or omissions.

Instructions may refer to the righthand or lefthand sides of the vehicle or the components. These are the same as the righthand or lefthand of an observer standing behind the vehicle and looking forward.

CHAPTER 1
THE ENGINE

1 :1 Description

The engine is an in-line, four cylinder, single overhead camshaft unit. The camshaft is driven by a double row roller chain from a sprocket on the crankshaft. Chain tension is controlled by a rubber pad which is operated by spring and oil pressure. The camshaft operates the valves through finger type rockers, threaded adjusters being provided at the rocker pivots for adjustment of valve clearances.

The cast iron cylinder block is integral with the upper half of the crankcase, the lower half of which is formed by the pressed steel sump. The five bearing counter-balanced crankshaft is a special steel casting. Crankshaft end thrust is taken by thrust rings at the centre main bearing position. The main and big-end bearings are provided with renewable shell type inserts. Cross sections through an L16 engine are shown in **FIG 1 :1**, this unit being typical of the range. Full details of engine types and specifications are given in **Technical Data**.

A rotor type oil pump, driven from a gear on the crankshaft, draws oil from the sump beneath the engine and forces it through the fullflow oil filter into the main oil gallery. From this point the oil is routed to the main and big-end bearings and to the camshaft support bearings. Oil from the camshaft bearings is fed to the rocker arms, valve stems and cam lobes through the oil gallery in the camshaft and the small channel at the base circle of each cam. The pistons and cylinders are lubricated directly by supply jets in the connecting rods and indirectly by oil splash from the big-end bearings. A relief valve is fitted to the system to limit the maximum oil pressure when the engine is cold. **FIG 1 :2** shows the layout of the engine lubrication system.

1 :2 Removing the engine

The standard operations of decarbonising and servicing the cylinder head can be carried out without the need for engine removal, as can the majority of engine servicing procedures. A major overhaul, however, can only be satisfactorily carried out with the engine removed and transferred to the bench. For some overhaul work, certain special tools are essential and the owner would be well advised to check on the availability of these factory tools or suitable substitutes before tackling the items involved. If the operator is not a skilled automobile engineer, it is suggested that much useful information will be found in **Hints on Maintenance and Overhaul** at the end of this manual and that it is read before starting work. It

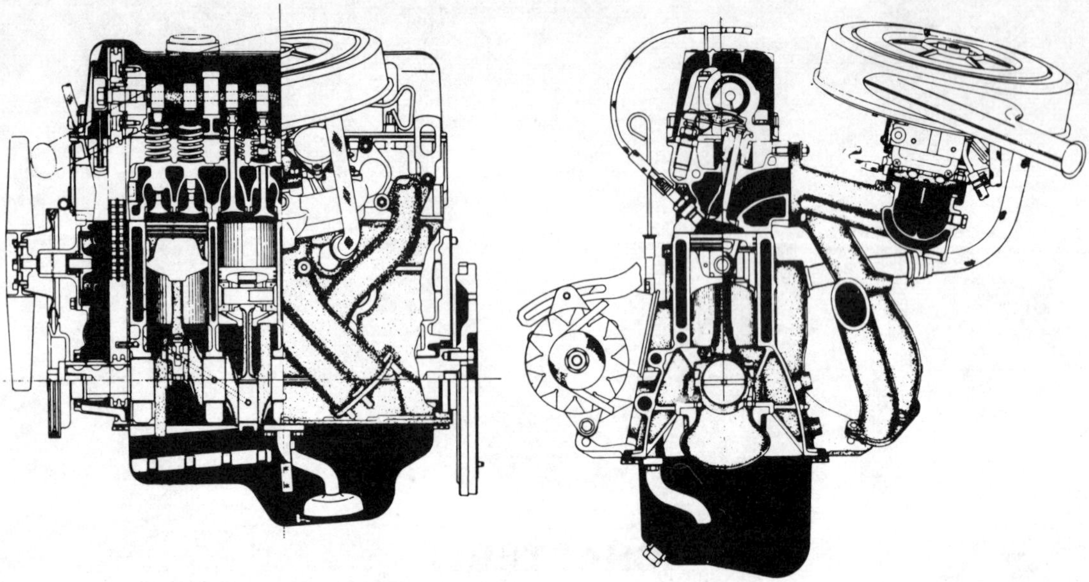

FIG 1:1 Sections through the L16 engine assembly

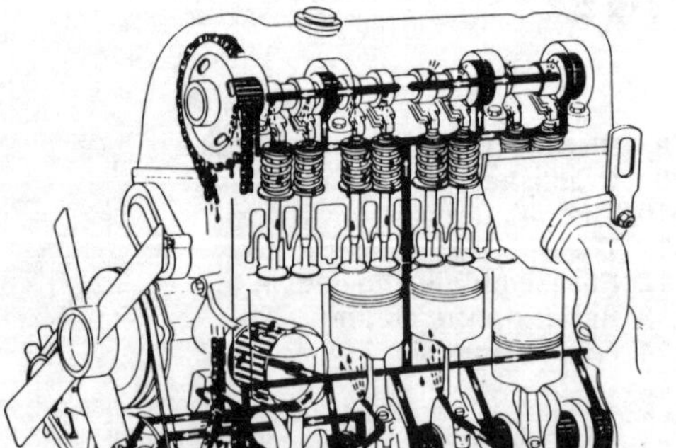

FIG 1:2 Layout of the engine lubrication system

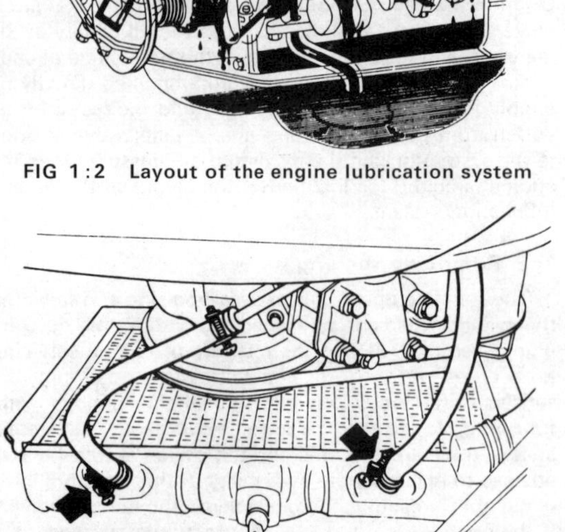

FIG 1:3 Removing automatic transmission oil cooler hoses

must be stressed that the lifting equipment used to remove the engine from the car should be sound, firmly based and not likely to collapse under the weight it will be supporting. The engine and transmission are removed as a single unit, then the transmission separated from the engine.

Owners of vehicles fitted with air-conditioning (refrigeration) systems should consult a Datsun service station before attempting engine removal procedures, so that advice can be obtained on any necessary system discharging and component removal procedures required. If the pressurised system is opened, liquid refrigerant will escape, immediately evaporating and instantly freezing anything it contacts. Uncontrolled release of the refrigerant will cause severe frostbite or possibly more serious injury if it contacts any part of the body. For this reason, all work involving air-conditioning system components should be entrusted only to a Datsun service station having the necessary special equipment and trained personnel.

Removal:

1 Disconnect the battery earth cable. Mark around the bonnet hinges to ensure correct refitting, then remove the bonnet.

2 Drain the cooling system and the engine sump. Remove the radiator grille. Disconnect the radiator upper and lower hoses.

3 On models fitted with automatic transmission, remove the splash board then disconnect the oil cooler hoses from the bottom of the radiator as shown in **FIG 1:3**. Plug the outlets and hoses to avoid loss of fluid. Disconnect the vacuum hose and disconnect the

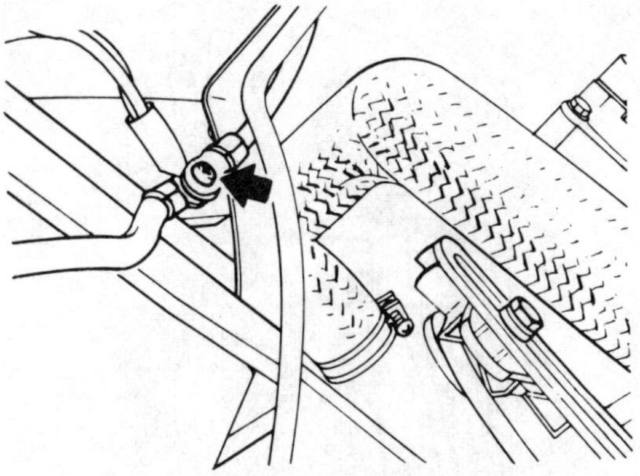

FIG 1:4 The engine earth cable connection

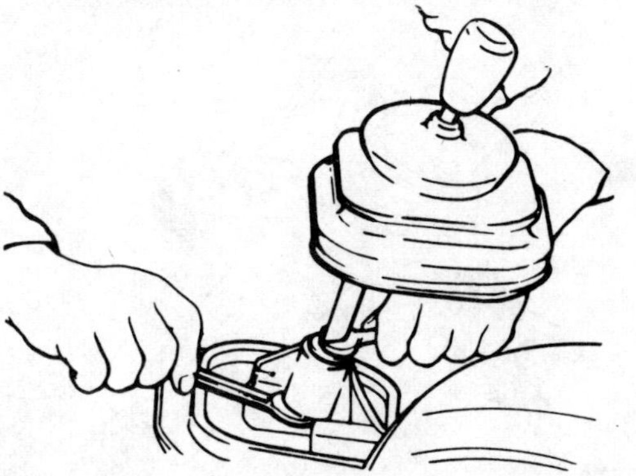

FIG 1:5 Removing the four-speed floor mounted gearlever

wiring connections from the inhibitor switch and downshift solenoid.

4 Remove the four bolts securing the radiator to the body and detach the radiator and radiator shroud if fitted.

5 Disconnect the engine earth cable at the body connection end as shown in **FIG 1:4**. Disconnect the hose(s) from the air cleaner then remove the air cleaner assembly.

6 Disconnect the accelerator linkage and choke cable at the carburetter, and the fuel hose at the fuel pump. Disconnect the high tension lead from the ignition coil.

7 Disconnect the two connector plugs for the engine compartment main wiring harness. Disconnect the vacuum hose from the servo unit, if fitted. Disconnect the heater hoses, if fitted.

8 On manual transmission models, remove the clutch slave cylinder without disconnecting the fluid hose.

9 Disconnect the speedometer cable from the transmission rear extension housing.

10 On models with the four-speed manual transmission, remove the gearlever as shown in **FIG 1:5**.
On models fitted with automatic transmission, disconnect the selector lever from the shaft as shown in **FIG 1:6**.
On models with the five-speed manual transmission, with the gearlever in neutral position remove the E clip indicated in **FIG 1:7** and withdraw the gearlever pivot pin and gearlever.

11 Disconnect the front exhaust pipe from the exhaust manifold. Disconnect the propeller shaft as described in **Chapter 8**.

12 On models fitted with five-speed transmission, remove the centre bearing bracket assembly from the floor panel, as shown in **FIG 1:8**.

13 Withdraw the sleeve yoke from the rear extension housing, plugging the end of the transmission to prevent oil leakage. Support the weight of the transmission with a suitable jack.

14 Refer to **FIG 1:9** and remove the two rear engine mounting nuts 1. Remove the four mounting member securing bolts 2 and detach the mounting member.

15 Securely attach the lifting equipment to the engine and raise sufficiently to take the weight of engine and

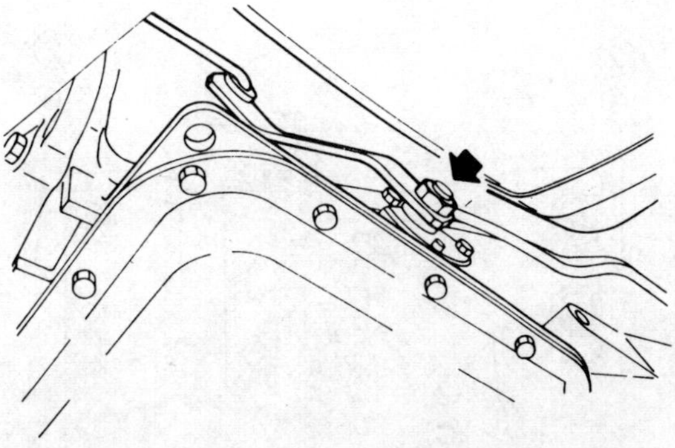

FIG 1:6 Disconnecting automatic transmission selector lever

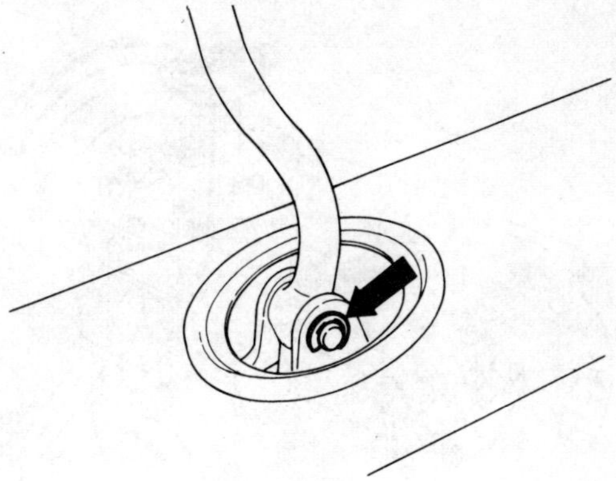

FIG 1:7 Removing the five-speed floor mounted gearlever

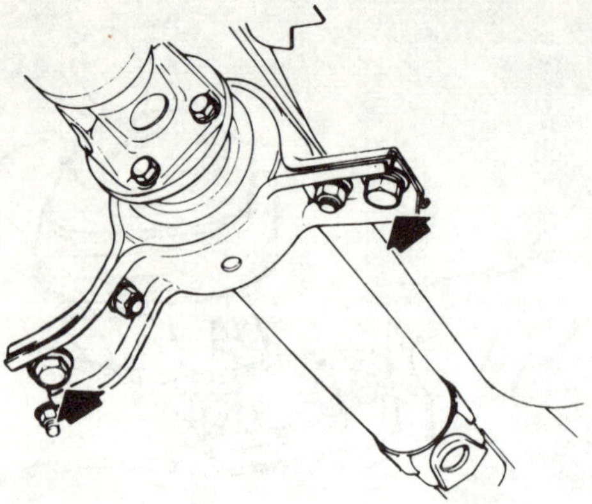

FIG 1:8 Five-speed transmission centre bearing removal

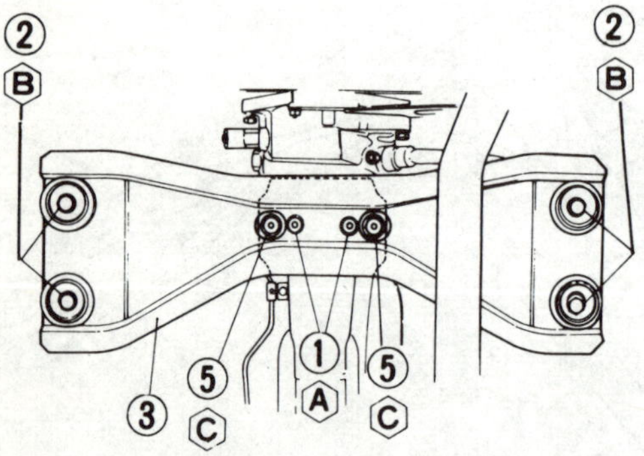

FIG 1:9 Engine rear mounting details. The numbers are referred to in the text

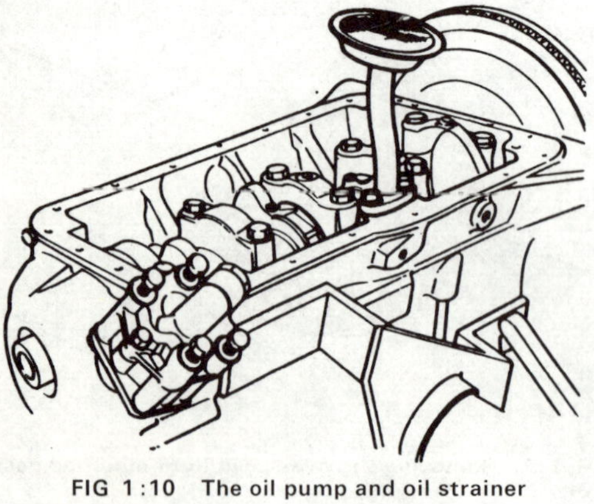

FIG 1:10 The oil pump and oil strainer

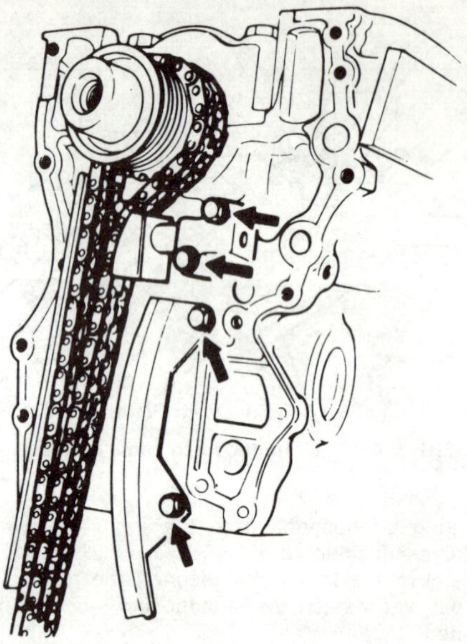

FIG 1:11 Removing timing chain, tensioner and guide

transmission assembly. Remove the bolts securing the engine support to the front mounting insulators. Raise the engine and transmission fully to remove from the car, tilting the assembly to clear the front and rear of the engine compartment. Detach the transmission from the engine.

1:3 Dismantling the engine

Before dismantling the engine, thoroughly clean and degrease the exterior of the unit to prevent contamination of the internal components. Use a suitable engine stand if available, or support the unit on wooden blocks during dismantling, to prevent damage.

1 Remove the alternator and drive belt. Remove the fan and fan pulley. Remove the righthand engine mounting. Unscrew and remove the oil filter, using a suitable tool if it is stiff to turn. Remove the oil pressure switch and the oil level dipstick.
2 Lock the flywheel against rotation by suitable means, then remove the crankshaft pulley. Refer to **Chapter 5** and remove the clutch assembly from the flywheel.
3 Remove the high tension cables and sparking plugs. Loosen the clamps and disconnect the hoses for the crankcase breathing, emission control and the heating system. Disconnect the fuel pipes. Remove the EGR valve if fitted (see **Chapter 14**).
4 Remove the thermostat housing and the rocker cover from the cylinder head.
5 Refer to **Chapter 2** and remove the fuel pump and carburetter(s). Remove the inlet and exhaust manifolds.
6 Remove the lefthand engine mounting. Remove the water pump, the distributor and the fuel pump drive cam.
7 Refer to **Section 1:4** and remove the camshaft sprocket and cylinder head assembly.
8 Invert the engine and remove the oil sump. Remove

the oil strainer and the oil pump with drive spindle as shown in **FIG 1:10**.

9 Remove the front cover from the crankcase, then remove the chain tensioner and side guide as shown in **FIG 1:11**. Remove the timing chain, oil thrower and crankshaft worm gear. Use a suitable puller to remove the chain drive sprocket as shown in **FIG 1:12**.

10 Mark the connecting rods and bearing caps so that they can be reassembled in their exact original locations. Unbolt and remove the connecting rod caps, then remove the piston and connecting rod assemblies through the top of the cylinder bores as shown in **FIG 1:13**. Keep all components in the correct order.

11 Remove the fixing bolts and detach the flywheel as shown in **FIG 1:14**. Mark the main bearing caps so that they can be refitted in their exact original positions, then remove the cap retaining bolts. Remove the caps, using tool ST1651S000 or similar to remove the centre and rear caps as shown in **FIG 1:15**.

12 Remove the two side seals. Remove the crankshaft rear oil seal as shown in **FIG 1:16**. Lift the crankshaft from the cylinder block. Remove the baffle plate and cylinder block net as shown in **FIG 1:17**.

1:4 Removing and refitting cylinder head

Removal:

Drain the cooling system, collecting the coolant in a clean container if it is to be re-used. Refer to **Chapter 2** and remove the air cleaner and carburetter(s).

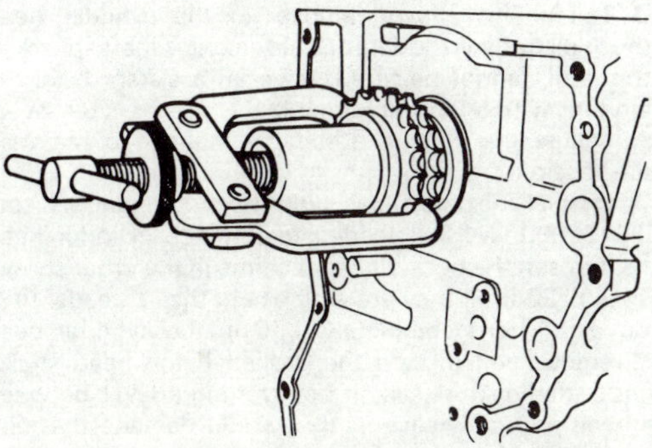

FIG 1:12 Removing timing chain drive sprocket

FIG 1:13 Removing pistons and connecting rods

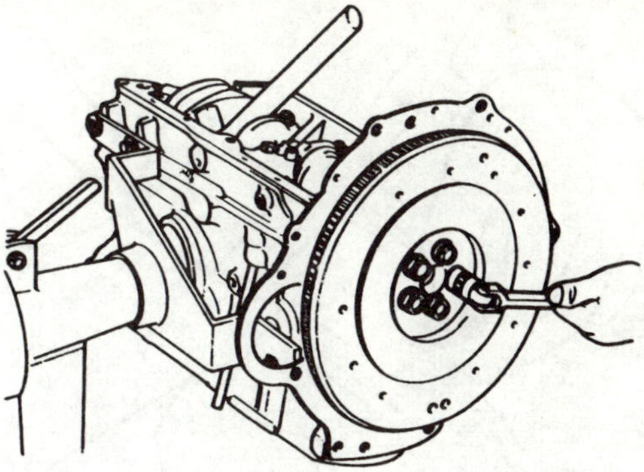

FIG 1:14 Flywheel removal

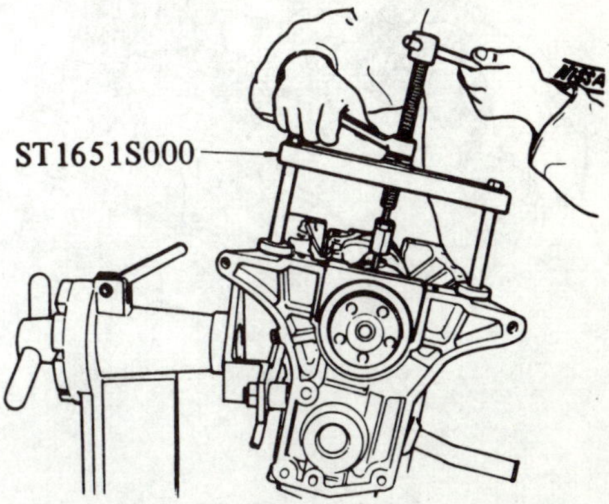

FIG 1:15 Removing rear main bearing cap

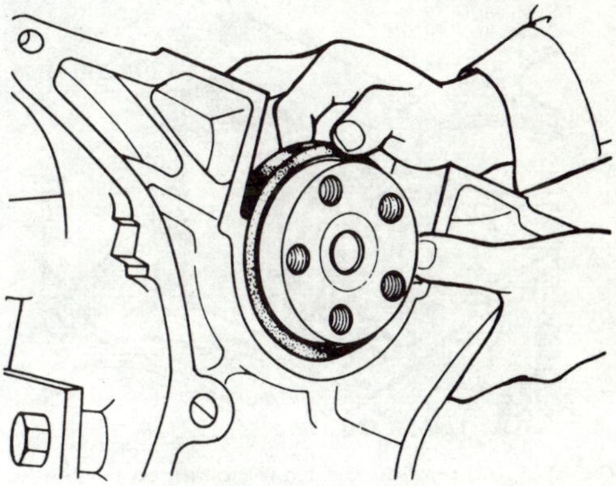

FIG 1:16 Crankshaft rear oil seal removal

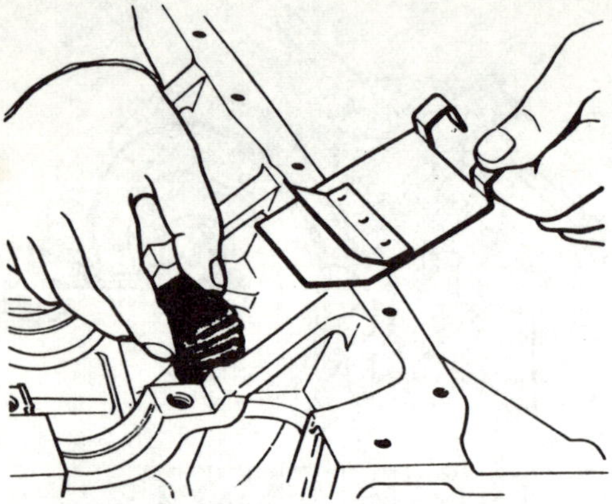

FIG 1:17 Removing baffle plate and net

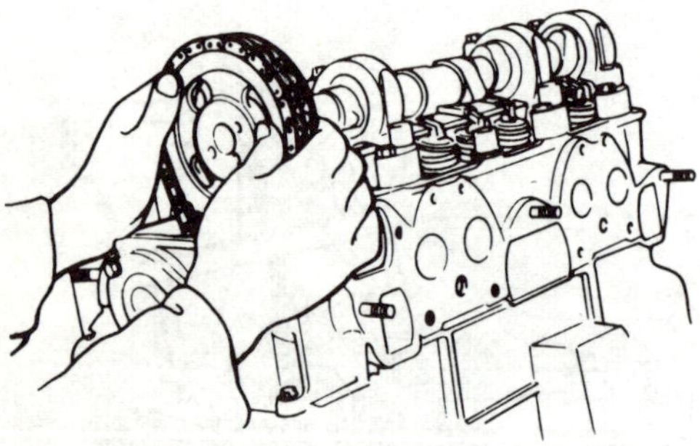

FIG 1:18 Camshaft sprocket removal

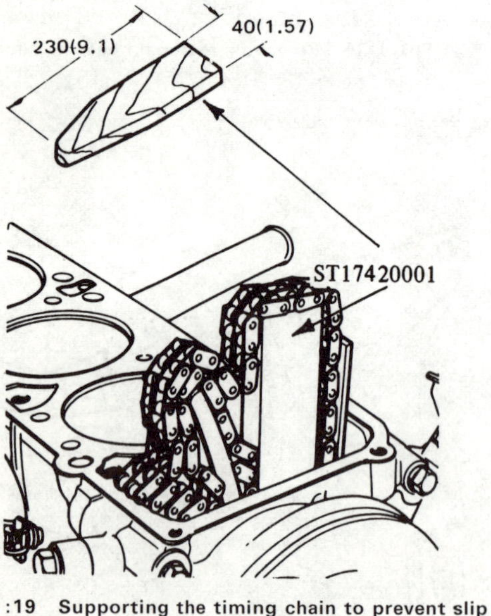

FIG 1:19 Supporting the timing chain to prevent slip on the crankshaft sprocket. Tool dimensions in mm (in) are shown

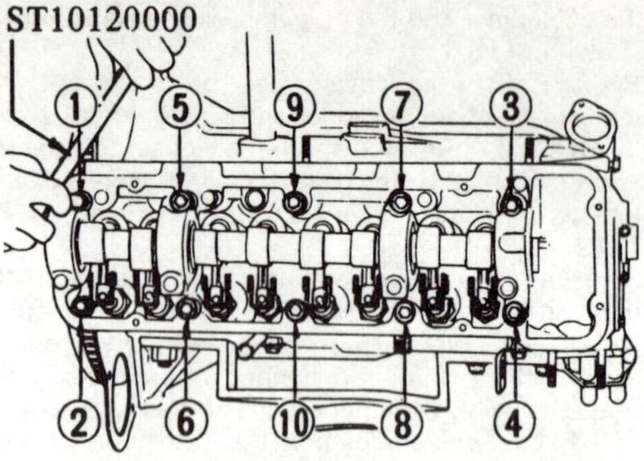

FIG 1:20 Cylinder head bolt loosening sequence

Remove the distributor cap and high tension leads. Detach any additional wiring from the cylinder head components.

Disconnect the radiator and heater hoses from the cylinder head. Remove the inlet and exhaust manifolds, the thermostat housing, the fuel pump and the rocker cover.

When the camshaft sprocket is removed from the camshaft, the timing chain must be kept taut so that it does not slip on the crankshaft sprocket. If this happens, the front cover must be removed in order to reset the valve timing correctly as described in **Section 1:6**. Remove the camshaft sprocket as shown in **FIG 1:18**. Special tool ST 17420001 can be made to support the timing chain when the sprocket is removed, as shown in **FIG 1:19**. This allows removal of the cylinder head without disturbing the settings at the crankshaft sprocket. If this tool cannot be fitted, have an assistant hold the chain taut with a loop of wire while the head is removed, then secure the wire in a suitable manner to maintain chain tension.

A special hexagon-key type wrench such as tool ST10120000, will be needed to turn the cylinder head bolts. Loosen the bolts a little at a time in the order shown in **FIG 1:20** until they are all loose in their threads, then remove the bolts completely. Lift off the cylinder head and remove and discard the gasket. If the head sticks, do not attempt to release it be inserting a lever between the head and crankcase as this would damage the joint faces. Gentle tapping with a hammer is permissible, provided that a thick piece of wood is interposed between the hammer and cylinder head to avoid damage, particularly as a light alloy head is fitted.

Refitting:

The camshaft must be correctly positioned with the timing mark on the sprocket aligned to mate with the timing mark on the chain. If the chain has been disconnected or allowed to slip on the crankshaft drive sprocket it is essential to remove the front cover and reset the valve timing as described in **Section 1:6**. **If this is not done the valves will contact the pistons and cause serious damage.**

Carefully fit a new cylinder head gasket to the cylinder block. Apply sealant to the front side of the cylinder block as described in **Section 1:12**. Make sure that the timing

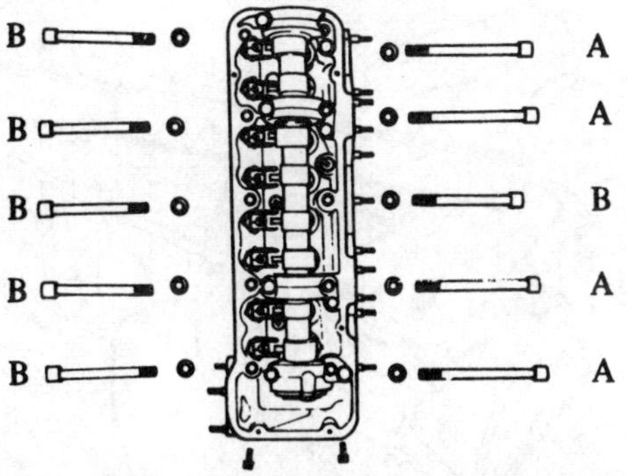

FIG 1 : 21 Locations of the cylinder head bolts, which differ in length

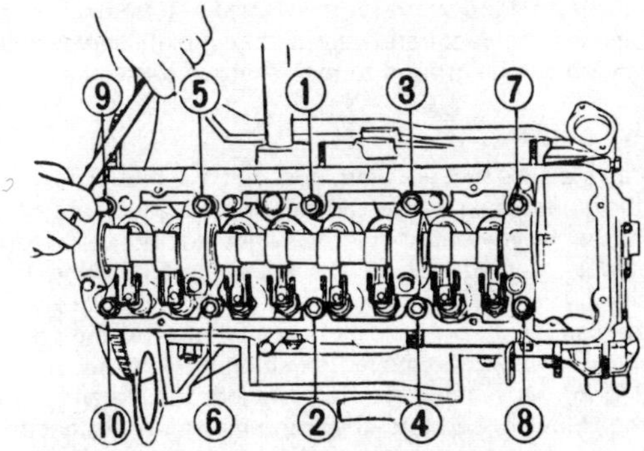

FIG 1 : 22 Cylinder head bolt tightening sequence

mark on the camshaft sprocket is set to align with the mark on the timing chain, then refit the cylinder head. Make sure that the cylinder head bolts are correctly located as shown in **FIG 1 : 21**, then install them finger tight.

Tighten the head bolts in the sequence shown in **FIG 1 : 22**, in three stages. At the first stage tighten to 4kgm (29lb ft), at second stage to 6kgm (43lb ft) and at final stage to 6.5 to 8.5kgm (47 to 61lb ft). This done, tighten the two small bolts at the front of the cylinder head.

Keeping the timing chain taut, fit the chain around the camshaft sprocket with the timing marks on chain and sprocket in alignment. Fit the sprocket to the camshaft, turning the camshaft fractionally if necessary to align the keyway. Refer to **Section 1 : 6** for details.

Install the remaining components in the reverse order of removal, using new gaskets throughout. On completion, refill the cooling system. Set the valve clearances as described in **Section 1 : 7**. Start the engine and allow it to run for a few minutes, then switch off and remove the rocker cover. Recheck the tightness of the cylinder head bolts in the correct order and to the final torque figure as described previously. Recheck the valve clearances.

1 : 5 Servicing cylinder head, camshaft and valves

Remove the cylinder head as described in **Section 1 : 4** and transfer it to the bench, taking care not to damage the joint surfaces.

Note that if the camshaft bearing assemblies are removed, or even if the mounting bolts are slackened, the alignment of the bearing bores will be disturbed. To correct misalignment it is necessary to use special in-line boring equipment and this is therefore a specialist job.

Remove the valve rocker springs. Loosen the valve rocker pivot locknut and remove the rocker arms by pressing the valve springs down, as shown in **FIG 1 : 23**. Take care not to lose the valve rocker guides. Keep all valve gear components in the correct order for refitting in their original positions. Remove the camshaft thrust plate, then carefully remove the camshaft taking care not to damage the bearings or lobes (see **FIG 1 : 24**).

Use a suitable valve spring compressor to remove the valve gear from the cylinder head. With the spring compressed, remove the split taper collets, then remove the compressor tool and collect the valve, springs, spring seats, washers, oil seal and rocker guide (see **FIG 1 : 25**). Note that L14 engines use a single inlet valve spring only. Keep all components in the correct order for refitting in their original positions.

Valves:

When the valves have been cleaned of carbon deposits, they must be inspected for serviceability. Valves with bent stems or badly burned heads must be renewed. Valves that are pitted can be recut at a service station,

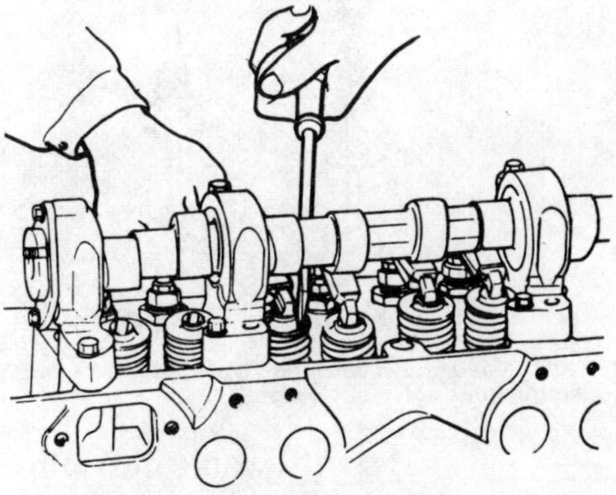

FIG 1 : 23 Rocker arm removal

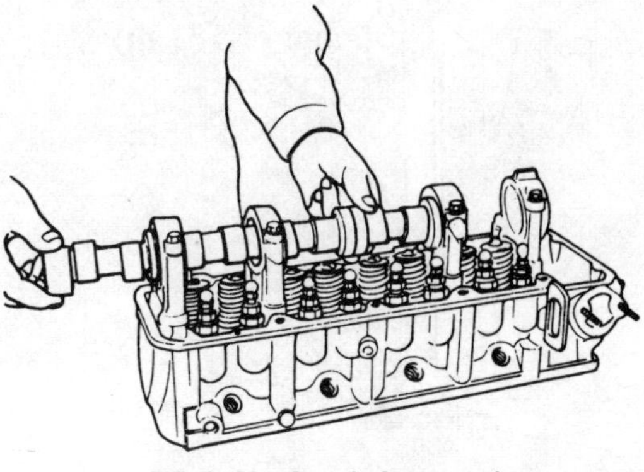

FIG 1 : 24 Camshaft removal

but if they are too worn for this remedial treatment, new valves will be required. Valves that are in serviceable condition can be ground to their seats as described later.

Valve guides:

Valve guides that are worn or scored must be renewed. As the guides must be pressed into or out of place, reamed, then the valve seat recut for concentricity, this work should be carried out by a service station having the necessary special equipment. Wear between valve and guide can be checked by refitting the valve to the guide from which it was removed, positioning it as shown in **FIG 1:26**. Move the valve stem towards the left and right of the cylinder head and check the maximum deflection.

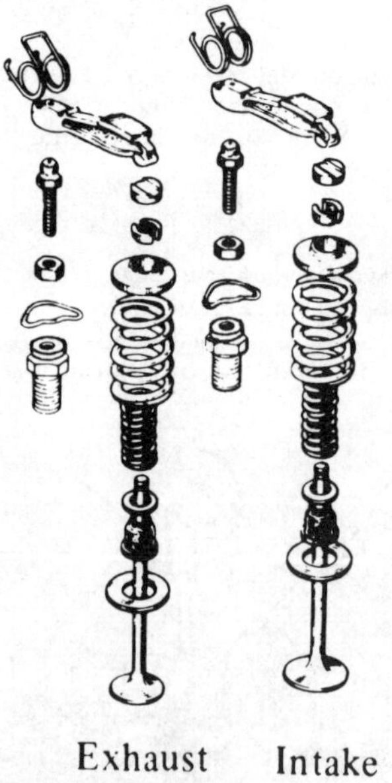

FIG 1:25 Valves and springs. Note that L14 engines use a single inlet valve spring only

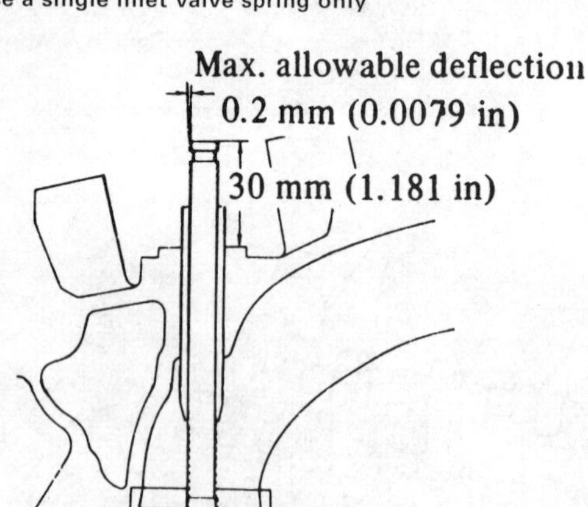

FIG 1:26 Checking valve stem clearance in guide

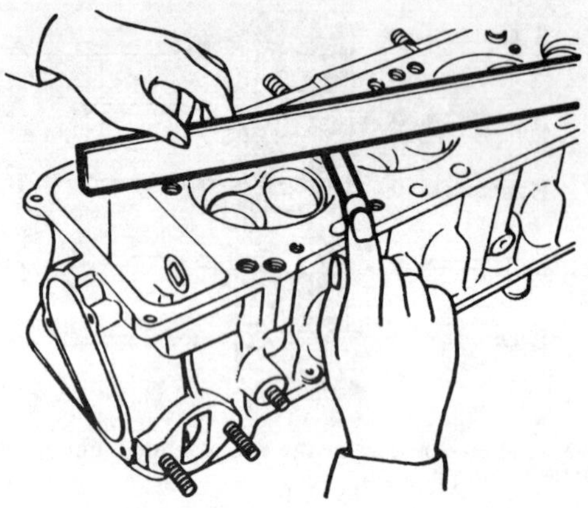

FIG 1:27 Checking cylinder head for warping

If this is 0.2mm (0.0079in) or more, it indicates that the clearance between stem and guide exceeds the maximum limit of 0.1mm (0.0039in) and the valve, guide, or both must be renewed.

Valve seat inserts:

Valve seat inserts are pressed into position in the light alloy cylinder head. Valve seats that are pitted or burnt must be refaced or, if the damage is too severe for refacing, renewed. As either operation requires the use of special equipment, the work should be carried out by a service station. If the valve seats are serviceable, they should be ground to the valves as described later.

Valve springs:

Test the valve springs by comparing with the figures given in **Technical Data**, or by comparing the efficiency of the old spring against that of a new spring. To do this, insert both the old and new springs end to end with a metal plate between them into the jaws of a vice. If the old spring is weakened, it will close up first when pressure is applied. Take care that the springs do not fly out of the vice under pressure. Any spring which is shorter or weaker than standard should be renewed.

Decarbonising and valve grinding:

Avoid the use of sharp tools which will damage the cylinder head or piston surfaces. Remove all traces of carbon deposits from the combustion chambers, inlet and exhaust ports and joint faces. If the pistons have not been removed and cleaned during previous engine dismantling, plug the waterways and oil holes in the top surface of the cylinder block with pieces of rag to prevent the entry of dirt, then clean the carbon from the piston crowns.

To grind-in valves, use medium grade carborundum paste followed by fine grade, unless the seats are in very good condition, when fine grade paste can be used at once. A light spring under the valve head will assist in the operation and allow the valve to be lifted from its seat

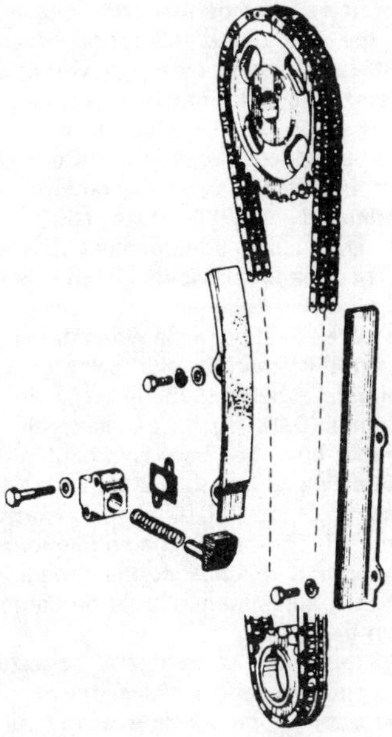

FIG 1:28 Timing gear components

without releasing the grinding tool. Use a suction cup tool and grind with a semi-rotary movement, letting the valve rise off its seat occasionally by pressure of the spring under the head, then turning to a new position before starting again. Use paste sparingly. When both valve and cylinder head seats have a smooth matt-grey finish, clean away every trace of grinding paste from port and valve.

Reassemble the valves to the cylinder head in the reverse order of removal, using new seals and making sure that all parts are fitted in their original positions. Lubricate the valve stems with engine oil before fitting.

Camshaft:

Check the camshaft lobes and bearing journals and the bores in the bearing assemblies mounted on the cylinder head. Measure the inside diameter of the camshaft bearings and the outside diameter of matching camshaft journals using suitable micrometers. Compare with the details in **Technical Data**. If a new camshaft or bearings are required, the work should be carried out by a service station having special in-line reaming equipment, as described previously.

Cylinder head:

Check the cleaned cylinder head mating surface for flatness. Lay a steel straightedge across the cylinder head lengthways, crossways and diagonally in turn, checking with feeler gauges each time as shown in **FIG 1:27**. If a 0.1mm (0.0039in) feeler can be fitted between the straightedge and cylinder head joint surface at any point, the head is warped beyond limits and must be refaced at a service station. Carry out a similar check on the joint surface of the cylinder block.

Reassembly:

Reassemble the components in the reverse order of dismantling. After refitting the camshaft and thrust plate, temporarily refit the camshaft sprocket and check the camshaft end float. This should be 0.08 to 0.38mm

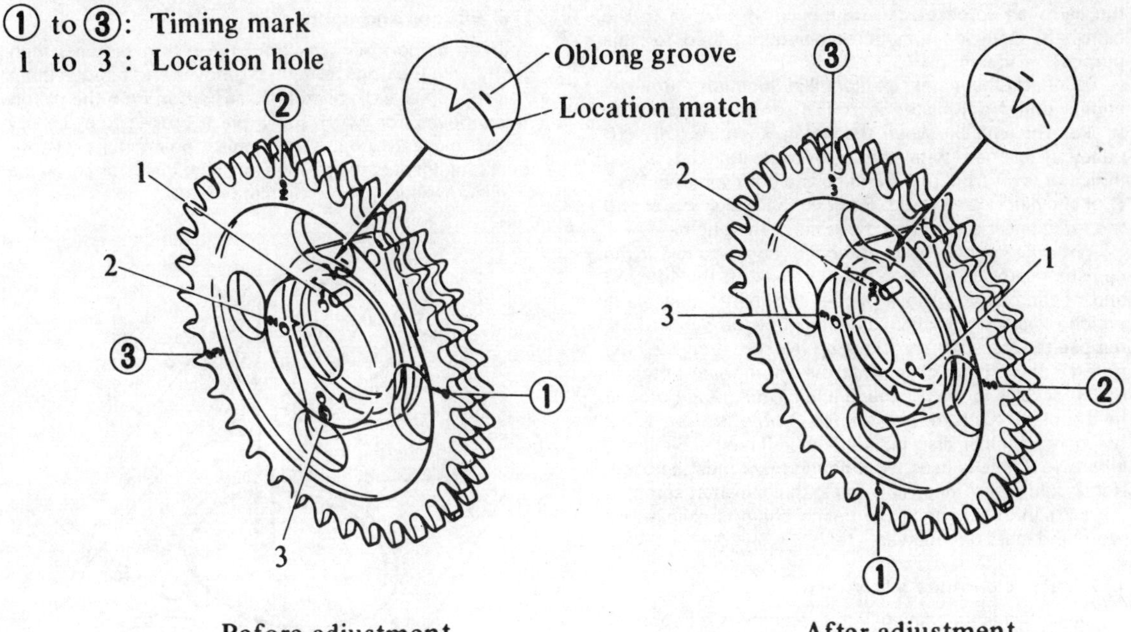

FIG 1:29 Adjusting camshaft sprocket location

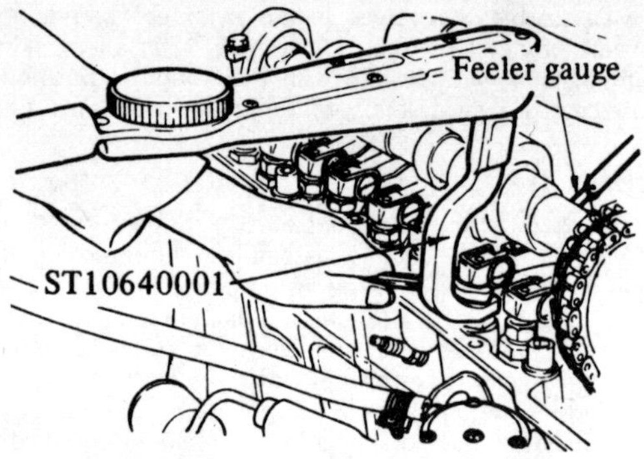

FIG 1:30 Valve clearance adjustment

(0.0031 to 0.0150in). If outside limits, renew the camshaft thrust plate.

Refit the cylinder head as described in **Section 1:4**. Make sure that the camshaft timing mark is set in the same position it occupied when the sprocket was removed, so that it will align with the mark on the chain. Do this before fitting the head and do not rotate the camshaft independently afterwards, otherwise the valves may be damaged by contacting the pistons.

1:6 Timing gear

The timing chain, sprockets, guides and tensioner components are shown in **FIG 1:28**. Check all components for wear or damage, renewing any found to be defective.

Check the chain for damage, excessive wear or stretch at its roller links. When the chain stretches due to normal wear, the valve timing is affected. To compensate for this, the camshaft sprocket can be moved in relation to the camshaft, three location holes being provided for this purpose as shown in **FIG 1:29**.

To check the camshaft sprocket location, turn the engine until No 1 piston is at TDC on its compression stroke. This will be when the notch on the crankshaft pulley is aligned with the zero mark on the timing indicator at the front of the engine and both valves at No 1 (front) cylinder are closed. Remove the rocker cover and the timing gear cover from the front of the engine.

With the engine set as described, check to see if the camshaft sprocket location notch comes off the lefthand end of the oblong groove on the camshaft thrust plate, which indicates that chain stretch is beyond limits. If so, remove the camshaft sprocket and relocate it on the next hole (2 or 3). Now check that the appropriate notch in the sprocket is to the righthand end of the oblong groove in the plate. Note that, when No 2 hole is used No 2 timing mark must also be used for reference. Similarly, when No 3 hole is used No 3 timing mark must be used. If it should prove impossible to set the camshaft sprocket correctly in this manner, the timing chain is excessively worn and must be renewed.

1:7 Valve clearance adjustment

The correct adjustment of valve clearances is important as they affect engine timing and performance considerably. Excessive clearance will reduce valve lift and opening duration and reduce engine performance, causing excessive wear on the valve gear components and noisy operation. Insufficient or zero clearance will again affect engine timing and, in some circumstances, can hold the valve clear of its seat. This will result in much reduced performance due to lost compression and the possibility of burnt valves and seats. Valve clearances should be checked and adjusted every 10,000km (6000 miles) as routine maintenance and, additionally, whenever the cylinder head has been serviced or the head bolts tightened.

Final adjustment should be made when the engine is at normal operating temperature, the correct clearances under these conditions being 0.25mm (0.010in) for inlet valves and 0.30mm (0.012in) for exhaust valves. However, if the cylinder head has been overhauled the valve clearances should first be set to 0.20mm (0.0008in) for inlet valves and 0.25mm (0.010in) for exhaust valves with the engine cold. This allows the engine to be started and safely run until it reaches normal operating temperature, when final adjustment should be carried out to the figures given previously.

Run the engine until it is at normal operating temperature, then switch off and remove the rocker cover. Turn the engine until the cam lobe over the valve to be checked is pointing upwards, away from the rocker. Use feeler gauges to check the clearance between the cam and the rocker as shown in **FIG 1:30**. If adjustment is needed, slacken the locknut and turn the adjuster to alter the clearance until the feeler gauge is a smooth sliding fit in the gap, being neither tight nor loose. Tighten the locknut and recheck the clearance. Repeat the checking and adjusting procedure on each valve in turn, noting the different clearances required for inlet and exhaust valves.

1:8 Pistons and connecting rods

Clean carbon deposits from the piston crowns, then gently ease the rings from their grooves and remove them over the top of each piston. Clean carbon from the piston ring grooves, for which job a piece broken from an old piston ring and ground to a chisel point will prove an ideal tool. Inspect the pistons for score marks or any signs of seizure, which would dictate renewal.

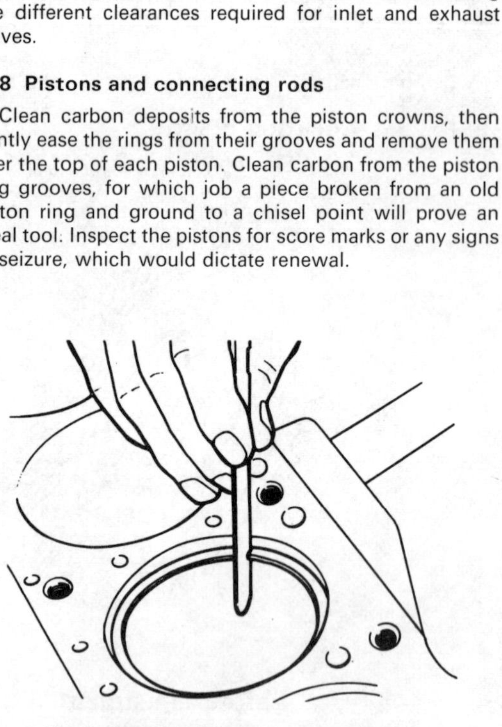

FIG 1:31 Checking piston ring end gap

Fit the piston rings one at a time into the bore from which they were removed, pushing them down with the inverted piston to ensure squareness. Measure the gap between the ends of the ring while it is positioned in the bore, using feeler gauges as shown in **FIG 1:31**. Compare the measurement with the figures given in **Technical Data**. Note that, if new piston rings are being fitted without cylinder reboring, the new rings should be pushed to the bottom of the cylinder bore before measurement, this being the minimum wear point. Hold each ring in the piston groove from which it was removed as shown in **FIG 1:32**, then measure the side clearance with feeler gauges. Compare the measurement with the figures given in **Technical Data**. If the clearance measurement in either test is at or near the wear limit, new rings must be fitted. Excessive ring clearance can be responsible for high oil consumption and poor engine performance.

Check the cylinder bores for score marks and remove glaze and carbon deposits. Badly scored or worn surfaces will dictate a rebore to accept new pistons, this being a specialist job. The fitting of new pistons to connecting rods must be carried out by a service station, due to the need for special press equipment to remove and refit the gudgeon pin.

Check the clearance of each piston in its bore, by measuring the inside diameter of the cylinder bore and the outside diameter of the piston skirt and comparing the two figures. Take the bore measurements at right angles to the cylinder block length as wear will be greatest in this direction. Measure piston diameter at right angles to and at a point about 20mm (0.8in) below the centre of the gudgeon pin bore, as shown in **FIG 1:33**. Correct piston to bore clearance is 0.025 to 0.045mm (0.0010 to 0.0018in). Excessive clearance will dictate the fitting of new pistons and, possibly, reboring of the cylinders.

Connecting rods:

If there has been a big-end bearing failure, the crankpin must be examined for damage and for transfer of metal to its surface. The oilway in the crankshaft must be checked to ensure that there is no obstruction. Big-end bearing clearance can be checked by the use of Plastigage, which is the trade name for a precisely calibrated plastic filament. The filament is laid along the bearing to be measured for working clearance, the bearing cap fitted and the bolts tightened to the specified torque.

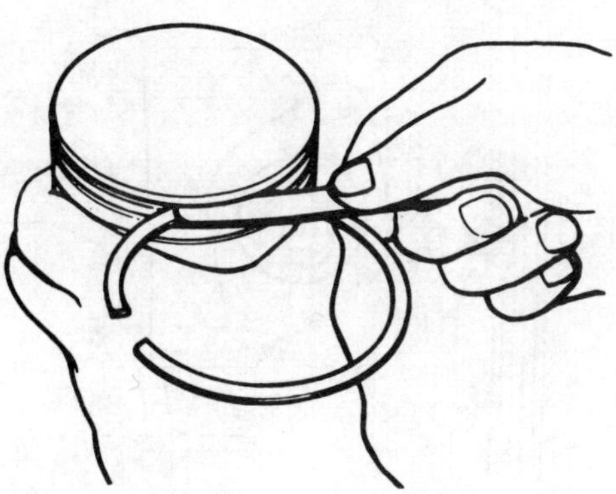

FIG 1:32 Checking piston ring side clearance

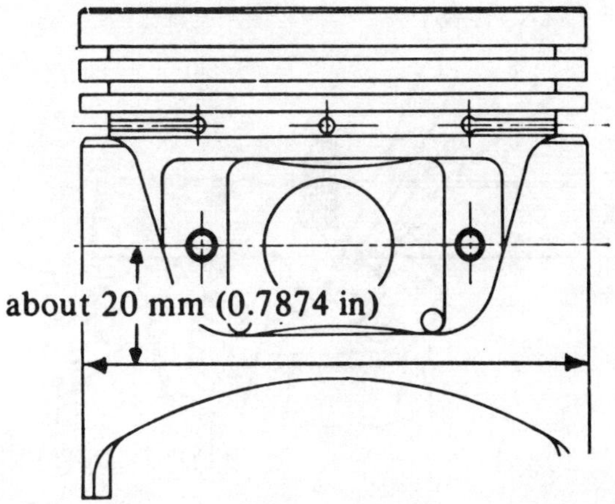

FIG 1:33 Checking piston diameter

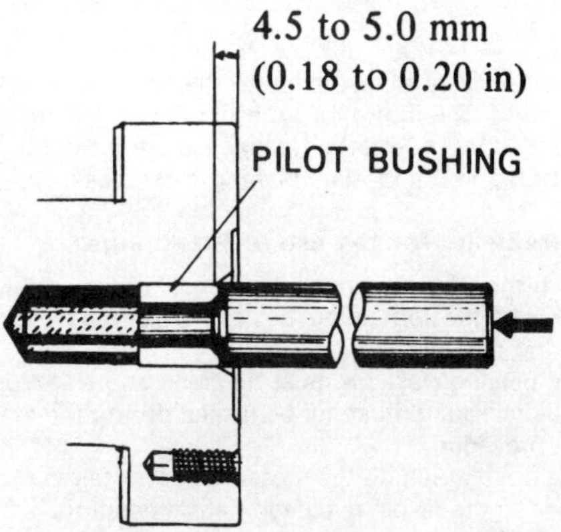

FIG 1:34 Fitting clutch pilot bush in flywheel

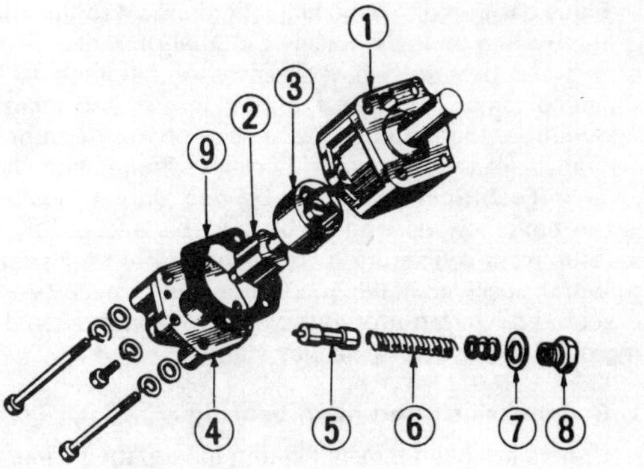

FIG 1:35 Oil pump components

Key to Fig 1:35 1 Oil pump body 2 Inner rotor and shaft 3 Outer rotor 4 Oil pump cover 5 Regulator valve 6 Regulator spring 7 Washer 8 Regulator cap 9 Cover gasket

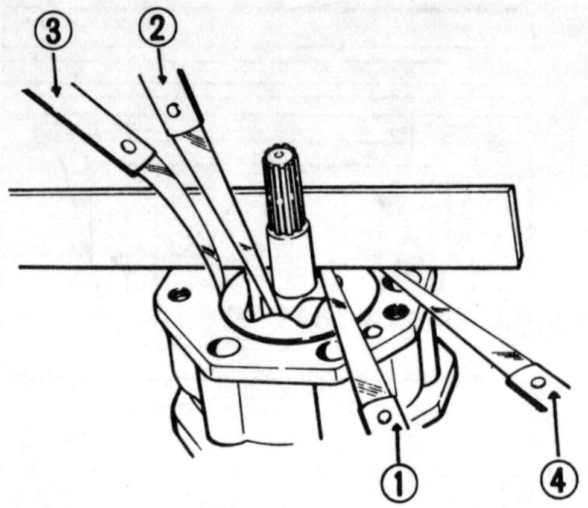

FIG 1:36 Checking pump component clearances

Key to Fig 1:36 1 Side clearance 2 Tip clearance 3 Outer rotor to body clearance 4 Rotor to bottom cover clearance

The bearing is then dismantled and the width of the flattened filament measured with the scale supplied with the material. The figure thus measured is the actual bearing clearance. The method of measurement is the same for both big-end and main bearing clearances.

Requirements for the use of Plastigage:

1 Each main bearing must be measured separately and none of the remaining bearing caps must be fitted during the operation.
2 The bearing surfaces must be clean and free from oil.
3 The crankshaft must not be turned during the measuring procedure.
4 The point at which the measurement is taken must be close to the respective dead centre position.
5 No hammer blows must be applied to the bearing or cap.

Procedure:

Place a length of plastic filament identical to the width of the bearing on the crankshaft journal then fit the main or big-end bearing cap with shells and tighten to the specified torque. Remove the bearing cap and measure the width of the flattened filament to obtain the running clearance for that bearing. Check the figure with those given in **Technical Data**. If the bearing running clearance is too high, new bearing shells must be selected by the measurement procedure to bring the running clearance to within specified limits. If any crankpin or main bearing is scored or worn out of round, the crankshaft should be reground at a specialist service station.

1:9 Crankshaft and main bearings

If there has been a main bearing failure, the crankshaft journal must be checked for damage and transfer of metal to its surface. The oilways in the crankshaft must be checked to ensure that there is no obstruction. Main bearing clearance can be checked by the use of Plastigage, in the manner described in **Section 1:8** for big-end bearings, the procedure being the same. If there is any doubt about the condition of the crankshaft it should be taken to a specialist for more detailed checks.

Examine the starter ring gear on the flywheel. If the teeth are broken or worn, a new ring gear should be fitted by a service station. If the clutch pilot bush in the centre of the flywheel is to be renewed, the old bush must be pulled out with tool ST16610001 or similar. Thoroughly clean the bore in the flywheel, then press in the new bush so that its height above the flange end is 4.5 to 5.0mm (0.18 to 0.20in), as shown in **FIG 1:34**. Do not oil the bush.

1:10 The oil pump

The oil pump is mounted on the bottom of the engine front cover and secured by four bolts, being gear-driven from the crankshaft.

The pump can be removed with the engine in situ. To do this, remove the distributor as described in **Chapter 3**, then remove the oil pump body and drive spindle assembly.

Servicing:

FIG 1:35 shows the oil pump components. Remove the cover attaching bolts, cover and cover gasket, then slide out the pump rotors. Remove the regulator cap, valve and spring.

Wash all parts in a suitable solvent and dry thoroughly. Inspect the pump body and cover for cracks or excessive wear. Examine the pump rotors for any signs of damage or excessive wear. Check the inner rotor shaft for looseness in the pump body and inspect the regulator valve

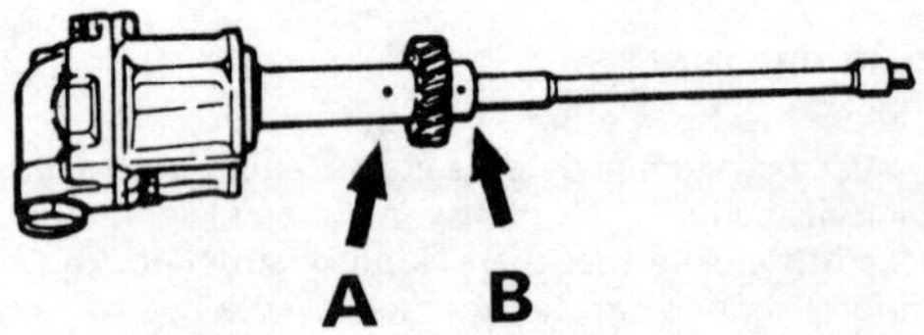

FIG 1:37 Aligning pump spindle and body

Key to Fig 1:37 A Oil hole B Punch mark

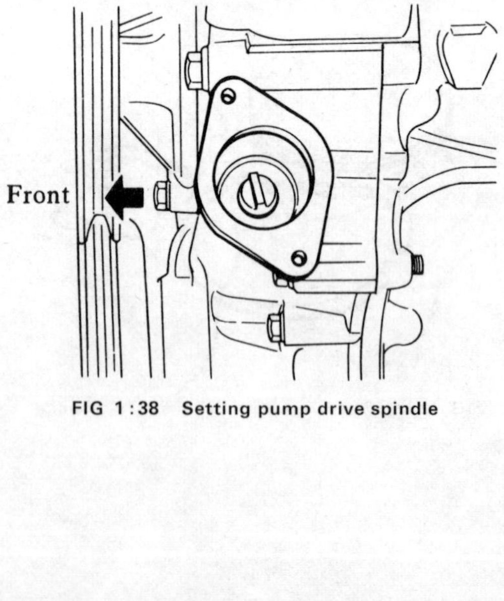

FIG 1:38 Setting pump drive spindle

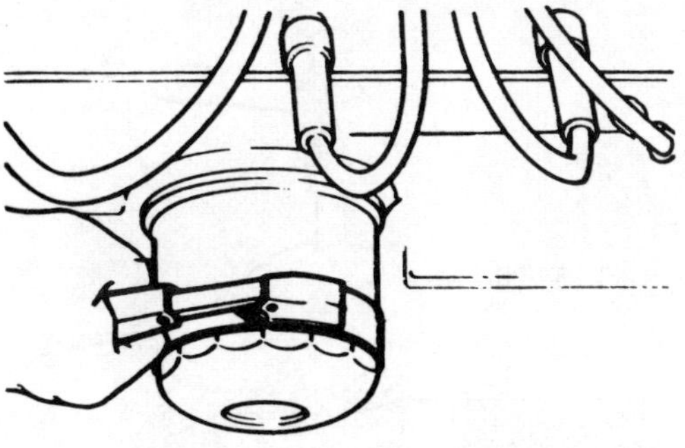

FIG 1:39 Oil filter removal

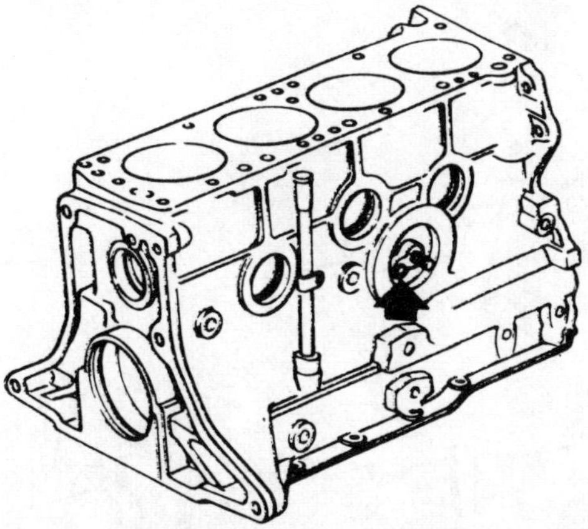

FIG 1:40 Oil pressure relief valve location

for wear or scoring. Check the regulator spring to make sure that it is not worn on one side or distorted. Use a steel straightedge and feeler gauges to check the pump working clearances as shown in **FIG 1:36**, then compare the measurements obtained with those given in **Technical Data**. If excessive clearance is found at any point, the entire pump assembly must be renewed as the internal components are not serviced separately.

Before refitting the oil pump, turn the crankshaft so that No 1 piston is at TDC on the firing stroke. Fill the oil pump housing with engine oil, then align the punch mark on the spindle with the hole in the pump as shown in **FIG 1:37**. Using a new gasket, fit the oil pump and drive spindle assembly so that the projection on its top is located as shown in **FIG 1:38**, with the smaller bow-shape towards the front. Make sure that the engagement is correct by checking the top of the spindle through the distributor fitting hole. Tighten the bolts securing the pump to the front cover. Refit the distributor as described in **Chapter 3**.

1:11 The oil filter

The oil filter is of the renewable cartridge type and should be renewed every 10,000km (6000 miles). To do this, unscrew the oil filter cartridge as shown in **FIG 1:39** and discard it.

While the oil filter is removed, check that the relief valve shown in **FIG 1:40** is not cracked or broken. If a new valve is required, remove the old valve by carefully levering out with a screwdriver. Fit a new valve by tapping it into place.

Clean the filter mounting face on the engine and lightly coat the new seal with engine oil. Make sure that the seal is correctly fitted, then screw the new filter into place until it just contacts its seating. From this point tighten a further three-quarters of a turn by hand only. Do not overtighten the filter or oil leaks may result. A strap type tool may be used to remove the filter if it is too stiff to be unscrewed by hand, but never use anything but hand pressure to tighten the unit. On completion, start and run the engine to check for oil leaks at the filter unit. Switch off the engine and top up the oil level to compensate for that used to fill the new filter element.

1:12 Reassembling the engine

When reassembling the engine, make sure that all parts are thoroughly clean and that oil holes are clear of

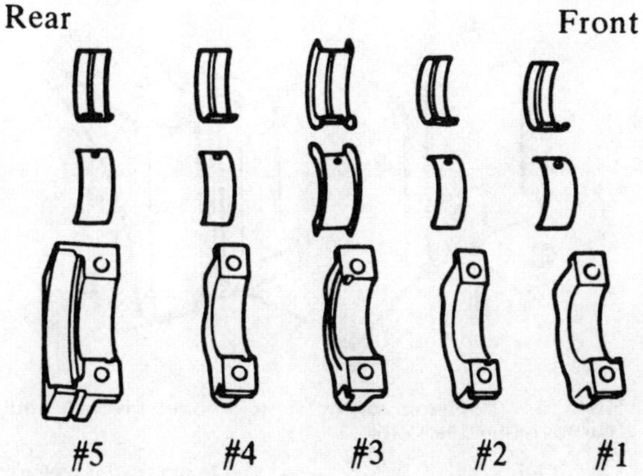

FIG 1:41 Main bearing shell locations

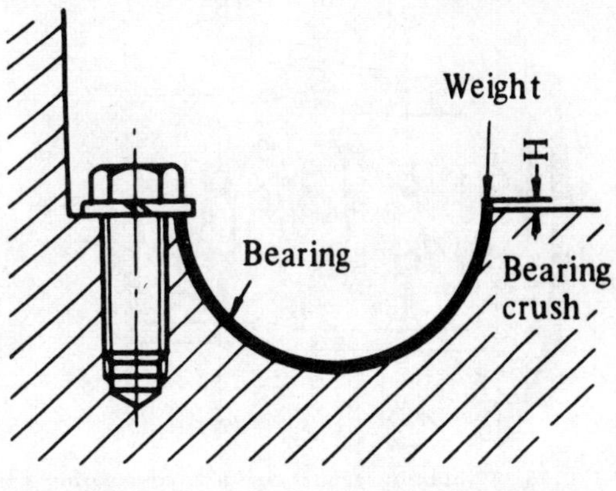

FIG 1:42 Checking main and big-end bearing crush

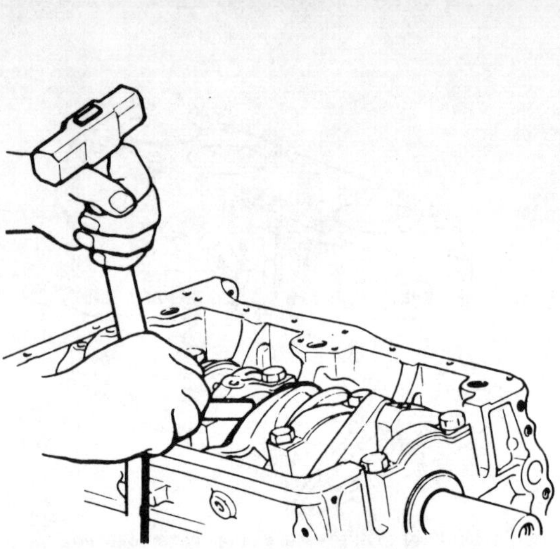

FIG 1:43 Checking crankshaft end float

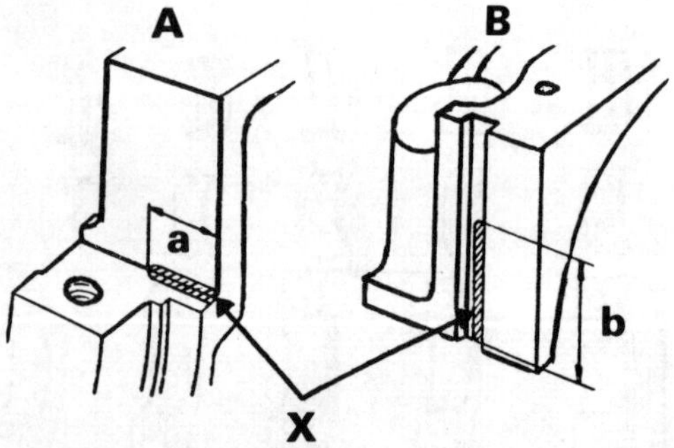

FIG 1:44 Applying sealant X to cylinder block A and rear main bearing cap B

Key to Fig 1:44 a = 20 to 25mm (0.75 to 1.0in) b = 25 to 30mm (1.0 to 1.2in)

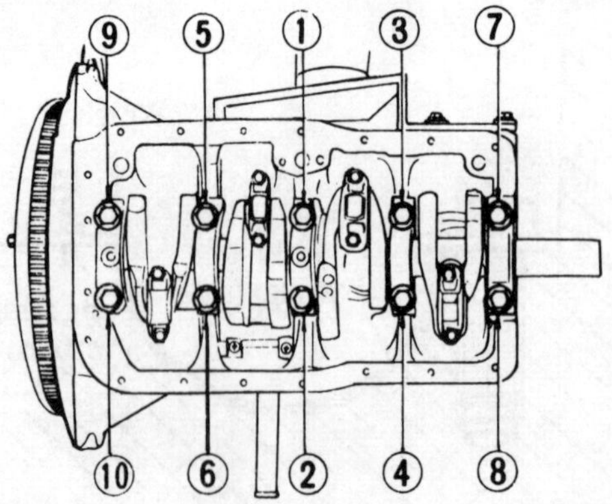

FIG 1:45 Tightening sequence for main bearing cap bolts

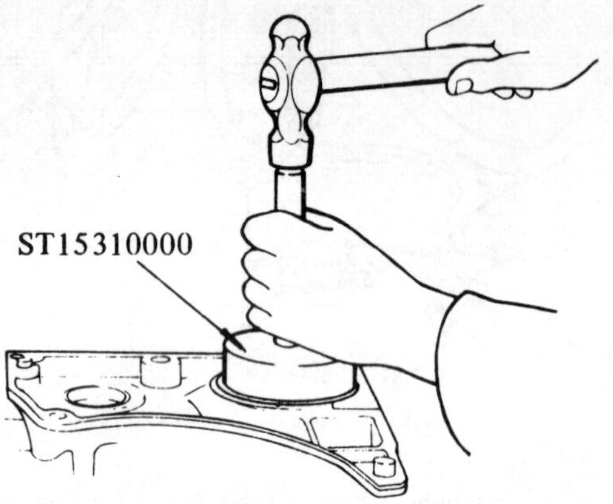

FIG 1:46 Installing rear oil seal

foreign matter. Use new gaskets and seals throughout and also renew all lockwashers. Lubricate all moving parts with engine oil before installation. Observe the torque wrench settings given in the text when tightening the various fixtures.

Fit the cylinder block net and baffle plate. Clean and dry the main bearing shells, then fit the shells to their respective cylinder block and cap positions as shown in **FIG 1:41**, lightly lubricate the bearing surfaces with engine oil. Note that the centre bearing incorporates thrust washers to control crankshaft end float. Bearings No 2 and 4 are of the same type. The front bearing (No 1) is the same type as the rear bearing (No 5) except that an oil hole is provided in the front bearing. All bearings except No 1 can be interchanged between upper and lower positions.

The main and big-end bearing shells are designed to compress slightly when the cap bolts are tightened. To check that this bearing crush will be correct, set the bearing shell in the cap recess or cylinder block recess and lock one side as shown in **FIG 1:42**. Press down on the other side of the bearing until the back surface touches the recess, then measure dimension H with a feeler gauge. For main bearing shells, this measurement should be 0 to 0.03mm (0 to 0.0012in). For big-end bearing shells the measurement should be 0.015 to 0.045mm (0.0006 to 0.0018in).

Carefully fit the crankshaft into place then fit and evenly tighten all the crankshaft bearing cap bolts and make sure that the crankshaft can rotate freely. Move the crankshaft fore and aft and check the end float at each side of the centre main bearing flanges as shown in **FIG 1:43**. End float should be between 0.05 and 0.18mm (0.0020 and 0.0071in). Excessive end float must be corrected by fitting new centre main bearing shells. Main bearing cap bolts must be tightened to 4.5 to 5.5kgm (33 to 40lb ft). Apply sealant to each side of the rear main bearing cap and at each corner of the cylinder block as shown in **FIG 1:44**. Make sure that the arrows marked on the bearing caps face towards the front of the engine and tighten the cap bolts gradually in two or three stages in the order shown in **FIG 1:45**.

Apply sealant to the rear main bearing cap side oil seals, then install the seals. Install the rear oil seal using

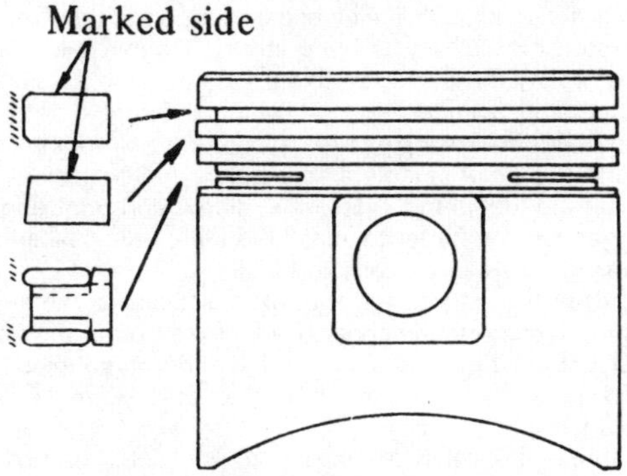

FIG 1:47 Piston ring installation

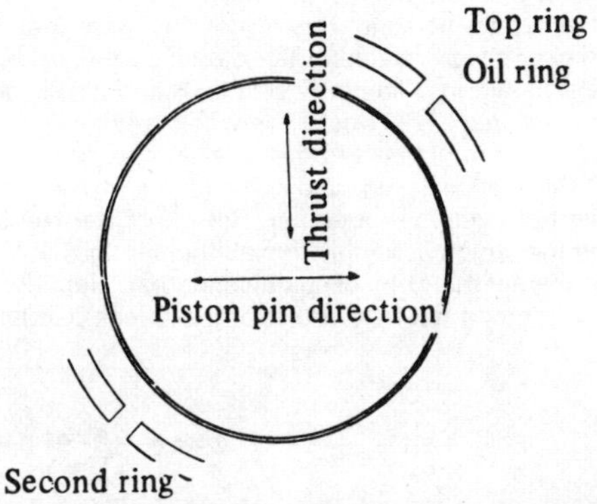

FIG 1:48 Spacing piston ring gaps around piston

a driver such as tool ST15310000 as shown in **FIG 1:46**. Apply lithium grease to the sealing lip of the seal. Install the rear end plate then fit the flywheel and tighten the bolts to 14 to 16kgm (101 to 116lb ft).

Fit the rings carefully to the pistons from which they were removed, as shown in **FIG 1:47**. Space the ring gaps around the piston as shown in **FIG 1:48**. Oil the pistons before inserting them into the cylinder bores, noting that the notch mark on the piston faces towards the front of the engine, as shown in **FIG 1:49**. Use a suitable ring clamp when entering the piston rings into the bores. Make sure that the big-end caps are fitted to their correct respective connecting rods, then fit the cap bolts and tighten to 3.2 to 3.8kgm (23 to 28lb ft) for L16 engines, 4.5 to 5.5kgm (33 to 40lb ft) for all other engines. Make sure that the rods and caps are set so that the cylinder numbers face in the same direction. Check the connecting rod big-end side play as shown in **FIG 1:50**, which should be 0.2 to 0.3mm (0.008 to 0.012in).

Turn the crankshaft until No 1 piston is at TDC on the firing stroke. Make sure that the camshaft sprocket location notch and plate oblong groove are aligned correctly as described in **Section 1:6**. Make sure that the crankshaft and camshaft keys point upwards. Make sure that all valves are apart from the piston heads when the cylinder head is installed. Do not rotate the crankshaft and camshaft separately or the valves will contact

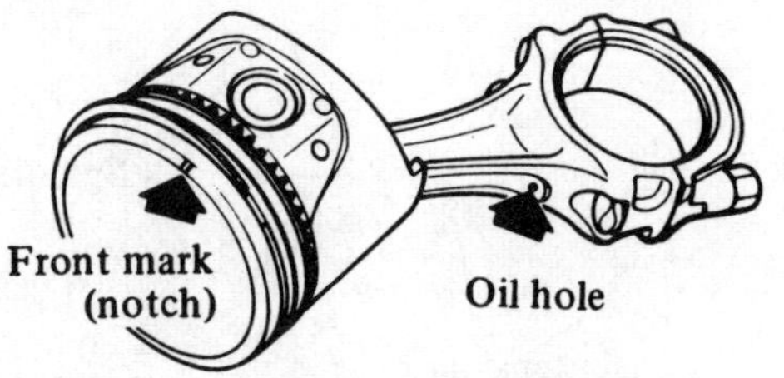

FIG 1:49 The notch mark on the front of piston

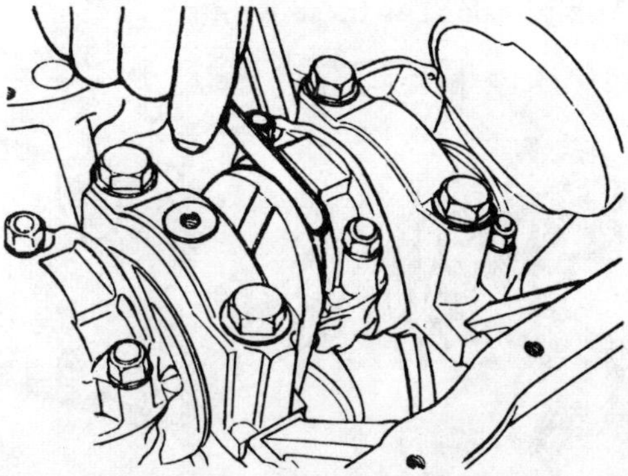

FIG 1:50 Checking big-end bearing side clearance

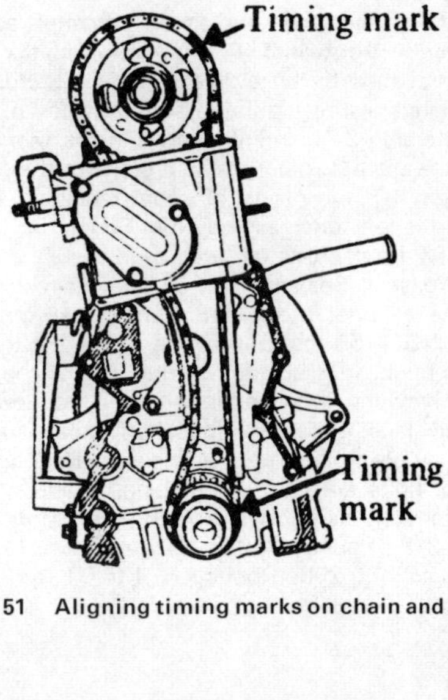

FIG 1:51 Aligning timing marks on chain and sprockets

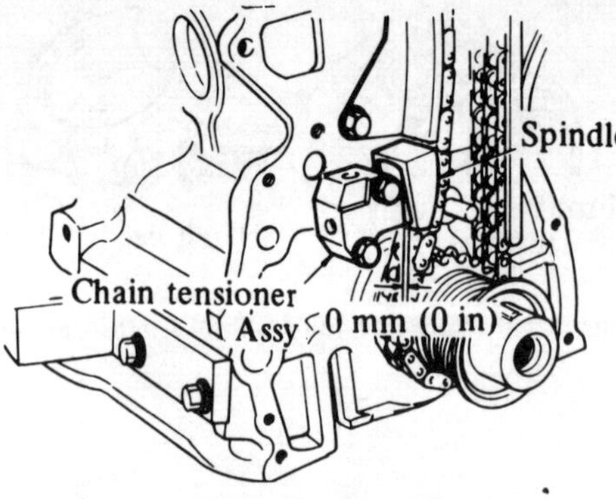

FIG 1:52 Installing chain tensioner

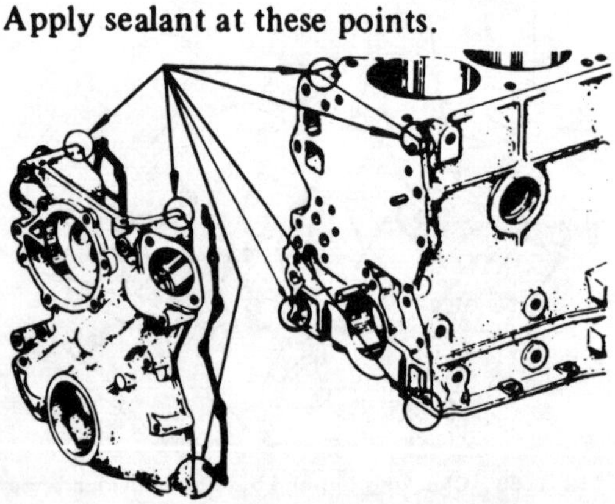

FIG 1:53 Applying sealant to front cover and cylinder block

the pistons. Fit the cylinder head with new gasket and temporarily tighten bolts 1 and 2 shown in **FIG 1:22**. Install the crankshaft sprocket and distributor drive gear and fit the oil thrower.

Install the timing chain and fit the camshaft sprocket as described in **Section 1:6**. The mating marks on the chain must align with those on the camshaft and crankshaft sprockets at the righthand side, as shown in **FIG 1:51**. There are 42 chain links between the two mating marks on the chain. Install the chain guide to the cylinder block. Adjust the protrusion of chain tensioner to zero and install the tensioner, as shown in **FIG 1:52**.

Fit a new front cover oil seal, then install the front cover and gasket. Sealant must be applied to the front side of the cylinder block and front cover gasket as shown in **FIG 1:53**, but at no other point. Fit the front cover with the head gasket in position. Check the height difference between cylinder block upper face and front cover upper face. Difference must not exceed 0.15mm (0.006in). Apply lithium grease to the sealing lip of oil seal. Cover bolts are of different lengths and must be installed correctly as shown in **FIG 1:54**. Tighten M8 (8mm or 0.315in) bolts to 1.0 to 1.6kgm (7.2 to 11.6lb ft) and M6 (6mm or 0.236in) bolts to 0.4 to 0.8kgm (2.9 to 5.8lb ft).

Fit the crankshaft pulley and water pump, then set No 1 piston at TDC on its firing stroke. Tighten the crankshaft pulley nut to 12 to 16kgm (87 to 115lb ft). Finally tighten the cylinder head bolts in the correct order as described in **Section 1:4**. Install the oil pump and distributor drive spindle as described in **Section 1:10**. Install the fuel pump, water inlet elbow and front engine slinger. Do not forget to install the fuel pump spacer and packing between spacer and block.

Install the oil strainer and apply sealant to the sump mating face on the cylinder block at the points shown in **FIG 1:55**. Fit the sump and gasket and tighten the sump bolts in a diagonal pattern to 0.6 to 0.9kgm (4.3 to 6.5lb ft).

Adjust the valve clearances to the cold settings as described in **Section 1:7**. Install the rear engine slinger, exhaust and inlet manifolds. Fit the distributor as described in **Chapter 3**. Refit the carburetter(s) as described in **Chapter** 2. Install the fuel pipes and vacuum hose. Install the thermostat housing, thermostat and water outlet. Fit the rocker cover, attaching the gasket to the cover with sealant before installation. Install EGR and check valve if fitted. Connect all hoses between the engine and associated components in the reverse order of removal.

Fit the sparking plugs and connect the HT leads. Install the lefthand engine mounting. Refer to **Chapter 5** and install the clutch assembly. Install the oil dipstick.

Fit the alternator bracket, adjusting bar, alternator, fan pulley, fan and fan belt in that order. Check belt tension

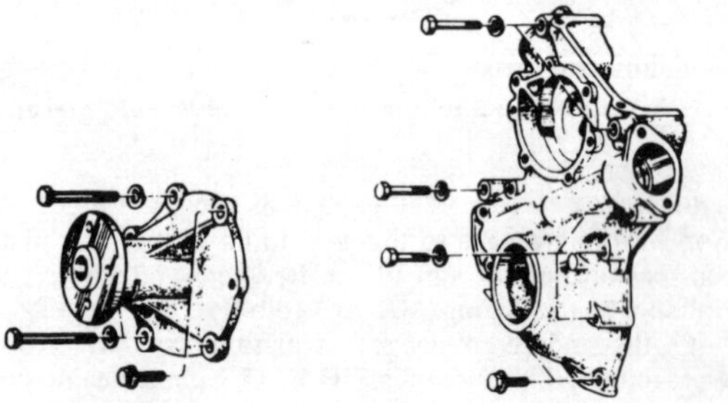

FIG 1:54 Front cover bolts

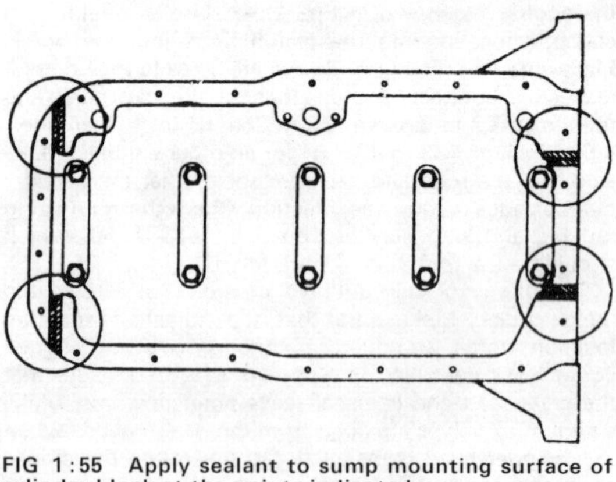

FIG 1:55 Apply sealant to sump mounting surface of cylinder block at the points indicated

as described in **Chapter 4**. Fit righthand engine mounting bracket, oil filter, oil pressure switch and water drain plug. Refer to **Section 1:11** when tightening the oil filter.

1:13 Refitting the engine

Refitting the engine is a reversal of the removal procedure given in **Section 1:2**, noting the following points:

Secure the rear engine mounting member to the body first. The bolts at the rear mounting are shown in **FIG 1:9**. Tighten bolts A to 0.9 to 1.2kgm (6.5 to 8.7lb ft), bolts B to 1.9 to 2.6kgm (14 to 19lb ft) and bolts C to 1.4 to 1.8kgm (10.1 to 13.0lb ft).

When installing the bonnet, align the hinges with the marks made on the bonnet panel during removal. Make sure that the bonnet is properly centred and that the lock operates securely. Refer to **Chapter 13** for bonnet adjustment details.

On completion, refill the engine sump with oil and the cooling system with clean coolant. Fit the air cleaner and ensure that all hoses, wires and plugs are firmly reconnected. Start the engine and run it up to normal operating temperature, then check for oil leaks. With the engine hot, reset the valve clearances as described in **Section 1:7**. Check manual transmission oil level or automatic transmission fluid level (see **Chapter 6** or **7**).

1:14 Fault diagnosis

(a) Engine will not start

1 Defective coil
2 Faulty distributor capacitor
3 Dirty, pitted or incorrectly set contact points
4 Ignition wires loose or insulation faulty
5 Water on spark plug leads
6 Battery discharged, corrosion of terminals
7 Faulty or jammed starter
8 Sparking plug leads wrongly connected
9 Vapour lock in fuel pipes
10 Defective fuel pump
11 Overchoking or underchoking
12 Blocked fuel filter or carburetter jet
13 Leaking valves
14 Sticking valves
15 Valve timing incorrect
16 Ignition timing incorrect

(b) Engine stalls

1 Check 1, 2, 3, 4, 5, 10, 11, 12, 13 and 14 in (a)
2 Sparking plugs defective or gaps incorrect
3 Retarded ignition
4 Mixture too weak
5 Water in fuel system
6 Fuel tank vent system blocked
7 Incorrect valve clearances

(c) Engine idles badly

1 Check 2 and 7 in (b)
2 Air leak at manifold joints
3 Carburetter adjustment wrong
4 Air leak in carburetter
5 Over-rich mixture
6 Worn piston rings
7 Worn valve stems or guides
8 Worn valve springs

(d) Engine misfires

1 Check 1, 2, 3, 4, 5, 8, 10, 12, 13, 14, 15 and 16 in (a)
2 Weak or broken valve springs

(e) Engine overheats (see Chapter 4)

(f) Compression low

1 Check 13 and 14 in (a); 6 and 7 in (c) and 2 in (d)
2 Worn piston ring grooves
3 Scored or worn cylinder bores

(g) Engine lacks power

1 Check 3, 10, 11, 12, 13, 14, 15 and 16 in (a); 2, 3, 4 and 7 in (b); 6 and 7 in (c) and 2 in (d). Also check (e) and (f)
2 Leaking joint washers or gaskets
3 Fouled sparking plugs
4 Automatic advance not working

(h) Burnt valves or seats

1 Check 13 and 14 in (a); 7 in (b) and 2 in (d). Also check (e)
2 Excessive carbon around valve seats and head

(j) Sticking valves

1 Check 2 in (d)
2 Bent valve stem
3 Scored valve stem or guide
4 Incorrect valve clearances

(k) Excessive cylinder wear

1 Check 11 in (a)
2 Lack of oil
3 Dirty oil
4 Piston rings gummed up or broken
5 Badly fitting piston rings
6 Connecting rod bent

(l) Excessive oil consumption

1 Check 6 and 7 in (c) and check (k)
2 Ring gaps too wide
3 Oil return holes in piston choked with carbon
4 Scored cylinders
5 Oil level too high
6 External oil leaks

(m) Connecting rod and crankshaft bearing failure

1 Check 2 in (k)
2 Restricted oilways
3 Worn journals or crankpins
4 Loose bearing caps
5 Extremely low oil pressure
6 Bent connecting rod

(n) Internal water leakage (see **Chapter 4**)

(o) Poor water circulation (see **Chapter 4**)

(p) Corrosion (see **Chapter 4**)

(q) High fuel consumption (see **Chapter 2**)

(r) Engine vibration

1 Loose ancillary components fixings
2 Engine mountings loose or defective
3 Misfiring due to mixture, ignition or mechanical fault

CHAPTER 2

THE FUEL SYSTEM

2:1 Description

Fuel from the rear-mounted tank is supplied to the carburetter(s) by a mechanical type fuel pump operated from a special eccentric on the engine camshaft.

Standard models use either a single dual-barrel carburetter or twin carburetters according to engine type. Models for USA export are fitted with a single dual-barrel carburetter of special design, which incorporates several ancillary systems to ensure that toxic exhaust emissions do not exceed the levels dictated by current Federal Regulations.

On standard models, fuel enrichment for cold starting is controlled by a manually operated choke unit, USA export models being provided with an electrically operated choke unit which is controlled automatically according to engine operating temperature.

All models are equipped with viscous paper cartridge type air cleaner units.

2:2 Routine maintenance

Under normal operating conditions, the air cleaner element should be renewed at 40,000km (24,000 mile) intervals, as described in **Section 2:3**. If the car is operated under very dusty conditions, the servicing period should be suitably reduced. No servicing is required between renewal intervals and no attempt should be made to clean the air filter element.

At 20,000km (12,000 mile) intervals, or before if contamination causes reduced fuel flow, the fuel filter element should be renewed. The condition of the element can be checked without removing the unit, as the casing is transparent. To renew the filter, detach the fuel pipes and catch fuel spillage in a suitable container. Remove and discard the old unit, then fit a new unit in its place (see **FIG 2:1**). Reconnect the fuel pipes, then run the engine and check for leaks.

On models fitted with twin carburetters, the oil in the carburetter dampers should be checked at 5000km (3000 mile) intervals. Unscrew the cap and remove the damper unit as shown in **FIG 2:2**. Check the level of oil against the two marks provided on the damper rod. If necessary, add 10W-30 engine oil to bring the level to the upper mark on the rod.

2:3 Air cleaner

To renew the air cleaner element, remove the screws securing the cover to the air cleaner body, then detach the cover and lift out the element. Wipe the inside of the

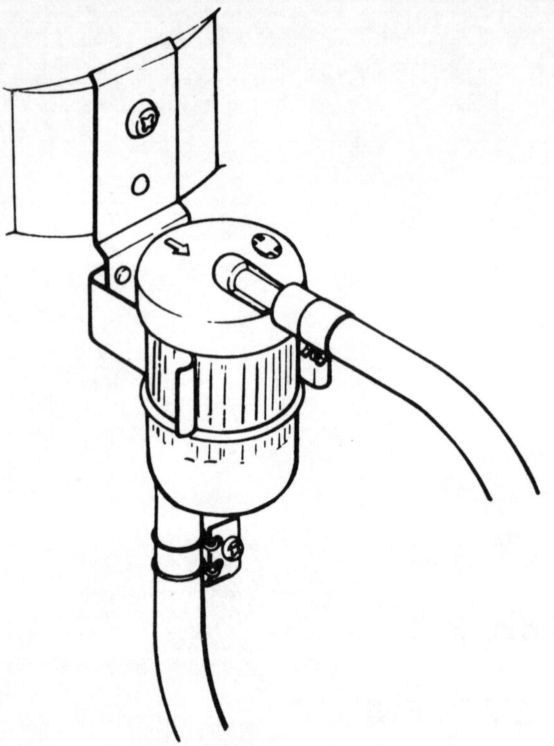

FIG 2:1 The cartridge type fuel filter unit

cover and body to remove any dirt or grease, then reassemble the air cleaner using a new element.

To remove the air cleaner assembly complete, remove the element as described previously then remove the screws attaching the air cleaner body to the carburetter(s). Detach any hoses connected between the air cleaner body and engine ancillary components, then remove the assembly from the car.

2:4 Fuel pump

Testing:

Before testing the pump, ensure that the fuel tank vent system is not blocked. If it is suspected that fuel is not reaching the carburetter, disconnect the carburetter feed pipe and hold a suitable container under the end of the pipe. Disconnect the HT lead from the centre of the coil so that the engine will not start and run on fuel in the carburetter float chamber, then turn the engine over a few times with the starter and watch for fuel squirting from the end of the pipe, which indicates that the pump is working. If so, check the float needle in the carburetter for possible sticking.

Reduced fuel flow can be caused by blocked fuel pipes or a clogged filter. Check the fuel filter as described in **Section 2:2**. If an obstructed pipeline appears to be the cause of the trouble, it may be cleared with compressed air. Disconnect the pipeline at the pump and carburetter. **Do not pass compressed air through the pump or the valves will be damaged.** If there is an obstruction between the pump and the tank, remove the tank filler cap before blowing the pipe through from the pump end.

If the pump delivers insufficient fuel, suspect an air leak between the pump and the tank, dirt under the pump valves or faulty valve seatings. If no fuel is delivered, suspect a sticking valve or a faulty pump diaphragm.

Servicing:

Disconnect the fuel pipes from the fuel pump and fit plugs to the pipes to prevent fuel loss before removing the pump from the engine. Remove the two nuts and washers and detach the pump, gasket and spacer from the cylinder head.

Test the action of the valves by gently blowing and sucking at the inlet and outlet points. It should be possible to blow air in through the pump inlet but not to suck air out, and it should be possible to suck air out of the pump outlet but not to blow air in. If the valves do not work properly according to this test, the valves and seats should be cleaned then the valve action tested again. If the fault persists, new valves or, possibly, a complete new pump upper body must be fitted.

FIG 2:3 shows the fuel pump components. Remove the setscrews and separate the upper and lower bodies. Remove the screws and detach the cap and gasket. Unscrew the elbow and connector. Remove the valve retainer by unscrewing the two screws and remove the two valves.

To remove the diaphragm, press the assembly down against spring pressure, then tilt the assembly until the end of the pull rod touches the inner wall of body (see **FIG 2:4**). Now release the diaphragm to unhook the pull rod. Take care not to damage the diaphragm or oil seal during the operation. Use a hammer and suitable drift to drive the rocker arm pin from the lower body.

Clean all parts and check for wear or damage. Check the diaphragm for pin holes, cracks or wear. Check the rocker arm for wear at the bearing surface which contacts the camshaft. Carefully inspect the rocker arm pin for wear, as this fault may cause oil leakage. Renew any faulty components.

Reassemble the fuel pump in the reverse order of dismantling. Lubricate the rocker arm, link and pin before installation.

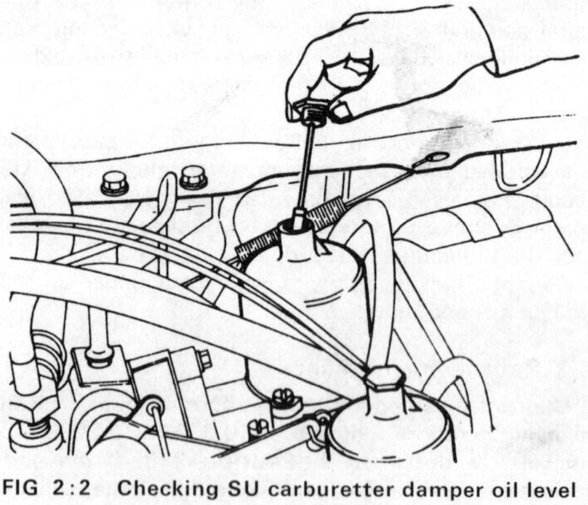

FIG 2:2 Checking SU carburetter damper oil level

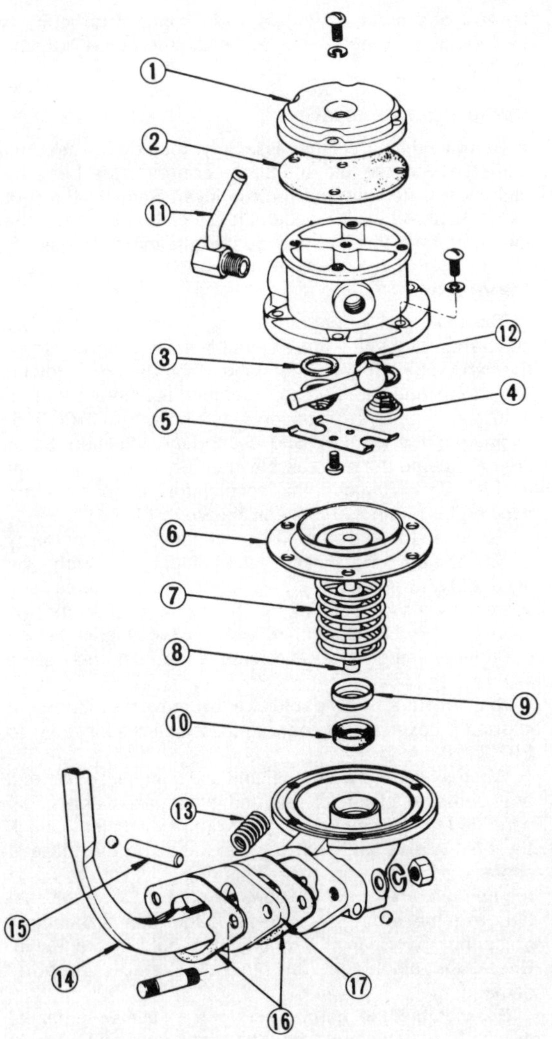

FIG 2:3 **Fuel pump components**

Key to Fig 2:3 1 Fuel pump cap 2 Cap gasket 3 Valve gasket 4 Fuel pump valve 5 Valve retainer 6 Diaphragm 7 Diaphragm spring 8 Pull rod 9 Lower body seal washer 10 Lower body seal 11 Inlet connector 12 Outlet connector 13 Rocker arm spring 14 Rocker arm 15 Rocker arm side pin 16 Fuel pump gasket 17 Spacer

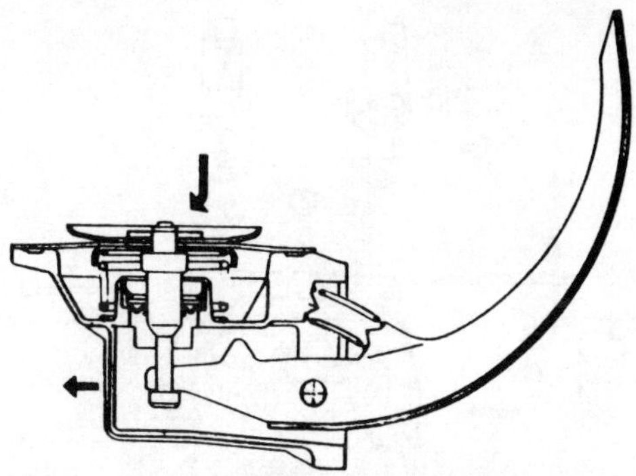

FIG 2:4 **Removing pump diaphragm assembly**

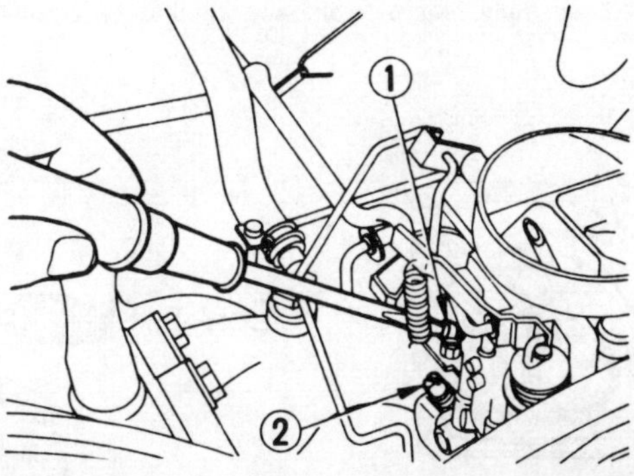

FIG 2:5 **Idle adjustment screws on standard single carburetter**

Key to Fig 2:5 1 Throttle adjustment screw 2 Idle mixture screw

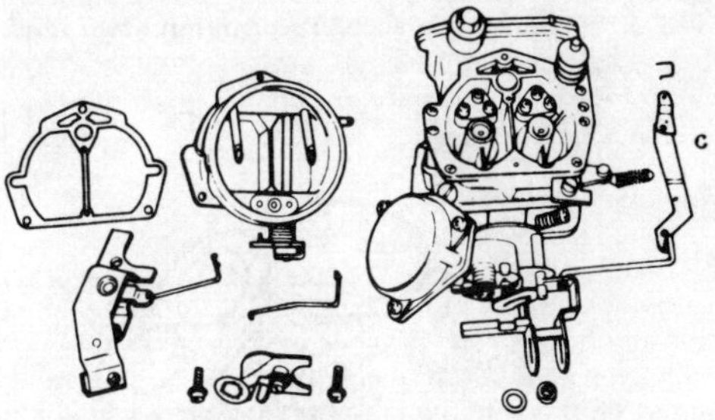

FIG 2:6 **Choke chamber removal**

2:5 Single carburetter

Slow-running adjustment:

If the carburetter has been overhauled and the idle settings lost, turn the idle mixture screw shown at 2 in **FIG 2:5** down gently to the stop then unscrew by two-and-a-quarter turns for L14 and L16 engines, or one-and-a-half turns for L18 engines. Slacken the throttle adjusting screw 1, tighten it until it just contacts the linkage, then tighten by a further two or three turns.

Start the engine and run it until it reaches normal operating temperature. With the engine idling, adjust screw 1 until an engine speed of approximately 600rev/min is obtained for manual transmission models, or 650rev/min on automatic transmission models. Now adjust the idle mixture screw to obtain the fastest possible idle speed. This done, adjust the throttle adjustment screw to return the idle to the specified speed. Repeat the procedure as necessary to obtain a smooth reliable idle.

Note that idle speed adjustments will only be effective if the sparking plugs, contact points and ignition system

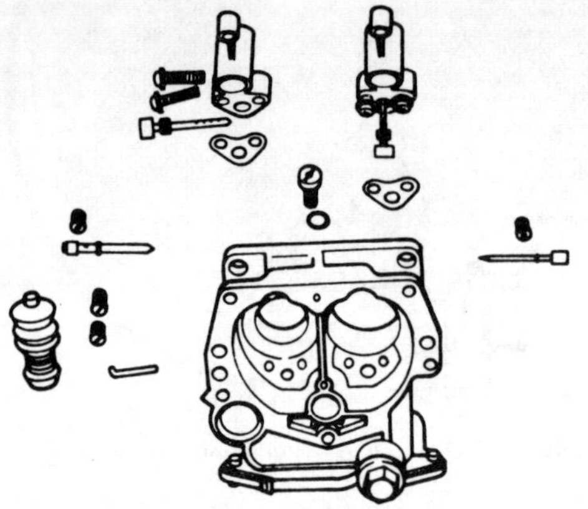

FIG 2:7 Removing primary and secondary emulsion tubes

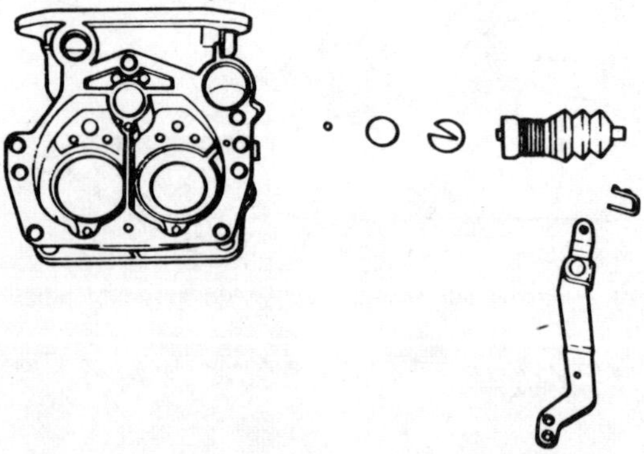

FIG 2:8 Removing accelerator pump assembly

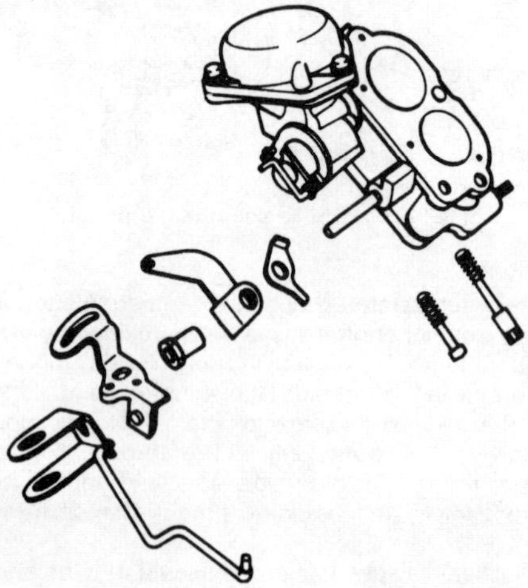

FIG 2:9 Removing throttle valve assembly

are in good order, so check these points if difficulty is experienced in obtaining a satisfactory slow-running setting.

Carburetter removal:

Remove the air cleaner assembly, then disconnect the fuel pipe, vacuum line and choke control cable from the carburetter. Remove the throttle lever. Remove the four fixing nuts and washers then lift the carburetter from the inlet manifold. Remove and discard the manifold gasket.

Servicing:

The main jets and slow-running jets on both primary and secondary sides are accessible from the outside of the carburetter. Detach the choke chamber by removing the connecting rod, pump connecting rod, return spring, stop pin and three setscrews as shown in **FIG 2:6**. Dismantle the primary and secondary emulsion tubes after removing the main air bleed on each side, as shown in **FIG 2:7**. Remove the accelerator pump arm and accelerator pump assembly as shown in **FIG 2:8**.

Remove the throttle valve chamber assembly by removing the rod linking the diaphragm with the secondary throttle valve and loosening the three setscrews, as shown in **FIG 2:9**. Do not remove the throttle valves unless component renewal is necessary. Detach the float chamber cover and remove the float and needle valve assemblies.

Remove the attaching screws and remove the diaphragm chamber, cover and diaphragm assemblies as shown in **FIG 2:10**.

Wash all parts in clean fuel and use compressed air or a tyre pump to clean all jets and passages. Examine all parts and renew any which are worn or damaged. Check the float needle and seat for wear and the throttle and choke shaft bores for wear or scoring. Inspect the tip of the idle mixture screw for burrs or ridges. Clean the fuel filter to remove dirt or sediment. If the filter is damaged or cannot be cleaned properly it should be renewed. Check the diaphragm for pin holes, cracks or other damage.

Reassemble the carburetter in the reverse order of dismantling, carrying out the following adjustment procedures.

FIG 2:10 Removing diaphragm assembly

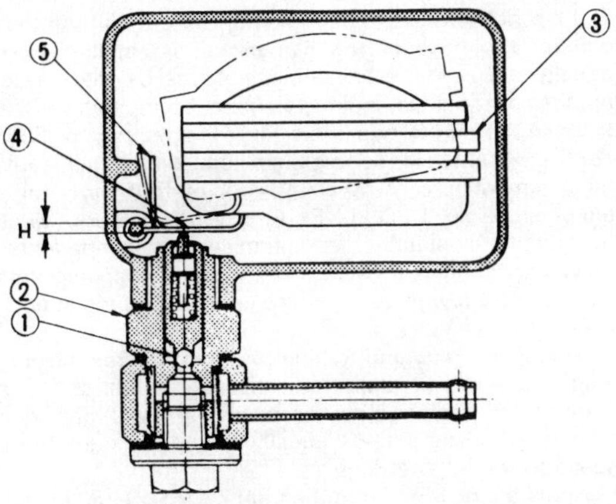

FIG 2:11 Checking float level and operating stroke

Key to Fig 2:11 1 Ball valve 2 Valve seat 3 Float 4 Float arm 5 Float stopper

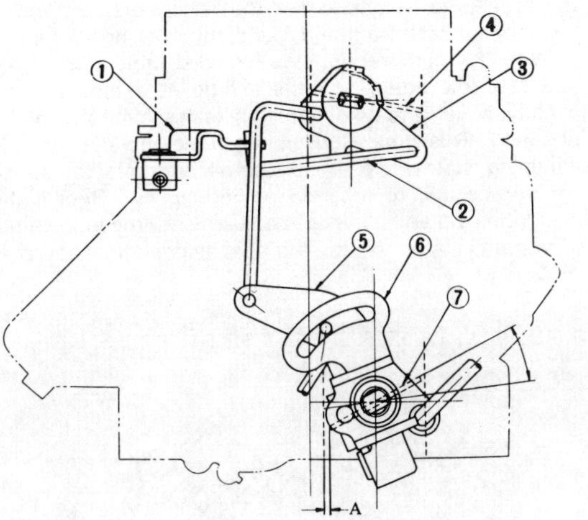

FIG 2:12 Fast-idle linkage

Key to Fig 2:12 1 Choke lever 2 Crank rod 3 Choke arm 4 Choke valve 5 Starting lever 6 Throttle arm 7 Throttle valve

Float level adjustment:

Assemble the float and needle valve components and invert the assembly as shown in **FIG 2:11**. The float should rest in a horizontal position as shown. From this position, raise the float until stopper 5 contacts the side of the float chamber. In this position, dimension H should be 1mm (0.0394in). Adjust the float level setting if necessary by carefully bending float arm 4, and correct float movement by carefully bending float stopper 5.

Fast-idle linkage adjustment:

Operate the linkage shown in **FIG 2:12** until choke valve 4 is fully closed. In this position, check that dimension A is 1.55mm (0.0610in) for L18 models, 1.3mm (0.0512in) for L16 models or 1.4mm (0.0563in) for L14 models. Use a suitable drill or round wire gauge to measure the gap, as shown in **FIG 2:13**. Adjust clearance A if necessary by carefully bending the choke connecting rod.

Adjusting throttle valve interlock opening:

When a primary throttle valve opens 50°, the connecting link contacts the righthand end of a groove on the primary throttle arm A. When the primary throttle valve opens further, the locking arm is detached from the secondary throttle arm, permitting the start of the

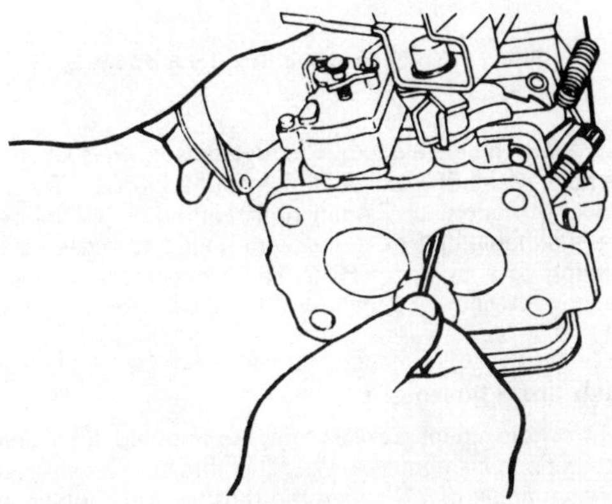

FIG 2:13 Measuring fast-idle setting

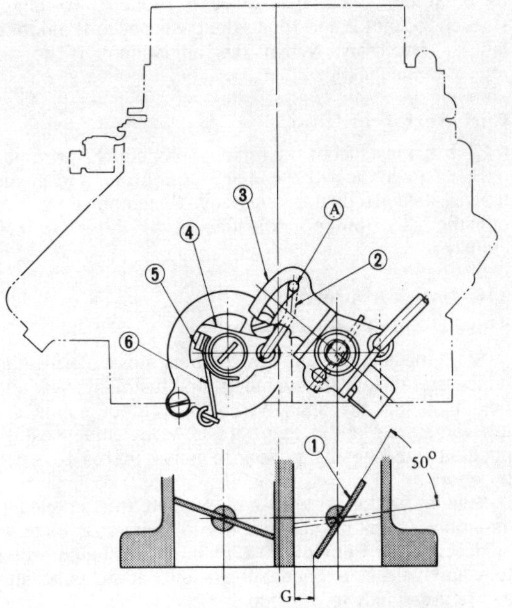

FIG 2:14 Throttle interlock linkage

Key to Fig 2:14 1 Throttle valve 2 Connecting link 3 Throttle arm 4 Rocking arm 5 Secondary throttle arm 6 Rocking arm return spring

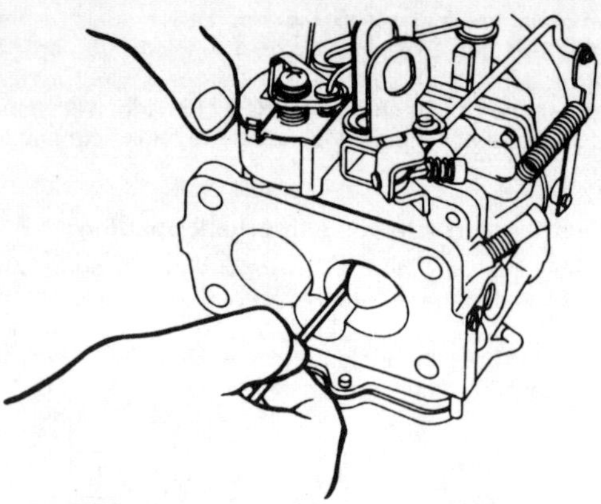

FIG 2:15 Measuring interlock opening

secondary throttle system. The linkage setting is correct if distance G in **FIG 2:14** is 6.3mm (0.2480in) for L18 and L14 models, or 7.4mm (0.2913in) for L16 models. Use a suitable drill or round wire gauge to measure the opening as shown in **FIG 2:15**. If necessary, adjust to the correct figure by carefully bending the connecting link.

Dash pot adjustment:

This adjustment applies only to models fitted with automatic transmission units. The throttle valve should be at an angle of 11° when the throttle arm touches the dash pot stem, as shown in **FIG 2:16**. In this position, clearance B will be 0.780mm (0.307in) on L18 models, or 0.586mm (0.0231in) on L16 models. To adjust, slacken locknut 2 and rotate the dash pot to the right or left as necessary. When the adjustment is correct, retighten the locknut.

Carburetter refitting:

This is a reversal of the removal procedure, using new gaskets. Reconnect the carburetter controls and ensure that all linkages operate correctly. On completion, carry out the slow-running adjustments as described previously.

2:6 Twin carburetters

Slow-running adjustment:

Start the engine and run it up to normal operating temperature. Note that carburetter adjustments will only be effective if the sparking plugs, contact points and ignition system are in good order. A flow meter will be necessary to check the balance between the two carburetters.

Switch off the engine and remove the air cleaner assembly. Check the oil level in the carburetter dampers as described in **Section 2:2**. Push the choke control in fully and make sure that the choke lever at the carburetter has returned fully to the stop.

Refer to **FIG 2:17** and loosen both front and rear carburetter throttle adjusting screws, the balance screw and the fast-idle setting screw. Make sure that the front and rear throttle shafts will now move independently.

Tighten both front and rear idle adjusting nuts until they contact the base of the carburetter assemblies. Now equally unscrew the idle adjusting nuts by the correct number of turns, according to ambient temperature. The standard setting is two turns for a temperature of 30°C (86°F). Alternative settings are one-and-a-half turns for a temperature of 40°C (104°F), or four turns for a temperature of −10°C (14°F). Adjust the number of turns to obtain a suitable compromise for temperatures between the figures stated. Note that the adjusting nuts must be unscrewed by the same number of turns at each carburetter.

Start the engine and tighten the front and rear throttle adjusting screws equally until the engine will idle at a comfortable speed. Now unscrew the front and rear throttle adjusting screws equally to reduce the engine speed to 600–700rev/min.

Apply the flow meter to the front carburetter air intake.

Apply the flow meter to the rear carburetter and check the reading. If the meter does not align with the position set at the front carburetter, carefully adjust the rear carburetter throttle adjusting screw until it does. This operation will synchronise the two carburetters. Repeat the procedure to check that the flow meter reading is the same at both front and rear carburetter positions.

With the carburetters synchronised, adjust the front and rear idle adjusting nuts a little at a time and by exactly equal amounts until the fastest smooth idle is obtained. This done, loosen the front and rear throttle adjusting screws by exactly equal amounts to reduce the engine idle to a speed of 650rev/min. Repeat the synchronising and idle speed adjustment procedures until a smooth, stable idle at the specified engine speed is obtained.

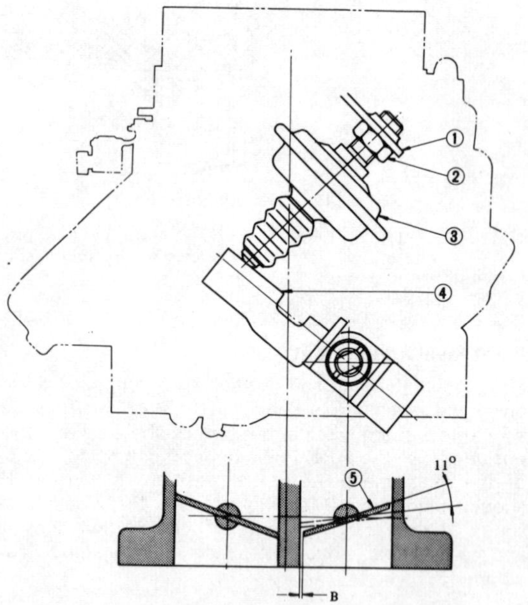

FIG 2:16 Measuring dash pot clearance

Key to Fig 2:16 1 Dash pot bracket 2 Locknut 3 Dash pot 4 Throttle lever 5 Throttle valve

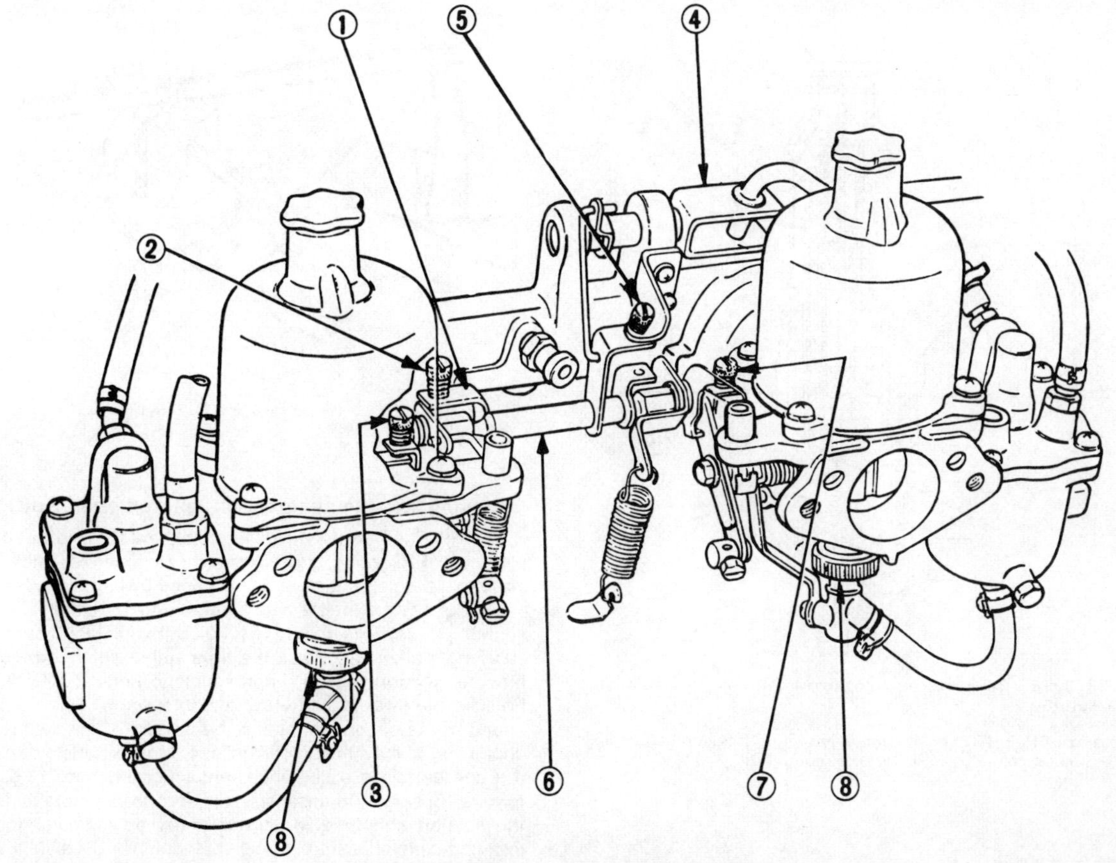

FIG 2:17 Twin carburetter operating linkage

Key to Fig 2:17 1 Throttle lever 2 Balance screw 3 Throttle adjusting screw (front) 4 Auxiliary shaft 5 Fast-idle setting screw 6 Throttle shaft 7 Throttle adjusting screw (rear) 8 Idle adjusting nuts

The throttle linkage must now be correctly set. Tighten the balance screw 2 until the screw head contacts the throttle connecting lever, making sure that the idling speed is not altered. Adjust the balance screw so that the carburetter pistons act simultaneously. Check the adjustment by moving the throttle shaft to rapidly accelerate the engine several times. The engine should return to the original idle speed setting.

Adjust the fast-idle setting screw 5 to increase the engine speed to approximately 1500rev/min, then use the flow meter to check that the flow is the same at each carburetter. If not, carefully readjust the balance screw 2.

Slacken the fast-idle setting screw to decrease engine speed. Move the throttle shaft to rapidly accelerate the engine a few times, then again check for equal flow at the carburetters. If the flow is uneven, adjust the front and rear throttle adjusting screws independently to obtain an equal flow at the specified idle speed. Repeat this final procedure to ensure correct carburetter synchronisation, then readjust the front and rear throttle adjusting screws by equal amounts to obtain the correct engine idle speed.

Set the throttle shaft so that the throttle valve is just starting to open, then adjust the clearance between the tip of the fast-idle setting screw 5 and the linkage to 1 to 2mm (0.039 to 0.078in). Switch off the engine and install the air cleaner assembly.

Removing carburetters:

Remove the air cleaner assembly from the carburetter flanges. Disconnect the fuel feed pipes and the distributor vacuum line. Disconnect the throttle and choke control linkages from the carburetters. Unscrew the securing nuts and remove the carburetters from the inlet manifold flanges. Remove and discard the flange gaskets.

Servicing:

The carburetters should not be dismantled unless absolutely necessary. If operational faults indicate that overhaul is essential, the work should be carried out with great care to avoid damage to the internal components.

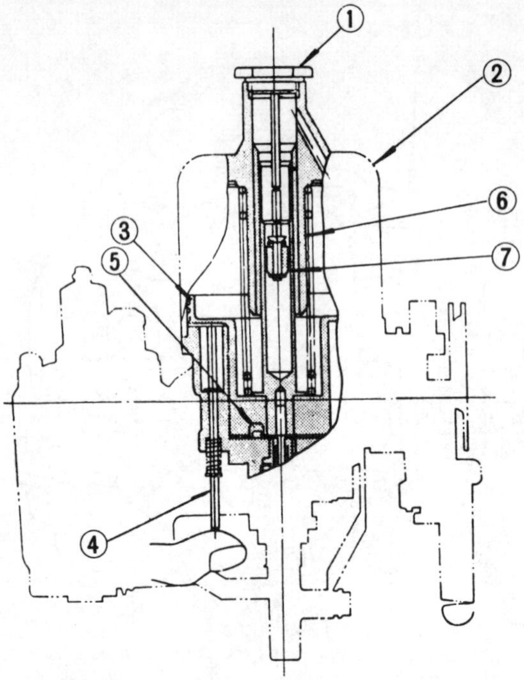

FIG 2:18 Carburetter suction chamber and piston assembly

Key to Fig 2:18 1 Oil cap nut 2 Suction chamber 3 Suction piston 4 Lifter 5 Stop pin 6 Oil damper 7 Plunger

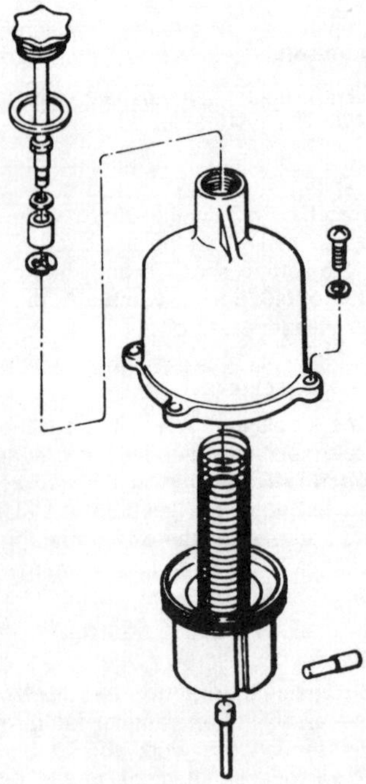

FIG 2:19 Suction chamber and piston removal

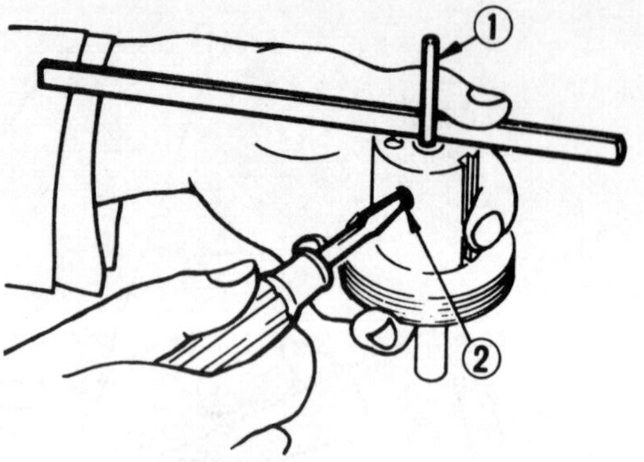

FIG 2:20 Installing jet needle

Key to Fig 2:20 1 Jet needle 2 Set screw

Checking suction chamber and piston operation:

With the carburetters installed, unscrew the cap nut 1 shown in **FIG 2:18** and remove the damper assembly. Note that the cap nut must be tightened by hand only.

Gradually raise lifter 4 with a finger until it contacts the suction piston. This should require approximately 1.5mm (0.06in) movement. Raise the lifter fully, which should lift the suction piston approximately 8mm (0.32in). Release the lifter to allow the piston to drop, when the sound of the piston contacting the bottom of the venturi should be clearly heard. Piston operation is satisfactory if it can be raised easily and drops smoothly back to its original position. If unsatisfactory results are obtained, the suction chamber and piston must be removed for cleaning and checking. Check the damper oil level as described in **Section 2:2**, refit the damper assembly then repeat the test. Resistance should be felt when the piston is lifted due to the action of the damper unit, but the piston should still drop smoothly when the lifter is released. If the piston sticks, suspect a bent damper rod.

Dismantling suction chamber and piston:

Refer to **FIG 2:19**. Take out the four screws and remove the suction chamber, then remove the spring, nylon washer and piston from the chamber. Take great care not to damage the piston sliding surfaces or the needle assembly.

Do not remove the needle unless renewal is necessary. If the needle must be removed, first loosen the jet needle setscrew and then hold the needle within 2mm (0.08in) from the shoulder with a pair of pliers then pull and turn very carefully to avoid bending the needle. When refitting, set the needle in the piston so that the shouldered part is flush with the bottom of the piston. Use a straight-edge to align needle shoulder and piston surface as shown in **FIG 2:20**, then tighten the retaining setscrew.

Wash the suction chamber and piston with a suitable solvent to remove dust and oil, then dry thoroughly with compressed air. Apply a few drops of light oil to the suction piston rod, then refit the piston to the chamber. Under no circumstances must oil be applied to the inside of the suction chamber or to the large end of the

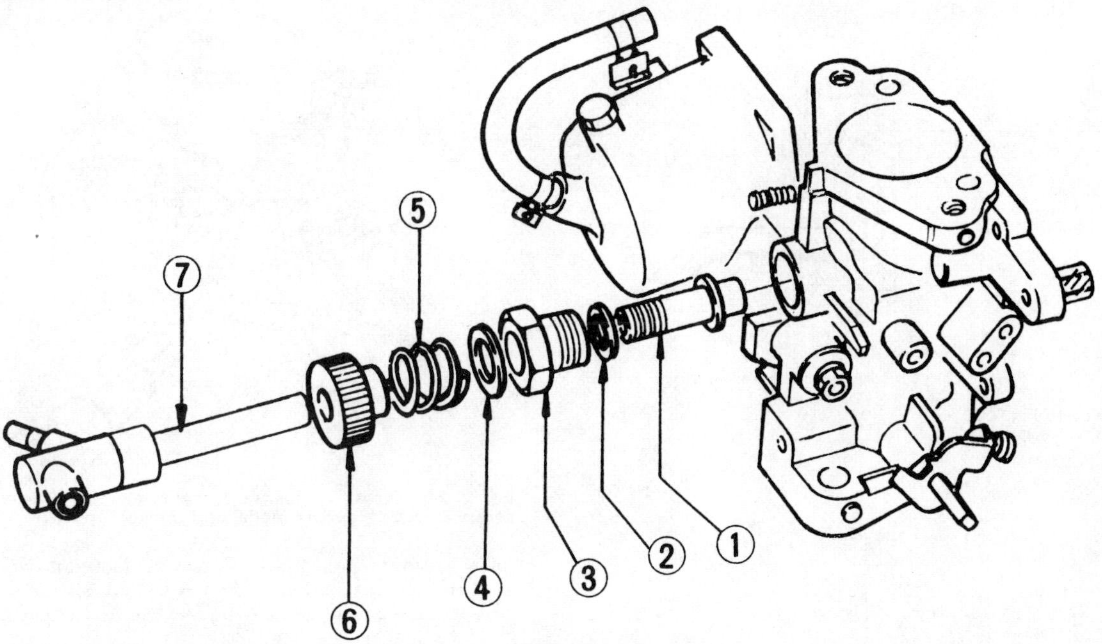

FIG 2:21 Jet nozzle components

Key to Fig 2:21 1 Nozzle sleeve 2 Washer 3 Nozzle sleeve set screw 4 Adjusting shim 5 Idle adjust nut spring 6 Idle adjust nut 7 Nozzle

piston. Refit the suction chamber assembly to the carburetter, then recheck piston operation as described previously.

Dismantling jet nozzle:

This work should only be carried out if it is absolutely essential, as accurate reassembly and alignment is extremely difficult.

The jet nozzle components are shown in **FIG 2:21**. Remove the 4mm (0.1575in) diameter screw, then remove the connecting plate from the nozzle head by pulling lightly on the choke lever. Loosen the clip and remove the fuel line. Remove the jet nozzle from the carburetter, taking care not to damage either the nozzle or jet needle. Remove the idle adjusting nut and spring. If it is essential to remove the jet nozzle sleeve, this can be carried out after removing the setscrew.

Carefully clean all parts in a suitable solvent and dry with compressed air.

Before refitting the jet nozzle assembly, unscrew the cap nut and remove the damper assembly from the top of the carburetter. The suction chamber, piston and needle valve must not be removed. Assemble the jet nozzle sleeve, washer and sleeve setscrew by tightening the setscrew temporarily. Make sure that the suction piston is in the fully closed position then insert the jet nozzle until it contacts the nozzle sleeve. When the jet contacts the needle, move the sleeve slightly until the needle enters the nozzle tube without contacting the sides of it. Without disturbing this setting, raise the suction piston and lower it slowly. If the piston drops smoothly until the stop pin lightly strikes the venturi, the installation is satisfactory. In this position, securely tighten the nozzle sleeve setscrew.

Remove the nozzle, fit the idle adjusting spring and adjusting nut on the nozzle sleeve, then refit the nozzle. Connect the fuel line to the nozzle nipple and fully tighten the retaining clip. Take care not to twist the fuel line.

With the choke lever lightly pulled out, fit the connecting plate between the washer and sleeve collar then fasten the plate to the nozzle head with the fixing screws. By moving the choke lever as necessary, make certain that the collar is fitted in the hole in the plate. Check again to ensure that the suction piston operates freely.

On completion, top up the damper with oil and carry out the slow-running adjustments as described previously.

Dismantling float chamber:

Disconnect the fuel pipes from the fittings on the float chamber cover. Remove the four fixing screws and lift off the cover and float lever assembly. Carefully remove the float from the float chamber.

Check the float for damage or leaks. If any faults are found a new float must be fitted. Remove the drain plug from the bottom of the float chamber and flush through with clean petrol to remove any dirt or sediment. Refit the drain plug and replace the float.

Check the float level by inverting the float chamber cover as shown in **FIG 2:22**. Lift up the float lever then

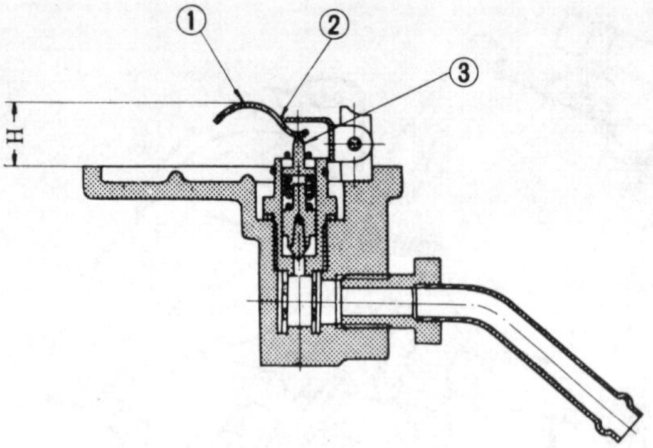

FIG 2:22 Checking float level setting

Key to Fig 2:22 1 Float lever 2 Adjustment point 3 Valve stem

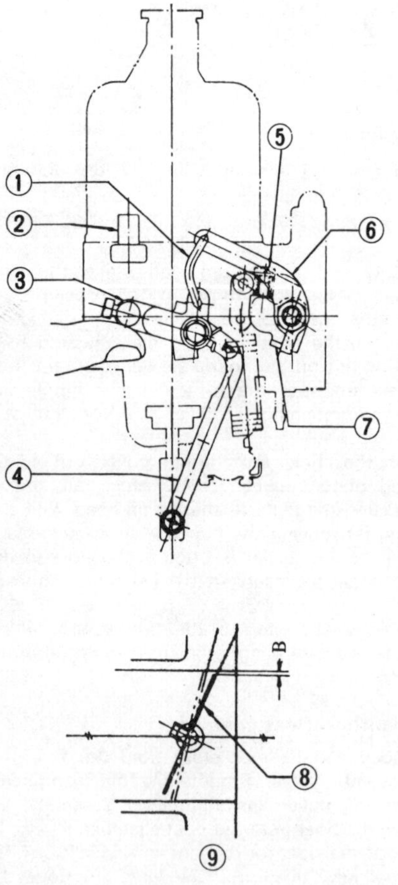

FIG 2:23 Interlock valve adjustment

Key to Fig 2:23 1 Connecting rod 2 Wire guard 3 Choke lever 4 Connecting plate 5 Throttle adjusting screw 6 Fast-idle lever 7 Throttle adjusting plate 8 Throttle valve 9 Throttle valve-to-chamber clearance

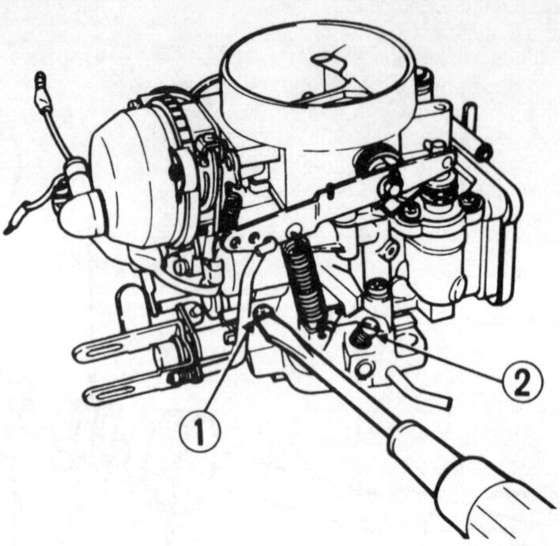

FIG 2:24 Throttle adjusting screw 1 and idle adjusting screw 2 on USA export model carburetter

lower it slowly until the lever seat contacts the valve stem. In this position, dimension H should be between 11 and 12mm (0.43 and 0.47in). Adjust if necessary by carefully bending the float lever.

Refit the float chamber cover and evenly tighten the fixing screws. Reconnect the fuel pipes.

Adjusting interlock valve:

The interlock valve mechanism is shown in **FIG 2:23**. Apply the choke fully by raising choke lever 3. In this position, the clearance between the throttle valve and the chamber wall should be 0.6mm (0.0236in), measured at point B. Adjust if necessary by carefully bending connecting rod 1.

Refitting carburetters:

This is a reversal of the removal procedure, using new gaskets. On completion carry out the slow-running adjustments as described previously.

2:7 USA export model carburetter

The carburetter fitted on models exported to the USA is a dual-barrel downdraught instrument incorporating special design features and sub-systems to ensure an optimum air/fuel mixture under all operating conditions. The main features of the carburetter are as follows:

1 A slow economiser unit to ensure a smooth transition between acceleration and deceleration during light load running. It also ensures a stable low speed performance.

2 Idle limiter to reduce harmful exhaust emissions to a minimum.

3 A boost controlled deceleration device to reduce HC emissions during coasting. The high manifold vacuum which occurs when the throttle is released at high engine speeds prevents the mixture from complete combustion which results in a large amount of HC emissions into the atmosphere. The BCDD system operates to provide an additional mixture of optimum ratio and quantity into the inlet manifold by opening

a separate mixture passage in the carburetter. This ensures complete combustion and greatly reduces the amount of HC contained in the exhaust gas.

4 An electrically operated automatic choke unit to finely control mixture strength during cold starting and running conditions.

5 An anti-dieseling solenoid to prevent a hot engine from running-on when the ignition is switched off. When the ignition is switched off, the anti-dieseling valve operates to completely shut off the supply of fuel to the carburetter idle circuit.

6 A vacuum actuated booster to ensure smooth high speed operation.

Carburetter servicing:

It is not recommended that owners attempt to dismantle the carburetter or to carry out any component adjustments, due to the need for special tools and gauge equipment to correctly set the various systems for optimum performance. Instead, all carburetter maintenance and overhaul operations should be carried out by a fully equipped Datsun service station.

Slow-running adjustment:

This work requires the use of an accurate CO meter to analyse the exhaust gas while the engine is idling.

Start the engine and run it to normal operating temperature, then allow to idle for one minute. Refer to **FIG 2:24**. Turn the throttle adjusting screw 1 to obtain an engine speed of 800rev/min with the gearlever in neutral. Check the ignition timing as described in **Chapter 3**, using a stroboscopic lamp. Now adjust the idle adjusting screw 2 until the CO percentage is 1.5.

Reset the throttle adjusting screw to obtain the correct engine idling speed if it has altered, then readjust screw 2 to bring CO emissions within limits. Repeat this procedure as necessary until the settings are correct.

On models fitted with automatic transmission, check the final setting with the road wheels chocked, the handbrake applied and the selector lever in the D position. Idle speed should then be 650rev/min with a CO percentage of 1.5. Readjust at screws 1 and 2 if necessary to obtain these conditions.

2:8 Fault diagnosis

(a) Leakage or insufficient fuel delivery

1 Air vent to tank restricted
2 Fuel pipes blocked
3 Air leaks at pipe connections
4 Fuel filter blocked
5 Pump gaskets faulty
6 Pump diaphragm defective
7 Pump valve sticking or seating badly

(b) Excessive fuel consumption

1 Carburetter requires adjustment
2 Fuel leakage
3 Sticking choke unit
4 Float level too high
5 Dirty air cleaner
6 Excessive engine temperature
7 Brakes binding
8 Idling speed too high

(c) Idling speed too high

1 Incorrect idle speed adjustment
2 Rich fuel mixture
3 Throttle control sticking
4 Choke unit sticking
5 Worn throttle valves or shafts

(d) Noisy fuel pump

1 Loose pump mountings
2 Air leaks on suction side of diaphragm
3 Obstruction in fuel pipeline
4 Clogged fuel filter

(e) No fuel delivery

1 Float needle valve stuck
2 Tank vents blocked
3 Defective pump diaphragm
4 Pump valves stuck
5 Pipeline obstructed
6 Bad air leak on suction side of pump

NOTES

CHAPTER 3

THE IGNITION SYSTEM

3:1 Description

The ignition system is conventional, comprising an ignition coil, distributor and contact breaker system. The distributor incorporates automatic timing control by means of centrifugal mechanism and a vacuum controlled unit. As engine speed increases, the centrifugal action of rotating weights pivoting against the tension of small springs moves the contact breaker cam relative to the distributor drive shaft and progressively advances the ignition. The vacuum unit is connected by a small bore pipe to a fitting on the carburetter. At high degrees of vacuum the unit advances the ignition, but under load, at reduced vacuum, the unit progressively retards the ignition. By these means, near optimum settings for the different engine speeds and loads are achieved.

The ignition coil is of the high output type with a series resistance wire incorporated. When the starter is switched on, the series resistor is disconnected and full battery voltage is fed to the coil to obtain the best possible spark at cranking speeds, but when the starter is switched off the resistor automatically functions to reduce the current to the coil.

California models from 1975 on have an electronic ignition system. The parts of the distributor are shown in **FIG 3:15**. Within the distributor the contact breaker assembly is replaced by a magnetic sensor which triggers the transistor unit. The transistor unit then breaks the primary coil current electronically. The centrifugal and vacuum advance systems operate normally. The contactor serves to eliminate vacuum and centrifugal advance hysteresis. The transistor ignition unit is located on the lefthand dash side panel in the passenger compartment.

3:2 Routine maintenance

Pull off the two spring clips and remove the distributor cap. Pull the rotor from the top of the shaft. Apply a tiny drop of oil to the moving contact pivot point and a light smear of grease to the cam lobes. Avoid allowing grease or oil to contaminate the contact breaker points, lubricating sparingly for this reason.

Adjusting the contact points:

Turn the engine until one of the cams has opened the points to the fullest extent, then check the gap between the points with a clean feeler gauge. The correct gap is 0.45 to 0.55mm (0.018 to 0.021in). To adjust the gap, slacken the adjuster screw so that the fixed contact

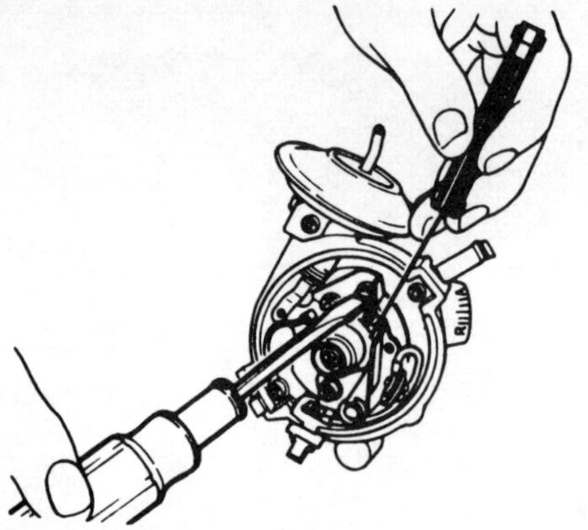

FIG 3:1 Adjusting contact points gap

point is just free to move, then move the fixed contact point until the feeler gauge is lightly nipped and a slight drag is felt on it as it is moved (see **FIG 3:1**). Tighten the adjuster screw and check that the adjustment has not altered.

Cleaning the contact points:

Use a fine carborundum stone or a special contact point file to polish the points if they are dirty or pitted, taking care to keep their faces flat and square. On

FIG 3:2 Contact breaker assembly and terminal connections

Key to Fig 3:2 1 Screw 2 Adjuster 3 Primary lead terminal 4 Earth lead wire 5 Set screw

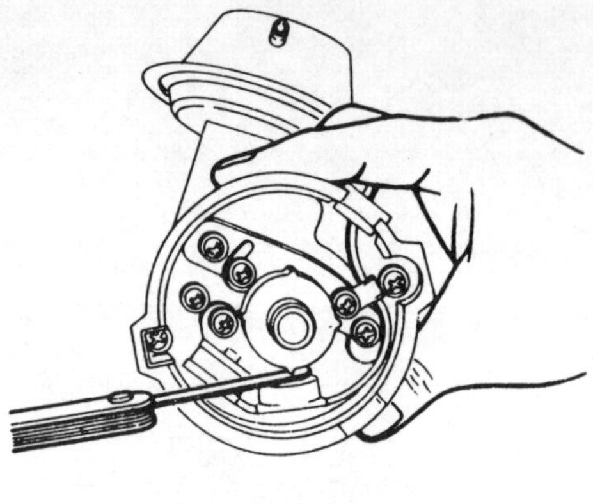

FIG 3:3 Electronic ignition. Checking the air gap

completion, wipe away all dust with a cloth moistened in petrol, then set the points gap as described previously. If the points are badly pitted or burned and will require excessive removal of material to clean up, the complete points set should be renewed.

Renewing contact points:

Remove the distributor cap and rotor arm, then disconnect the contact breaker plate fixing screws and the terminal connections at the points shown in **FIG 3:2**. Lift out the contact breaker plate assembly, taking care not to lose the steel balls fitted between the breaker spring and breaker plate. Clean the mating faces of the new contact points with a cloth moistened in petrol or methylated spirits, to remove the protective coating applied at the factory, Fit the new points set in the reverse order of removal, adjusting the points gap as described previously.

Adjusting the air gap (electronic ignition models only):

Turn the engine until one of the ridges of the reluctor is opposite the pick-up coil. Check the air gap with a clean feeler gauge as shown in **FIG 3:3**. The gap should be between 0.2 and 0.4mm (0.008 and 0.016in).

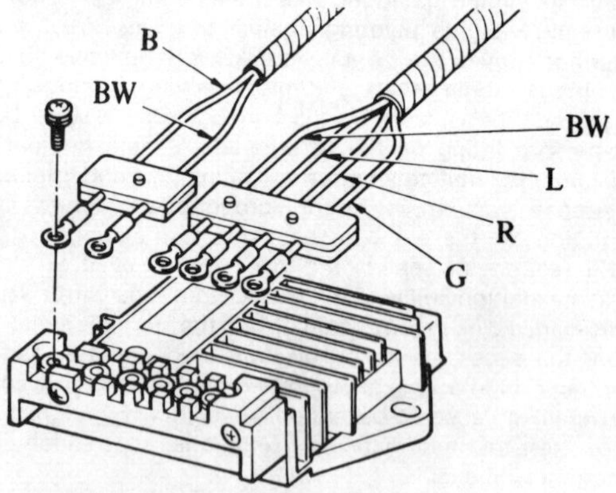

FIG 3:4 Electronic ignition unit and wiring connectors

Adjustment is made by loosening the pick-up coil screws. Remove any foreign matter from the air gap.

3:3 Ignition faults

If the engine runs unevenly, set it to idle at about 1000rev/min and, taking care not to touch any metal part of the plug leads, remove and replace each lead from its sparking plug in turn. Doing this to a plug which is firing properly will accentuate the uneven running but will make no difference if that plug is not firing. To avoid shocks during this test, it is advisable to wear a thick glove or use a pair of insulated pliers to pull off the leads. Always pull on the moulded caps at the plugs themselves, never directly on the leads.

Having located the faulty cylinder, stop the engine and remove the plug lead. Remove the plug connector from the lead so that the end of the lead is exposed. If the plug connector cannot be removed, insert a drill or suitable metal bar into the connector to act as an extension. Start the engine and hold the lead carefully to avoid shocks so that the end is about $\frac{1}{8}$in away from the cylinder head. A strong, regular spark confirms that the fault lies with the sparking plug, which should be cleaned as described in **Section 3:7** or renewed if defective.

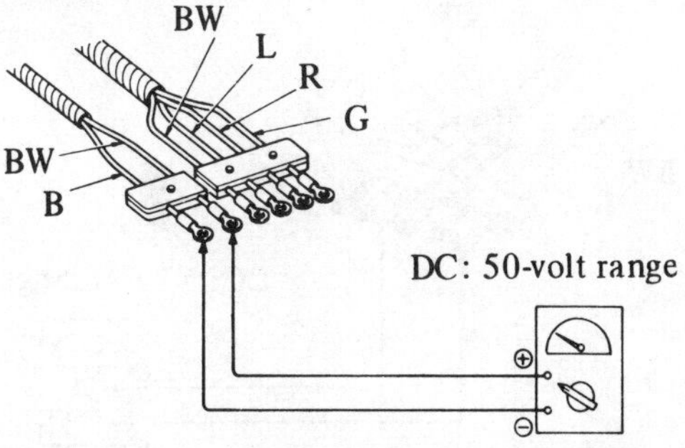

FIG 3:5 Checking the power supply wiring and the battery

If the spark is weak and irregular, check the condition of the lead and, if it is perished or cracked, renew it and repeat the test. If no improvement results, check that the inside of the distributor cap is clean and dry and that there is no sign of tracking, which can be seen as a thin black line between the electrodes or to some metal part in contact with the cap. Tracking can only be rectified by

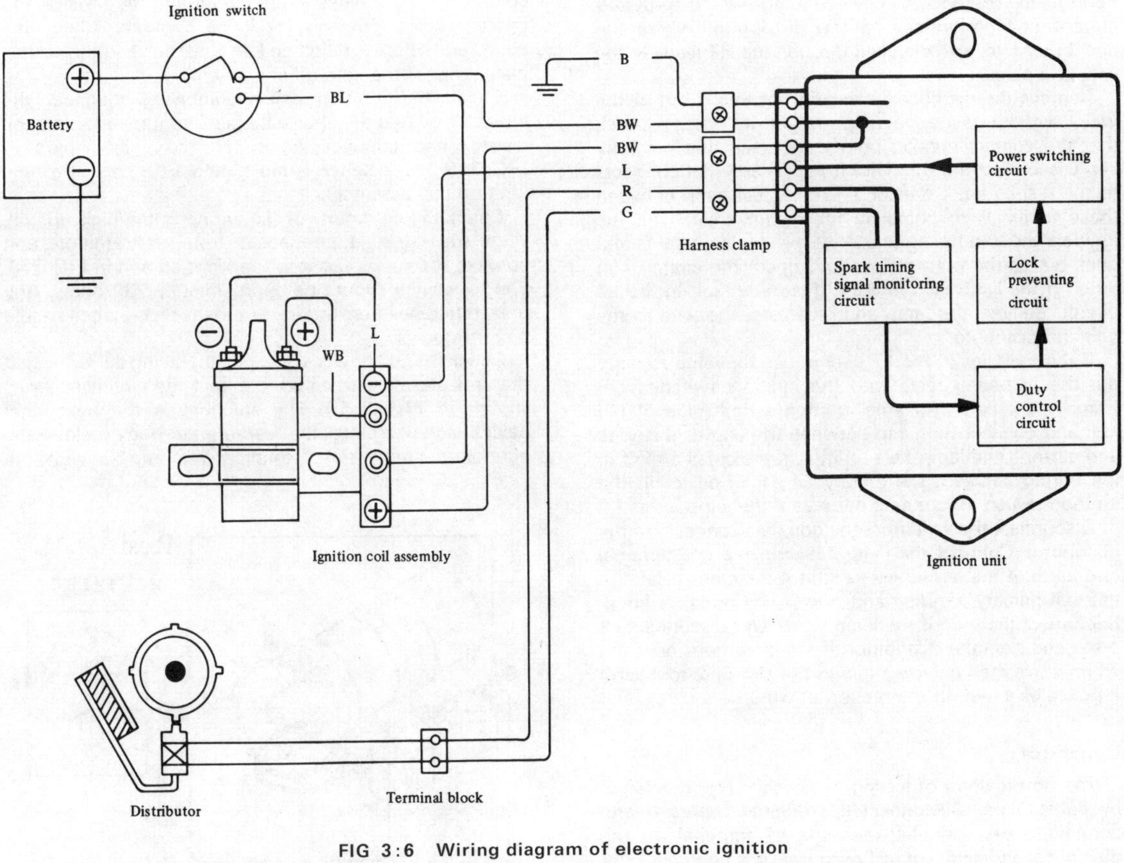

FIG 3:6 Wiring diagram of electronic ignition

Wiring colour code: **B** Black **BW** Black and white **BL** Black and blue **L** Blue **R** Red **G** Green

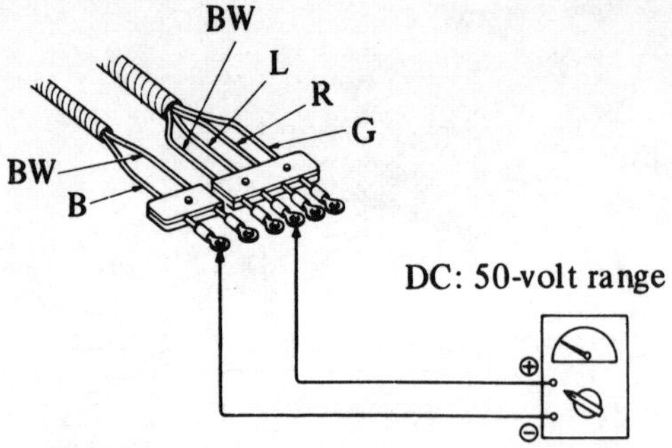

FIG 3:7 Checking primary circuit

fitting a new cap. Check that the carbon brush in the centre of the cap is clean and that it moves freely against its spring to make good contact with the rotor arm.

Testing the LT circuit:

The LT circuit connects the battery, ignition switch, coil primary winding and the contact breaker assembly and provides timed pulses of current to the coil primary windings as the contacts open and close. These pulses control the secondary coil winding which provides current at high voltage to the distributor, where the distributor rotor arm directs it through the HT leads to the sparking plugs.

Remove the distributor cap and position it out of the way, without disconnecting any of its leads. Check that the contact breaker points are clean and correctly set. Disconnect the thin wire from the coil that connects to the distributor. Connect a 12-volt test lamp between these terminals to complete the circuit, switch on the ignition and turn the engine slowly. If the lamp lights and goes out as the points close and open, the circuit is in order. If the lamp fails to light, there is a fault in the LT circuit. Remove the lamp and reconnect the wire to the coil and distributor.

If the fault lies in the LT circuit, use the lamp to carry out the following tests with the ignition switched on. Remove the wire from the ignition switch side of the coil and connect the lamp between the end of this wire and earth. If the lamp fails to light, it indicates a fault in the wiring between the battery and the coil, or in the ignition switch. Reconnect the wire if the lamp lights.

Disconnect the wire from the coil that connects to the distributor. Connect the lamp between the coil terminal and earth. If the lamp fails to light it indicates a fault in the coil primary winding and a new coil must be fitted. Reconnect the wire if the lamp lights and disconnect its other end from the distributor. If the lamp does not light when connected between the end of this wire and earth it indicates a fault in the section of wire.

Capacitor:

The best method of testing a capacitor (condenser) is by substitution. Disconnect the original capacitor and connect a new one between the LT terminal on the distributor and earth for test purposes. If a new capacitor is proved to be required, it can then be properly fitted.

An alternative check for the capacitor is to charge it from a DC source, such as the car battery, then leave it for about five minutes. The terminal and case of the capacitor should then be shorted with a piece of wire and, if the capacitor is in good condition, a noticeable spark should result. If a new capacitor is required, the capacity of the replacement unit should be 0.22 to 0.44 microfarad.

Electronic ignition models:

Should any fault develop in the transistor ignition unit the unit must be renewed. Ensure when fitting a new unit that the car's battery is disconnected and that the wires to the unit are connected as shown in **FIG 3:4**. Incorrect connection will damage the unit.

The operation of the electronic ignition can be checked using a circuit testing meter and the series of tests described here.

First check that the battery voltage is registered when the tester is connected as shown in **FIG 3:5** and the ignition switch is on. If not then check the battery condition and the continuity of the wiring from the battery. The layout of the ignition system wiring is shown in **FIG 3:6**.

Check the continuity of the primary circuit by connecting the meter as shown in **FIG 3:7**. Again normal battery voltage should be registered. If it is not check the continuity of the wires in the circuit and the resistor and ignition coil's terminals for loose contacts. Check the continuity of the ignition coil and resistor and the white/black wire of the ignition coil assembly.

Check the ignition coil assembly. Disconnect the ignition coil and distributor harness from the ignition coil resistor and connect the circuit tester as shown in **FIG 3:8**. If resistance is more than 1.8 ohms fit a new ignition coil assembly.

Check the continuity of the wiring in the pick-up coil. With the wires disconnected from the ignition unit connect the circuit tester to the wires shown in **FIG 3:9**. The resistance should be approximately 720 ohms. Any great difference from this value and the pick-up coil should be renewed.

Check the coil power signal pulse. Having disconnected the anti-dieseling solenoid, connect the circuit tester as shown in **FIG 3:10**. The solenoid is the hexagonal device screwed into the carburetter body below the automatic choke unit. Rotating the engine with the

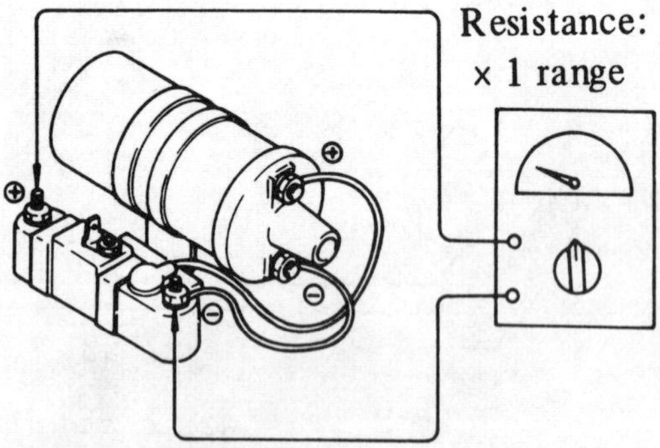

FIG 3:8 Checking ignition coil assembly

starter motor the pointer of the circuit tester should deflect slightly. If it does not deflect at all fit a new pick-up coil assembly.

Check the operation of the transistor ignition unit. Connect the ignition coil and distributor harness to the ignition coil external resistor and the wiring harness to the ignition unit. Disconnect the anti-dieseling solenoid as for the coil power signal check. Hold the end of the coil HT lead, 4 to 5mm away from the engine block keeping the fingers away from the end. Rotate the engine with the starter motor and check that the sparks fly across the gap. If no sparks cross the gap then either the ignition unit or the HT lead is at fault and should be replaced.

Check the lock preventive circuit. Connect the circuit tester as shown in **FIG 3:11**. With the ignition switched on battery voltage should be registered within 10 seconds. If it is not replace the transistor ignition unit.

3:4 Removing and refitting distributor

To remove the distributor from the engine, first disconnect the HT leads to the sparking plugs and remove the distributor cap. Disconnect the LT lead from the terminal on the side of the distributor.

Time may be saved in setting up after maintenance if the precise position of the rotor in relation to one of the terminals is noted and the engine crankshaft is not turned while distributor maintenance is being carried out. Do not slacken the distributor clamp bolt at all, but remove the bolt(s) securing the clamp plate to the cylinder block. Lift the distributor away from the engine. Cover the distributor mounting hole with a clean, lint-free rag to prevent the entry of dirt while the distributor is being serviced.

Refitting:

If the crankshaft position has not been altered since the distributor was removed, turn the rotor to the approximate position it was in and insert the spindle into the drive dog in the engine. Turn the rotor a little as necessary until proper engagement is achieved. Correctly set the ignition timing as described in **Section 3:6**.

Should the crankshaft position have been altered, it is necessary to first set piston No 1 at the top of its compression stroke. To do this, remove the rocker cover and examine the position of the cams. Turn the engine until both cams for No 1 cylinder have their lobes pointing upwards away from the rockers. Now turn the engine a little from this position until the timing marks are correctly aligned as described in **Section 3:6**. Turn the rotor of the distributor until the rotor arm is pointing towards terminal 1 on the distributor cap. Insert the distributor shaft home in the drive dog and set the ignition timing as described in **Section 3:6**. Refit the rocker cover. Refit the distributor cap and connect the HT leads to the respective sparking plugs. Reconnect the LT lead to the terminal on the side of the distributor.

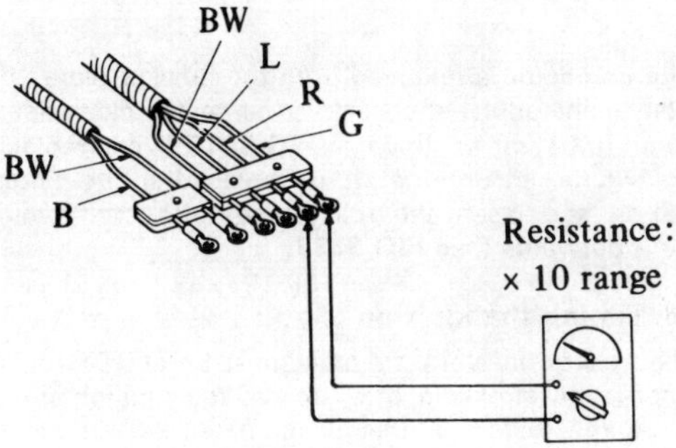

FIG 3:9 Checking pick-up coil

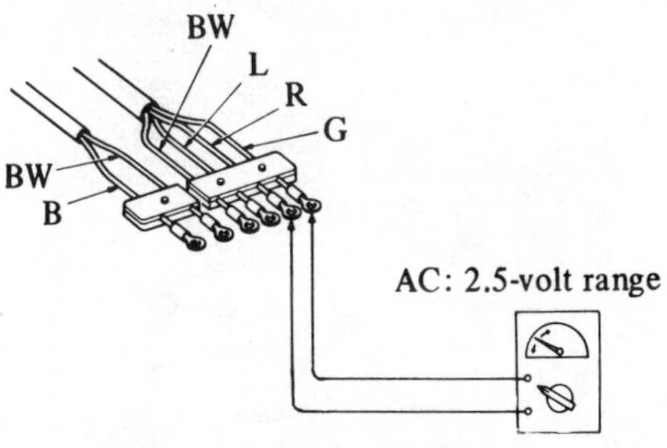

FIG 3:10 Checking pick-up power signal

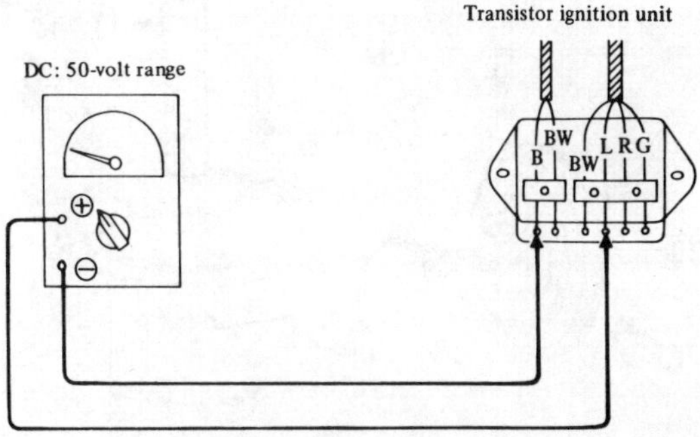

FIG 3:11 Checking lock preventive circuit

3:5 Distributor overhaul

The distributor components are shown in **FIG 3:12** or **FIG 3:13**. Remove the distributor as described in **Section 3:4**. Pull off the rotor arm and remove the vacuum control unit from the distributor body. Remove the contact breaker plate assembly as described previously. Drive the retaining pin from the lower end of the shaft, then withdraw the shaft and centrifugal advance mechanism from the top of the distributor body. If the cam is to be removed from the shaft, make a match mark across cam and shaft so that it will be refitted in its original position. Remove the screw from the upper end of the shaft and detach the cam assembly. If the centrifugal weights and springs are disconnected, take care not to stretch or deform the springs.

Thoroughly clean all components with a suitable solvent, then examine for wear or damage. Renew any faulty components.

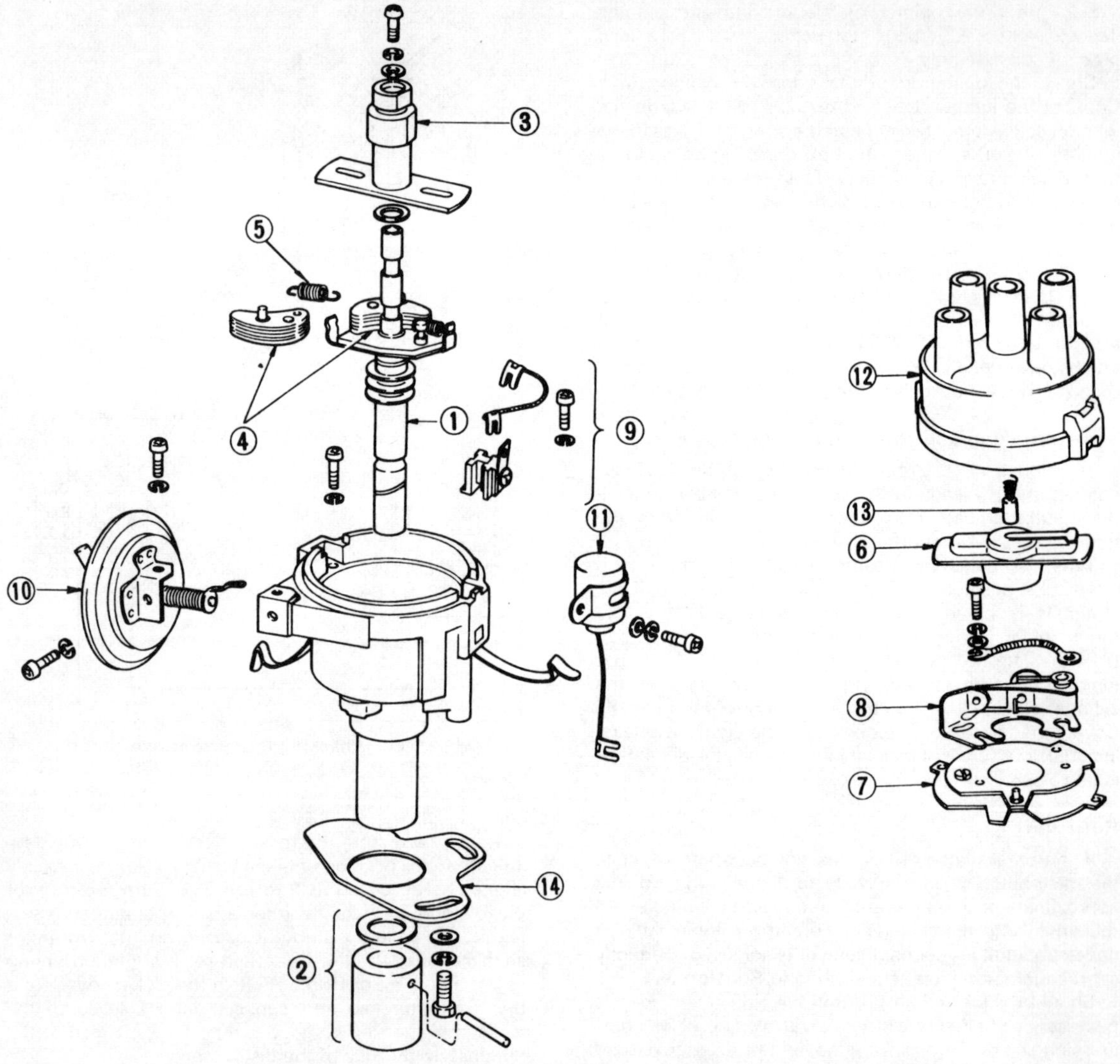

FIG 3:12 Standard distributor components

Key to Fig 3:12 1 Shaft assembly 2 Drive collar assembly 3 Cam assembly 4 Centrifugal advance mechanism 5 Spring 6 Rotor 7 Contact breaker plate 8 Contact points 9 LT terminal 10 Vacuum control unit 11 Capacitor 12 Cap 13 Carbon brush 14 Clamp plate

Reassemble the distributor in the reverse order of dismantling. Reassemble the centrifugal advance mechanism and cam, referring to **FIG 3:14** for alignment details. Lubricate the centrifugal weights with grease. On completion, refit the distributor assembly, lubricate the contact breaker mechanism and set the contact points gap all as described previously. Check the ignition timing as described in the next section.

Electronic ignition models:

Dismantling the distributor is largely the same as for the conventional type. The reluctor is removed by levering it from the shaft and then removing its locating roll pin. If the contactor is removed from the breaker plate, after replacement adjust the cam to contactor clearance to 0.3mm (0.012in) as shown in **FIG 3:16**. When replacing the reluctor ensure that it is replaced in its original position and insert the roll pin with the roll pin slit facing outwards (see **FIG 3:17**).

3:6 Timing the ignition

The piston in No 1 cylinder must be at TDC on the compression stroke in order to set the ignition timing. To set the piston in this position, either remove the rocker cover and turn the engine until both cam lobes for No 1 cylinder are pointing away from the rockers, or

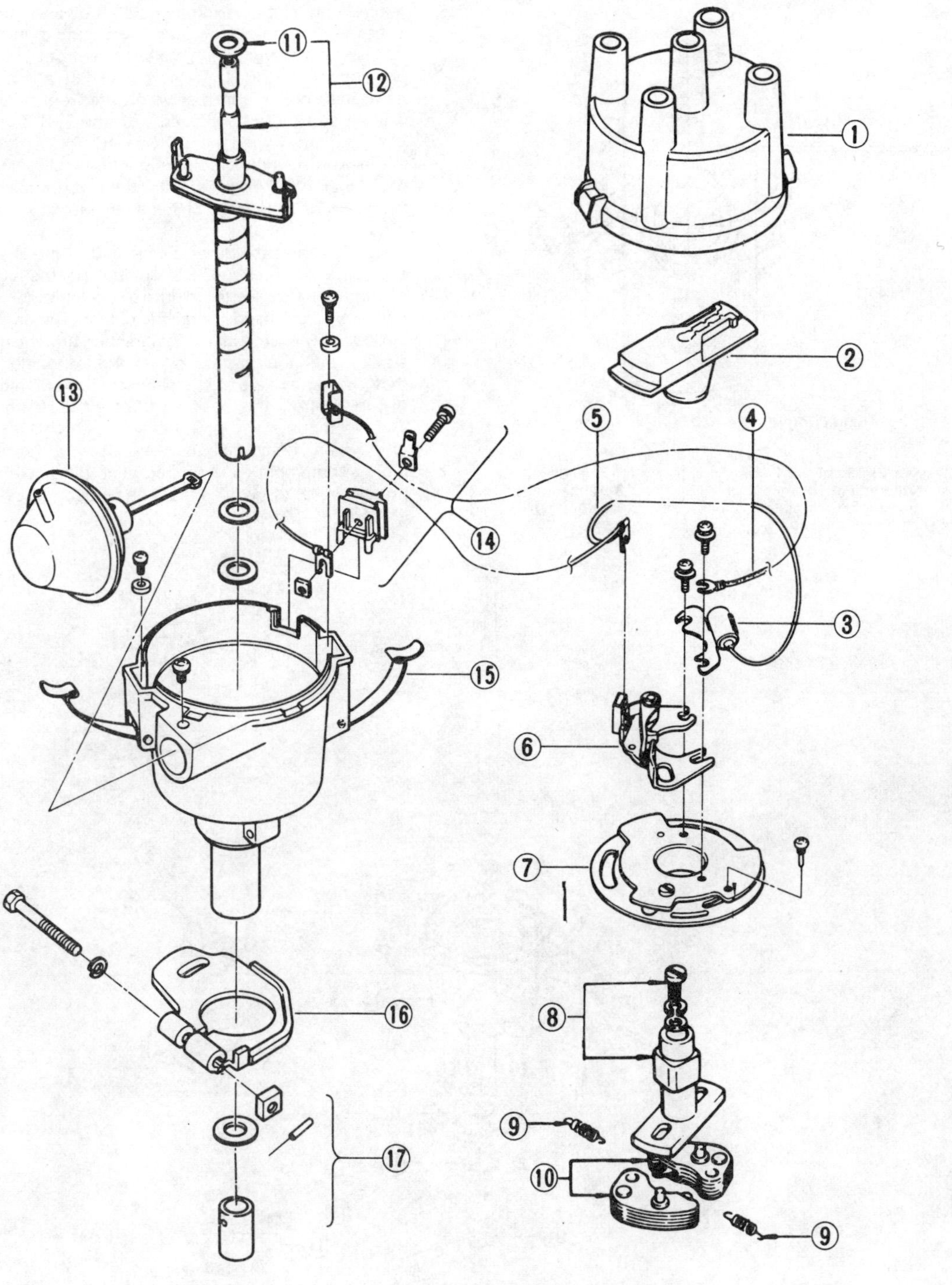

FIG 3:13 Standard distributor components for USA models

Key to Fig 3:13 1 Cap 2 Rotor 3 Capacitor 4 Earth wire 5 Lead wire 6 Contact points 7 Contact breaker plate 8 Cam 9 Spring 10 Centrifugal weight 11 Thrust washer 12 Shaft assembly 13 Vacuum control unit 14 Terminal 15 Clip 16 Clamp plate 17 Drive collar assembly

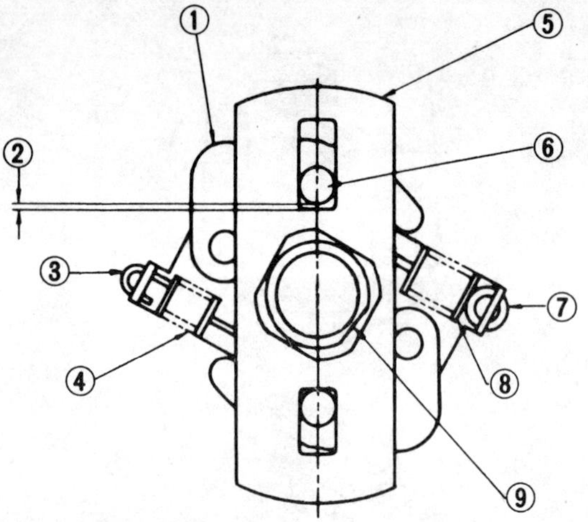

FIG 3:14 **Setting the centrifugal advance mechanism and cam**

Key to Fig 3:14 1 Centrifugal weight 2 Clearance for start and end of advance angle 3 Rectangular hook 4 Spring 5 Cam plate 6 Pin 7 Circular hook 8 Spring 9 Flat for rotor location

remove the sparking plug from No 1 cylinder and turn the engine until compression can be felt by a thumb pressed over the plug hole. Now turn the engine a little more as necessary until the timing marks at the front of the engine are correctly aligned. These consist of a notch in the crankshaft pulley and a scale on the front timing cover. The notch should be aligned with the 8° BTDC mark for L14 engines, with the 10° BTDC for L16 and L18 engines with single carburetter, with the 14° BTDC mark for L16 and L18 engines with twin carburetters and with the 12° BTDC mark for L18 engines fitted to USA export models.

Loosen the distributor clamp and connect a 12-volt test lamp between the LT terminal on the side of the distributor and earth. Turn the distributor body if necessary to ensure that the contact points are fully closed. Now switch on the ignition and turn the distributor slowly until the test lamp just lights, which indicates that the points are just opening. Without moving the distributor from this position, tighten the clamp securely. This method provides a fairly accurate static setting, after which the setting must be checked with stroboscopic timing equipment as described next. If this equipment is not available, the work should be carried out by a service station.

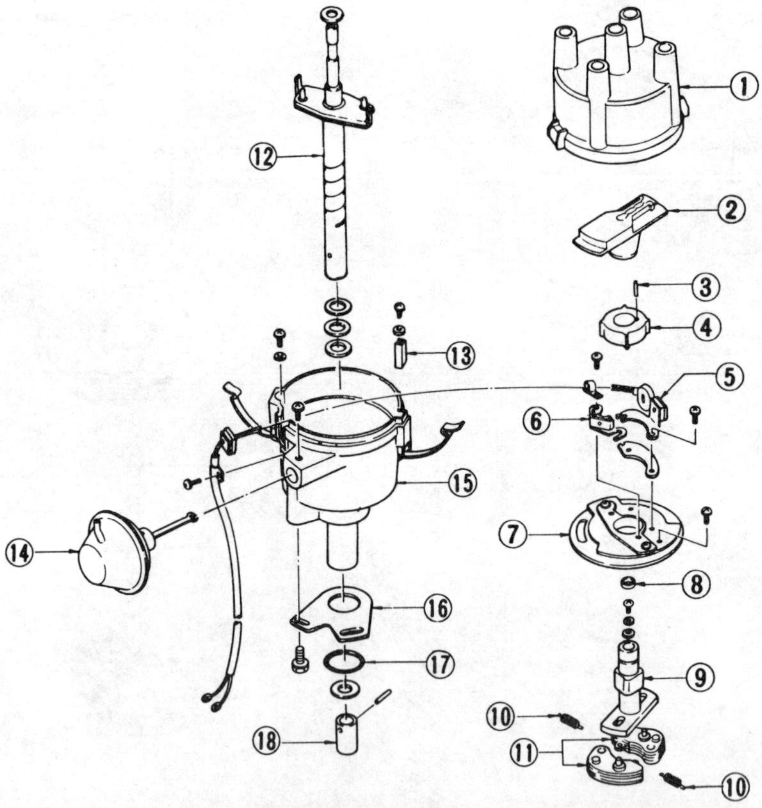

FIG 3:15 **Electronic ignition distributor**

Key to Fig 3:15 1 Cap 2 Rotor arm 3 Roll pin 4 Reluctor 5 Pick-up coil 6 Contactor 7 Breaker plate 8 Packing 9 Rotor shaft 10 Spring 11 Weight 12 Shaft assembly 13 Cap setter 14 Vacuum control unit 15 Body 16 Clamp plate 17 'O' ring 18 Collar

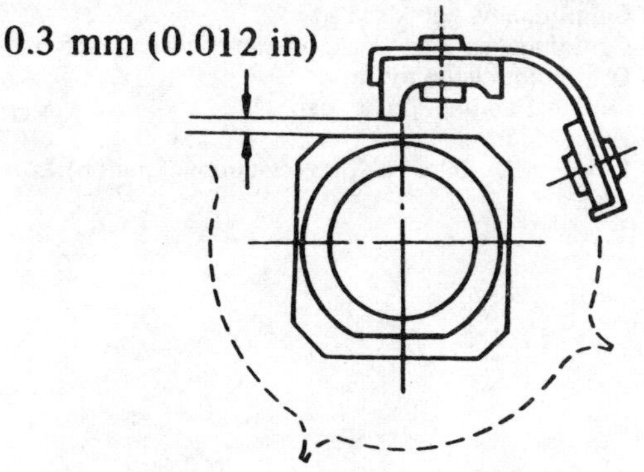

FIG 3:16 Contactor clearance

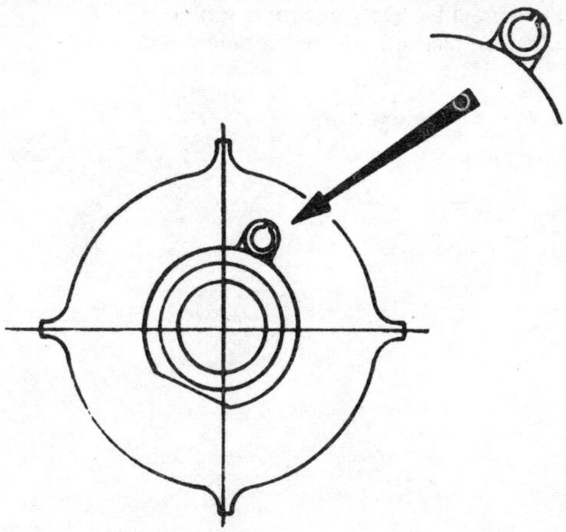

FIG 3:17 Roll pin position

Stroboscopic timing:

This should be carried out after setting the ignition by the test lamp method just described. Run the engine until it is at normal operating temperature. Connect the timing light to the ignition circuit of No 1 cylinder and connect a suitable tachometer in accordance with the manufacturer's instructions. The correct ignition advance and the engine idling speed at which it should be measured will be found in **Technical Data**. Direct the timing light onto the timing marks, then slacken the distributor clamp and turn the distributor body until the marks are correctly aligned. When the correct setting is achieved, tighten the distributor clamp securely. Disconnect the tachometer and stroboscopic lamp equipment.

3:7 Sparking plugs

Inspect and clean sparking plugs regularly. When removing sparking plugs, ensure that their recesses are clean and dry so that nothing can fall into the cylinders. Plug gaskets can be re-used, providing that they are not less than half their original thickness. Have sparking plugs cleaned on an abrasive-blasting machine and tested under pressure with the electrode gaps correctly set at between 0.8 and 0.9mm (0.031 to 0.035in) on standard models. For USA models see **Technical Data**. The electrodes should be filed until they are bright and parallel. The gaps must always be set by adjusting the earth electrodes. Do not try to bend the centre electrode. Renew plugs at approximately 16,000km (10,000 mile) intervals, or before if badly worn.

Before refitting the plugs, clean the threads with a wire brush. Clean the threads in the cylinder head if the plugs cannot be screwed in by hand. Failing a proper tap for this purpose, use an old sparking plug with cross cuts down the threads. Plugs should be tightened with a proper plug spanner, as other types of spanner may slip off during tightening and crack the plug insulation. Do not overtighten the plugs.

Inspections of the deposits on the plug electrodes can be helpful when tuning. Normally, from mixed periods of high and low speed driving, deposits will be powdery and range in colour from brown to greyish tan. There will also be slight wear of the electrodes. Long periods of constant speed driving or low speed city driving will give white or yellowish deposits. Dry, black fluffy deposits are due to incomplete combustion and indicate running with a rich mixture, excessive idling and, possibly, defective ignition. Overheated plugs have a white blistered look about the centre electrode and the side electrode may be badly eroded. This may be caused by poor cooling, a weak mixture, incorrect ignition timing or sustained high speeds with heavy loads.

Black, wet deposits result from oil in the combustion chamber from worn pistons, rings, valve stems or guides. Sparking plugs which run hotter may alleviate the problem, but the cure is an engine overhaul.

3:8 Fault diagnosis

(a) Engine will not fire

1 Battery discharged
2 Contact points dirty, pitted or wrongly adjusted
3 Distributor cap dirty, cracked or tracking
4 Contact inside distributor cap not touching rotor
5 Faulty cable or loose connection in LT circuit
6 Distributor rotor arm cracked or dirty
7 Faulty coil
8 Broken contact breaker spring
9 Contact points stuck open
10 Defective pick-up coil (electronic ignition)
11 Air gap too wide (electronic ignition)
12 Faulty ignition unit (electronic ignition)

(b) Engine misfires

1 Check 2, 3, 4, 7 and 12 in (a)
2 Weak contact breaker spring
3 HT plug or coil lead defective
4 Sparking plugs loose
5 Sparking plug insulation cracked
6 Sparking plug gaps incorrectly set
7 Ignition timing incorrect
8 Faulty capacitor

9 Incorrect air gap (electronic ignition)
10 Dirt on pick-up coil (electronic ignition)

(c) Poor acceleration

1 Ignition retarded
2 Centrifugal weights seized
3 Centrifugal springs weak, broken or disconnected
4 Distributor clamp loose
5 Incorrect contact points gap
6 Worn plugs
7 Dirt in pick-up coil air gap (electronic ignition)

CHAPTER 4

THE COOLING SYSTEM

4:1 Description

The cooling system is pressurised and thermostatically controlled. Water circulation is assisted by a centrifugal pump which is mounted at the front of the cylinder block and the cooling fan, which draws air through the radiator, is fitted to the same shaft as the pump impeller. The pump and fan and the alternator are driven from a pulley on the crankshaft by an endless belt. The tension of this belt is adjustable at the alternator mountings.

The pump takes coolant from the bottom of the radiator and delivers it to the cylinder block from which it rises to the cylinder head. At normal operating temperatures the thermostat is open and the coolant returns from the head to the top of the radiator. At lower temperatures, the thermostat valve is closed and the coolant bypasses the radiator and returns to the pump inlet to provide a rapid warm-up.

4:2 Routine maintenance

The cooling system should be checked regularly for correct coolant level when the engine is cool. When removing the radiator filler cap on a hot engine, hold the cap with a large piece of rag. Turn the cap anticlockwise and wait a few moments for the pressure to release before lifting off the cap. It is recommended that an antifreeze solution is maintained in the system all year round. Topping up should therefore be carried out with the correct mixture of antifreeze and water to avoid weakening the solution in use. The correct coolant level is approximately 30mm (1.2in) below the bottom of the radiator filler neck. If the radiator is filled above this level, excess coolant will be lost through the overflow due to expansion as the engine warms up.

Every two years the cooling system should be drained, flushed to remove sediment and refilled with fresh antifreeze mixture. Check that the clips are tight on all hoses and that the radiator pressure cap is in good condition and sealing effectively. Loss of system pressure due to a leaking filler cap can be a cause of overheating.

Regular checks should be made on the condition and tension of the drive belt, as described in **Section 4:6**. **FIG 4:1** shows the layout of the cooling system and the flow of coolant through the radiator and engine water passages.

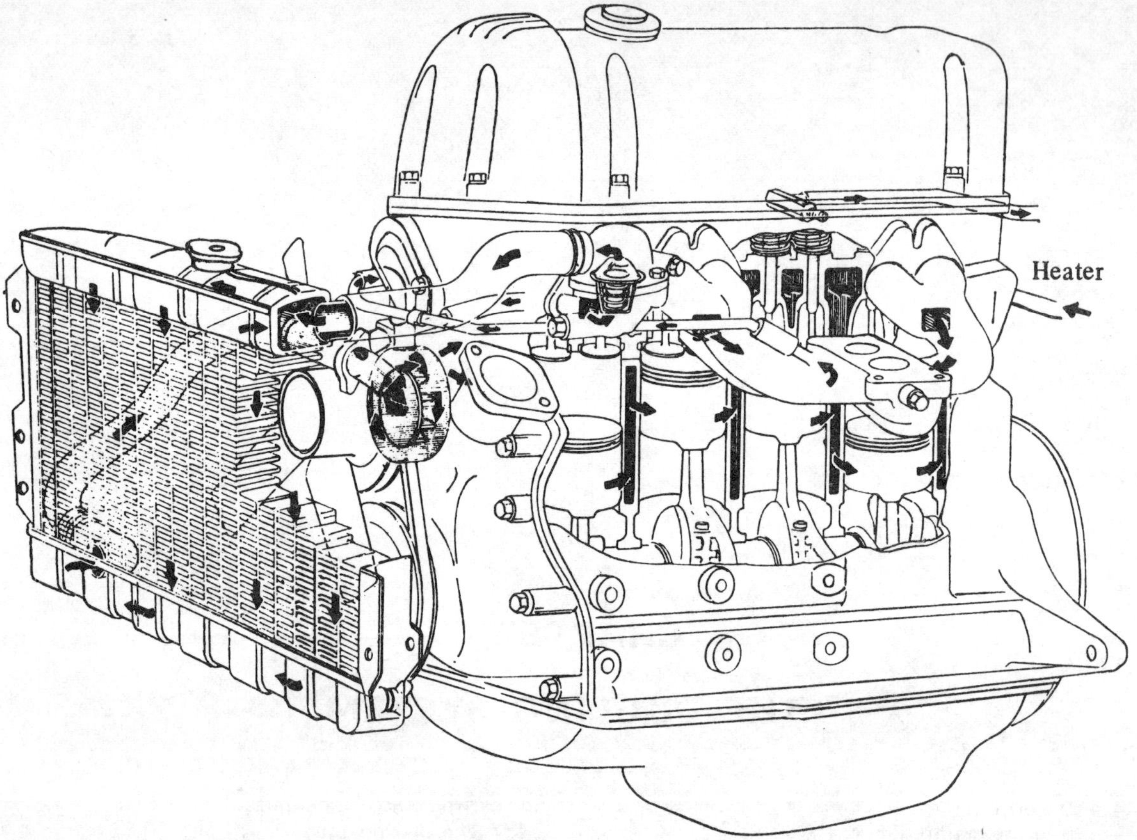

FIG 4:1 Layout of the cooling system

Draining the system:

If a heater is fitted, place the heater temperature control in the car to the maximum heat position. Make sure that the system is cool, then remove the radiator cap. Remove the drain plugs from the bottom of the radiator and from the righthand side of the cylinder block. Collect the coolant in a clean container if it is to be re-used.

Flushing:

When all old coolant has drained, refit the drain plugs. Fill the system with clean water and run the engine until the top radiator hose feels warm, which indicates that the thermostat has opened for complete circulation. Now completely drain the system again before the sediment has time to settle.

Filling:

Check that the drain plugs are properly fitted and that all hose clips are tight. Leave the heater control in the maximum heat position. Prepare the new antifreeze mixture according to the manufacturer's instructions. If the system is still warm, allow it to cool down as adding the cold liquid when the system is warm may crack the engine cylinder block. Fill the system to the correct level as described previously, then check the level again after running the engine for some time and top up if necessary.

4:3 The radiator

Removal:

Drain the radiator as described in **Section 4:2**. Remove the front grille then disconnect the radiator upper and lower hoses. If automatic transmission is fitted, disconnect the fluid lines from the radiator, plugging the lines and outlets to prevent loss of fluid. Remove the four bolts securing the radiator to the side supports. On some models two hooks are installed on the front top face of the radiator, which must be pulled out through the holes in the radiator upper support.

Refit the radiator in the reverse order of removal, refilling the cooling system on completion as described previously.

4:4 Cooling fan

The standard cooling fan is mounted directly on the water pump drive shaft and is therefore driven by the belt at the same speed as the pump unit. However, some models are equipped with a special fan assembly as shown in **FIG 4:2**. In this case, the fan is driven through

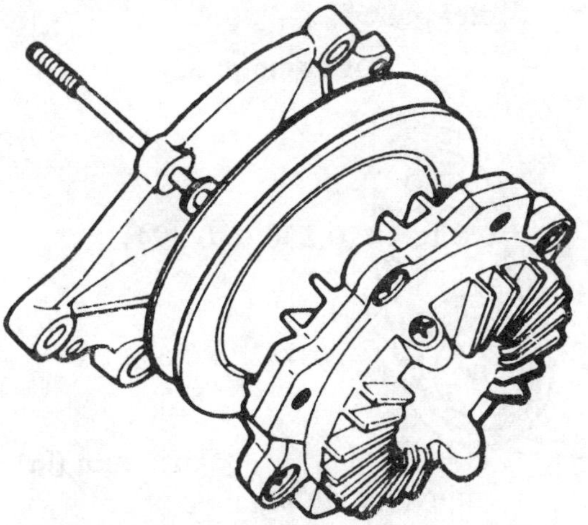

FIG 4:2 The viscous fan coupling fitted to some models

a viscous coupling which allows direct drive through the coupling to the fan up to engine speeds of approximately 3000rev/min. As engine speed increases further, drive through the coupling to the fan is progressively decreased to reduce fan noise and power absorption without impairing cooling efficiency. If the viscous coupling unit should stick, or if oil leaks are noticed, the car should be taken to a service station for checks to be carried out.

4:5 The water pump

Removal:

Drain the cooling system as described previously. Loosen the four bolts retaining the fan shroud to the radiator and remove the shroud. Remove the fan, then slacken the drive belt as described in **Section 4:6**. Disconnect the hose, then remove the water pump from the engine front cover as shown in **FIG 4:3**.

Inspection:

Check for badly corroded vane and body components, and for excessive end play or roughness of the bearings. If any faults are found the pump unit must be renewed complete, as the internal parts are not serviced separately. Note that excessive bearing noise or squeak can sometimes be cured by applying Nissan water seal lubricant. This will not, of course, effect a cure if the problem is excessive wear or damage to the bearings or shaft.

Refitting:

Make sure that the joint faces on pump and front cover are clean. Refit the pump, using a new gasket. Tighten the bolts alternately and evenly to avoid distortion. Reconnect the hose, then fill the cooling system as described previously. Install the fan and fan pulley, tightening the fixing bolts securely. Fit the drive belt and tension as described in **Section 4:6**. Fill the cooling system as described previously, then run the engine and check for coolant leaks.

4:6 Drive belt tensioning

A tight drive belt will cause rapid wear of the driven component bearings, a loose belt will slip and wear excessively with the consequent possibility of poor output from the driven components and, possibily, a squealing noise. The tension is correct when the belt can be deflected 8 to 12mm (0.32 to 0.47in) by firm thumb pressure applied midway between two pulleys, as shown in **FIG 4:4**.

To adjust the alternator and water pump drive belt, slacken the alternator mounting bolts and pivot the alternator away from the engine. If a lever is used to move the alternator, it must be applied to the drive end bracket only, never to the body of the unit. When the tension is correct, hold the alternator in place and tighten all the mounting bolts.

On models fitted with air conditioning systems, the compressor drive belt must be tensioned in the same manner as that for the alternator and water pump. To tighten the belt, turn the adjuster bolt located at the top of the idler pulley bracket. The correct settings are shown in **FIG 4:5**.

On models equipped with the emission control air injection system, the air injection pump drive belt must also be correctly tensioned. To tighten the belt slacken

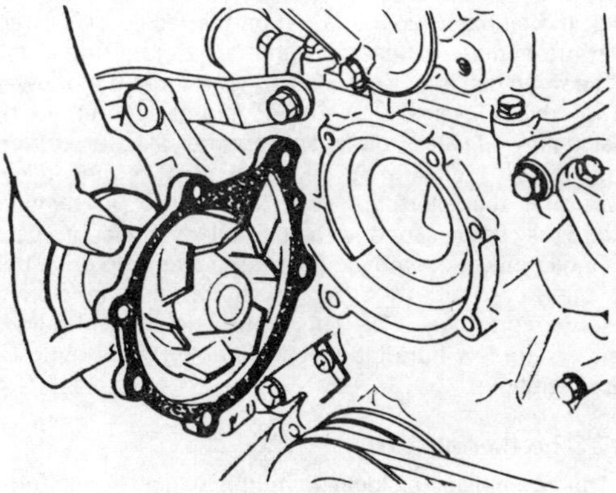

FIG 4:3 Water pump removal

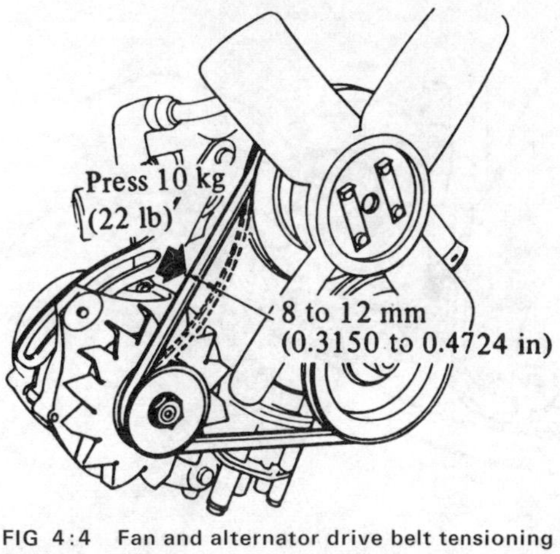

FIG 4:4 Fan and alternator drive belt tensioning

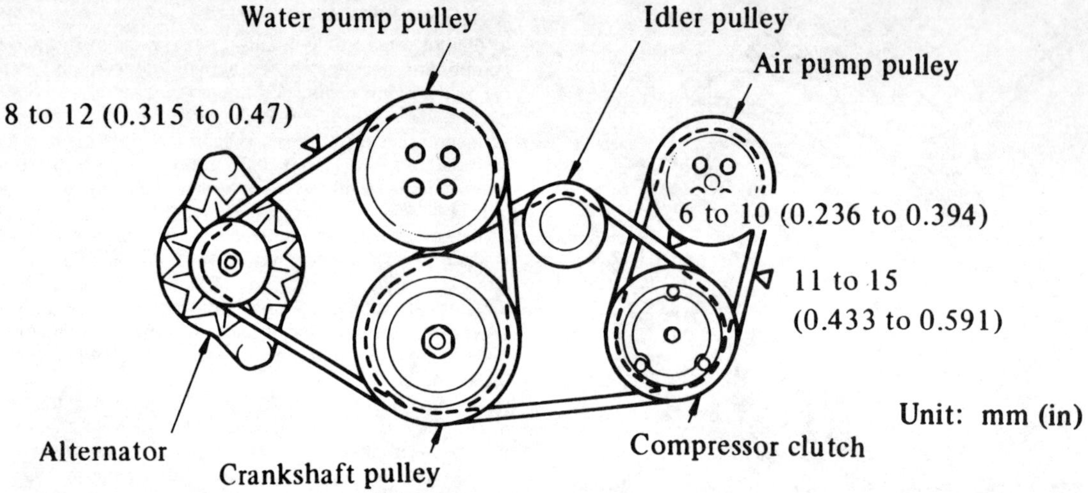

FIG 4:5 Belt tensioning on models fitted with air conditioning systems

the pivot bolt nut and the nut on the support arm and pivot the air pump upwards. When the tension is correct, hold the pump in place and tighten the mounting nuts.

If a drive belt is worn or damaged, it must be renewed. To do this, loosen the alternator mounting bolts or the idler pulley adjuster bolt as appropriate. Slacken the belt sufficiently to allow it to be removed over the pulleys. Note that the alternator drive belt must be removed before the compressor drive belt. Similarly, the compressor drive belt must be removed before the air pump drive belt. Fit the new belt, then set to the correct tension as described previously. The tension of a new belt should be reset after a few hundred miles of driving, to take up the initial stretch.

4:7 The thermostat

The thermostat is located in the water pump outlet adjacent to the inlet manifold.

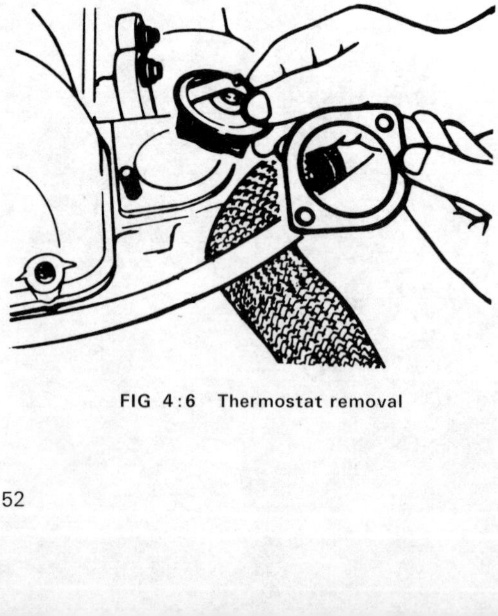

FIG 4:6 Thermostat removal

Removal:

Drain sufficient coolant so that the level is below the thermostat, then disconnect the upper radiator hose at the water outlet. Remove the two securing nuts then detach the water outlet, gasket and thermostat as shown in **FIG 4:6**.

Testing:

Clean the thermostat and immerse it in a container of cold water together with a 0° to 100°C thermometer. Heat the water, keeping it stirred, and observe the operation of the valve. The valve should begin to open at the appropriate temperature. For the standard thermostat the figure is 82°C, on models exported to cold areas 88°C, or models exported to tropical areas 76.5°C. On all models, the valve should be open more than 8mm when the water boils. The valve should close tightly when the thermostat is removed and placed into cold water. If the thermostat does not operate correctly it must be renewed.

Refitting:

Refit the thermostat in the reverse order of removal, using a new gasket. Refill the cooling system, run the engine and check for coolant leaks.

4:8 Frost precautions

With the correct coolant solution in use as described in **Section 4:2**, no additional frost precautions should be necessary. However, it is advisable to have the solution tested at intervals during the winter to make certain that it has not weakened. An hydrometer calibrated to read both specific gravity and temperature for the type of coolant in the system must be used, most garages having such equipment. Always ensure that the antifreeze mixture used for filling the system is of sufficient strength to provide protection against freezing, according to the manufacturer's instructions.

4:9 Fault diagnosis

(a) Internal water leakage

1 Cracked cylinder wall
2 Loose cylinder head nuts
3 Cracked cylinder head
4 Faulty head gasket

(b) Poor circulation

1 Radiator core blocked
2 Engine water passages restricted
3 Low water level
4 Loose drive belt
5 Defective thermostat
6 Perished or collapsed radiator hoses

(c) Corrosion

1 Impurities in the coolant
2 Infrequent draining and flushing

(d) Overheating

1 Check (b)
2 Sludge in crankcase
3 Faulty ignition timing
4 Low oil level in sump
5 Tight engine
6 Choked exhaust system
7 Binding brakes
8 Slipping clutch
9 Incorrect valve timing
10 Weak fuel mixture

NOTES

CHAPTER 5

THE CLUTCH

5:1 Description

The clutch is a single dry-plate unit of either diaphragm spring or coil spring type, according to model. The main components are the driven plate, pressure plate assembly and release bearing. The two types of clutch unit are shown in **FIGS 5:1** and **5:2**.

The driven plate consists of a resilient steel disc attached to a hub which slides on the splined gearbox input shaft. The friction linings are riveted to both sides of the disc.

The pressure plate assembly consists of the pressure plate, diaphragm spring or coil springs, and the clutch housing. The release bearing is a ballbearing of special construction with an elongated outer ring that presses directly against the diaphragm spring or spring release levers when the clutch pedal is operated.

The clutch is operated by hydraulic pressure from the master cylinder transmitted to the slave cylinder mounted on the transmission housing. The slave cylinder pushrod acts against the clutch release lever.

When the clutch is fully engaged, the driven plate is nipped between the pressure plate and the engine flywheel and transmits torque to the gearbox through the splined input shaft (main drive shaft). When the clutch pedal is depressed, the pressure plate is withdrawn from the driven plate by hydraulic pressure, the driven plate then ceasing to transmit torque. The design of the slave cylinder is such that compensation for clutch plate wear is made automatically, no additional adjustment being required.

5:2 Routine maintenance

Regularly check the fluid level in the clutch master cylinder reservoir. If necessary, top up the level to the mark provided on the side of the reservoir. It is essential to use the correct fluid, which is one conforming to Specification SAE.J1703a or DOT3 for USA models. **Do not use any other type of fluid.**

Wipe the filler cap before unscrewing it so that dirt cannot fall inside. Check that the small vent hole in the cap is clear. At the same intervals, check the condition of the pipe and hose in the clutch hydraulic system.

5:3 Bleeding the clutch system

This will be necessary if the clutch hydraulic system has been dismantled or if there is a spongy feel to clutch pedal operation, with the possibility of the clutch not fully disengaging.

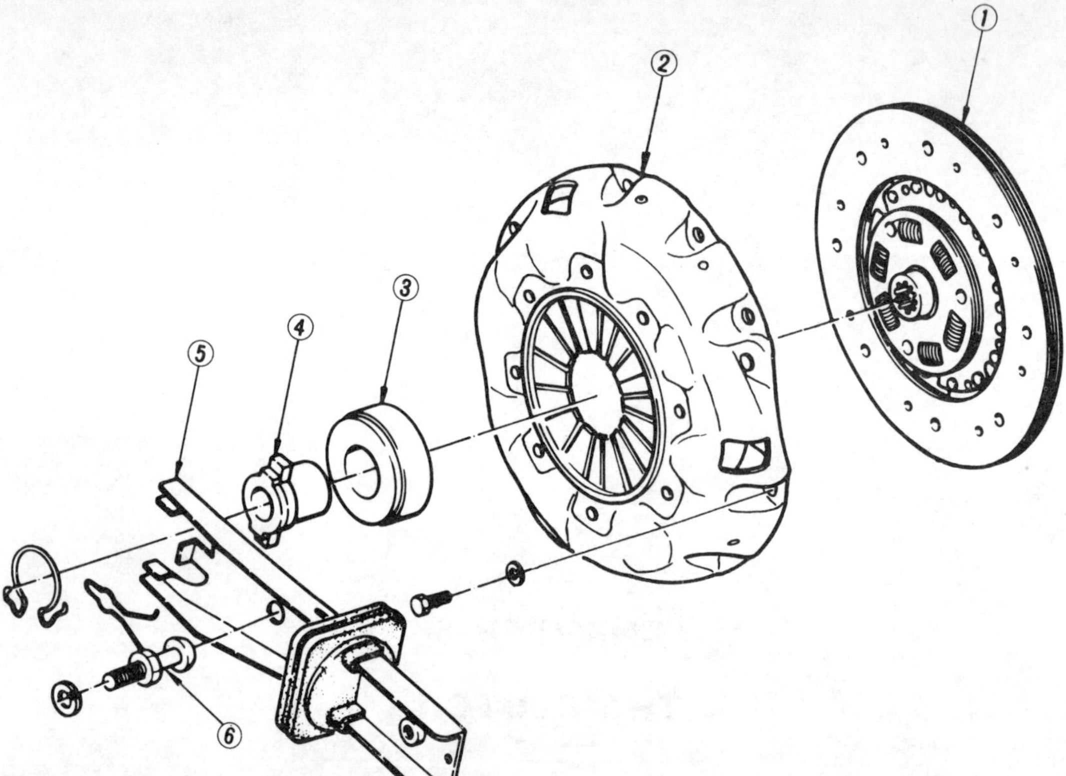

FIG 5:1 The diaphragm spring clutch and release mechanism

Key to Fig 5:1 1 Clutch disc 2 Clutch cover 3 Release bearing 4 Release sleeve 5 Release lever 6 Release lever ball pin

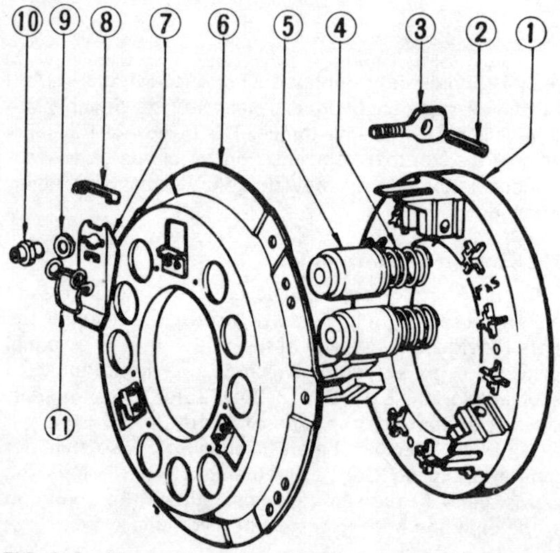

FIG 5:2 The coil spring clutch unit which may be fitted on some models

Key to Fig 5:2 1 Pressure plate 2 Pin 3 Eye bolt 4 Spring 5 Spring retainer 6 Clutch cover 7 Release lever 8 Release lever stop 9 Release lever seat 10 Eye bolt nut 11 Retaining lever spring

The bleed screw is on the clutch slave cylinder. Remove the dust cap and attach a rubber or plastic tube to the nipple. Immerse the free end of the tube in a small quantity of clean brake fluid in a glass jar. Make sure that the reservoir is topped up with the correct fluid. Check this level during the operation to make sure that it does not fall too low.

Get an assistant to depress the clutch pedal three times and hold it to the floor at the end of the last stroke. With the pedal held down, open the bleed screw about three-quarters of a turn. When fluid ceases to flow into the jar, tighten the bleed screw and have the pedal released. Wait a few seconds before repeating the operation. Continue with this sequence, watching the immersed end of the tube for air bubbles. When they cease, tighten the bleed screw with the pedal held to the floor, then release the pedal and remove the bleed tube. Check the fluid level in the reservoir and refit the dust cap to the bleed screw.

5:4 Removing and refitting clutch

Removal:

Remove the gearbox as described in **Chapter 6**. Mark the clutch cover and flywheel with a small dab of paint so that on reassembly the clutch will be in the same

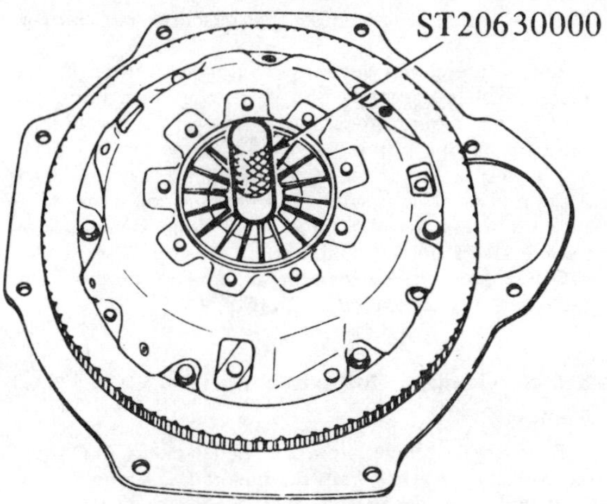

FIG 5:3 Fitting the clutch alignment tool

relative position to retain the original balance of the assembly.

Fit the special tool, a spare gearbox main drive shaft or other suitable mandrel through the centre of the clutch assembly and into the clutch pilot bearing in the flywheel (see **FIG 5:3**). Loosen the bolts attaching the clutch cover to the flywheel alternately and evenly until spring pressure is released. Remove the bolts and lift off the clutch assembly complete with alignment tool. The release bearing assembly can be removed from the clutch housing on the gearbox. Remove the spring from the bearing sleeve then disconnect the clutch release lever from the sleeve. Remove the release bearing and sleeve from the mainshaft as an assembly.

Servicing:

If necessary, use a suitable puller and adaptor to remove the clutch release bearing from the sleeve, as shown in **FIG 5:4**. Thoroughly clean all parts in a suitable solvent, with the exception of the driven plate friction linings and the release bearing. The release bearing must not be cleaned with solvent as this would wash the internal lubricant from the bearing, so simply wipe it clean with a cloth.

The diaphragm spring clutch cover, spring and pressure plate assembly is an integral unit and must not be dismantled. If any part is defective the assembly must be renewed complete. If faults are suspected with a coil spring pressure plate, the unit should be taken to a service station for overhaul as special tools are required to dismantle and reassemble the unit.

Inspect the surface of the flywheel where the driven plate makes contact. Small surface cracks or scratches are unimportant, but if there are any deep scratches the flywheel should be machined smooth or renewed. Check the pressure plate for scoring or damage and that the operating surface is flat and true. Check the release bearing for roughness when it is pressed and turned by hand. Any worn or damaged parts must be renewed.

Check the driven plate for loose rivets and broken or very loose torsional springs. The friction linings should be well proud of the rivets and have a light colour, with a polished glaze through which the grain of the material is clearly visible. A dark, glazed deposit indicates oil on the facings and, as this condition cannot be rectified, a new or relined unit will be required. Any signs of oil in the clutch will call for examination of the crankshaft rear oil seal, as described in **Chapter 1**. Check the disc for run-out at the outer circumference, preferably using a dial gauge as shown in **FIG 5:5**. Measure at a point 95mm (3.74in) from the hub centre (85mm [3.35in] for L14 engine models). Run-out should not exceed 0.5mm (0.020in). Excessive run-out can usually be cured by sliding the disc onto the gearbox splined shaft and twisting the disc as necessary by hand or with a suitable tool until it is true. If this method does not succeed, however, the disc should be renewed. A warped driven disc will cause clutch judder and wear out very quickly in service.

If the driven plate is defective in any way, a new or reconditioned unit should be obtained and fitted. Check the driven plate hub for a smooth, sliding fit on the splined shaft, removing any burrs on the shaft or in the hub with a fine stone.

Refitting:

Assemble the release bearing to the sleeve, using a press or suitable vice. Press only on the inner race, never on the outer race. Pack the inner recess of the release bearing with grease as shown in **FIG 5:6**. Similarly lubricate the contact surfaces of the release lever, lever

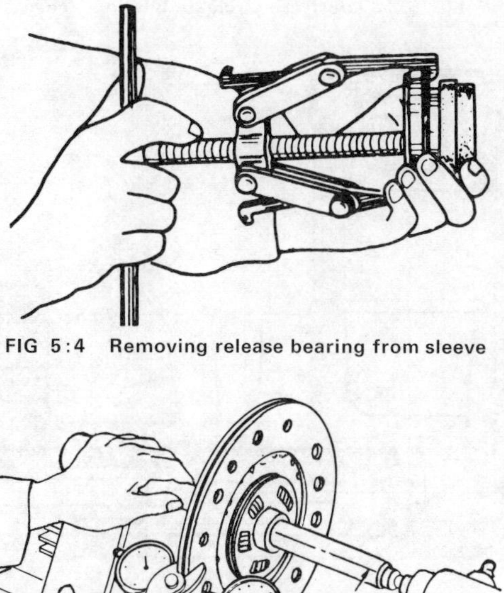

FIG 5:4 Removing release bearing from sleeve

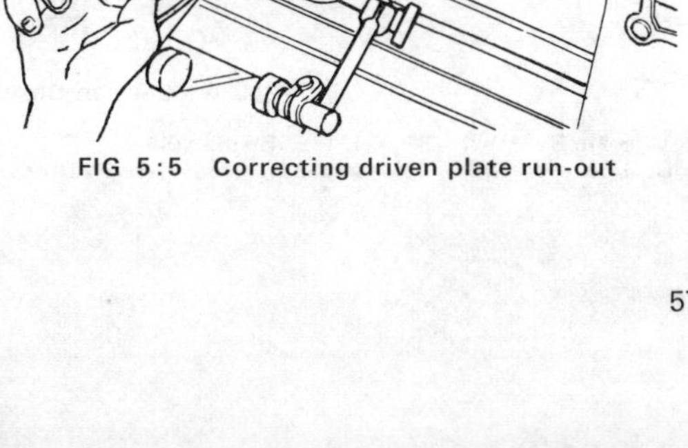

FIG 5:5 Correcting driven plate run-out

ballpin and bearing sleeve, contact surfaces of transmission front cover and the contact surfaces of the splined gearbox input shaft. Do not over-lubricate, or lubricant may contaminate the clutch friction surfaces.

Install the release lever, release bearing and sleeve on clutch housing. Inspect the clutch pilot bushing in the flywheel and renew if necessary as described in **Chapter 1**.

Locate the clutch driven disc in position, then fit the pressure plate assembly and insert the special tool or spare shaft through the whole clutch assembly and into the pilot bearing in the flywheel. With the tool in place, fit and evenly tighten the clutch mounting bolts to 1.6 to 2.1kgm (12 to 15lb ft). After installing the coil spring type of clutch, remove the three stops from beneath the release levers on the clutch cover. A stop is shown in **FIG 5:2** (item 8). Remove the alignment tool, then refit the gearbox as described in **Chapter 6**.

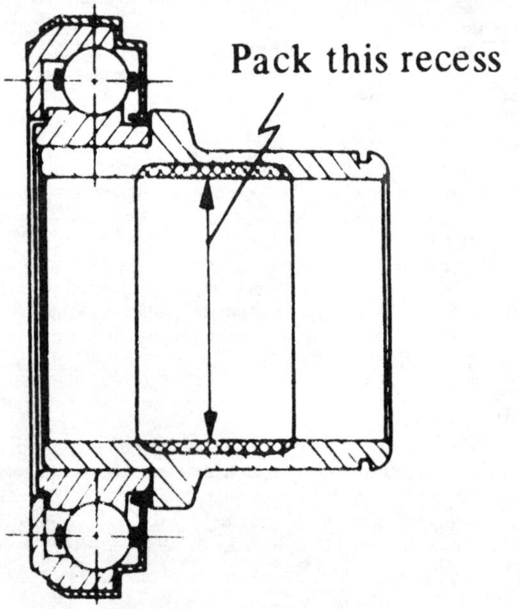

FIG 5:6 Lubricating release bearing sleeve

5:5 Servicing the master cylinder

Removal:

Remove the circlip from the pedal clevis pin, then remove the clevis pin from the pushrod. Disconnect the fluid pipe from the master cylinder then drain the fluid into a suitable container by pumping the clutch pedal. Remove the nuts securing the master cylinder to the dash panel then remove the cylinder from the engine compartment.

Dismantling:

Refer to **FIG 5:7**. Detach the dust cover and remove the stop ring from the body. Remove the pushrod and piston assembly. Remove the spring seat from the piston and, if necessary, detach the piston cup. If the piston cup is removed it must be renewed on reassembly. **FIG 5:8** shows the piston components.

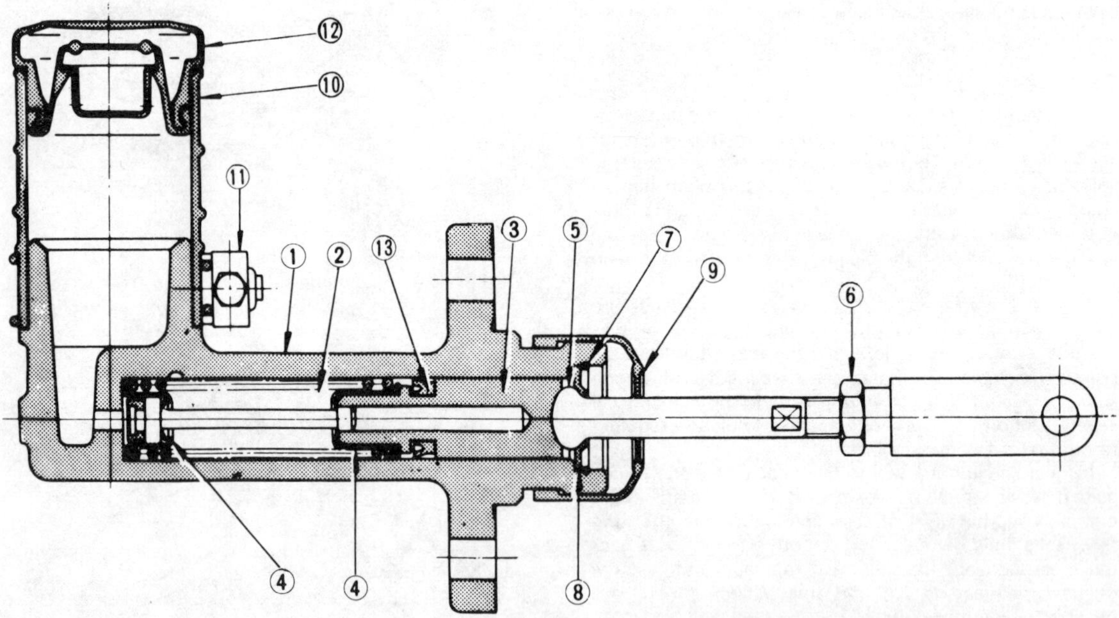

FIG 5:7 Section through the master cylinder assembly

Key to Fig 5:7 1 Cylinder 2 Return spring 3 Piston 4 Spring seat 5 Pushrod 6 Nut 7 Stop ring 8 Stop 9 Dust cover 10 Fluid reservoir 11 Reservoir band 12 Cap 13 Piston cup

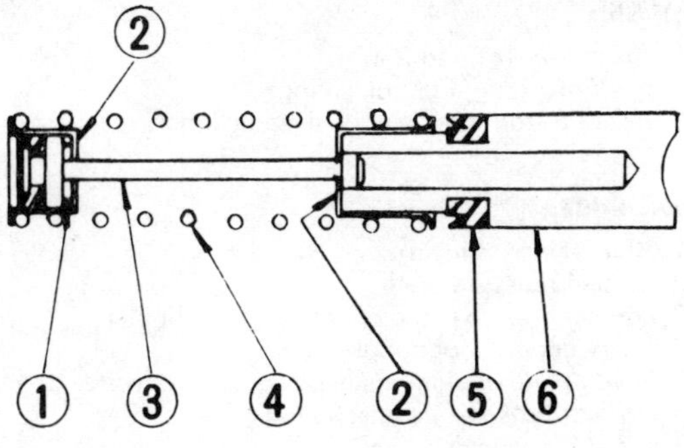

FIG 5:8 Master cylinder piston assembly

Key to Fig 5:8 1 Valve spring 2 Spring seat 3 Valve assembly 4 Return spring 5 Piston cup 6 Piston

Cleaning and inspection:

Clean all parts in methylated spirit or approved brake fluid only. Examine the cylinder bore for scoring or corrosion. If the bore is not smooth and polished in appearance, or if the clearance between cylinder and piston is more than 0.15mm (0.0059in), the cylinder must be renewed. Examine all other parts for wear or damage, renewing as necessary.

Reassembly:

Observe absolute cleanliness during reassembly to avoid contamination by dirt or grease. Dip the internal parts in the correct brake fluid and assemble them wet.

Assemble the components in the reverse order of dismantling, making sure that the piston cup is correctly located as shown in **FIG 5:8**.

Refitting:

This is a reversal of the removal procedure. On completion, adjust the clutch pedal height to 180mm (7.087in) for lefthand drive and all USA export models or 175mm (6.890in) for righthand drive models. Refer to **FIG 5:9** and turn the pedal stop bolt until the clutch pedal height is correct, then tighten locknut A1 to 0.8 to 1.1kgm (5.8 to 8.0lb ft). Adjust the pedal free play until the clearance between the clevis pin and clutch pedal is 1 to 5mm (0.039 to 0.197in) measured on the top face of the pedal pad. Adjust by turning in or out the pushrod. After adjustment, tighten locknut B2 to 0.8 to 1.1kgm (5.8 to 8.0lb ft). Finally, bleed the clutch system as described in **Section 5:3**.

5:6 Servicing the slave cylinder

Removal:

Disconnect the fluid pipe from the fluid hose, then detach the hose from the slave cylinder. Remove the two securing bolts and detach the slave cylinder from the clutch housing.

Servicing:

Refer to **FIG 5:10**. Remove the pushrod and dust cover then withdraw the piston and spring. If the piston cup is removed it must be renewed when reassembling. Remove the bleed screw.

Clean all parts in methylated spirit or correct brake fluid only. Renew the cylinder if bore is pitted, scored or corroded. Examine all other parts and renew any found worn or damaged. Dip all internal parts in approved brake fluid and assemble wet.

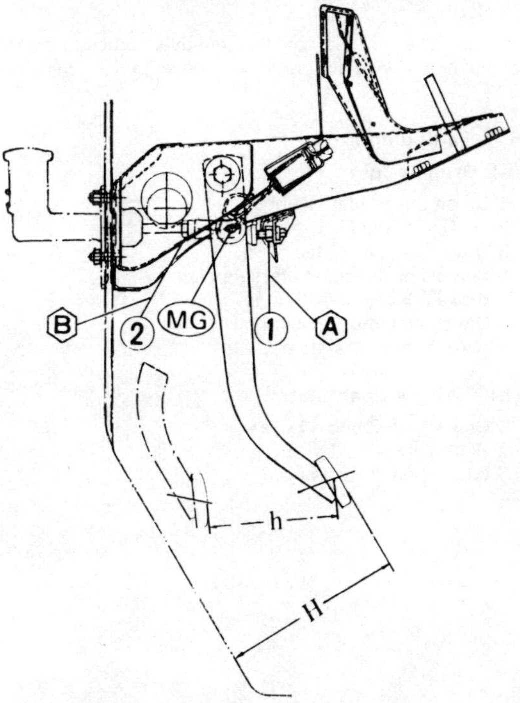

FIG 5:9 Clutch pedal adjustment

Key to Fig 5:9 A1, B2 Locknuts MG Multipurpose grease H Pedal height h Pedal full stroke of 135mm (5.315in)

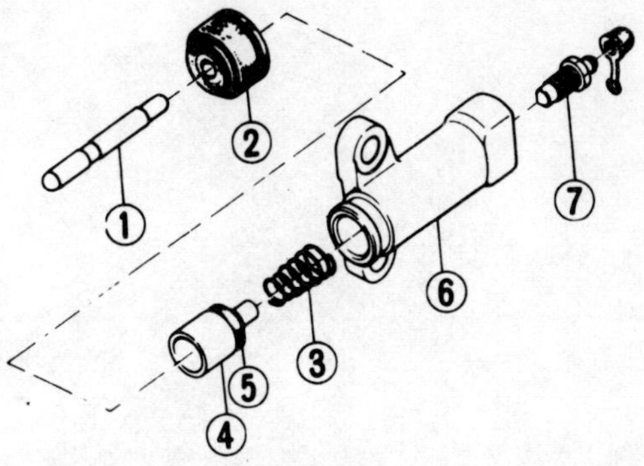

FIG 5:10 Slave cylinder components

Key to Fig 5:10 1 Pushrod 2 Dust cover 3 Piston spring 4 Piston 5 Piston cup 6 Slave cylinder 7 Bleed screw

Refitting:

This is a reversal of the removal procedure. On completion, bleed the system as described in **Section 5:3**.

5:7 Fault diagnosis

(a) Drag or spin

1 Oil on driven plate linings
2 Leaking hydraulic system
3 Driven plate distorted
4 Warped or damaged pressure plate
5 Broken driven plate linings
6 Driven plate hub binding on splines
7 Air in hydraulic system

(b) Fierceness or snatch

1 Check 1, 2, 3 and 4 in (a)
2 Worn linings
3 Worn release mechanism

(c) Slip

1 Check 1 in (a) and 2 in (b)
2 Weak diaphragm or coil springs
3 Seized piston in master or slave cylinder

(d) Judder

1 Check 1 and 3 in (a)
2 Warped pressure plate
3 Contact area of linings not evenly distributed
4 Faulty engine mountings
5 Driven plate or shaft splines excessively worn
6 Worn or broken torsional springs

(e) Tick or knock

1 Check 5 and 6 in (d)
2 Worn release bearing
3 Faulty drive pinion on starter
4 Loose parts in clutch cover

CHAPTER 6

MANUAL TRANSMISSION

6 : 1 Description

Either a four-speed or five-speed gearbox may be fitted, according to model specification and market territory, these units being designated type F4W63L and type F5W63A respectively. The two types of gearbox are basically similar in design and construction, so component descriptions and servicing instructions given in this chapter will apply to all types unless otherwise stated.

Synchromesh is provided on all forward speeds, the reverse gear being of the sliding mesh type using spur gears. The main drive gear is meshed with the countergear and the forward speed gears on the countershaft are in constant mesh with the main gears on the mainshaft. When the gearlever is operated, the mechanism causes the coupling sleeve to slide on the synchroniser hub. This engages the hub inner teeth with the teeth on the mainshaft gear. When the gearlever is moved to the reverse position, the mainshaft reverse gear provided on the outer side of the first and reverse coupling sleeve moves into mesh with the reverse idler gear.

FIGS 6 : 1 and **6 : 2** show sectional views of the transmission assemblies.

6 : 2 Routine maintenance

The gearbox oil level should be checked at intervals of 5000km (3000 miles). Remove the combined filler and level plug from the side of the gearbox and check that the oil is up to the lower edge of the hole. Top up if necessary using an approved grade of gearbox oil. Oil should be to specification API-GL-4 and of viscosity SAE 80W for temperatures below 80°F. For temperatures up to 100°F use oil of viscosity SAE 90W and for greater temperatures use oil of viscosity SAE 140W. Allow any surplus oil to drain out of the filler hole before installing the plug.

At intervals of 50,000km (30,000 miles) drain out the oil into a suitable container by removing the gearbox drain plug. Refill to the correct level with fresh lubricant.

6 : 3 Removing the gearbox

1 Disconnect the earth cable from the battery. Raise the front of the car and safely support on floor stands. Remove the centre console if fitted.
2 On four-speed units, loosen the securing nut and remove the gearlever as shown in **FIG 6 : 3**. On five-speed units, remove the 'E' ring and lever pin from the

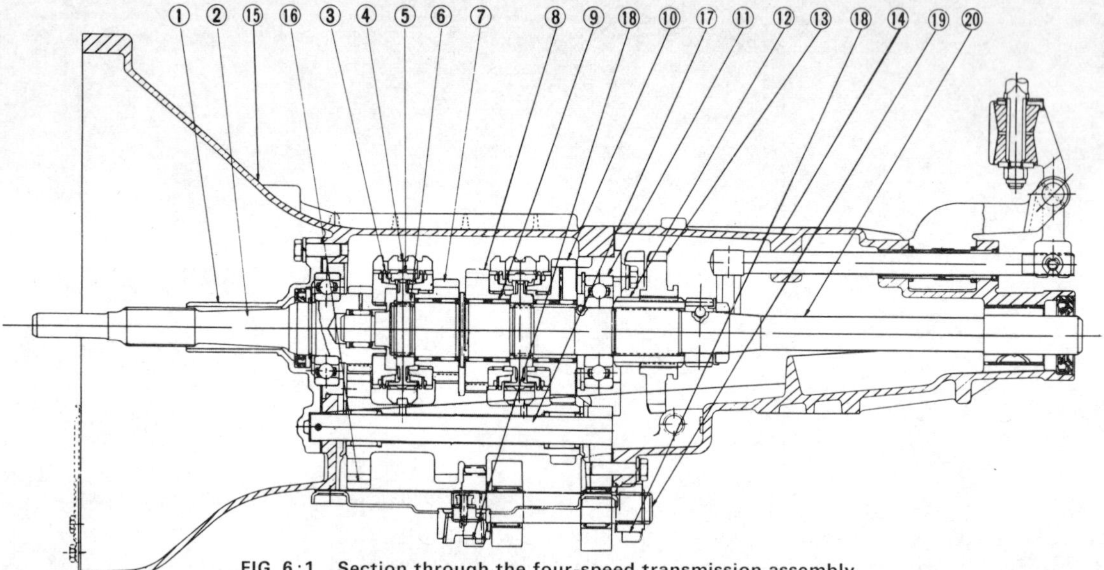

FIG 6:1 Section through the four-speed transmission assembly

Key to Fig 6:1 1 Front cover 2 Main drive shaft 3 Baulk ring 4 Coupling sleeve 5 Shifting insert 6 Synchroniser hub 7 3rd speed gear, mainshaft 8 2nd speed gear, mainshaft 9 Needle bearing 10 1st speed gear, mainshaft 11 Mainshaft bearing 12 Reverse hub 13 Reverse gear 14 Rear extension housing 15 Transmission case 16 Counter gear 17 Countershaft 18 Reverse idler gear 19 Reverse idler shaft 20 Mainshaft

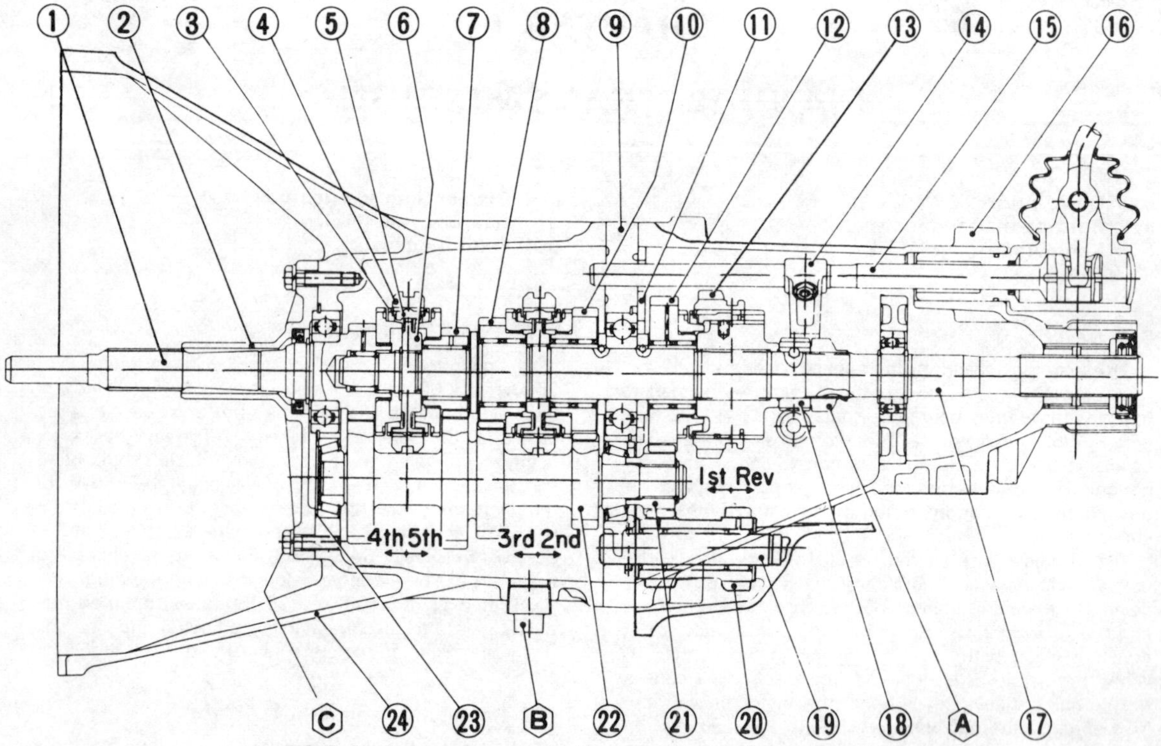

FIG 6:2 Section through the five-speed transmission assembly

Key to Fig 6:2 1 Main drive gear 2 Front cover 3 Baulk ring 4 Coupling sleeve 5 Shifting insert 6 Synchroniser hub 7 5th gear, mainshaft 8 3rd gear, mainshaft 9 Adapter plate 10 2nd gear, mainshaft 11 Bearing retainer 12 1st gear, mainshaft 13 Reverse gear, mainshaft 14 Striking lever 15 Striking rod 16 Rear extension 17 Mainshaft 18 Speedometer drive gear 19 Reverse idler shaft 20 Reverse idler gear 21 1st counter gear 22 Counter gear 23 Counter gear bearing shim 24 Transmission case

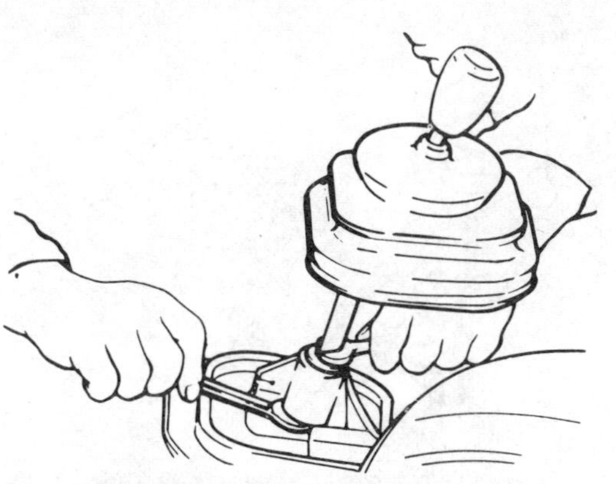

FIG 6:3 Removing gearlever on four-speed units

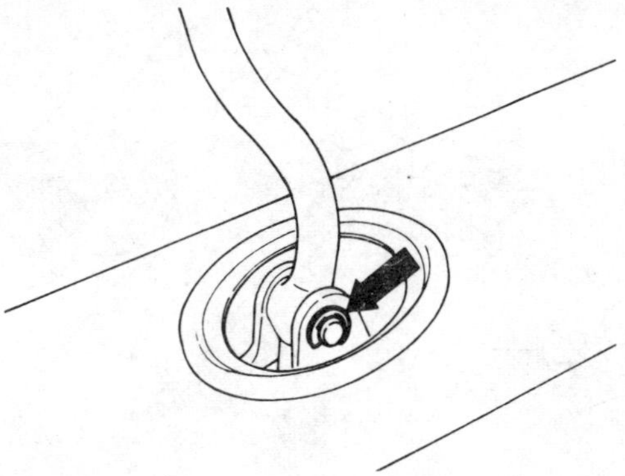

FIG 6:4 Removing gearlever on five-speed units

striking rod guide, then remove the gearlever as shown in **FIG 6:4**.

3 Disconnect the front exhaust pipe and disconnect the wires from the reversing lamp switch on the transmission. Refer to **Chapter 5** and remove the clutch operating cylinder without disconnecting the hose. Wire the cylinder away from the work area so that the hose is not strained. Disconnect the speedometer cable from the transmission rear extension housing.

4 Refer to **Chapter 8** and disengage the propeller shaft Plug the opening in the rear of the transmission to prevent oil leakage. Support the engine with a jack placed beneath the oil sump, interposing a block of wood between sump and jack head. Similarly, support the transmission with a second suitable jack. Detach the transmission mounting crossmember from both transmission and car body. Lower the jack beneath the transmission to facilitate the remaining removal procedures.

5 Remove the starter motor. On four-speed units, remove the four bolts securing engine to gussets, then remove three bolts securing gussets to engine rear plate and transmission case and separate gussets from engine box and transmission case, as shown in **FIG 6:5**.

6 Remove the bolts securing transmission to engine, then carefully slide the transmission rearwards to slide the input shaft from the clutch assembly. Lower the jack and remove the transmission from beneath the car. **Do not allow the weight of the gearbox to hang on the splined input shaft while it is in the clutch unit, or severe damage to the clutch driven plate and hub may occur.**

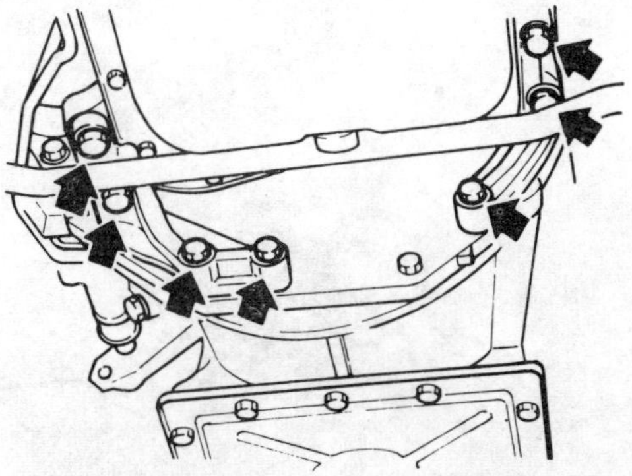

FIG 6:5 Gusset mounting bolts on four-speed units

Refitting:

The gearbox is installed in the reverse order of removal. Make sure that the mating surfaces of engine and gearbox case are clean and dry. Lightly apply an approved grade of grease to the splines on the gearbox input shaft. On completion, fill the gearbox to the correct level with an approved grade of gear oil as described in **Section 6:2**. Check that the gears engage smoothly and freely.

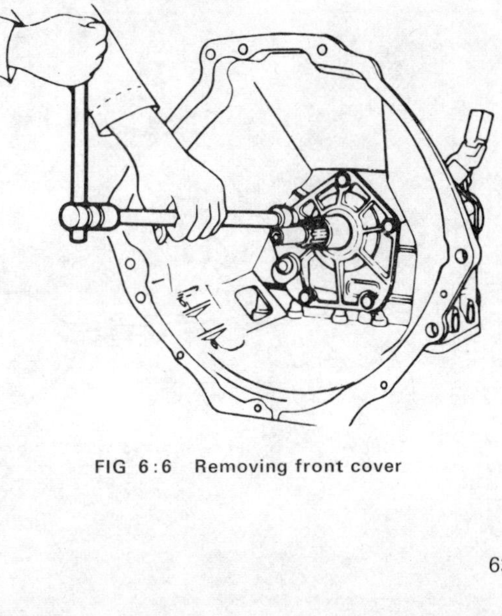

FIG 6:6 Removing front cover

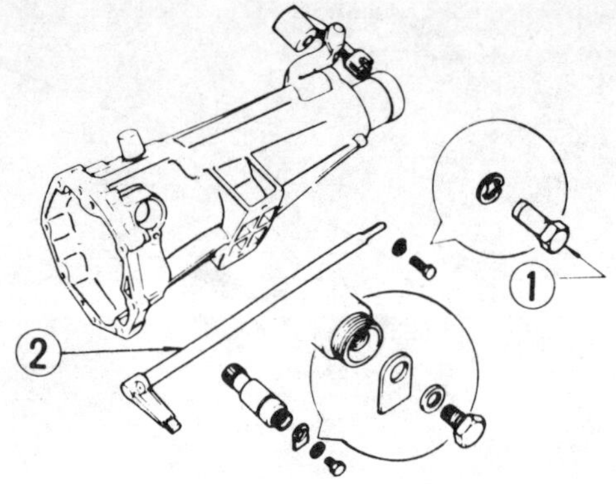

FIG 6:7 Removing pin 1, striking rod 2 and extension housing on four-speed units

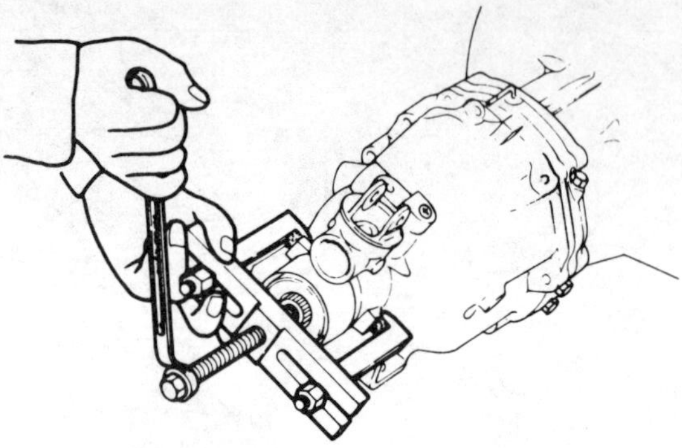

FIG 6:10 Removing rear extension housing on five-speed units

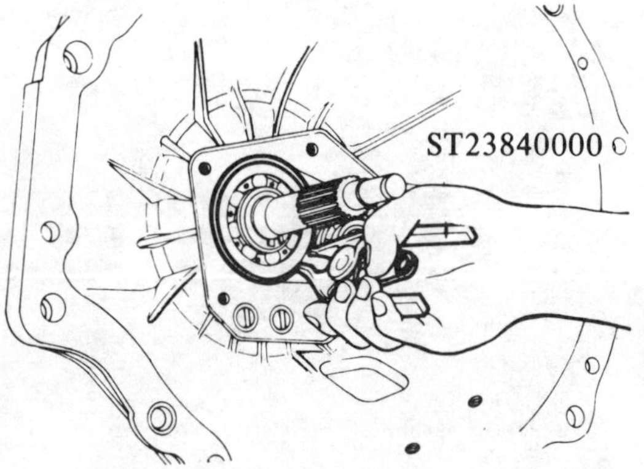

FIG 6:8 Removing main drive bearing on five-speed units

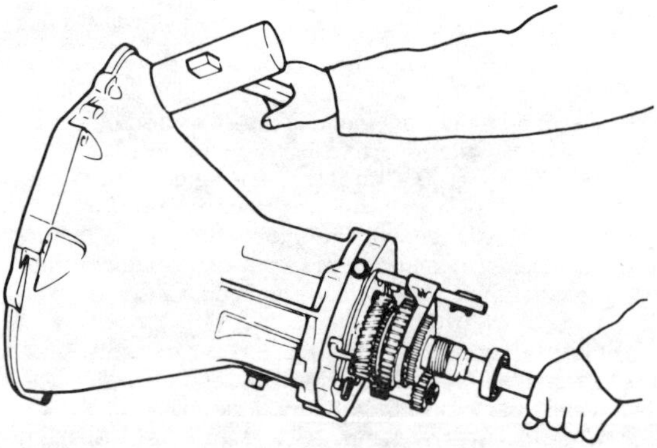

FIG 6:11 Removing transmission case from adaptor plate on five-speed units

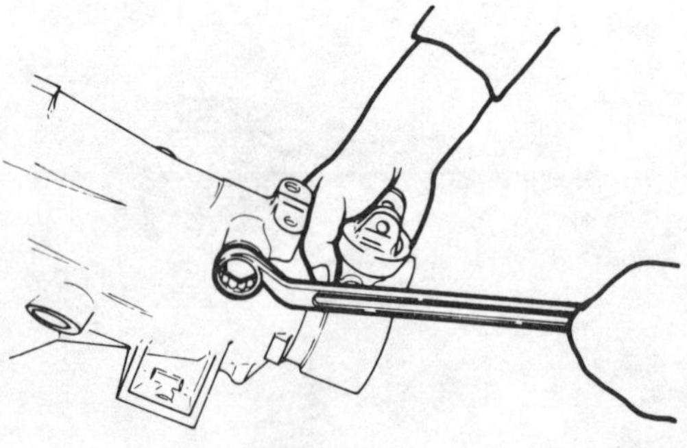

FIG 6:9 Removing reverse selector return plug on five-speed units

6:4 Dismantling the gearbox

Note that complete dismantling of the gearbox assembly requires the use of certain special tools and the owner will be well advised to check on the availability of these factory tools or suitable substitutes before tackling the items involved.

1 Thoroughly clean the exterior of the unit to remove all road dirt and grease. Drain the lubricant from the gearbox.
2 Detach the dust cover from the transmission case, then refer to **Chapter 5** and remove clutch release lever and release bearing.
3 Remove the reversing lamp switch and the speedometer pinion complete with pinion sleeve. Remove the fixing bolts and detach the front cover from the transmission as shown in **FIG 6:6**.
4 Detach bottom cover from transmission case. Make sure that the gears are in neutral.

On four-speed units, refer to **FIG 6:7** and pull out striking rod pin 1. Remove the fixing bolts then detach the rear extension housing by lightly tapping it with a soft-faced hammer.

On five-speed units, detach the countershaft front bearing shim then remove the main drive bearing circlip with tool ST23840000 or other suitable circlip

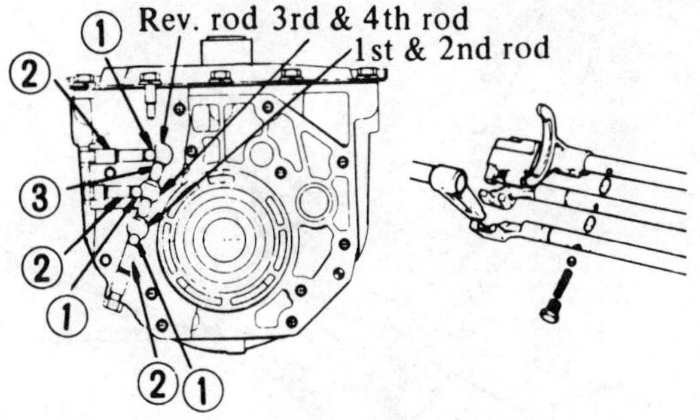

FIG 6:12 Dismantling interlock mechanism on four-speed units

Key to Fig 6:12 1 Check ball 2 Locking spring 3 Interlock plunger

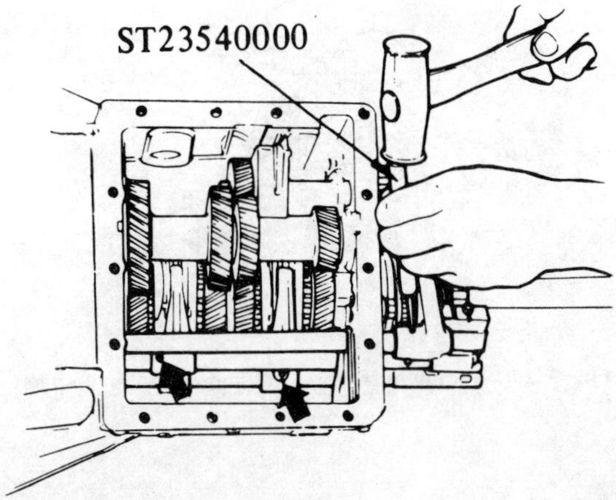

FIG 6:13 Retaining pin removal on four-speed units

pliers, as shown in **FIG 6:8**. Remove reverse selector return plug, return spring and plunger from rear extension as shown in **FIG 6:9**.

5 Remove the securing bolts then extract the rear extension housing with a suitable puller, as shown in **FIG 6:10**. Separate transmission case from adaptor plate with a soft-faced hammer, as shown in **FIG 6:11**.

6 On four-speed units, loosen check ball plugs then remove three locking springs and check balls as shown in **FIG 6:12**. Using pin punch ST23540000 or similar, drive retaining pins from fork rod as shown in **FIG 6:13**. Pin punch ST23540000 is shown in **FIG 6:14**. Draw out fork rods, taking care not to lose the two plungers.

On five-speed units, use tool ST23540000 or similar pin punch to drive retaining pins from each fork rod, as shown in **FIG 6:14**. Refer to **FIG 6:15** and remove the three check ball plugs, then drive out fork rods from adaptor plate by lightly tapping on the front end. Take care not to lose the three check balls and two interlock plungers.

Removing gears and shafts:

Four-speed units:

1 Engage two gears at once to lock the assembly in position, then straighten the lockwasher and loosen the mainshaft nut.

2 Use tool ST23100000 to push out countershaft from transmission case as shown in **FIG 6:16**. Take care not to drop needle bearings into case. Remove countergear together with needle bearings and washers, making sure that washers used between countergear and case are removed.

3 Remove circlip retaining reverse idler gear in place. Remove idler gearshaft from rear of transmission case as shown in **FIG 6:17**.

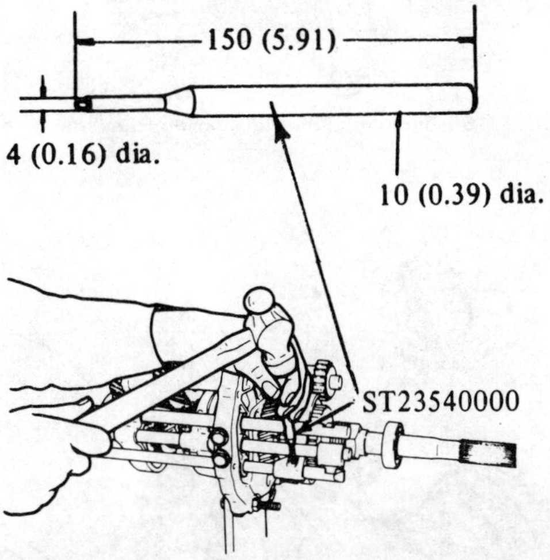

FIG 6:14 Retaining pin removal on five-speed units

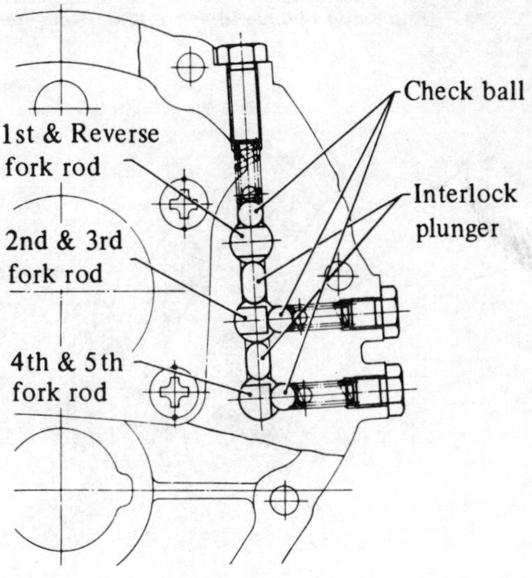

FIG 6:15 Dismantling interlock mechanism on five-speed units

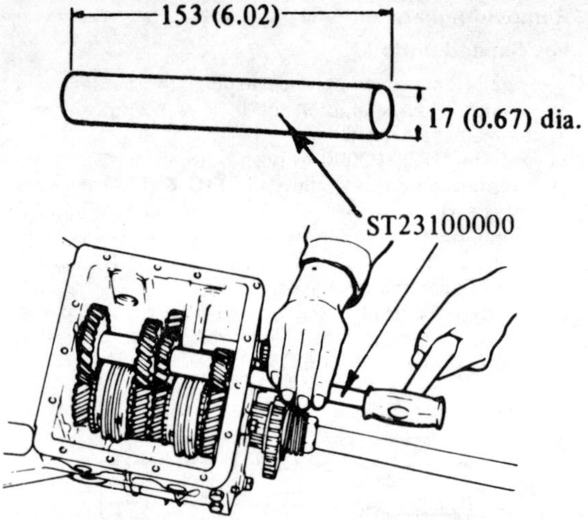

FIG 6:16 Removing countergear on four-speed units

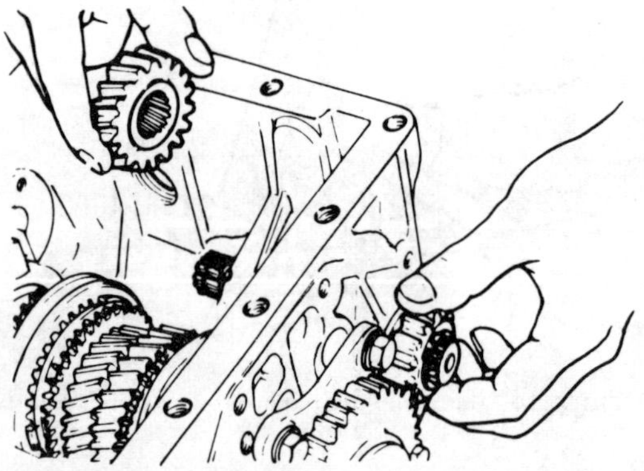

FIG 6:17 Removing reverse idler shaft on four-speed units

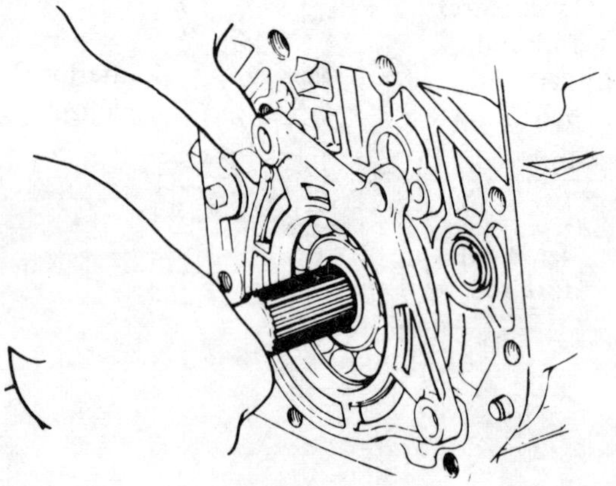

FIG 6:18 Removing mainshaft assembly on four-speed units

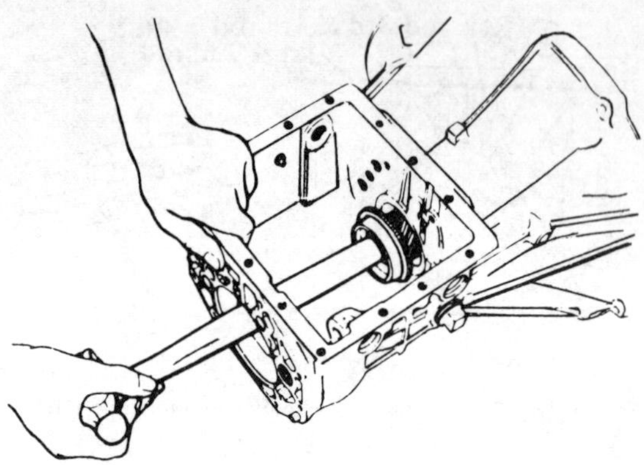

FIG 6:19 Main drive gear removal on four-speed units

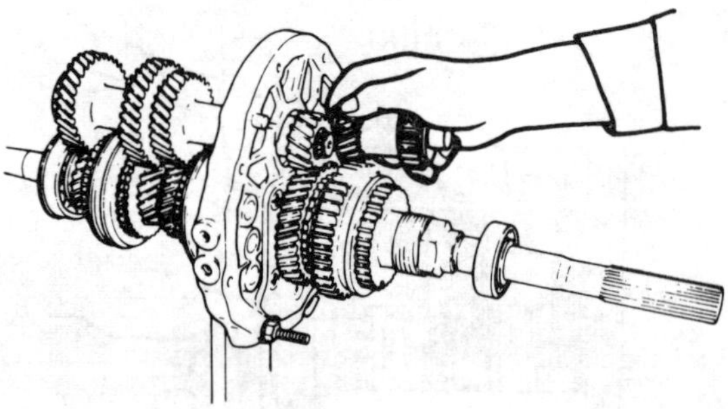

FIG 6:20 Removing reverse idler gear on five-speed units

4 Remove bolts securing mainshaft bearing retainer, then withdraw mainshaft assembly from rear of transmission case as shown in **FIG 6:18**.
5 Remove pilot bearing located between mainshaft and main drive gear. Use a hammer handle to drive out main drive gear as shown in **FIG 6:19**.

Five-speed units:

1 Remove reverse idler gear complete with shaft as shown in **FIG 6:20**.
2 Remove retaining circlip then pull off mainshaft end bearing with tool ST22460001 as shown in **FIG 6:21**. Remove second circlip for mainshaft end bearing.
3 Engage both first and second gears, then release the staking of the mainshaft nut as shown in **FIG 6:22**. Remove mainshaft nut, then remove speedometer drive gear, synchroniser hub with reverse and first gear together with needle bearing (see **FIG 6:23**). Remove thrust washer. Take care not to lose steel ball retaining speedometer drive gear and thrust washer.
4 Remove circlip and thrust washer from rear end of first countergear. Use tool ST22480000 to remove first countergear, as shown in **FIG 6:24**.
5 Use tool ST22471000 to remove mainshaft gear assembly, as shown in **FIG 6:25**. Remove main

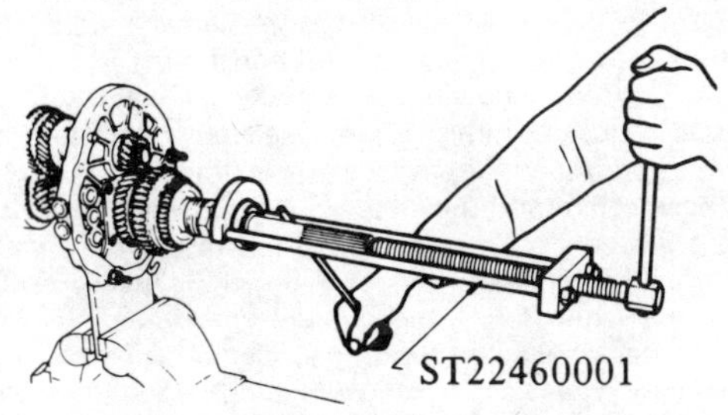

FIG 6:21 Removing mainshaft end bearing on five-speed units

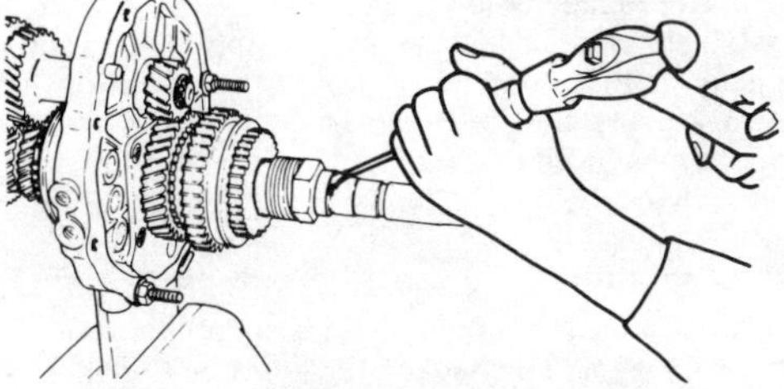

FIG 6:22 Releasing staking of mainshaft nut

drive gear and countergear as shown in **FIG 6:26**, then draw out mainshaft about 10mm (0.4in). Take care not to drop the gear assemblies.

Servicing gear assemblies:

Gear assembly dismantling involves the use of a hydraulic press and a number of special press tools. Reassembly of the components again involves the use of a press and also the selective fitting of circlips. For these reasons, it is recommended that the work is carried out only by a fully equipped Datsun service agent.

6:5 Gearbox reassembly

Four-speed units:

Clean all metal components in a suitable solvent and examine for wear or damage. Any faulty components must be renewed. Do not allow solvent to come into contact with rubber seals, as this can cause damage. Renew all gaskets and seals. Reassembly is a reversal of the removal procedure, noting the following points:

Refer to **FIG 6:27** when installing countershaft. To fit needle roller bearing 3 in position, insert countershaft guide ST23100000 in countergear 1 then install washer 2, bearing 3 and second washer in place. Install these parts together with washers 4 and 5 to transmission case, then insert countershaft 6 into countergear through hole of case and retaining pin 7 into its hole on the front side of countershaft. Select and install rear thrust washer 5 of suitable thickness to obtain countergear end play of 0.05 to 0.15mm (0.0020 to 0.0059in).

With gears meshed in two positions, tighten mainshaft nut to 9 to 11kgm (65 to 80lb ft), then bend lockplate to secure the nut.

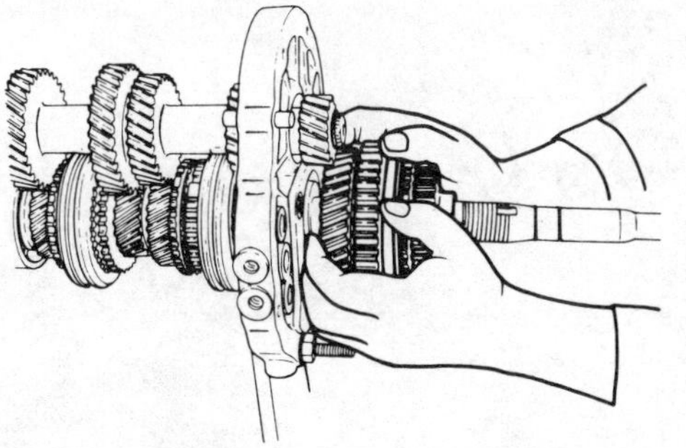

FIG 6:23 Removing first and reverse gears on five-speed units

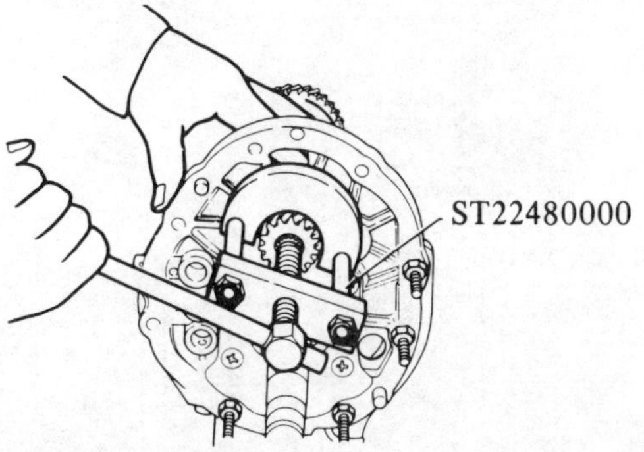

FIG 6:24 Removing first countergear on five-speed units

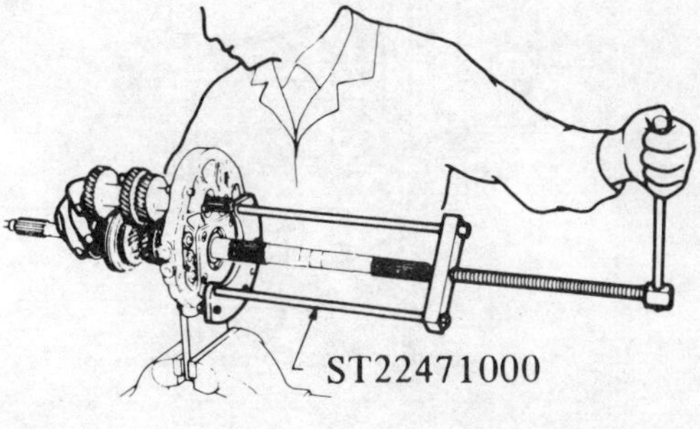

FIG 6:25 Removing mainshaft gear on five-speed units

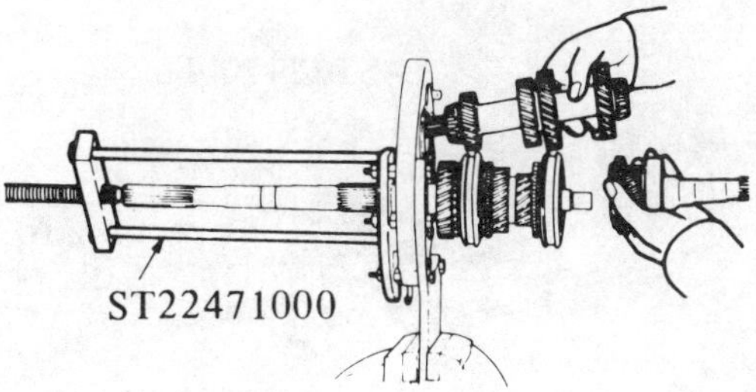

FIG 6:26 Removing main drive gear and countergear on five-speed units

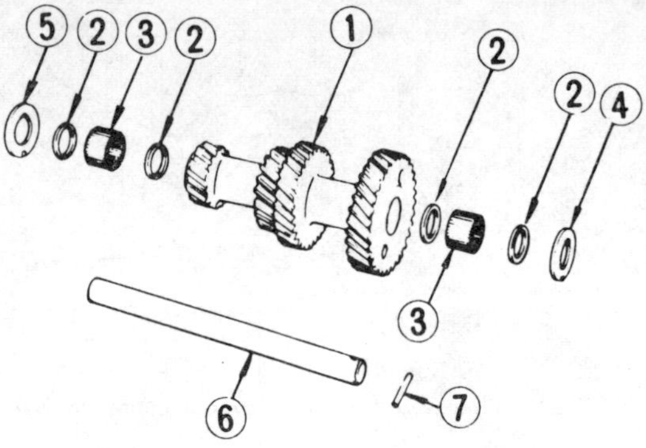

FIG 6:27 Countershaft assembly on four-speed units

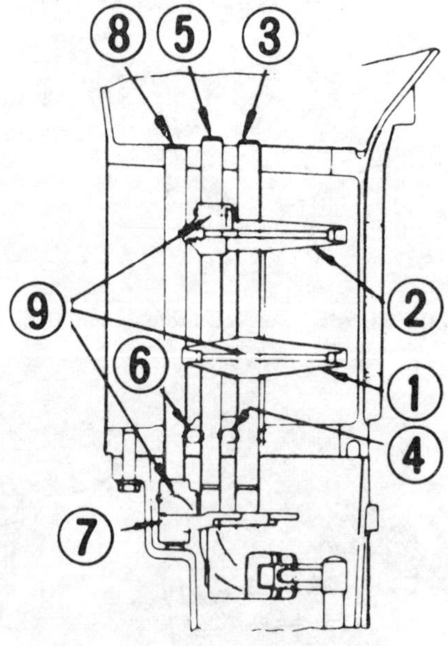

FIG 6:28 Selector rod and fork installation on four-speed units

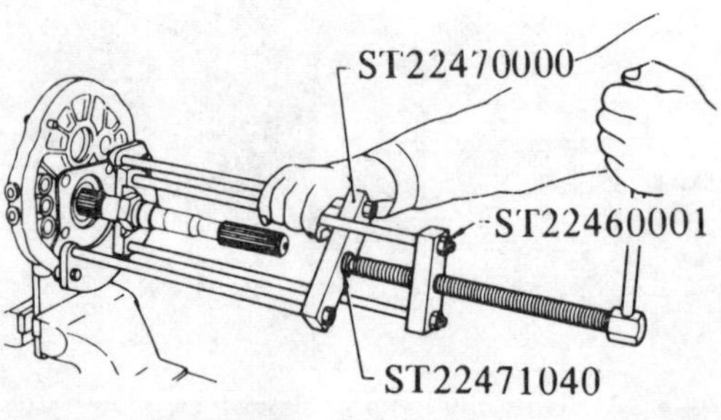

FIG 6:29 Mainshaft installation on five-speed units

Refer to **FIG 6:28** for selector fork installation. Align first and second fork 1 and third and fourth fork 2 with grooves on coupling sleeves respectively. Insert first and second rod 3 and drive in pin 9 securely. With first and second rod in neutral position, install interlock plunger 4 and insert third and fourth rod 5 into position then drive in pin 9 securely. Place third and fourth rod 5 in neutral position then install interlock plunger 6. Install reverse rod 8 into shift fork 7, then secure with retaining pin 9. Install check balls and locking springs at three places in transmission case and tighten with plugs, applying sealing compound to plug threads.

Apply gear oil to all sliding parts and make sure that gears mesh smoothly. Make sure that gears are in neutral positions and install extension housing to transmission case by properly aligning striking lever with selector rod brackets. Fit transmission front cover.

Install clutch release lever and bearing as described in **Chapter 5**. Install bottom cover to transmission case, then make sure that main drive shaft rotates smoothly without any sign of binding.

Five-speed units:

Clean all metal components in a suitable solvent and examine for wear or damage. Any faulty components must be renewed. Do not allow solvent to come into contact with rubber seals, as this can cause damage. Renew all gaskets and seals. Reassembly is a reversal of the removal procedure, noting the following points:

Fit the reverse idler gear assembly so that the thrust washers on the shaft have their brown surfaces facing towards the gears. Place the mainshaft assembly into the adaptor plate and fit the mainshaft nut. Pull the mainshaft assembly into the adaptor plate using special tools shown in **FIG 6:29**, until thrust washer to bearing clearance reaches approximately 10mm (0.394in). Fit baulk ring on cone surface of main drive gear. Lubricate mainshaft pilot bearing with gear oil and fit in place. Fit drive gear assembly on front end of mainshaft. Assemble counter-gear assembly to mainshaft and main drive gear. Use special tools to pull mainshaft assembly into adaptor plate together with main drive gear and countergear. Hold gears carefully by hand to prevent them from falling. Press first countergear onto countershaft using special tools as shown in **FIG 6:30**.

Fit spacer on rear end of first countergear and secure with new circlip. Install components to rear of mainshaft in the following order: steel ball, thick thrust washer, first gear bushing, needle bearing, first gear, first gear baulk ring, first synchroniser together with reverse gear, steel ball, speedometer drive gear and mainshaft nut. With both first and second gears engaged, tighten mainshaft nut to 14 to 17kgm (101 to 123lb ft). A torque wrench adaptor tool will be required for this operation. The Datsun tool is shown in **FIG 6:31**. Using the following formula the torque read on the torque wrench can be calculated:

$$C = A \times \left(\frac{L}{L + M}\right)$$

where C is the torque value read on the torque wrench, A is the required torque, L the length of the torque wrench and M the distance between the centres of the two holes of the adaptor (the Datsun tool is 0.1m (0.33ft) between the centres). Stake mainshaft nut to groove in mainshaft with a suitable punch.

When fitting selector forks and rods, place three selector forks in groove in each coupling sleeve, taking care not to drop selector forks. Install first and reverse fork rod through first and reverse selector fork and adaptor plate. Secure with a new retaining pin. Install check ball, check ball spring and check ball plug, applying sealant to plug threads. Align centre notch in first and reverse selector rod with check ball. Note that ball plug for first and reverse fork rod is longer than those for second and third and fourth and fifth fork rods (see **FIG 6:15**). Install interlock plunger on adaptor plate. Install second and third fork rod through adaptor plate, second and third fork and fourth and fifth fork, then secure with a new retaining pin. Install check ball and check ball spring. Install check ball plug, using sealant on threads. Align centre notch in second and third fork rod with check ball. Install interlock plunger on adaptor plate. Install fourth and fifth rod through adaptor plate and fourth and fifth fork, then secure with a new retaining pin. Install check ball and check ball spring. Fit check ball plug, using sealant on threads. Apply gear oil to all sliding surfaces and check that selector rods operate correctly and that gears engage smoothly.

Clean mating surfaces of adaptor plate and rear extension, then apply sealant to these surfaces. With selector forks in their fifth positions, gradually slide rear extension onto adaptor plate. Take care not to move selector arm off striking lever pin. Install selector arm onto fourth and fifth fork rod, then fit striking lever pin into other fork rods. Check that rods operate correctly.

Clean mating surfaces of adaptor plate and transmission case, then apply sealant to these surfaces. Slide transmission case onto adaptor plate, tapping lightly with a soft hammer. Carefully fit main drive bearing and countershaft front bearing, then make sure that mainshaft rotates freely. Install washers and through bolts, tightening to 1.3 to 1.8kgm (9.4 to 13.0lb ft). Fit main drive bearing circlip fully into groove.

When fitting front cover assembly, the correct thickness of countershaft front bearing shim must be selected. Support transmission with front side up, then place setting gauge ST22500000 on countershaft front bearing then turn main drive shaft until bearing is settled. Refer to **FIG 6:32** and measure clearance B between gauge and front end of transmission case, using a thickness gauge. Depth H, which is the required shim thickness, is obtained by applying the formula $H = A - B$, where H is depth from front end of transmission case to countershaft front bearing, A is figure marked on setting gauge and B is measured value obtained from thickness gauge. The correct thickness of shim should be obtained and fitted, according to measurement H. Shims are supplied for this purpose in 18 different thicknesses.

Clean mating surfaces of front cover and transmission case. Apply grease to selected shim and retain on countershaft front bearing, then install front cover to transmission case. Apply sealant to front cover and transmission case mating surfaces before installation. Install through bolts with washers and tighten to 1.3 to 1.8kgm (9.4 to 13.0lb ft). Apply sealant to through bolt threads before installation.

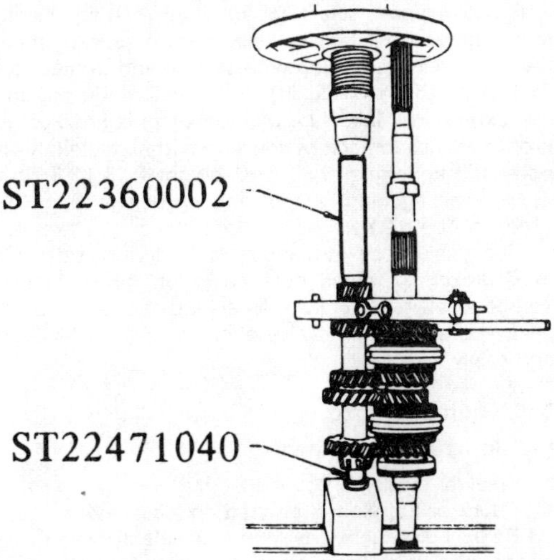

FIG 6:30 Installing first countergear on five-speed units

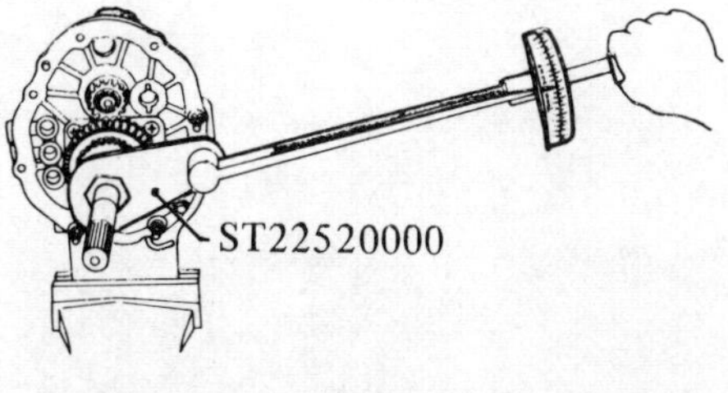

FIG 6:31 Tightening mainshaft nut

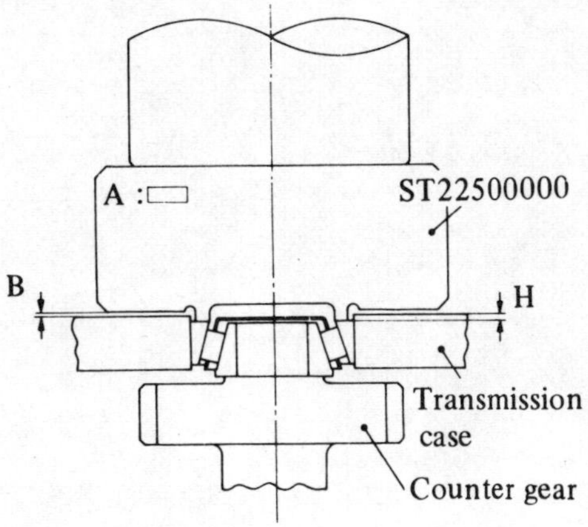

FIG 6:32 Selecting countershaft front bearing shim thickness on five-speed units

Grease reverse select return plunger then install in rear extension. Fit reverse select return springs, then fit reverse select return plug with sealant and tighten to 0.8 to 1.0kgm (5.8 to 7.2lb ft). Fit speedometer pinion on rear extension. Make sure that lockplate is lined up with groove in speedometer pinion sleeve, then install through bolts and tighten to 0.32 to 0.44kgm (2.3 to 3.2lb ft).

Fit reversing lamp switch and tighten to 2 to 3kgm (14.5 to 21.7lb ft).

Fit clutch release lever and release bearing as described in **Chapter 5**. Install dust cover on clutch housing. Temporarily install control lever and move through all gear ranges to check that gears can be selected smoothly and easily.

6:6 Fault diagnosis

(a) Jumping out of gear

1 Weak or broken check ball spring
2 Check ball broken or omitted on reassembly
3 Badly worn check ball groove in selector shaft
4 Worn baulk rings or synchromesh units
5 Selector fork loose on shaft
6 Worn selector fork

(b) Noisy gearbox

1 Insufficient or incorrect lubricant
2 Excessive end floats and clearances
3 Worn or damaged bearings
4 Worn or damaged gear teeth

(c) Oil leaks

1 Lubricant level too high
2 Defective oil seals
3 Leaks at component joint flanges
4 Damaged joint faces

(d) Difficult gearchanging

1 Excessively worn clutch
2 Faults in clutch release mechanism
3 Defective pilot bearing in flywheel
4 Worn synchromesh cones
5 Stiff selector linkage

CHAPTER 7

AUTOMATIC TRANSMISSION

7:1 Description

Automatic transmission is supplied as an optional extra to take the place of the usual clutch and gearbox. The automatic transmission consists of a torque converter and hydraulically controlled automatic epicyclic gearbox with three forward speeds and one reverse. In all gears the drive is through the torque converter which results in maximum flexibility, especially in top gear. The gears are selected automatically as the hydraulic control system engages clutches and/or applies brake bands in various combinations. The hydraulic control system and the torque converter assembly are supplied with pressure oil from an oil pump mounted within the transmission case. A manually controlled mechanical parking pawl is incorporated so that the transmission output shaft can be locked when the vehicle is stationary.

The torque converter consists of an impeller connected through a drive plate to the engine crankshaft, a turbine which is splined to the transmission input shaft and a stator connected to the unit by a one-way clutch. The impeller, driven by the engine, transmits torque by means of the transmission fluid to the turbine which drives the automatic gearbox. The stator redirects the flow of fluid as it leaves the turbine so that it re-enters the impeller at the most effective angle.

When the engine is idling, the converter impeller is being driven slowly and the energy of the fluid leaving it is low, so little torque is imparted to the turbine. For this reason, with the engine idling and drive engaged, the vehicle will have little or no tendency to move from rest. As the throttle is opened impeller speed increases and the process of torque multiplication begins. As the turbine picks up speed and the slip between it and the impeller reduces, the torque multiplication reduces progressively until, when their speeds become substantially equal, the unit acts as a fluid coupling. In this condition, the stator is no longer required to redirect the fluid flow and the roller clutch permits it to rotate with the impeller and turbine. **FIG 7:1** shows a sectional view of the automatic transmission assembly.

The maintenance and adjustment procedures which can be carried out by a reasonably competent owner are given in this chapter. More serious performance faults which require pressure take-off points to be opened and pressure measurements taken to diagnose the fault, adjustment of the governor or clutches and bands, partial or complete dismantling to replace worn or failed internal components dictate that the services of a fully equipped specialist should be enlisted. Quite apart from the specialised knowledge which is required, test

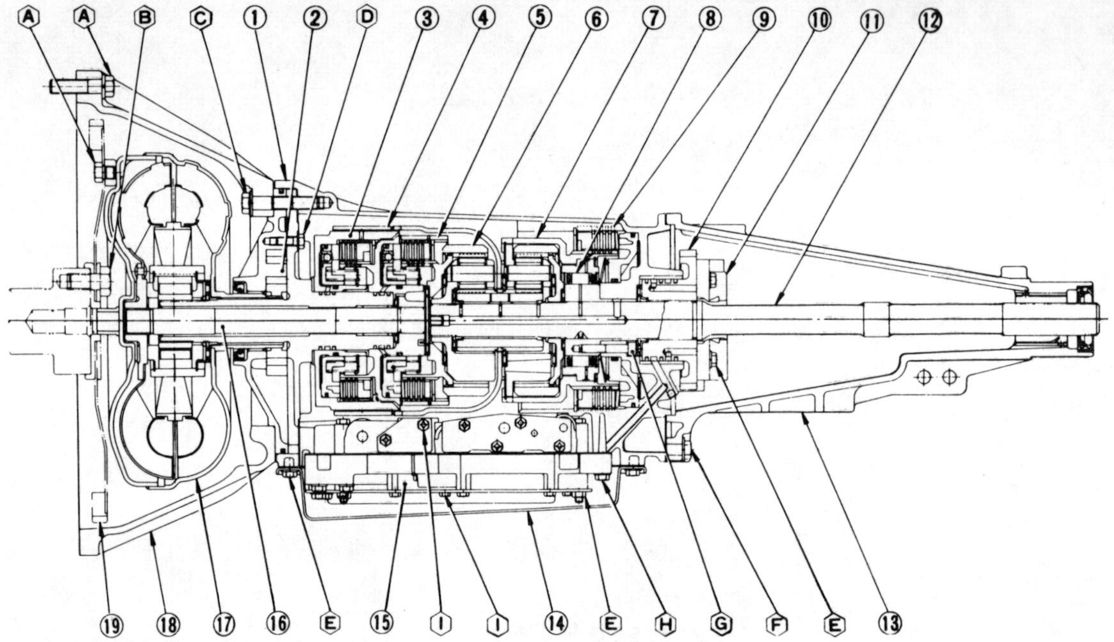

FIG 7:1 Sectional view of the automatic transmission assembly

Key to Fig 7:1 1 Transmission case 2 Oil pump 3 Front clutch 4 Band brake 5 Rear clutch 6 Front planetary gear 7 Rear planetary gear 8 One-way clutch 9 Low and reverse brake 10 Oil distributor 11 Governor 12 Output shaft 13 Rear extension 14 Oil pan 15 Control valve 16 Input shaft 17 Torque converter 18 Converter housing 19 Drive plate

equipment and a large number of special tools are essential. It should be noted that the torque converter is supplied as an assembly only, no internal parts being available separately.

7:2 Routine maintenance

Every 5000km (3000 miles) the fluid in the automatic transmission should be checked. The car should be taken for a run of at least five miles to ensure that the automatic transmission is at normal operating temperature. Apply the handbrake and start the engine. Move the transmission selector lever through all drive positions then place it in P (Park) position. Leave the engine idling while the fluid level is checked. Remove the automatic transmission dipstick as shown in **FIG 7:2**, wipe it clean on a non-fluffy cloth and refit it fully. Remove the dipstick again and check the level of fluid against the marks. Top up through the dipstick tube if necessary to bring the fluid level to the upper mark on the dipstick. Approximately 0.4 litre ($\frac{7}{8}$ US pint, $\frac{3}{4}$ Imp. pint) separates the H and L marks on the dipstick. **Do not overfill.** Use an approved grade of Dexron Automatic Transmission Fluid. **Never use anything but the recommended fluid in the automatic transmission.**

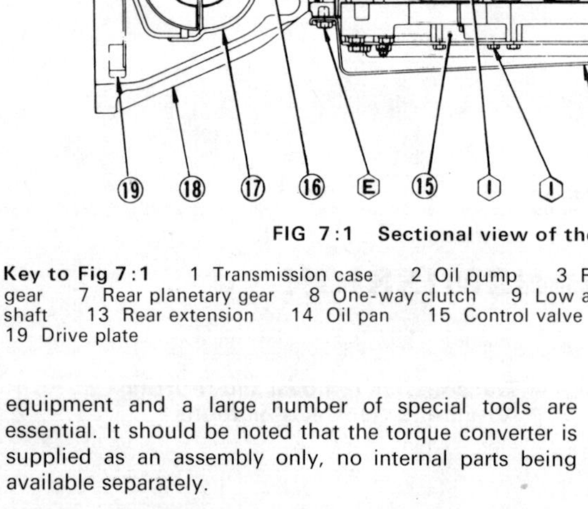

FIG 7:2 Automatic transmission dipstick and fluid filler tube

7:3 Gear selector linkages

A manual selector, located on the floor in the centre of the driver's compartment, offers a choice of six positions by moving a T-handled lever in a quadrant. These positions are marked P–R–N–D–2–1 and give the following services:

P or Park:

In this position the engine may be started and run without any drive being transmitted to the road wheels. At the same time a mechanical lock is applied and the car cannot be moved in either direction. P must never be selected while the car is in motion.

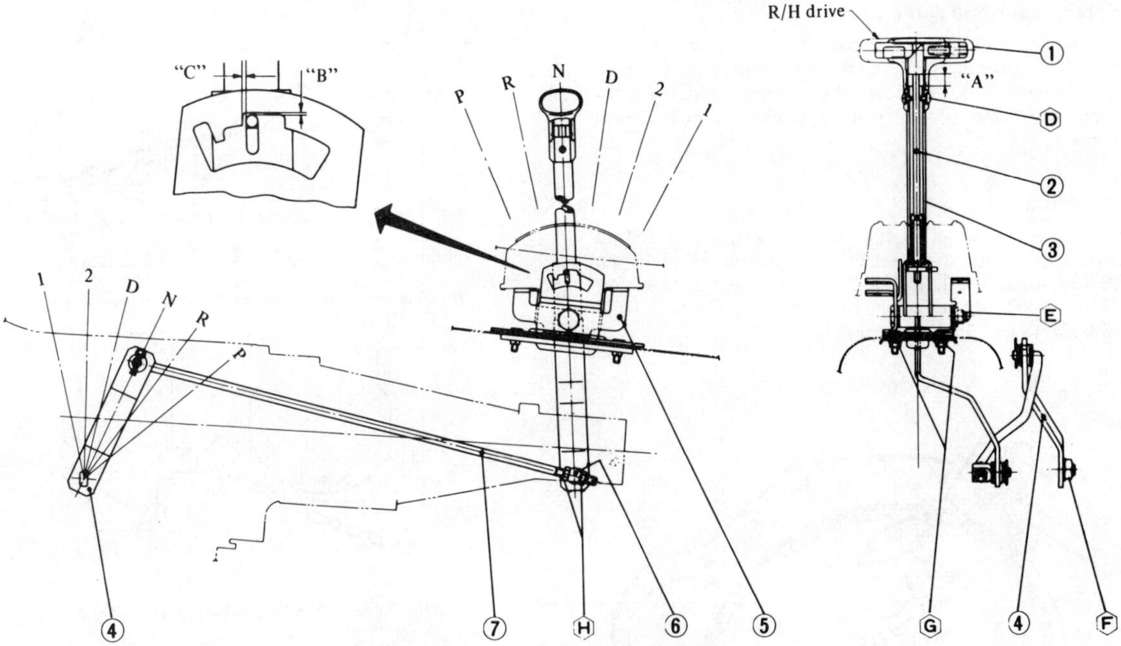

FIG 7:3 Control linkage details

Key to Fig 7:3 1 Control lever knob 2 Pusher 3 Control lever assembly 4 Selector range lever 5 Control lever bracket 6 Joint trunnion 7 Selector rod
Tightening torque (T) of nuts and screws kgm (lb ft): **D** T:0.07 to 0.13 (0.51 to 0.94) **E** T:1.6 to 2.2 (12 to 16)
F T:3 to 4 (22 to 29) **G** T:0.35 to 0.45 (2.5 to 3.3) **H** T:0.8 to 1.1 (5.8 to 8.0)

R or Reverse:

The car should always be brought completely to a halt before reverse is selected.

N or Neutral:

Similar in application to P, but the lock is not applied.

D or Drive:

This position is used for all normal running. When D is selected from rest the car will move off in first gear and the transmission will change automatically to second and third gears, and down again, at speeds appropriate to road speed and throttle position.

2 or Second:

As for D, but there will be no upward change into top gear. If selected while running in top gear, a change down to second will be made, thus providing engine braking or the possibility of improved acceleration.

1 or First

In this position there will be no upward change from first gear. If selected while running in top gear, a downchange to second will occur and the transmission will remain in second gear until the vehicle speed is reduced to approximately 40 to 50km/hr (25 to 31 mile/hr). This is due to the incorporation of a safety device to prevent a downchange to first gear at too high an engine or road speed.

Selector lever release catch:

A spring loaded button on the selector lever is incorporated to engage or release a catch mechanism in the selector quadrant to prevent accidental selection of certain positions. The button must be pressed for the following position changes—P-R, R-P, N-R and D-2.

Also included in the specification is a starter inhibitor switch, the purpose of which is to ensure that the starter can be operated only when the selector lever is in the P or N positions.

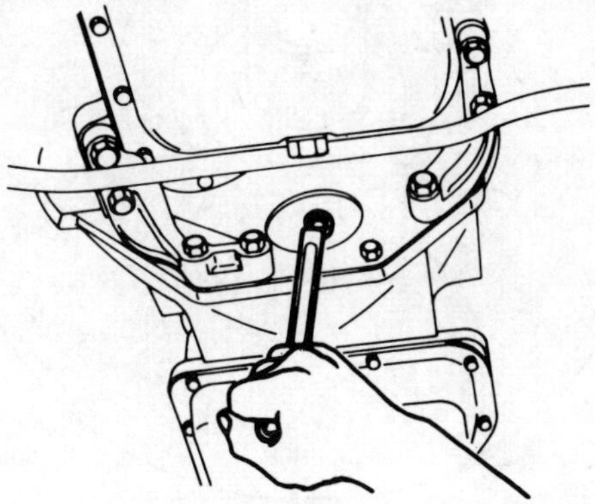

FIG 7:4 Removing torque converter to drive plate bolts

Selector linkage removal:

Refer to **FIG 7:3**. Remove the two fixing screws and detach the control handle from the lever. Remove the console box. Remove the selector rod, selector range lever and control lever assembly complete with bracket.

Refitting:

This is a reversal of the removal procedure. Before installing control knob, set dimension A to 11 to 12mm (0.433 to 0.472in). Install the control knob, checking dimension B and adjusting if necessary to 0.1 to 1.1mm (0.0039 to 0.331in) by turning pusher 2.

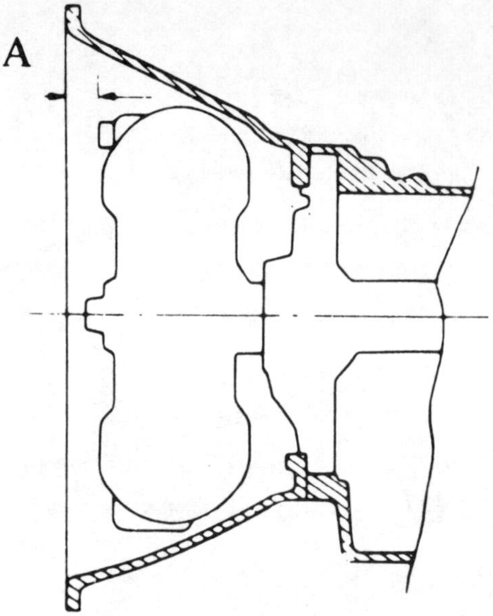

FIG 7:7 Installing torque converter

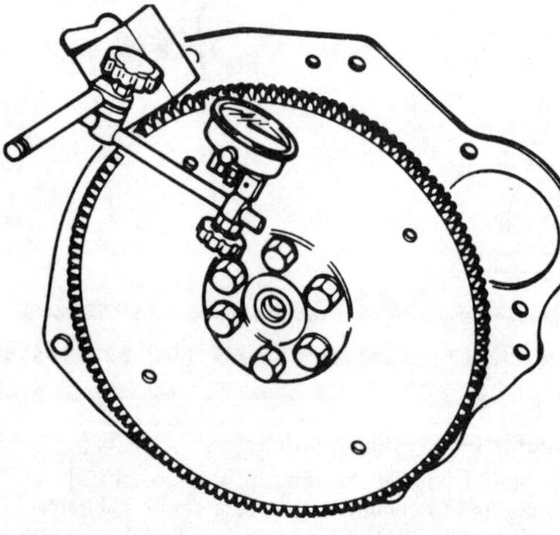

FIG 7:5 Checking drive plate run-out

Selector linkage adjustment:

Refer to **FIG 7:3**. Loosen adjusting nuts H. Set control lever 3 and selector lever 4 at the N position. Set clearance C to 1mm (0.039in) by turning in or out adjusting nuts at trunnion 6. On completion, make sure that the selector control lever can be set in any position correctly and moves freely through all positions with no sign of binding. If operation is unsatisfactory, recheck the adjustment before checking for worn or damaged selector linkage components.

7:4 Transmission removal and refitting

Removal:

Disconnect the earth cable from the battery terminal. Disengage the torsion shaft from accelerator linkage. Raise the vehicle and safely support on floor stands. Refer to **Chapter 8** and remove the propeller shaft. Plug the opening in the rear transmission extension to prevent oil leakage.

Disconnect the front exhaust pipe. Disconnect the selector range lever from the manual shaft. Detach the wiring connections from the inhibitor switch.

Disconnect the tube from the vacuum diaphragm and the wiring connections at the downshift solenoid. Disconnect speedometer cable from rear extension.

Disconnect the oil charging pipe. Disconnect oil cooler inlet and outlet tubes at transmission case. Plug ends of tubes and holes in transmission case to prevent leakage.

Support the engine by means of a jack placed beneath the sump, interposing a wooden block between sump and jack to prevent damage. Use a second suitable jack to support the weight of the transmission. Detach the rubber plug and remove the bolts securing torque

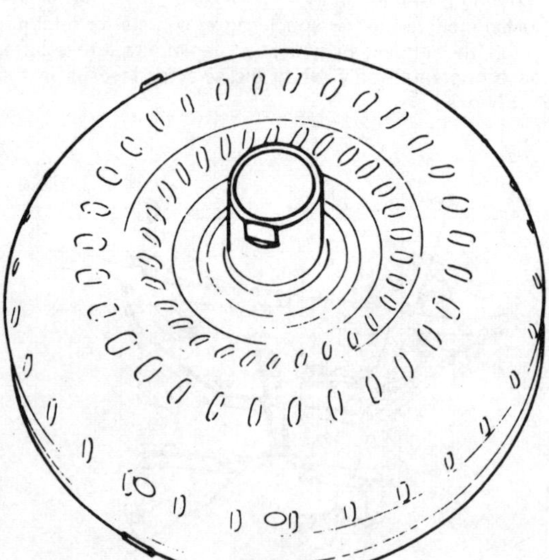

FIG 7:6 Torque converter alignment notch

converter drive plate, turning the engine for access to each bolt in turn (see **FIG 7:4**). Note that match marks must be made on the torque converter and drive plate before removing torque converter, so that the components can be replaced in their original positions.

Remove rear engine mount bolts and crossmember bolts. Remove starter motor. Remove bolts securing transmission to engine, then gradually lower the jack until transmission can be moved from beneath the car.

Refitting:

Refitting is a reversal of the removal procedure, noting the following points:

Check drive plate run-out, preferably using a dial gauge as shown in **FIG 7:5**. Rotate crankshaft one full turn and check total indicator reading. The drive plate must be renewed if run-out is in excess of 0.5mm (0.020in).

When installing torque converter, line up notch shown in **FIG 7:6** with notch in oil pump. Take great care not to cause undue stress in components while installing torque converter. When connecting torque converter to transmission, check that distance A in **FIG 7:7** is more than 21.5mm (0.846in).

Bolt the converter to drive plate, aligning the marks made when dismantling. When converter is installed, rotate crankshaft several times to check that transmission rotates freely without binding.

Connect selector linkage and correctly adjust as described in **Section 7:3**. Connect inhibitor switch wires and check that starter will only operate in selector lever positions P and N. Check also that the reversing lamp operates when lever is placed in R position.

On completion, add fluid if necessary until the level is at the lower mark on the dipstick, then drive the car until the transmission is at normal operating temperature before finally correcting the level as described in **Section 7:2**.

7:5 Automatic transmission faults

Serious automatic transmission faults are certain to require specialist attention because of the equipment needed for diagnosis and rectification. But in the event of unsatisfactory operation, always check first that the fluid level is correct (see **Section 7:2**). Incorrect fluid level can give rise to a wide range of faults including lack of drive, slip, poor acceleration, failure to change, overheating and noise.

If the fluid level is correct, the next check should be on the adjustment of the selector linkage (see **Section 7:3**), particularly if the faults include difficulty in manual selection of the required range, impaired automatic changes or slip.

If the starter motor will not operate, or if it will operate with the selector lever in positions other than N or P, there may be a fault in the inhibitor switch or its associated wiring. Reversing lamp operation is also controlled by the switch which is incorporated behind the selector lever on the side of the transmission unit.

NOTES

CHAPTER 8

THE PROPELLER SHAFT, REAR AXLE AND REAR SUSPENSION

8:1 Description

Power is transmitted from the transmission output shaft to the differential unit pinion shaft by a tubular propeller shaft, this shaft being fitted with universal joints to accommodate suspension movement.

On Standard and De Luxe models, the rear suspension is integrated with the rear axle assembly, which is of the semi-floating type. The rear axle is attached to the car frame by means of semi-elliptic leaf springs and telescopic hydraulic dampers. On Super Sport models independent rear suspension is provided by means of universally jointed drive shafts between differential and road wheels, coil springs and telescopic hydraulic dampers. The rear wheel hubs are carried on semi-trailing arms attached to pivot points on the rear body crossmember.

The items of maintenance and overhaul which can be carried out by a reasonably competent owner/mechanic are given in this chapter, but it is not advised that any further operations be attempted. Special tools and equipment are essential to overhaul the drive shaft and differential components and set the necessary preloads, so, for these reasons, the components mentioned should be dismantled and serviced only by a Datsun agent having the necessary equipment and trained fitters.

8:2 Routine maintenance

At 5000km (3000 mile) intervals the lubricant level in the differential unit must be checked. With the car standing on level ground and the axle cold, wipe dirt from around the filler plug on the differential casing and remove the plug. The oil level is correct if it reaches to the lower edge of the filler hole. If the level is low, top up with an approved grade of transmission oil as supplied by a Datsun agent. Allow the surplus to drain out before refitting the filler plug.

At intervals of 50,000km (30,000 miles) remove the drain plug from beneath the differential and allow the old oil to drain out. Draining will be easier if it is carried out after a run when the oil is hot. Fit the drain plug, remove the filler plug and slowly fill the axle to the correct level with new oil.

8:3 Propeller shaft

On models fitted with five-speed transmission and independent rear suspension, the propeller shaft is of the three-joint type and incorporates a centre bearing assembly as shown in **FIG 8:1**. On all other models, the propeller shaft is a two-joint type without a centre bearing, as

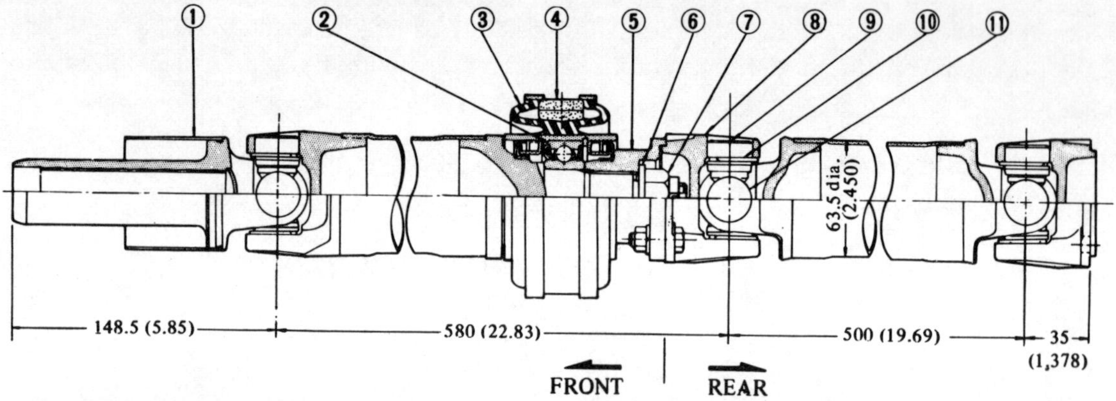

FIG 8:1 Propeller shaft fitted to models with five-speed transmission and independent rear suspension

Key to Fig 8:1 1 Sleeve yoke assembly 2 Centre bearing 3 Centre bearing insulator 4 Cushion rubber 5 Companion flange 6 Plain washer 7 Locking nut 8 Flange yoke 9 Bearing race assembly 10 Circlip 11 Journal assembly

shown in **FIG 8:2**. Note that diameter D and length L vary slightly between model types, so care should be taken to obtain a new shaft of the correct type if replacement is necessary.

All propeller shaft assemblies are dynamically balanced during manufacture. For this reason, propeller shaft dismantling or renewal of universal joint assemblies should only be carried out by a service station having the necessary equipment to rebalance the assembly afterwards.

Removal:

Raise the vehicle for access to the underside and safely support on floor stands. Mark both the propeller shaft flange and pinion flange so that the components can be refitted in their original balanced positions. Remove flange bolts.

Remove the centre bearing support, if fitted, by removing bolts 1 in **FIG 8:3**.

Move the propeller shaft rearwards to disengage the splines from the transmission output shaft, then remove assembly from beneath car. Fit a plug to the rear of transmission housing to prevent oil leakage.

Refitting:

This is a reversal of the removal procedure. Be sure to align the match marks when connecting propeller shaft and pinion shaft flanges. Tighten flange bolts to 2.5 to 3.2kgm (18 to 23lb ft). Tighten centre bearing bracket fixing nuts to 1.9 to 2.6kgm (14 to 19lb ft). Tighten the mounting bolts shown in **FIG 8:3** to 3.6 to 4.8kgm (26 to 35lb ft).

Centre bearing:

Renewal of the propeller shaft centre bearing should be carried out only by a fully equipped service station, as it is necessary to dynamically balance the propeller shaft after the work has been carried out.

8:4 Rear axle

Rigid axle removal:

Raise the rear of the car and support securely on floor stands placed beneath rear body members. Chock front wheels to prevent movement and release the handbrake fully. Place a jack beneath the centre of the rear axle

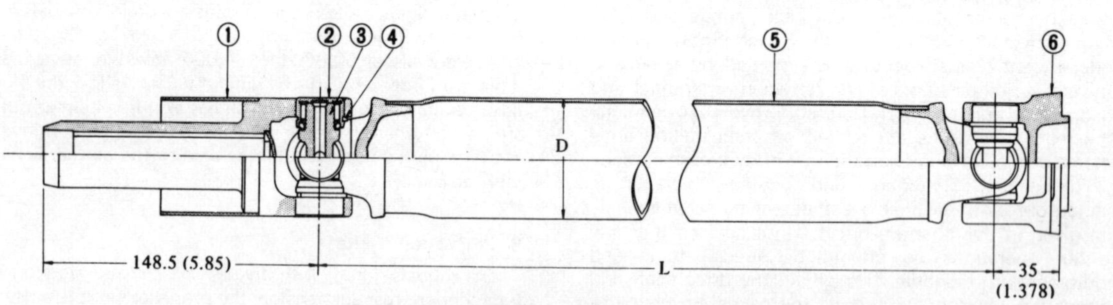

FIG 8:2 Standard propeller shaft assembly

Key to Fig 8:2 1 Sleeve yoke assembly 2 Bearing race assembly 3 Journal assembly 4 Circlip 5 Propeller shaft tube assembly 6 Flange yoke

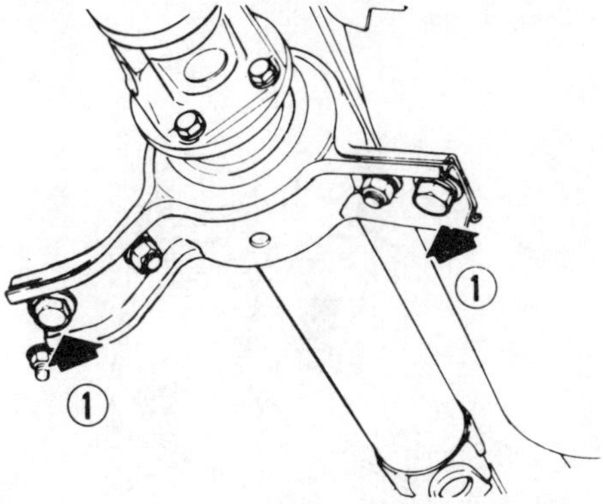

FIG 8:3 Removing centre bearing support

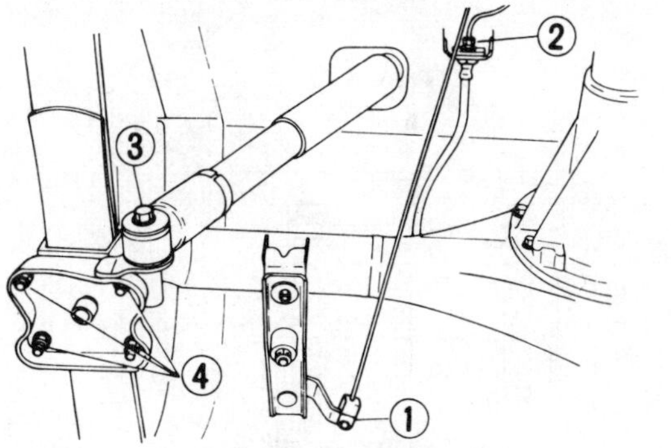

FIG 8:4 Components to be detached for rigid axle removal

assembly and raise sufficiently to just take the weight of the axle.

Remove propeller shaft as described in **Section 8:3**. Refer to **FIG 8:4** and disconnect handbrake cable at clevis pin 1. Disconnect rear brake hose at 2 and cover hose and pipe openings to prevent entry of dirt. Disconnect dampers at 3 and push upwards to clear work area. Lower jack beneath axle assembly, then remove spring U-bolts 4. Raise the jack to lift axle assembly clear of springs, then remove axle through space above one spring as shown in **FIG 8:5**.

Refitting:

This is a reversal of the removal procedure. Tighten U-bolts to 3.5 to 4.8kgm (25 to 35lb ft) as described in **Section 8:5**, and damper lower bolt to 1.6 to 2.2kgm (12 to 16lb ft). On completion, bleed the brakes as described in **Chapter 11**.

Differential carrier, IRS models:

Removal:

Raise the rear of the vehicle and safely support on floor stands. Mark the mating flanges for correct reassembly, then disconnect the propeller shaft from the differential carrier. Refer to **FIG 8:6** and disconnect drive shafts 1 from flanges at differential sides. Support the differential carrier with a jack, then remove nuts 2 on both ends of differential member. Remove four bolts 3 that hold differential carrier to suspension member, then move jack rearwards to detach differential carrier assembly.

Refitting:

This a reversal of the removal procedure, noting the following points. Fit gear carrier to rear suspension member and temporarily tighten with four bolts together with differential mounting spacer (see **FIG 8:7**). Fit differential mounting member to fitting bolts by pushing forwards, then tighten nuts to 7 to 10kgm (51 to 72lb ft). Secure carrier assembly to rear suspension member with four bolts, tightening to 5 to 7kgm (36 to 51lb ft). Tighten drive shaft flange bolts to 1.9 to 2.6kgm (14 to 19lb ft). On completion, check the oil level as described in **Section 8:2**.

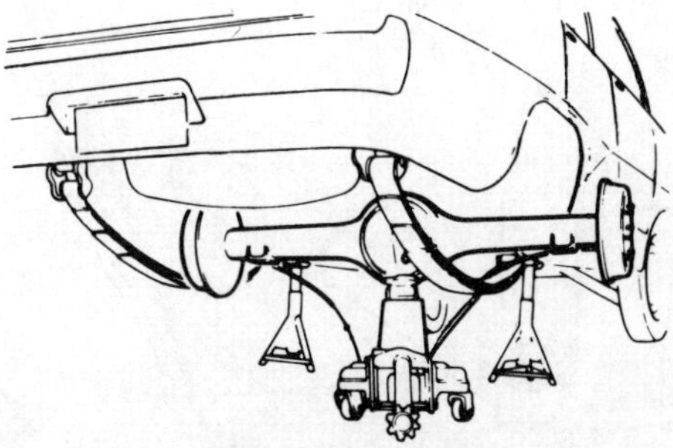

FIG 8:5 Axle removal

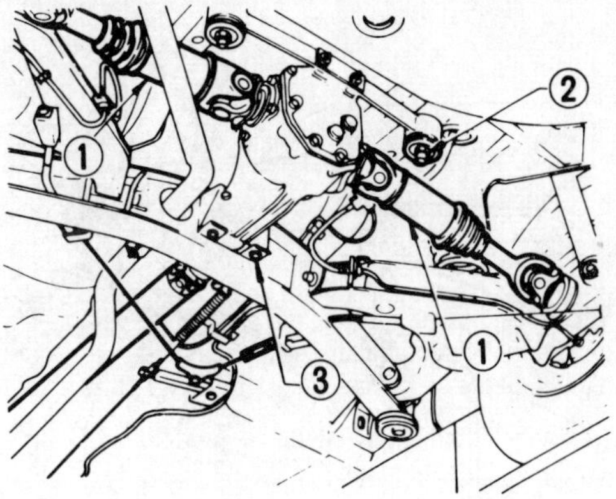

FIG 8:6 Differential carrier removal on IRS models

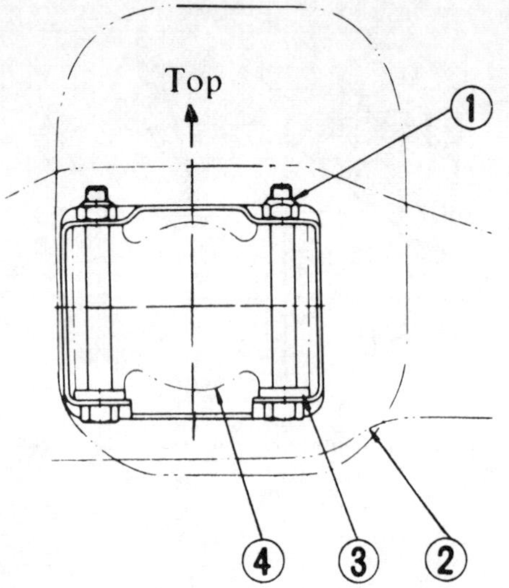

FIG 8:7 Differential mounting spacer details

Key to Fig 8:7 1 Nut 2 Suspension member 3 Spacer 4 Differential carrier assembly

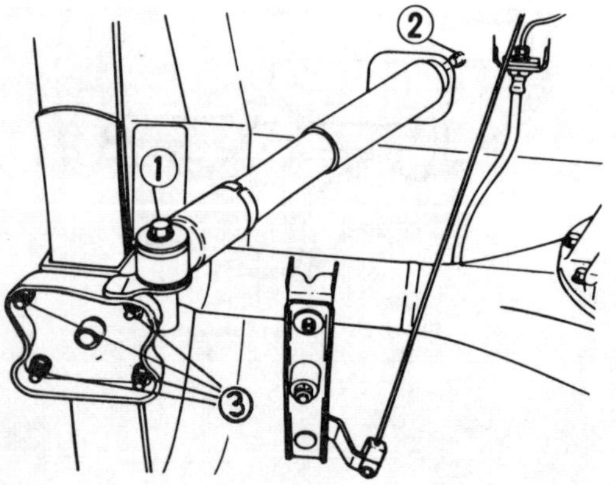

FIG 8:8 Damper mountings 1 and 2 and spring U-bolts 3

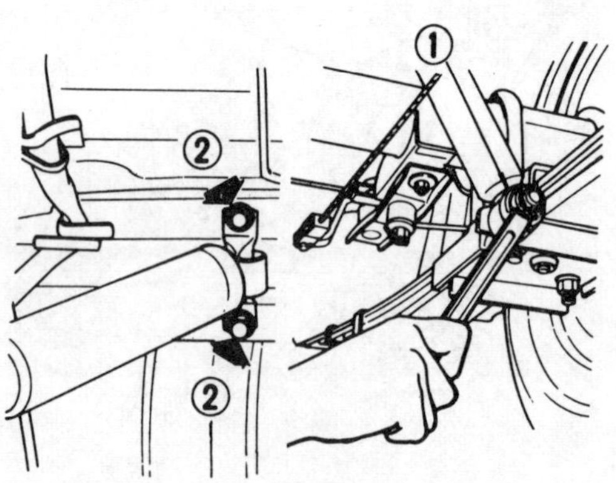

FIG 8:9 Station Wagon damper mountings 1 and 2

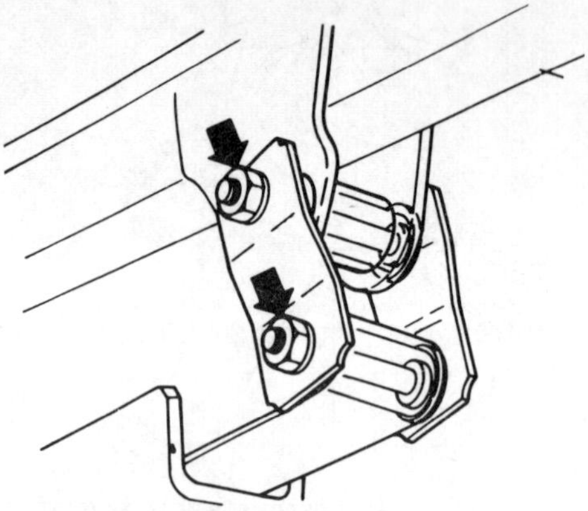

FIG 8:10 Removing spring shackle

8:5 Rigid axle rear suspension

Damper removal:

Raise the rear of the car and support on floor stands placed beneath the axle assembly on both sides. Refer to **FIG 8:8** or **FIG 8:9** and disconnect damper by removing bolts 1 and 2. No attempt must be made to dismantle a damper and heat must not be applied to the damper body.

Refitting:

This is a reversal of the removal procedure. Note that the car weight must be resting on the road wheels when tightening damper upper and lower bolts. When tightening upper bolt, securely tighten underside nut of the pair of nuts until it can be tightened no further, then tighten upper nut to lock. Tighten lower mounting bolt to 1.6 to 2.2kgm (12 to 16lb ft).

On Station Wagon models torque the upper end bolts to 0.9 to 1.2kgm (6.5 to 8.8lb ft) and the lower mounting nut to 3.6 to 4.8kgm (26 to 35lb ft).

Rear spring removal:

Raise rear of car and safely support on floor stands placed beneath body members on both sides. Refer to **FIG 8:8** or **FIG 8:9** and disconnect damper lower mounting 1 and remove U-bolts. Place a jack beneath the axle and raise sufficiently for axle housing to clear spring seat.

Remove nuts arrowed in **FIG 8:10** to disconnect rear spring shackle. Refer to **FIG 8:11** and disconnect spring front pin by removing nuts 1 and 2. On Station Wagon models remove the three nuts shown in **FIG 8:12**.

Use a wire brush to clean the spring assembly, then examine spring leaves for fractures or cracks. Check front bracket and pin, shackle, U-bolts and spring seat for wear, cracks or damaged threads. Inspect all rubber parts for wear, perishing or deformation. Renew any worn or damaged component.

Refitting:

This is a reversal of the removal procedure, noting the following points:

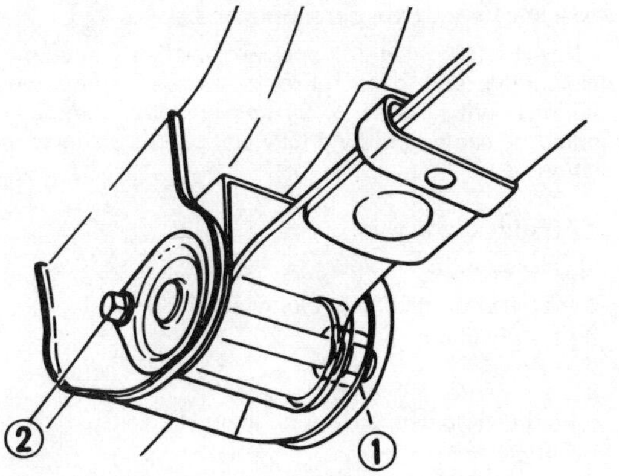

FIG 8:11 Removing front spring pin

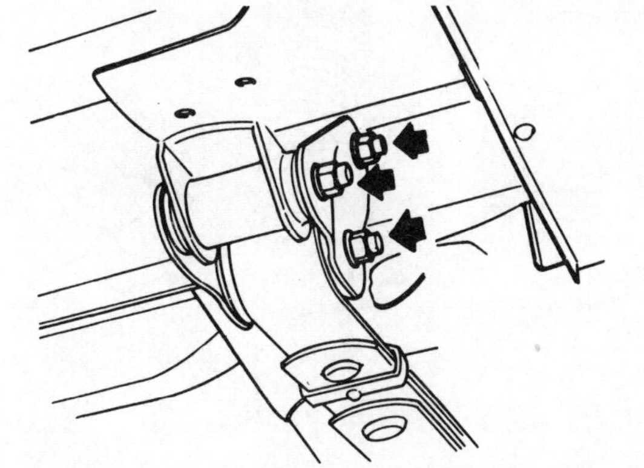

FIG 8:12 Removing the front spring hanger (Station Wagon)

when tightening front pin, shackle and damper lower bolt. Tighten nut 1 to 5.1 to 6.9kgm (37 to 50lb ft) and nut 2 to 0.8 to 1.0kgm (5.8 to 7.2lb ft), as shown in **FIG 8:10**. Tighten shackle nut to 5.1 to 6.9kgm (37 to 50lb ft). Tighten damper lower bolt to 1.6 to 2.2kgm (12 to 16lb ft).

On Station Wagon models torque the front spring nuts, the rear spring shackle nuts and the U-bolt nuts to a torque of 6.0 to 6.5kgm (43 to 47lb ft). Tighten the shock absorber lower mounting nut to 3.6 to 4.8kgm (26 to 35lb ft).

8:6 Independent rear suspension

Damper removal:

If the car is raised for better access to the underside, support securely on floor stands. Open the boot and remove the boot finisher assembly. Remove the double nuts which fasten the upper end of the damper to body (see **FIG 8:13**). Remove the lower fixing bolt and detach the damper unit.

Refitting:

This is a reversal of the removal procedure. Note that the car weight must be resting on the road wheels when damper attachments are tightened. Tighten the first upper damper nut as far as it will go, then tighten the second nut 4.8kgm (29 to 35lb ft). Car weight must be on rear wheels

When refitting U-bolts, apply soapy water to each side of spring pad. Fit nuts to U-bolts and tighten evenly so that a similar number of threads are exposed on each side. Make sure that the U-bolts are square to the axle casing. Tighten nuts alternately and evenly to a torque of 4.0 to to lock. Tighten lower mounting bolt to 1.6 to 2.2kgm (12 to 16lb ft).

Coil spring removal:

Raise rear of car and support safely on stands placed beneath rear body members. Chock front wheels against rotation and fully release the handbrake. Remove the rear road wheel.

Refer to **FIG 8:14**. Disconnect handbrake cables by removing adjusting nut at adjuster 1 and removing

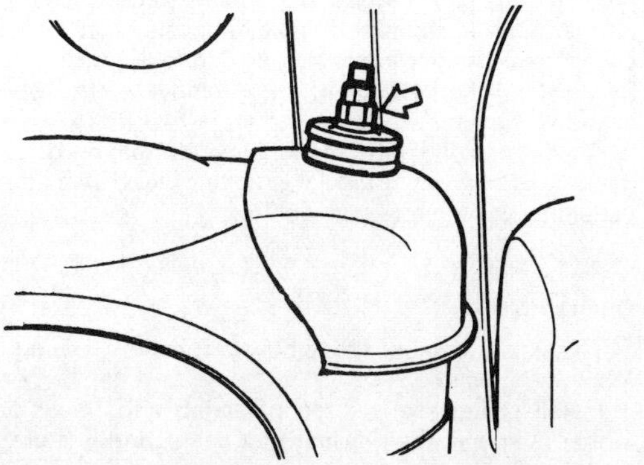

FIG 8:13 Damper upper fixing nuts

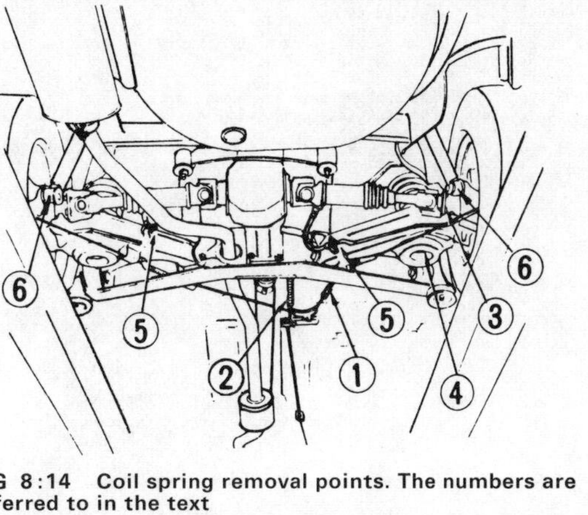

FIG 8:14 Coil spring removal points. The numbers are referred to in the text

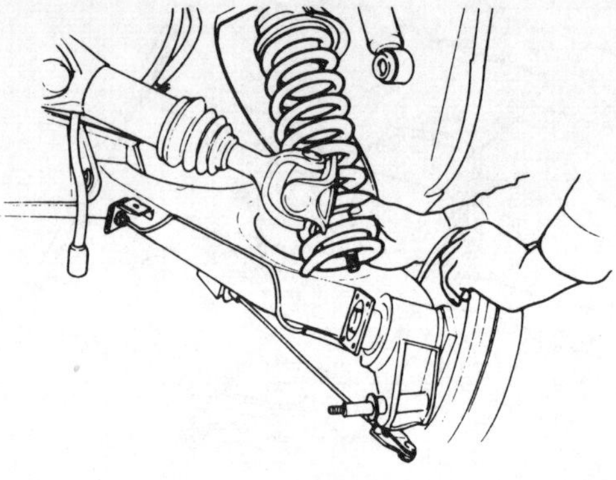

FIG 8:15 Removing coil spring

return spring. Remove drive shaft flange nuts 3 on wheel side and remove rebound rubber fixing nut 4. Disconnect rear brake hose 5 at suspension arm, plugging the hose to prevent entry of dirt. Place a jack beneath the suspension arm and raise slightly to relieve tension on damper. Disconnect damper lower bolt 6. Carefully lower jack to fully extend the coil spring, then remove spring, spring seat and rebound rubber as shown in **FIG 8:15**.

Check the coil spring for cracks, deformation or other damage. Check all rubber parts for wear, damage or perishing. Renew any faulty parts.

Refitting:

This is a reversal of the removal procedure, noting the following points:

Install spring seat on top of spring and fit rebound rubber in spring, then ensure that coil spring is correctly positioned with flat face of spring at the top. Tighten rebound rubber nut to 1.6 to 2.2kgm (12 to 16lb ft) and drive shaft flange bolts to 5 to 6kgm (36 to 43lb ft). Tighten damper lower bolt with car weight on road wheels as described previously. On completion, bleed the braking system as described in **Chapter 11**.

Axle shafts and suspension arms:

Due to the need for special tools and equipment, dismantling and overhaul of rear axle shafts, wheel bearings, drive shafts or suspension arm components should be carried out by a fully equipped Datsun service station.

8:7 Fault diagnosis

(a) Noisy axle

1 Incorrect or insufficient lubricant
2 Worn bearings
3 Worn gears
4 Damaged or broken gear teeth
5 Incorrect adjustments in differential
6 General wear

(b) Excessive backlash

1 Worn gears or bearings
2 Worn drive shaft splines
3 Worn universal joints
4 Loose wheel attachments

(c) Oil leaks

1 Defective oil seals
2 Defective gasket or distorted casing
3 Overfilled rear axle

(d) Vibration

1 Propeller shaft out of balance
2 Defective centre bearing
3 Worn universal joints

(e) Rattles

1 Worn universal joints
2 Worn suspension rubber bushings
3 Loose or worn damper mountings

(f) Knock

1 Check (a)
2 Badly worn splines on drive shafts
3 Worn universal joints

CHAPTER 9

FRONT SUSPENSION AND HUBS

9:1 Description

Independent front wheel suspension is by means of helically coiled springs controlled by double-acting hydraulic telescopic dampers. The damper units also act as pivots for the front wheel stub axle assemblies to accommodate steering movement. The suspension springs are fitted co-axially to the damper struts between two pressed steel support cups.

The front wheel hubs rotate on the stub axle assemblies, each wheel being carried on a pair of taper roller bearings.

The front wheel stub axle assembly is located at the lower end of the suspension strut. The suspension strut assemblies are attached to the car bodywork at their upper ends, the lower ends being located by means of transverse links pivoted at the outer ends of the suspension crossmember and tension rods mounted between the outer ends of the transverse links and brackets attached to the car bodywork. Ball joints are used at the transverse link to suspension strut attachment points to accommodate movement during suspension travel. An anti-roll bar is fitted across the front suspension, being journalled in bushes mounted on the car bodywork and attached to the outer ends of the transverse links through short connecting rods. **FIG 9:1** shows the layout of front suspension components.

9:2 Routine maintenance

Every 50,000km (30,000 miles), the suspension ball joints should be lubricated with multipurpose grease. To do this, remove the blanking plug from the ball joint lower housing, then install a suitable grease nipple in its place. After lubrication, remove the grease nipple and replace the blanking plug. At the same intervals, the front wheel bearings should be dismantled, cleaned and greased as described in the next section.

9:3 The front hubs

Bearing adjustment:

Jack up the front of the car and remove the road wheel. On models with front drum brakes, remove the brake drums; on models with disc brakes, remove the brake pads as described in **Chapter 11**. Use two screwdrivers to lever off the grease cap as shown in **FIG 9:2**, loosening the cap by tapping carefully with a soft-faced hammer if necessary. Take care to avoid damaging the 'O' ring. Remove the splitpin and adjusting cap.

Tighten the hub securing nut to a torque of 3.0 to 3.5kgm (22 to 25lb ft) for early models, 2.5 to 3.0kgm (18 to 22lb ft) for models from 1975. Rotate the wheel hub a few turns in each direction to seat the wheel bearing correctly, then retighten the nut to the torque specified. Now loosen the hub nut by quarter-of-a-turn on early models, 60° on models from 1975, and install adjusting cap. Tighten cap a little if necessary to align splitpin holes with hole in wheel spindle. Again rotate the wheel hub in each direction to check that it moves freely with no sign of binding.

Check the adjustment by measuring the turning torque of the hub assembly, using a spring balance hooked around a wheel stud as shown in **FIG 9:3**. For early models, if new bearings have been fitted, the hub should start to turn under a load of 1.22kg (2.7lb) or less. When readjusting original bearing assemblies, the hub should start to turn under a load of 0.7kg (1.5lb).

For models from 1975, if new bearings have been fitted, the hub should start to turn under a load 1.49kg (3.3lb) or less. When readjusting original bearing assemblies, the hub should start to turn under a load of 0.79kg (1.7lb).

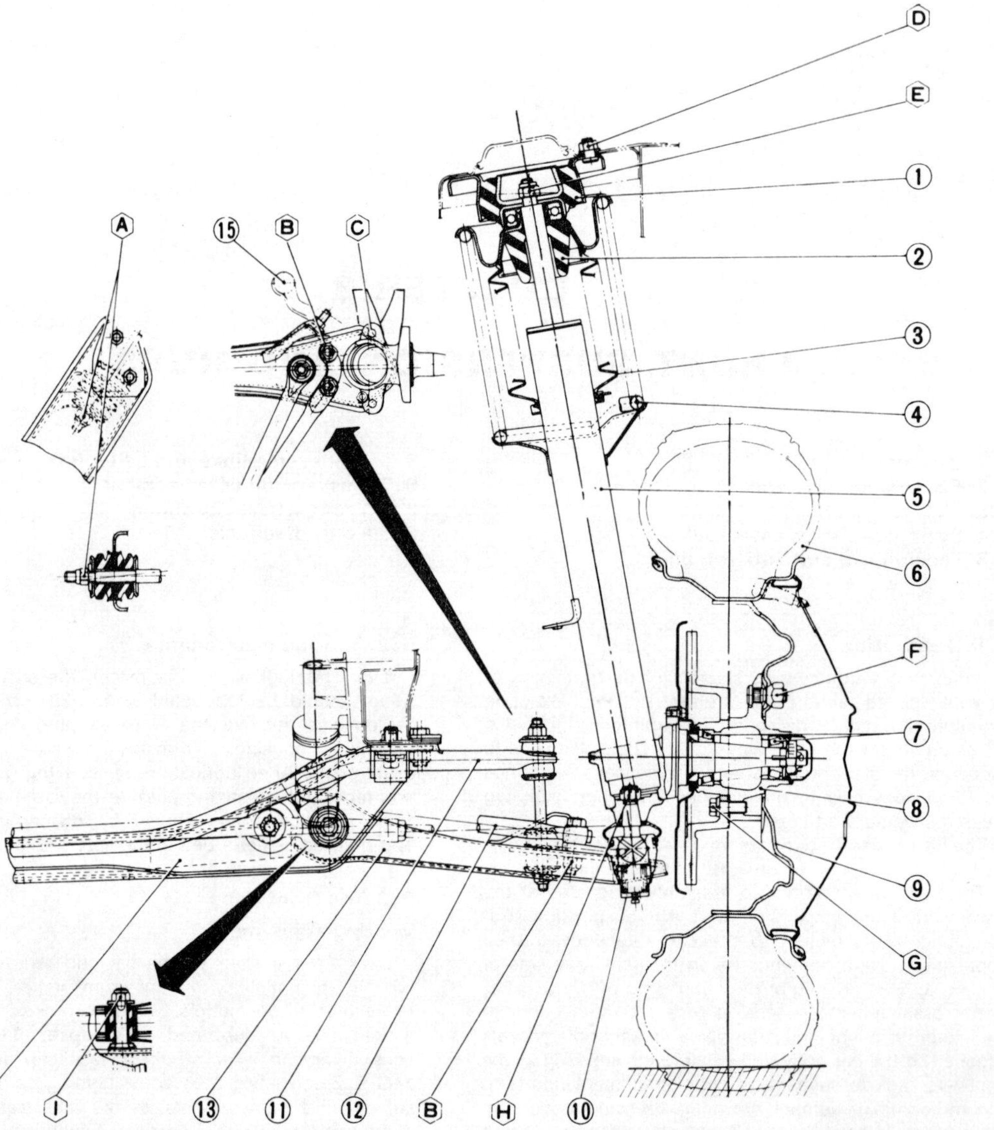

FIG 9:1 Layout of the front suspension. The letters refer to torque wrench settings which are given in the text

Key to Fig 9:1 1 Strut mounting insulator 2 Bump rubber 3 Dust cover 4 Coil spring 5 Strut assembly 6 Tyre 7 Wheel bearing 8 Wheel hub 9 Road wheel 10 Suspension ball joint 11 Anti-roll bar 12 Tension rod 13 Transverse link 14 Crossmember

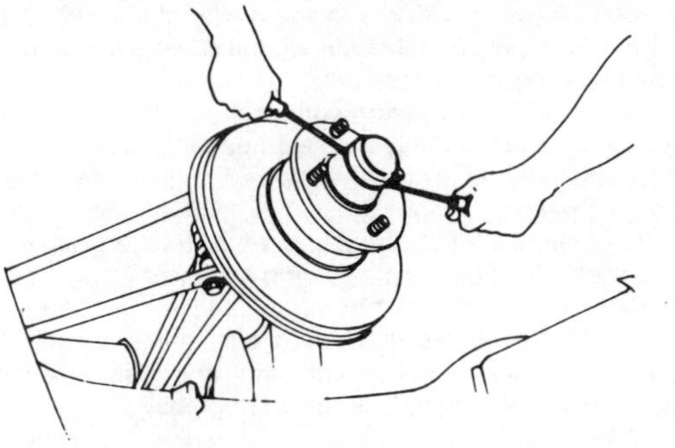

FIG 9:2 Removing grease cap

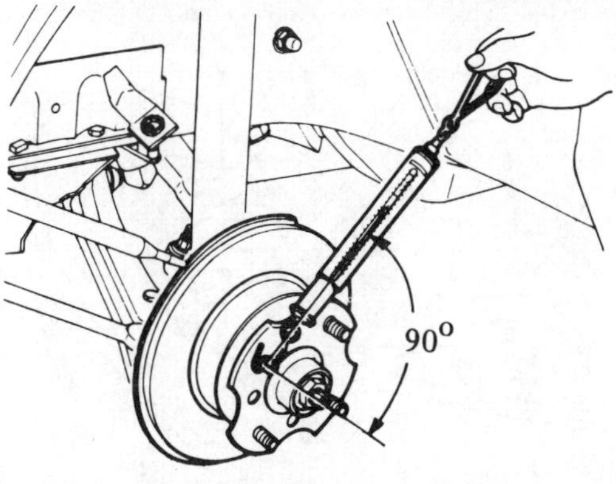

FIG 9:3 Measuring wheel bearing preload

Repeat the adjustment procedures described until the correct setting is achieved. If difficulty is experienced in correctly adjusting the bearings, or if binding or roughness is apparent when the hub is turned, the bearings should be dismantled for cleaning and inspection as described next. On completion, lock the bearing adjusting cap with a new splitpin. Bend the splitpin legs outwards and around the adjusting cap to secure. Refit the grease cap.

Hub and bearing removal:

Jack up the front of the car and remove the road wheel. Remove the grease cap as shown in **FIG 9:2**. Remove the splitpin and detach the adjusting cap and wheel bearing locknut.

On models fitted with disc front brakes, remove the hanger spring from the clip on the brake pipe then remove the brake caliper as described in **Chapter 11**. Support the caliper away from the work area so that the hose is not strained. Do not touch the brake pedal while the caliper is removed.

On models fitted with drum front brakes, remove the brake drum as described in **Chapter 11**.

Pull the hub assembly from the wheel spindle. On models fitted with disc front brakes, the hub is removed complete with the brake disc. Remove the wheel bearings. It is not necessary to remove the bearing outer races unless they are to be renewed. Remove the grease seal from the hub.

Thoroughly clean all parts in a suitable solvent and check for wear or damage. Check that the wheel bearings turn freely with no sign of roughness. Renew any worn or damaged parts. If the outer races are to be renewed, drive them out of the hub with a brass drift as shown in **FIG 9:4**, two grooves being provided in the hub for access. Work evenly on each side of the race to keep it square.

Reassembly:

If new bearing outer races are to be fitted, clean the recesses in the hub and drive the races carefully into place, keeping them square. Observe absolute cleanliness during the reassembly procedure to avoid contamination by dirt or grit. Take great care to avoid traces of dirt or grease from contaminating the brake disc. Lubricate the hub and bearings with a recommended grade of multi-

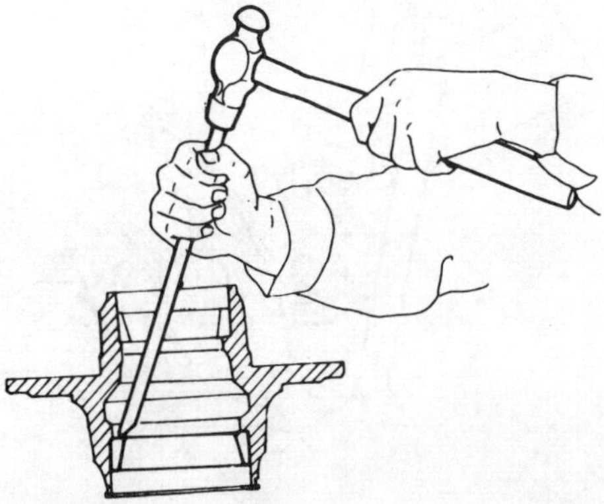

FIG 9:4 Removing bearing outer races

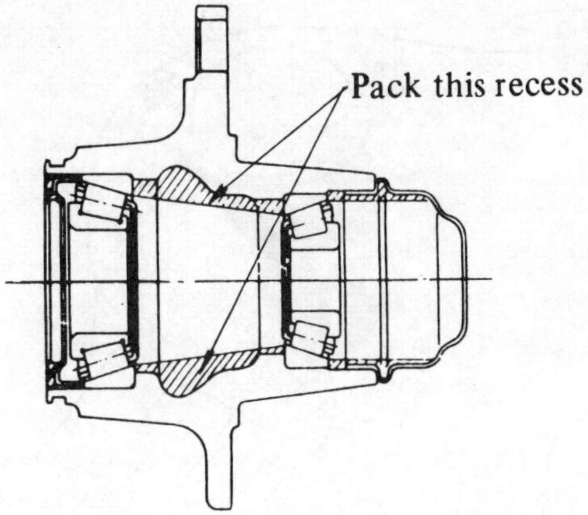

FIG 9:5 Lubricating wheel hub

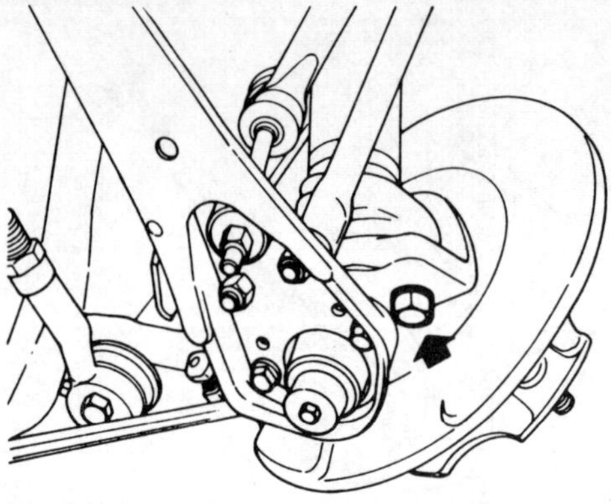

FIG 9:6 One of the two steering knuckle securing bolts

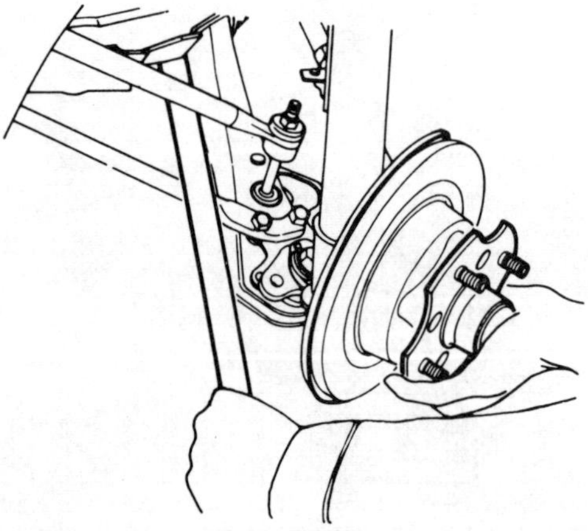

FIG 9:7 Removing steering knuckle

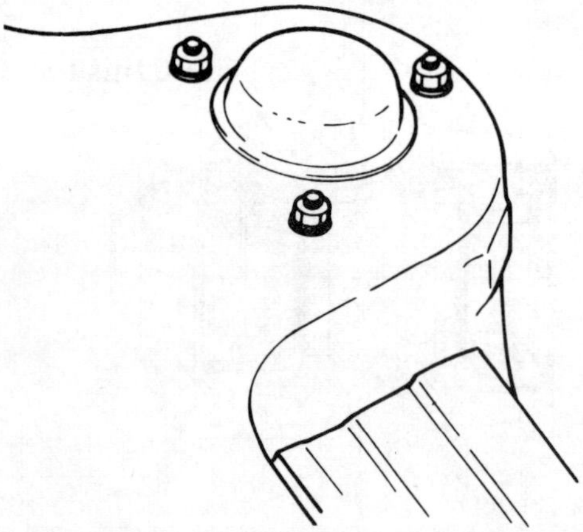

FIG 9:8 Suspension strut upper attachment nuts

purpose grease. Pack the inside of the hub and hub cap with grease (see **FIG 9:5**). Pack the cavities in each taper roller bearing with grease.

Place the inner bearing cone in hub and install a new grease seal, lubricating the seal lips with grease. Fit the hub assembly on wheel spindle and install outer bearing cone. Sparingly apply grease to washer and threaded parts of spindle and hub retaining nut. Fit the washer and nut, then adjust the wheel bearing as described previously.

Refit the remaining parts in the reverse order of removal. On models fitted with disc brakes, make sure that the brake disc is clean and dry. Use a suitable solvent to clean away any traces of grease.

9:4 Spring and strut assembly

Removal:

Jack up the front of the car and safely support on floor stands so that the front suspension hangs free. Remove the road wheel. On models fitted with drum front brake units, disconnect the brake hose from the brake pipe as described in **Chapter 11**. Plug the end of the pipe to prevent the entry of dirt. On models fitted with disc front brake units, detach the brake hose clip from the spring hanger, then detach the caliper as described in **Chapter 11**. Support the caliper away from the work area so that the hose is not strained.

Remove bolts connecting strut to steering knuckle as shown in **FIG 9:6**. Detach steering knuckle from bottom of strut by forcing down the transverse link with a suitable lever as shown in **FIG 9:7**. Place a jack or stand beneath the strut assembly to support it when the upper nuts are removed. Raise the bonnet and remove the upper fixing nuts shown in **FIG 9:8**. Support the weight of the strut assembly and lower it carefully to remove from beneath the car.

No further dismantling of the suspension strut assembly should be attempted by the owner, as spring compressor equipment and several special tools are required to carry out the work. All repair and overhaul work should be entrusted to a fully equipped service station.

Refitting:

This is a reversal of the removal procedure, noting the following points:

When installing the strut mounting insulator (item 1 of **FIG 9:1**) position it with the painted mark on the engine side.

When installing steering knuckle to strut assembly, apply a suitable sealing compound to the points marked by arrows in **FIG 9:9**. This procedure is to prevent rusting of the ball stud. Tighten the strut upper mounting nuts to 2.5 to 3.5kgm (18 to 25lb ft), steering knuckle to strut bolts to 7.3 to 9.9kgm (53 to 72lb ft). Note that the strut upper mounting nuts are of the self-locking type and should be renewed whenever the strut assembly is refitted.

9:5 Tension rod and anti-roll bar

Removal:

Jack up the front of the car and safely support on floor stands placed beneath the front crossmember. Remove the road wheels. Remove the splash board.

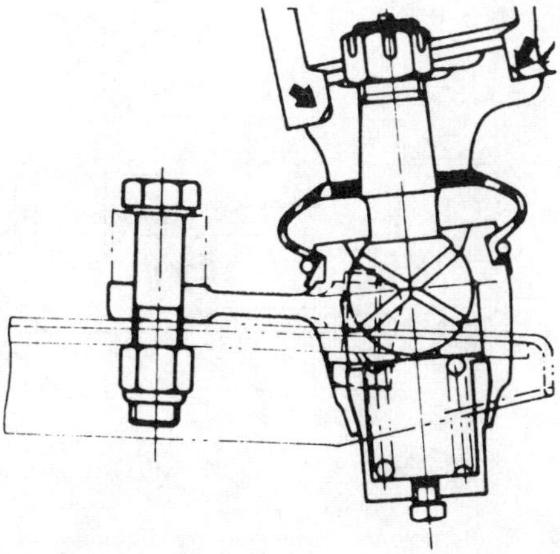

FIG 9:9 Applying sealant during steering knuckle installation

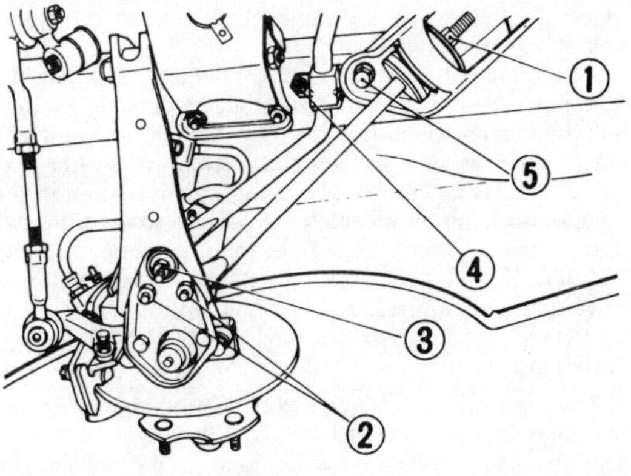

FIG 9:10 Removing tension rod and anti-roll bar. The numbers are referred to in the text

Refer to **FIG 9:10**. Loosen nut 1 securing tension rod to bracket, then remove bolts 2 securing tension rod to transverse link. Detach the tension rod. Remove nut 3 connecting anti-roll bar connecting rod to transverse link. Loosen bolts 5, then remove bolts 4 securing anti-roll bar in position. Remove anti-roll bar from beneath the car.

Check the anti-roll bar and tension rod for any signs of deformation or cracks. Check all rubber bushings for wear, damage or deterioration. Renew any faulty parts.

Refitting:

This is a reversal of the removal procedure, noting the following points. Make sure that the anti-roll bar is correctly installed on each side of the car. Check that the tension rod bushing is properly centred in its seat. Check that the clearance between tension rod and anti-roll bar is equal on both sides, as shown in **FIG 9:11**. Tighten the bolt securing tension rod to tension rod bracket before tightening transverse link side bolt. Tighten anti-roll bar to frame bolts to 1.4 to 1.8kgm (10 to 13lb ft), anti-roll bar connecting rod nut to 1.2 to 1.7kgm (8.7 to 12.0lb ft), tension rod bracket bolt to 5.1 to 6.9kgm (37 to 50lb ft), tension rod installation nut to 5.0 to 5.5kgm (36 to 40lb ft) and tension rod to transverse link bolt to 4.9 to 6.3kgm (35 to 46lb ft).

9:6 Transverse links and ball joints

Ball joint removal:

Jack up the car and safely support on floor stands. Remove the road wheel and the splash board. Remove splitpin and castle nut from steering tie rod ball joint, then separate tie rod from steering knuckle.

Remove bolts securing steering knuckle in position, then separate steering knuckle from lower end of suspension strut as described in **Section 9:4**. Disconnect tension rod and anti-roll bar from transverse link as described in **Section 9:5**.

Remove splitpin and castle nut from transverse link ball joint, then separate ball joint from lower end of strut

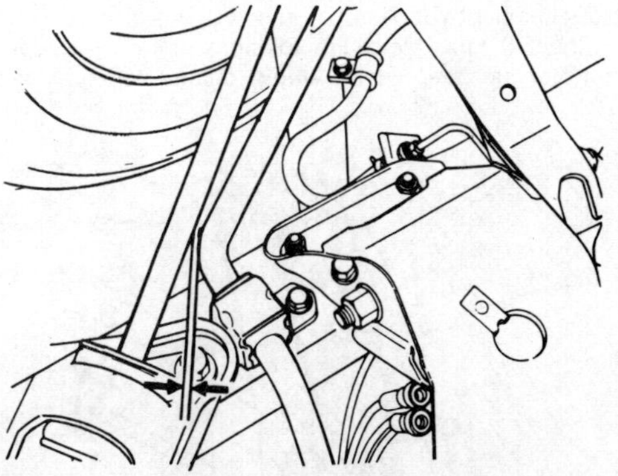

FIG 9:11 Clearance between tension rod and anti-roll bar must be the same on both sides of the car

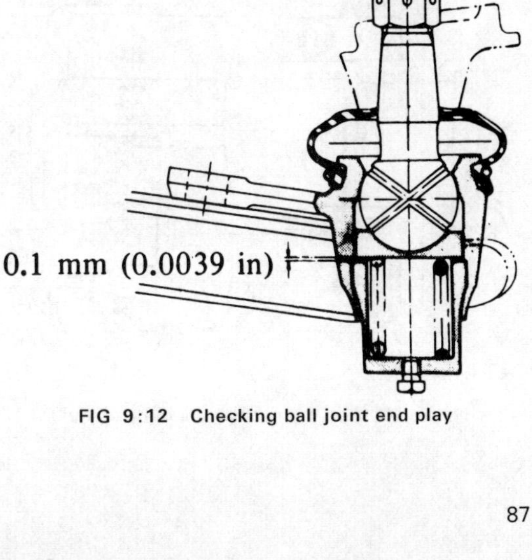

FIG 9:12 Checking ball joint end play

assembly. Remove bolt securing ball joint to transverse link, then detach ball joint.

Check the ball joint for wear or damage. Examine the dust cover and, if it is cracked, split or perished, a new ball joint assembly should be fitted. Check ball joint end play, which should not exceed 0.1mm (0.0039in) as shown in **FIG 9:12**. Hook a spring balance through the splitpin hole and check the force needed to start the ball joint moving. This should be approximately 11.3kg (24.9lb). If the balance reading is significantly higher or lower than the figure stated, the ball joint is faulty.

Refitting:

This is a reversal of the removal procedure. Tighten ball joint to transverse link bolt to 1.9 to 2.5kgm (14 to 18ft lb) and ball joint castle nuts to 5.5 to 7.6kgm (40 to 55ft lb). Use new splitpins to lock the castle nuts.

Transverse link removal:

Detach the transverse link outer ball joint from the suspension strut assembly as described previously, then remove the pin connecting transverse link to suspension crossmember by loosening nuts arrowed in **FIG 9:13**.

Check the transverse link for signs of cracks, distortion or other damage, which would dictate renewal. If the rubber bushing shows signs of wear, damage or deterioration, it should be renewed. As this procedure requires the use of press equipment and a special removal/installation tool, the work should be carried out by a fully equipped service station.

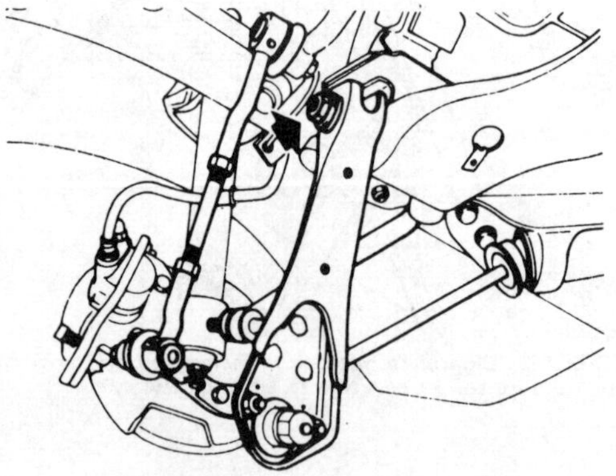

FIG 9:13 Transverse link removal

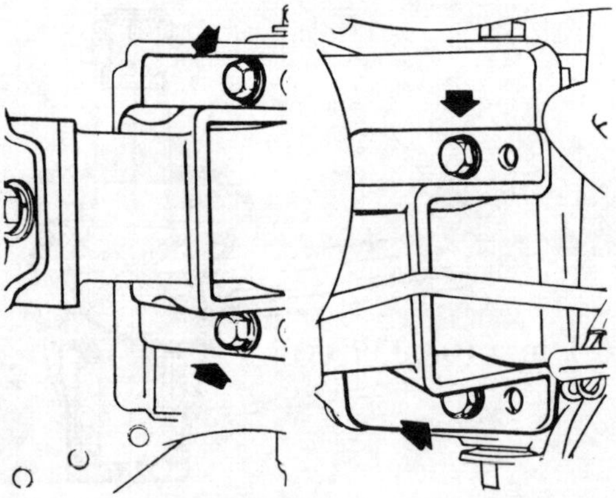

FIG 9:14 Removing engine mounting nuts

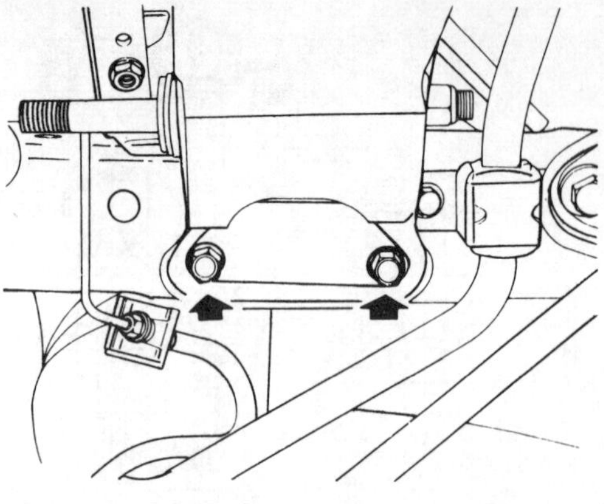

FIG 9:15 Removing suspension crossmember to body bolts

Refitting:

This is a reversal of the removal procedure. Tighten the transverse link mounting nuts loosely until the remaining components have been reassembled, then finally tighten early models to 4.9 to 6.3kgm (35 to 46lb ft) and models from 1976 to 9 to 10kgm (65 to 72lb ft) with the weight of the car resting on the road wheels.

9:7 Suspension crossmember

Removal:

Jack up the front of the car and safely support on floor stands placed beneath body members. Remove front road wheels and the splash board. Remove the transverse links as described in **Section 9:6**.

Attach suitable lifting equipment to the engine, then raise sufficiently to remove the engine weight from its mountings. Remove engine mounting bolts and nuts indicated by arrows in **FIG 9:14**. Centrally locate a suitable jack beneath the crossmember. Raise the jack a little if necessary to ensure that the suspension struts are fully extended. Make sure that the engine is properly supported if this is done. Remove the crossmember to body mounting bolts on each side (see **FIG 9:15**), then lower to remove the crossmember from beneath the car.

Refitting:

This is a reversal of the removal procedure. Tighten bolts securing suspension crossmember to body to 4 to 5kgm (29 to 36lb ft).

9:8 Front wheel alignment

The front wheel camber and caster angles are pre-set at the factory and cannot be adjusted. The only adjustment which can be made is the setting of toe-in as described in **Chapter 10**.

If steering faults or abnormal tyre wear indicate incorrect camber or caster angles, the suspension components should be checked for wear or damage, particularly if the car has been involved in a front-end collision.

9:9 Fault diagnosis

(a) Wheel wobble (see also **Chapter 10**)

1 Worn hub bearings
2 Weak front springs
3 Uneven tyre wear
4 Worn suspension bushes

(b) Car pulls to one side

1 Unequal tyre pressures
2 Incorrect suspension geometry
3 Defective suspension bushes or damaged parts
4 Weak spring on one side
5 Fault in steering system

(c) Bottoming of suspension

1 Bump rubbers worn or damaged
2 Broken or weak front coil spring
3 Defective damper

(d) Excessive body roll

1 Check 2 and 3 in (c)
2 Anti-roll bar weak or damaged

(e) Rattles

1 Defective suspension mounting bushes
2 Anti-roll bar broken or loose
3 Suspension strut attachments loose

NOTES

CHAPTER 10

THE STEERING GEAR

10:1 Description

Steering gear of the worm and recirculating ball type is fitted, with the steering wheel splined directly to the main steering shaft. An arm is fitted to the steering box output shaft and this is connected directly to the centre tie rod which passes under the car. The other end of the centre tie rod is supported by an idler lever which pivots on a bracket mounted to the car body. The outer ends of the centre tie rod are connected to adjustable outer tie rods which in turn are connected to the arms of the steering knuckles. Ball joints are used throughout the steering linkage to ensure positive and free movement with the minimum of play.

The ball joints are integral with the tie rod ends or centre tie rod and if a ball joint is defective the complete component must be renewed. The outer tie rods are adjustable for length so that front wheel alignment can be set.

A collapsible steering column assembly, designed to progressively collapse in the event of heavy load being applied to either end during a collision, is fitted to some models as standard equipment and may be fitted to other models as optional equipment.

10:2 Routine maintenance

At 10,000km (6000 mile) intervals, the level of oil in the steering gear should be checked and topped up if necessary. Remove the oil filler plug which is near the centre of the cover on the steering gear housing (see **FIG 10:15**). The oil level should be at the bottom of the threaded hole. If not, top up with an approved grade of steering gear oil. Allow excess oil to drain away fully, then refit the filler plug.

At 50,000km (30,000 mile) intervals, the ball joints in the steering linkage should be lubricated with multi-purpose grease. To do this, remove the grease plug from the ball joint housing and fit a suitable grease nipple in its place. On completion, remove the grease nipple and refit the plug. Grease the idler body and idler side joint (see **FIG 10:21**).

10:3 Steering wheel removal

Remove the horn pad from the steering wheel spokes. On two-spoke types, the pad must be turned anticlockwise then pulled off, or the pad slid upwards then pulled

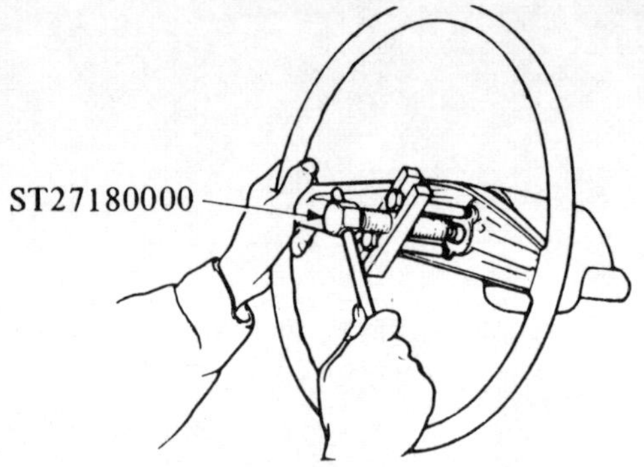

FIG 10:1 Steering wheel removal

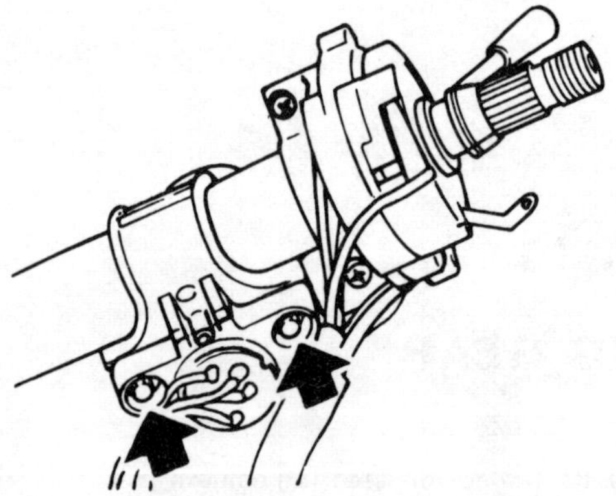

FIG 10:2 Steering lock mounting bolt locations

off, according to model. The pad on three-spoke units is simply pulled straight away from the spokes.

Remove the steering wheel nut then fit a suitable puller such as tool ST27180000 as shown in **FIG 10:1**. Tighten the puller centre bolt to remove steering wheel from the shaft splines. Do not strike the puller or steering column shaft as this may cause damage.

Refitting is a reversal of the removal procedure. Make sure that the front wheels are in the straightahead

FIG 10:4 Rubber coupling securing bolt

position, then refit the steering wheel with the main spokes in a horizontal position. Tighten the fixing nut to 3.8 to 5.2kgm (27 to 38lb ft).

10:4 Steering lock

To ensure that the steering lock cannot be easily detached, it is mounted to the steering column assembly by means of two shearhead bolts in the positions arrowed in **FIG 10:2**. To remove the lock, drill a hole down the centre of each bolt and use a suitable extractor tool to unscrew them. When refitting, align the steering lock hole in column jacket tube with the mating part of steering lock. Install new shearhead bolts and tighten them evenly until the heads break off.

10:5 Standard steering column

A section through the standard steering column assembly is shown in **FIG 10:3**.

Removal:

Remove the rubber coupling securing bolt arrowed in **FIG 10:4**. Remove the steering wheel as described in **Section 10:3**.

Remove the fixing screws and detach upper and lower steering column shell covers. Remove the fixing screws and detach the turn signal switch assembly. Remove the four bolts securing jacket tube flange to dash panel as shown in **FIG 10:5**. Remove the two bolts securing the steering column clamp, then remove the steering column assembly from the passenger compartment side.

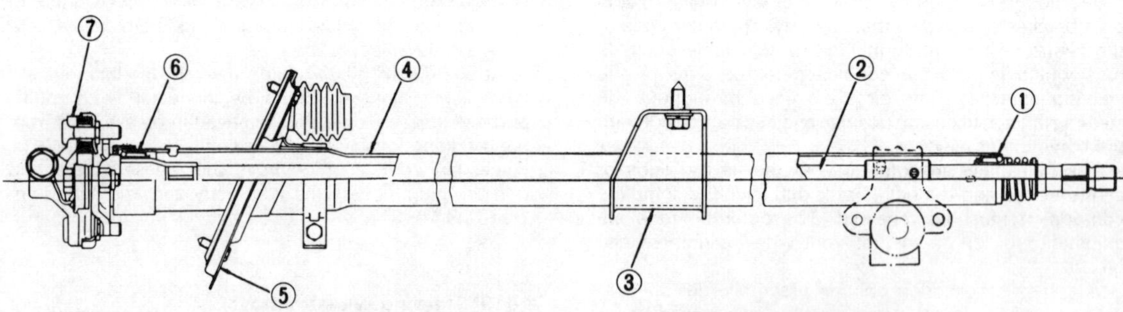

FIG 10:3 Section through the standard steering column assembly

Key to Fig 10:3 1 Upper bearing 2 Steering column shaft 3 Steering post clamp 4 Jacket tube 5 Jacket tube flange 6 Lower bearing 7 Rubber coupling

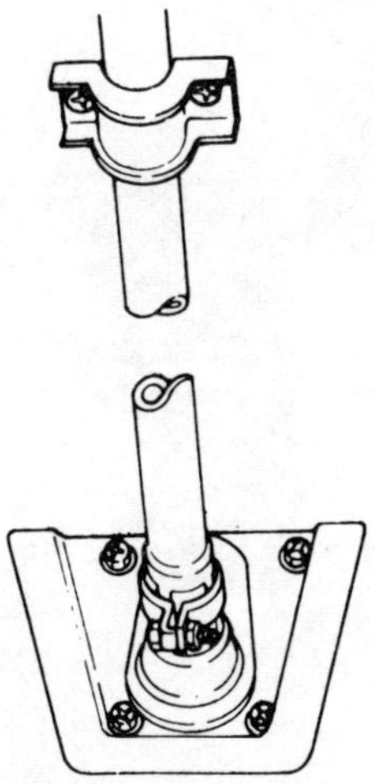

FIG 10:5 Jacket tube flange securing bolts

Dismantling:

Remove the circlip from steering column shaft upper end then withdraw washers and spring. Withdraw column shaft and column cover from jacket tube. Take care not to damage upper and lower bearings.

Servicing:

Check column bearings for wear or damage. The bearings are not serviced separately, so if faulty the column assembly must be renewed complete. If the bearings are in serviceable condition, they should be lubricated with multi-purpose grease. Check the jacket tube for deformation or damage and renew if necessary. Renew the column spring if damaged or weakened.

Reassembly:

This is a reversal of the dismantling procedure, noting the following points:

Apply multi-purpose grease to column bearings, spring, dust seal and sliding parts. Fit column cover as shown in **FIG 10:6**. Take care not to subject the column assembly to impact or bending loads.

Refitting:

This is a reversal of the removal procedure, noting the following points:

Set the front road wheels in the straightahead position.

Refer to **FIG 10:7**. Fit steering column assembly through dash panel onto wormshaft serrations and tighten bolt A. Align the column shaft so that the punch mark at the top end of the shaft is uppermost. Tighten column clamp bolts B to 0.8 to 1.1kgm (5.8 to 8.0lb ft).

Slide jacket tube flange to dash panel then tighten four nuts C to 0.35 to 0.45kgm (2.5 to 3.3lb ft). Refit the remaining components in the reverse order of removal, then check that the steering wheel turns smoothly and that the rubber coupling is not eccentric.

10:6 Collapsible steering column

A section through the collapsible steering column assembly is shown in **FIG 10:8**. Great care must be taken when handling the assembly to avoid impact or bending loads on any part of the column or shaft, as this could cause irreparable damage.

Removal:

Removal of the collapsible steering column is carried out in the same manner as that described for standard units in **Section 10:5**.

Servicing:

Check the column bearings for wear or damage. The bearings are not serviced separately, so if they are unserviceable the column assembly must be renewed complete. Check the jacket tube for deformation and breakage and the column spring for damage or weakness. Renew any faulty parts. If the car has been involved in a collision, or if damage to the collapsible column is suspected for any other reason, carry out the following inspection procedures:

Refer to **FIG 10:9**. Check that the dimension shown is the correct figure. If less than stated, the jacket tube is damaged. Measure dimension B in **FIG 10:10**, which should be zero. If the jacket tube is crushed, dimension B will be greater than zero. Check the steering wheel for axial play as shown in **FIG 10:11**. The steering jacket shaft is damaged if axial play can be felt. Check the serrated part of the sector shaft for deformation as shown in **FIG 10:12**. Renew any faulty parts found during the inspection procedures.

Refitting:

This is carried out in the same manner as that described for standard steering column assemblies in **Section 10:5**.

Note, however, that on USA models from 1976, the bolts B should be tightened to a torque of 1.3 to 1.8kgm (9.4 to 13.0lb ft).

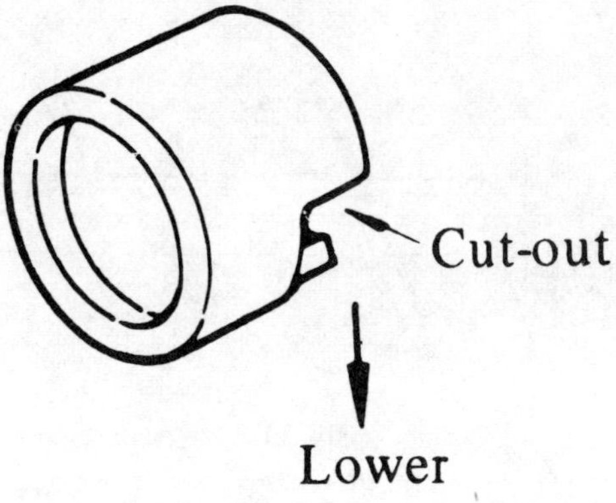

FIG 10:6 Column cover installation

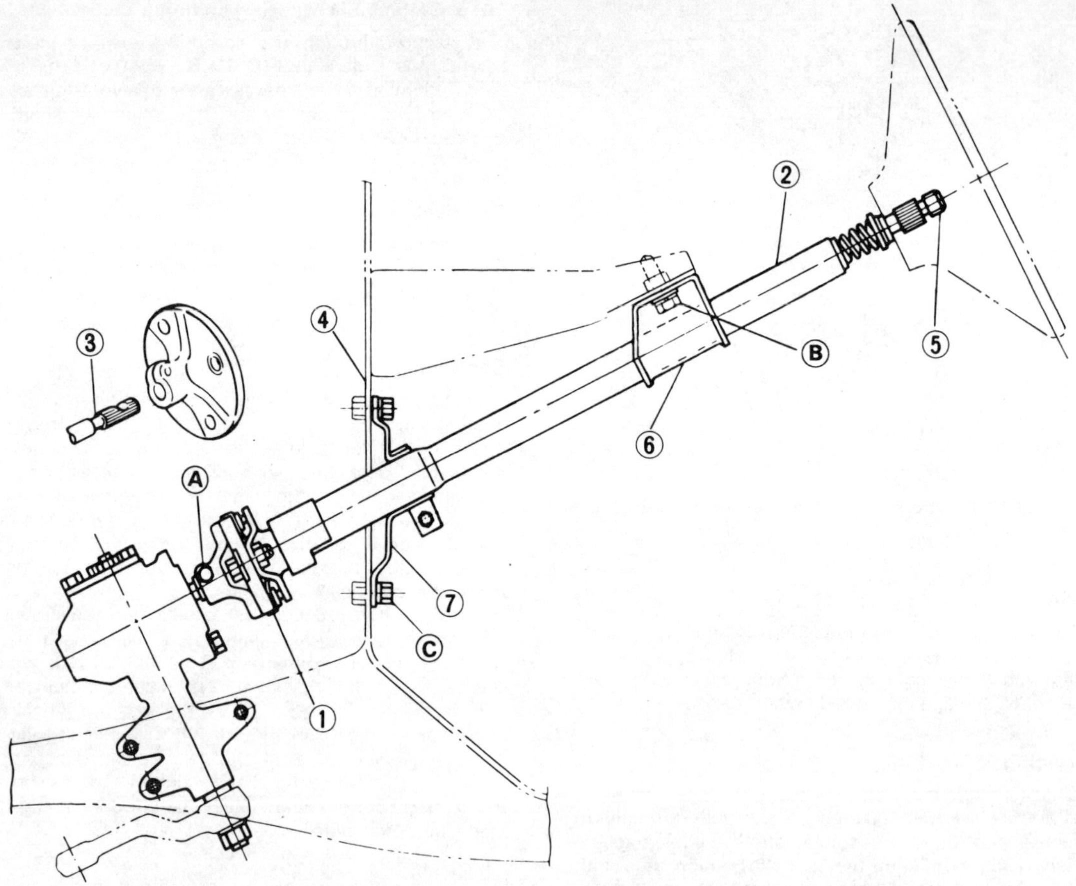

FIG 10:7 Standard steering column installation

Key to Fig 10:7 1 Rubber coupling 2 Steering column assembly 3 Worm shaft 4 Dash panel 5 Column shaft 6 Column clamp 7 Jacket tube flange

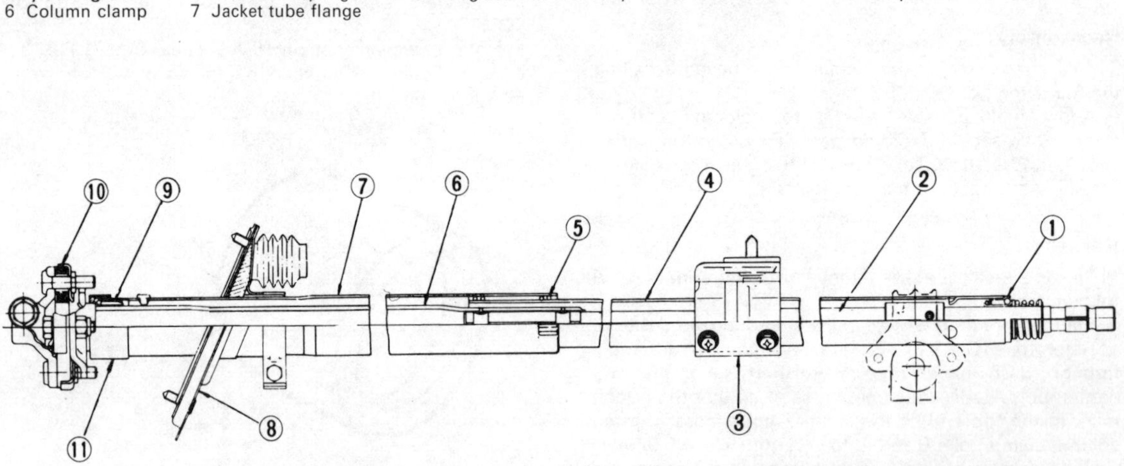

FIG 10:8 Section through the collapsible steering column assembly

Key to Fig 10:8 1 Upper bearing 2 Upper jacket shaft 3 Steering post clamp 4 Upper jacket tube 5 Steel ball 6 Lower jacket shaft 7 Lower jacket tube 8 Lower jacket tube flange 9 Lower bearing 10 Rubber coupling 11 Column dust cover

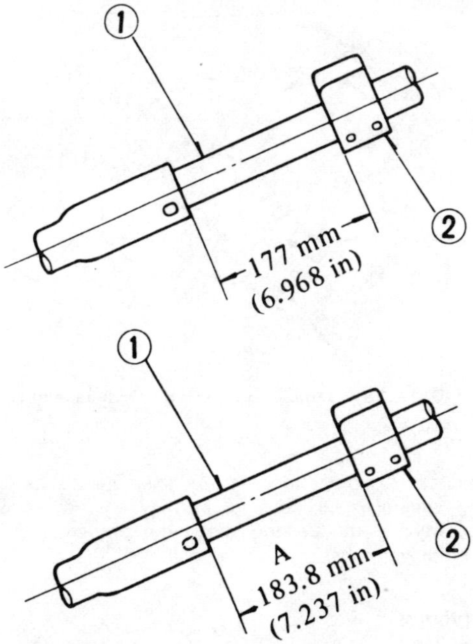

FIG 10:9 **Checking collapsible column jacket. Upper, European models; lower, USA and Canada**

Key to Fig 10:9 1 Jacket tube 2 Column clamp

10:7 Steering gear

Removal:

If a heat shield is fitted to the sidemember, remove the shield by detaching the two screws arrowed in **FIG 10:13**, Remove the bolt retaining rubber coupling to steering wormshaft, which is arrowed in **FIG 10:4**.

Remove nut and lockwasher securing steering gear arm to sector shaft. Remove arm from shaft using tool ST27200000, ST27140001 or other suitable puller (see **FIG 10:14**). Remove three bolts securing steering gear housing to body sidemember, then remove steering gear from engine compartment.

Dismantling:

Refer to **FIG 10:15**. If the special mounting tool shown in the illustration is available, it should be fitted at this stage. Thoroughly drain steering gear oil by removing filler plug 1. Loosen locknut 2 and remove bolts 3 attaching sector shaft cover. Note that some units have four bolts attaching sector shaft cover instead of three as shown. Remove cover complete with sector shaft, then remove sector shaft by turning adjusting screw clockwise.

Remove the three securing bolts and detach rear cover. Remove bearing adjusting shim(s) and steering worm assembly as shown in **FIG 10:16**. Take care not to allow the ball nut to run down to either end of the worm. If this happens, the ends of ball guides may be damaged. Do not detach ball nut from wormshaft assembly. If wear or damage is found, the assembly must be renewed

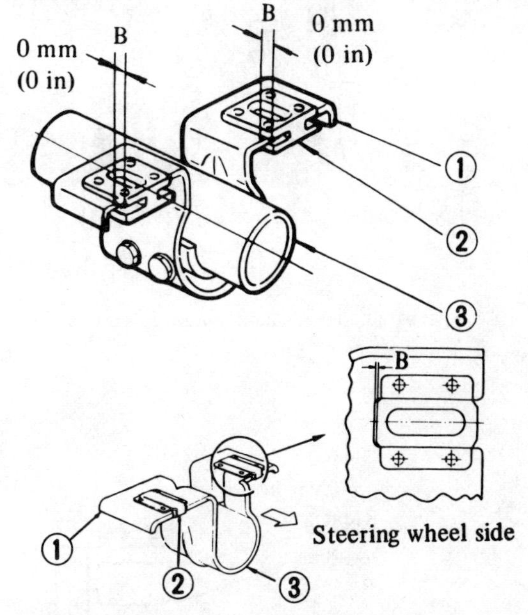

FIG 10:10 **Checking collapsible column clamp. Upper, European models; lower, USA and Canada**

Key to Fig 10:10 1 Column clamp 2 Block 3 Jacket tube

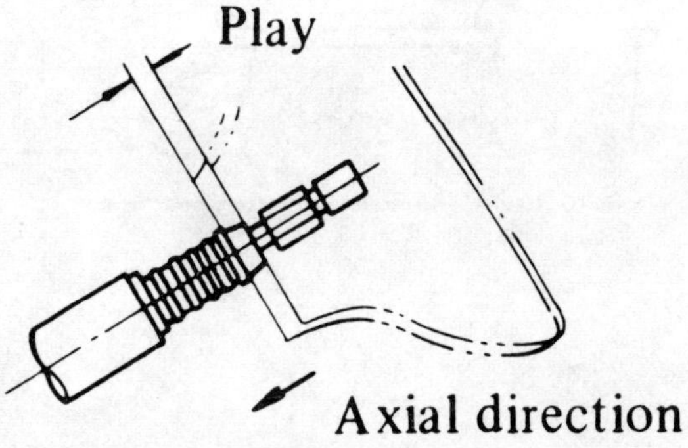

FIG 10:11 **Checking for axial play at steering wheel**

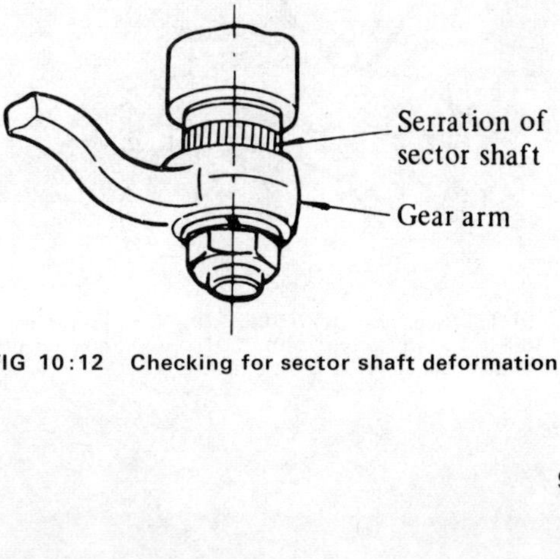

FIG 10:12 **Checking for sector shaft deformation**

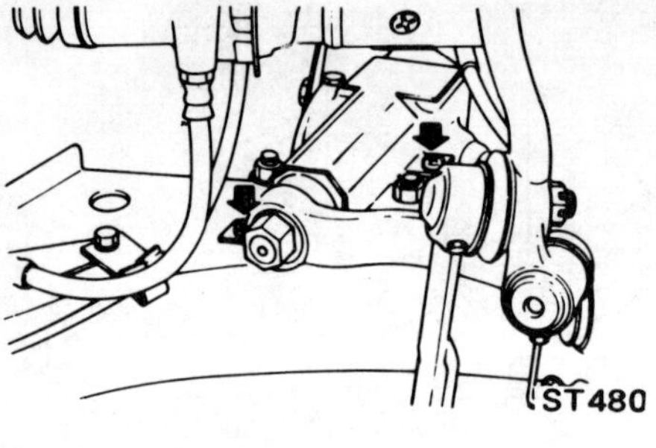

FIG 10:13 Heat shield mounting screws

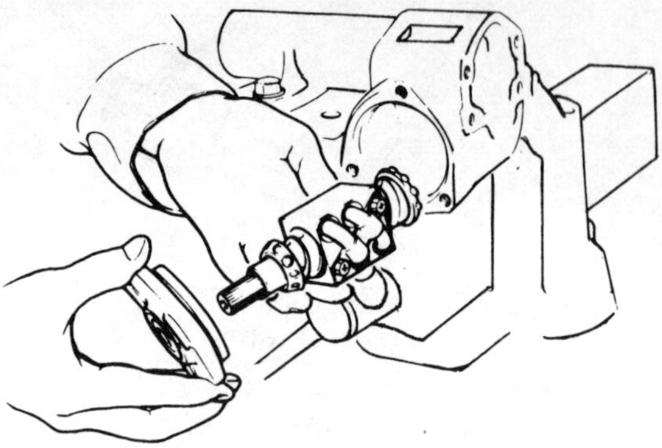

FIG 10:16 Removing steering worm assembly

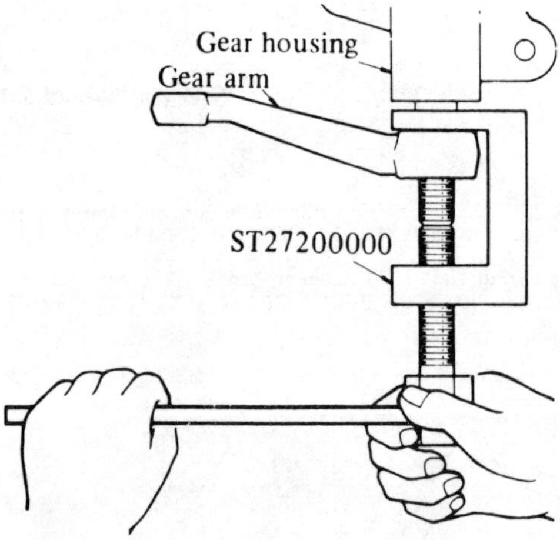

FIG 10:14 Removing steering gear arm

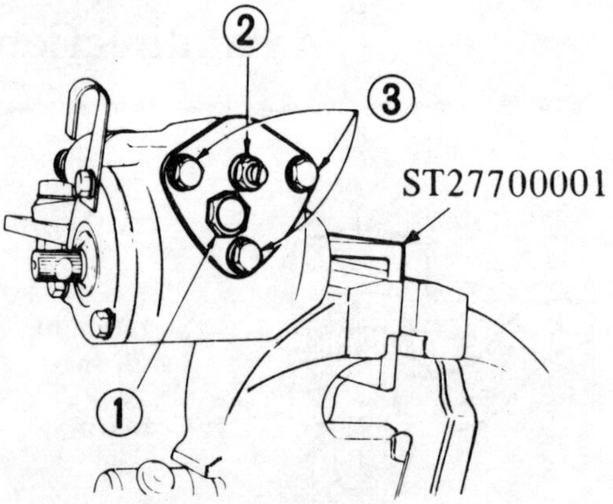

FIG 10:15 Steering gear filler plug 1, adjuster screw and locknut 2 and cover bolts 3. Note that some units have four cover bolts

complete. Do not remove sector shaft needle bearings from steering gear housing, as they are not serviced separately. If the bearings are worn or damaged, the gear housing must be renewed complete.

Servicing:

Thoroughly clean all parts in a suitable solvent. Remove and discard the oil seals (see **FIG 10:17**). Check the gear tooth surface for pitting, burrs, cracks or any other damage and renew if defective. Check sector shaft for distortion at serrated part and renew if necessary. Also check steering gear housing and steering gear worm for deformation if the sector shaft is damaged.

Inspect ball nut gear tooth surface and renew if found pitted, burred or otherwise damaged.

The ball nut must rotate smoothly on worm gear. If the assembly binds on the gear, it should be renewed.

To check, move ball nut to either end of worm gear, then place the worm gear and ball nut assembly flat on the bench and gradually lift the assembly at the ball nut end. The ball nut should travel smoothly along the worm gear under its own weight.

If the ball nut does not move freely over the entire stroke, wear or damage is indicated and the assembly should be renewed. Always handle the ball nut and worm assembly carefully to avoid damage to the ball nut guide tube.

Inspect wormshaft bearings and renew if found defective. Check sector shaft needle bearings for wear or damage, renewing the gear housing and bearings as an assembly if bearings are defective.

Reassembly and adjustment:

Reassembly is a reversal of the dismantling procedure, noting the following points and carrying out the adjustment procedure described in the following paragraphs.

Make sure that all parts are thoroughly clean. Lubricate worm bearings, sector shaft bearings and gear teeth with correct grade of lubricant when reassembling.

Fit a new oil seal to the gear housing and rear cover, filling the space between seal lips with multi-purpose grease. Press oil seal into place with lettered side towards outside of gear housing.

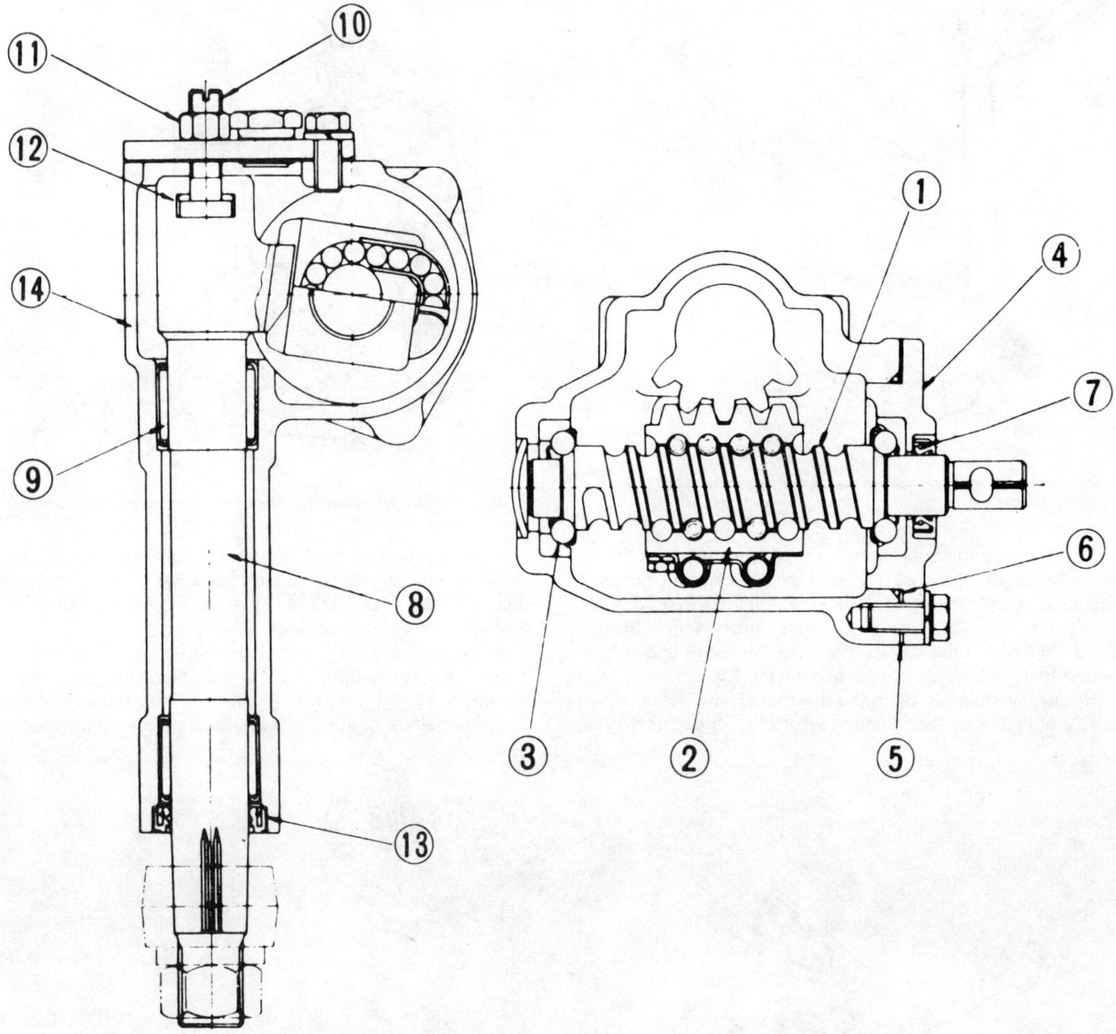

FIG 10:17 Section through the steering gear assembly

Key to Fig 10:17 1 Worm shaft 2 Ball nut 3 Worm bearing 4 Rear cover 5 Bearing shim 6 'O' ring 7 Oil seal 8 Sector shaft 9 Sector shaft bearing 10 Adjusting screw 11 Locknut 12 Adjusting shim 13 Oil seal 14 Steering gear housing

Place steering worm assembly in gear housing with worm bearings. Fit rear cover on housing with 'O' ring and worm bearing shims. Tighten rear cover fixings to 1.5 to 1.8kgm (11 to 13lb ft). Make sure that the thicker shims are fitted to gear housing side. Standard shim thickness is 1.5mm (0.051in), but four alternative shim thicknesses are available to correctly set worm bearing preload. Select and fit suitable bearing shims so that the initial turning torque of worm assembly is 4 to 6kg cm (56 to 83oz in), using a wrench and spring balance as shown in **FIG 10:18**. Rotate the wormshaft a few turns in each direction to settle the bearing before taking the measurement.

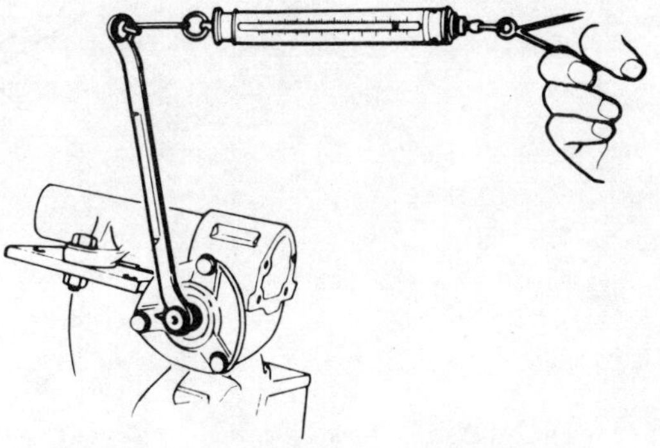

FIG 10:18 Checking worm bearing preload

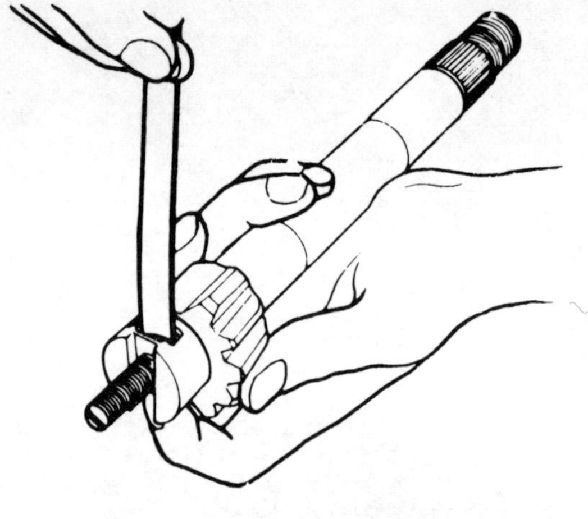

FIG 10:19 Checking play between sector shaft and adjusting screw

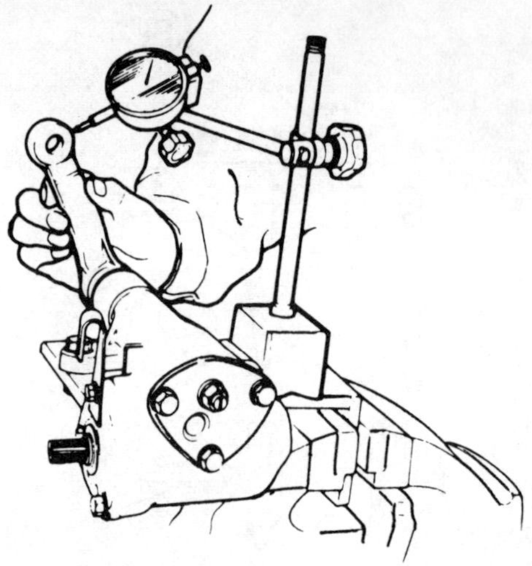

FIG 10:20 Measuring backlash at end of gear arm

Insert adjusting screw into T-shaped groove at sector shaft head, then adjust the end play between sector shaft and adjusting screw until it is within 0.01 to 0.03mm (0.0004 to 0.0012in) by selecting suitable shims from the six different thicknesses available. Measure end play with a feeler gauge as shown in **FIG 10:19**.

Rotate wormshaft by hand until ball nut is at the centre of its travel, then install sector shaft together with adjusting screw in gear housing, ensuring that centre tooth of sector shaft engages between centre teeth of ball nut (see **FIG 10:17**). Take care not to damage oil seal lips during the operation.

Install sector shaft cover to gear housing, using a new gasket. Apply suitable sealant to each side of gasket before fitting. By turning adjusting screw anticlockwise, fit sector shaft cover to gear housing and temporarily

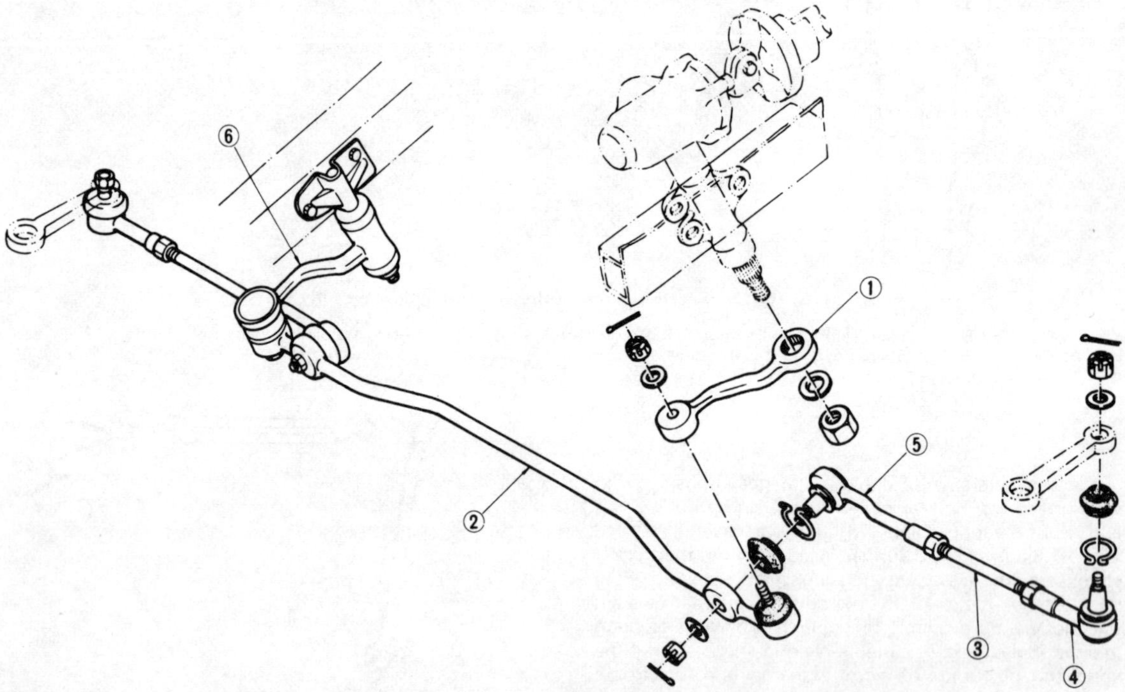

FIG 10:21 Steering linkage components

Key to Fig 10:21 1 Steering gear arm 2 Centre tie rod 3 Outer tie rod 4 Outer ball joint 5 Inner ball joint 6 Idler arm assembly

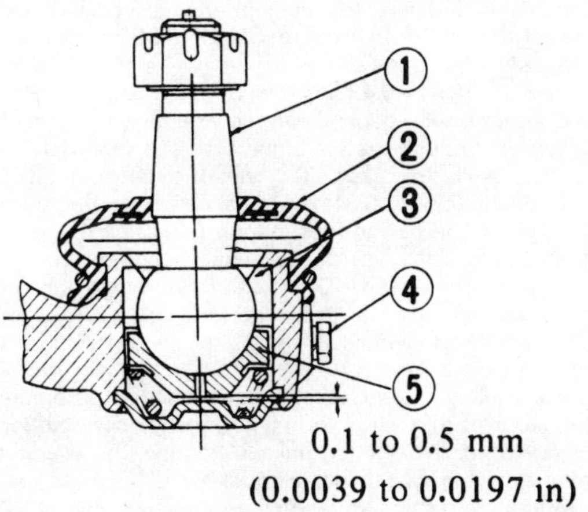

FIG 10:22 Section through a ball joint assembly

Key to Fig 10:22 1 Ball stud 2 Dust cover 3 Ball seat 4 Plug 5 Spring seat

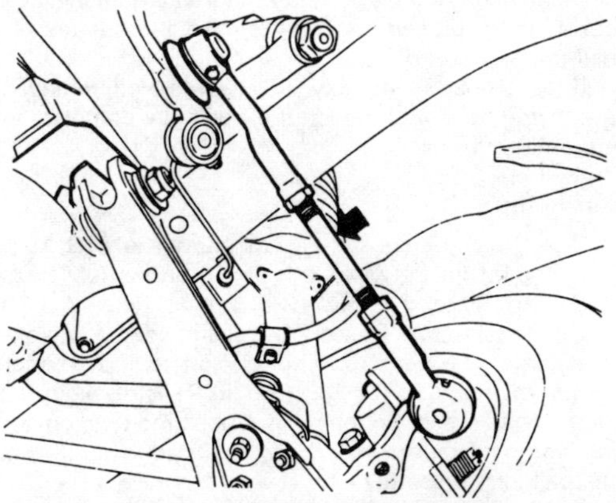

FIG 10:23 Toe-in is adjusted by rotating outer tie rods

secure with the fixing bolts. Pull sector shaft towards cover by approximately 2 to 3mm (0.079 to 0.118in) by turning adjusting screw anticlockwise, then tighten sector shaft cover fixing bolts to 1.5 to 2.5kgm (11 to 18lb ft). Push sector shaft against ball nut by gradually turning adjusting screw clockwise until sector shaft gear lightly meshes with ball nut gear, then temporarily secure adjusting screw with locknut.

Install steering gear arm to sector shaft and move sector shaft several times to make sure that it moves smoothly. Adjust steering gear backlash at central position of gear arm by turning adjusting screw in or out until free movement at top end of gear arm is less than 0.1mm (0.0039in). The most accurate method of checking free play is by using a dial gauge as shown in **FIG 10:20**. Now turn the adjusting screw clockwise by approximately one-eighth to one-sixth of a turn and tighten locknut to 2.0 to 2.5kgm (14 to 18lb ft) after moving sector shaft several times.

Refitting:

This is a reversal of the removal procedure, noting the following points:

Position steering gear and rubber coupling in place, then install and tighten bolts securing steering gear housing to body sidemember to 7 to 8kgm (51 to 58lb ft). Tighten bolt securing rubber connector to wormshaft to 4 to 5kgm (29 to 36lb ft). Make sure that the groove in wormshaft is aligned with bolt hole in rubber coupling flange yoke and pass coupling bolt through the undercut section of wormshaft. Align four grooves of gear arm serrations with four projections of sector shaft serrations, then install and tighten lockwasher and nut to 14kgm (101lb ft). On completion, fill the steering gear housing with the recommended grade of gear oil until the level is at the bottom of the filler plug hole, then fit and tighten filler plug.

10:8 Steering linkage

FIG 10:21 shows the steering linkage components.

Removal:

Raise the front of the car and support safely on floor stands. Remove splitpins and castle nuts attaching outer tie rod ball studs to steering knuckle arms. Use a suitable wedge-type tool such as tool ST27850000 to detach the ball joints from steering knuckles. Insert the wedge points between ball joint and steering knuckle, then drive tool into place with a hammer. Take care not to

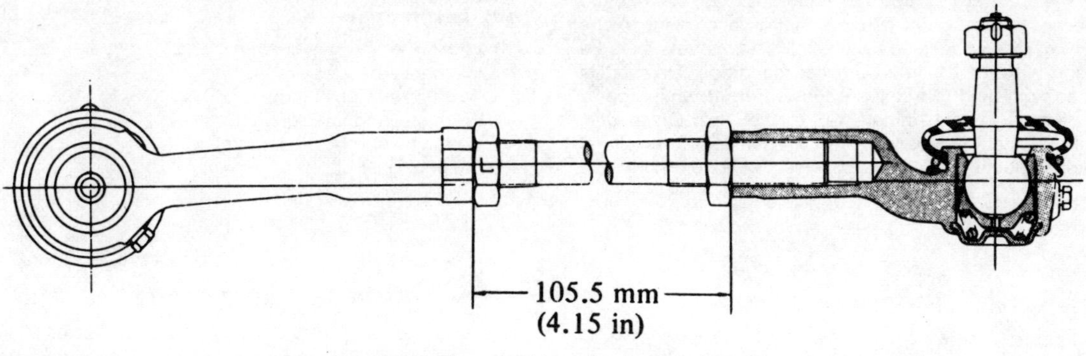

FIG 10:24 Standard length of outer tie rods

strike any part of the ball stud or tie rod assemblies. Carry out a similar procedure to disconnect the centre tie rod ball joints.

If the idler arm assembly is to be removed, remove the two fixing bolts and detach the assembly complete with mounting bracket.

Servicing:

Check ball joint axial play as shown in **FIG 10:22**. This should be between 0.1 and 0.5mm (0.0039 and 0.0197in). Excessive play will dictate renewal of the ball joint assembly. Check the force needed to pivot the ball joints. The ball stud should start to move when a torque of less than 0.5kgm (3.62lb ft) is applied. If the joint is stiff it must be renewed. Check the dust cover for damage or deterioration. If any faults are found, renew the ball joint assembly.

If a centre tie rod ball joint is defective, the tie rod must be renewed complete. If an outer tie rod ball joint is defective, slacken the locknut and unscrew the ball joint assembly, counting the number of turns taken to do so. Fit the new ball joint assembly by the same number of turns, then tighten the locknut.

Check the idler arm rubber bushing and nylon bushing in centre tie rod joint for damage, wear or play, renewing faulty components as necessary.

Refitting:

This is a reversal of the removal procedure, noting the following points:

Make sure that the ball stud tapered section is completely free of grease or oil. Tighten ball stud nuts to 5.5 to 10.0kgm (40 to 72lb ft), then tighten a little further as necessary to align the splitpin holes. Fit and lock a new splitpin to secure the nut.

If the idler arm has been dismantled for bushing renewal, apply multi-purpose grease to the sliding parts of idler arm and rubber bushings. Apply soapy water to bushing outer circumference. Press bushing into idler body carefully until it protrudes. Tighten idler assembly nut to 4 to 5kgm (29 to 36lb ft). Tighten idler body to frame bolts to 4.4 to 6.1kgm (32 to 44lb ft).

On completion, lubricate the steering linkage as described in **Section 10:2**, then check the toe-in setting as described in the next section.

10:9 Toe-in setting

The front wheel tracking should be set so that the wheels toe-in by the correct amount, according to the type or rear suspension installed. Measurements must be made with the car in an unladen condition. On models fitted with rigid axle rear suspension, front wheel toe-in should be 11 to 14mm (0.433 to 0.551in). On models with standard independent rear suspension, front wheel toe-in should be 11 to 14mm (0.433 to 0.551in). On models with hard independent rear suspension, front wheel toe-in should be 9 to 12mm (0.354 to 0.472in). On early USA models, front wheel toe-in should be 8 to 11mm (0.315 to 0.433in). On USA models from 1976 the toe-in setting depends on the type of tyres fitted; for radial ply tyres the toe-in should be 4 to 6mm (0.16 to 0.24in) while for bias belted tyres the toe-in should be 6 to 8mm (0.24 to 0.31in). Adjustment is carried out by slackening the tie rod locknuts on each side of the car, then rotating the tie rods by equal amounts until the setting is correct (see **FIG 10:23**). It is not recommended that owners attempt this work themselves, as great accuracy is essential. Instead, the work should be entrusted to a Datsun service station or a wheel and tyre specialist having optical setting equipment, the complete procedure taking only a short time under these conditions. However, if the steering linkage has been reassembled after servicing operations, the outer tie rods should be set to the correct standard lengths as shown in **FIG 10:24**. Slacken the locknuts and turn the outer tie rods until the distance between the backs of the locknuts on each side is 105.5mm (4.15in). Firmly tighten the locknuts to secure the adjustment.

10:10 Fault diagnosis

(a) Wheel wobble

1 Unbalanced wheels and tyres
2 Slack steering connections
3 Incorrect steering geometry
4 Excessive play in steering gear
5 Faulty suspension
6 Worn or loose hub bearings

(b) Wander

1 Check 2, 3 and 4 in (a)
2 Uneven tyre pressures
3 Ineffective dampers
4 Uneven tyre wear

(c) Heavy steering

1 Check 3 in (a)
2 Very low tyre pressures
3 Lack of lubrication
4 Wheels out of track
5 Steering gear adjustment too tight
6 Tight or damaged bearings

(d) Lost motion

1 Loose steering wheel connections
2 Worn steering gear
3 Worn steering ball joints
4 Worn steering knuckle joints
5 Worn steering gear bearings
6 Steering gear out of adjustment

CHAPTER 11

THE BRAKING SYSTEM

11 :1 Description

Either floating caliper disc brakes or twin leading shoe drum brakes are fitted at the front wheels, according to model type and export territory. All models are fitted with single leading shoe drum brakes at the rear wheels. The brakes on all four wheels are hydraulically operated from the brake pedal, the handbrake operating on the rear brakes only through a mechanical linkage. Standard drum brakes are provided with adjustment mechanism to take up clearance caused by normal friction lining wear, but models supplied to the European market may be optionally fitted with self-adjusting mechanisms actuated by handbrake movement. All disc brake units are self-adjusting. On models fitted with disc front brakes, a vacuum servo unit is connected directly between the brake pedal and the master cylinder and, by using the depression in the engine inlet manifold, assists the pressure applied by the driver on the brake pedal.

All models are fitted with a tandem braking system. A special master cylinder is fitted so that the rear and front brakes are hydraulically independent. The master cylinder is so designed that failure in one half of the system will still allow the other half to operate, though with increased pedal stroke, so that the car can be safely stopped. As well as increased pedal stroke the overall efficiency of the braking system will be reduced as only two brakes will be operating.

11 :2 Routine maintenance

Brake fluid:

Regularly check the fluid level in the brake master cylinder reservoirs. If necessary, top up the levels to the marks provided on the sides of the reservoirs. It is essential to use the correct fluid, which is one conforming to specification SAE.J1703a or DOT 3 for USA models. **Do not use any other type of fluid.**

Wipe the filler caps before removing them so that dirt cannot fall inside. Remove caps as described in **Section 11 :6**. Check that the small vent hole in each cap is clear. At the same intervals, check the condition of the pipes and hoses in the brake hydraulic system.

Brake pedal adjustment:

Brake pedal free play should be checked at 10,000km (6000 miles) intervals.

Refer to **FIG 11 :1**. Adjust brake lamp switch bolt until its end face is flush with the front face of locknut, as shown at A, then tighten locknut securely. Adjust pedal stop until pedal pad is 185mm (7.283in) above the car

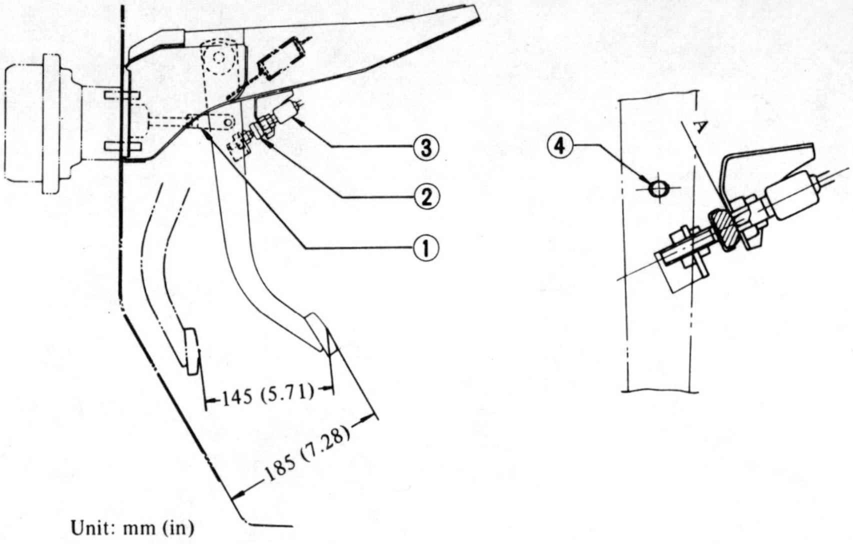

FIG 11:1 Brake pedal adjustment

Key to Fig 11:1 1 Pushrod adjusting screw 2 Pedal stop 3 Brake lamp switch 4 Clevis pin

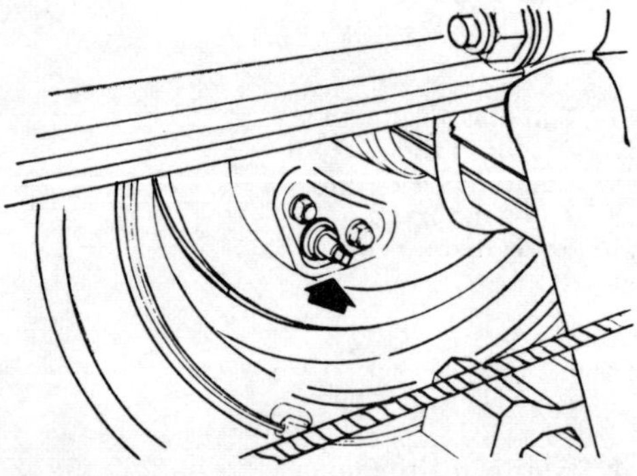

FIG 11:2 Typical rear drum brake adjuster

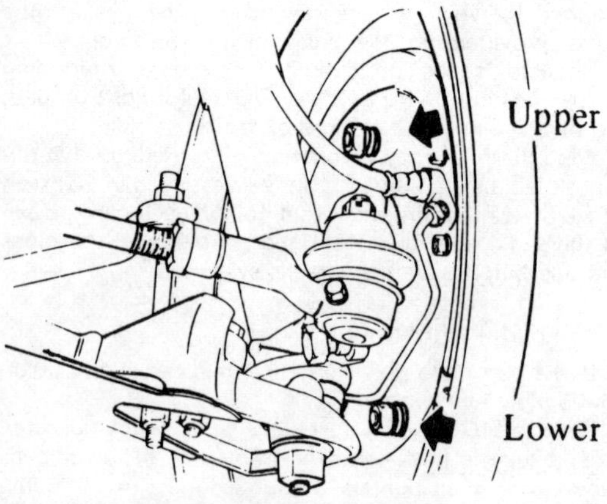

FIG 11:3 Front drum brake adjusters

floor. Tighten the locknut to secure the adjustment. Adjust length of pushrod until a pedal free play of 1 to 5mm (0.039 to 0.197in) is obtained at the pedal pad. This done, securely tighten locknut. When adjustments are completed, depress and release brake pedal several times to make sure that it travels through its full stroke smoothly, with no sign of binding. Lubricate the pedal pivot bushing with multi-purpose grease.

Drum brake adjustment:

Models fitted with self-adjusting rear brake units require no separate adjustment procedures to be carried out, but as no indication of lining wear is given at the brake pedal, the rear drums should be removed for a check on remaining lining thickness at 20,000km (12,000 miles) intervals, as described in **Section 11:4**. Self-adjusting units can be easily recognised as no adjuster will be found on the brake backplate (see also **Section 11:9**).

On models fitted with manual adjustment mechanisms, the drum brakes should be adjusted whenever excessive foot pedal or handbrake lever travel is noted. At 20,000km (12,000 miles) intervals or every second time that brake adjustment becomes necessary, whichever occurs first, the brake drum should be removed for a check to be made on friction lining thickness (see **Section 11:4**).

Rear brakes:

Pump the brake pedal several times to centre the shoes. Chock the front wheels against rotation and fully release the handbrake. Raise the rear of the car and support safely on floor stands. Make sure that each wheel cylinder lever for the handbrake mechanism is fully returned to the off position. Turn the adjuster shown in **FIG 11:2** in the direction of forward wheel rotation, turning the road wheel by hand while doing so. Tighten the adjuster until the wheel is stiff to turn, then loosen the adjuster until the wheel is just free. Operate the brake pedal and handbrake lever several times, then recheck the adjustments on each side. The wheels must turn without binding when the brakes are released.

Front brakes:

Pump the brake pedal several times to centre the shoes. Apply the handbrake, raise the front of the car until the wheels are clear of the ground and safely support on floor stands.

Refer to **FIG 11:3**. To tighten, the adjusters must be turned clockwise for left drum, anticlockwise for right drum. Act on one adjuster at a time, turning the adjuster while spinning the road wheel until the road wheel is stiff to turn. Now loosen the adjuster a fraction until the wheel is just free. Repeat the adjustment procedure at the second adjuster on the same brake unit. On completion, operate the brake pedal several times then recheck the adjustment on both sides.

Checking disc brake pads:

Two different types of front disc brake caliper are fitted, the swinging caliper type shown in **FIG 11:16** or the sliding caliper type shown in **FIG 11:21**.

Swinging caliper type:

Disc brake pad thickness should be checked at 5000km (3000 miles) intervals. To do this, remove the pad

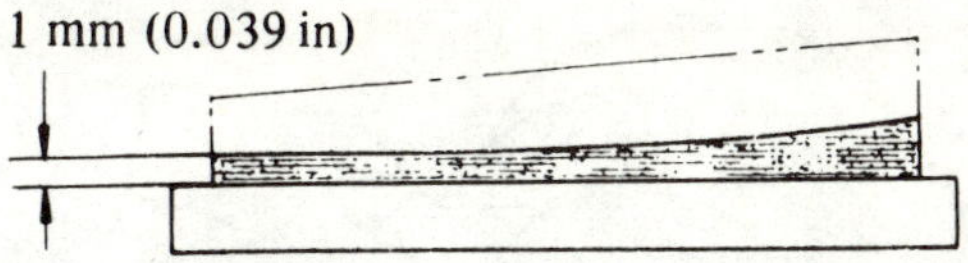

FIG 11:4 Disc brake pad friction lining wear limit

retaining clip as described in **Section 11:5**, then look into the caliper assembly to inspect the pads. The friction linings on the pads are tapered and, if any lining has worn down to a thickness of 1mm (0.039in) at its thinnest point (see **FIG 11:4**), all four front brake pads must be renewed as described in **Section 11:5**. **Do not renew pads singly or on one side only or unbalanced braking will result.** If the linings in any caliper are above the wear limit but unevenly worn, their positions in the caliper should be reversed. All four brake pads should also be renewed if any lining is broken or contaminated with grease or oil.

Sliding caliper type:

Disc brake pad thickness should be checked at 5000km (3000 miles) intervals. To do this look through the aperture in the caliper. The friction lining material next to the brake disc can be clearly seen and if any have worn

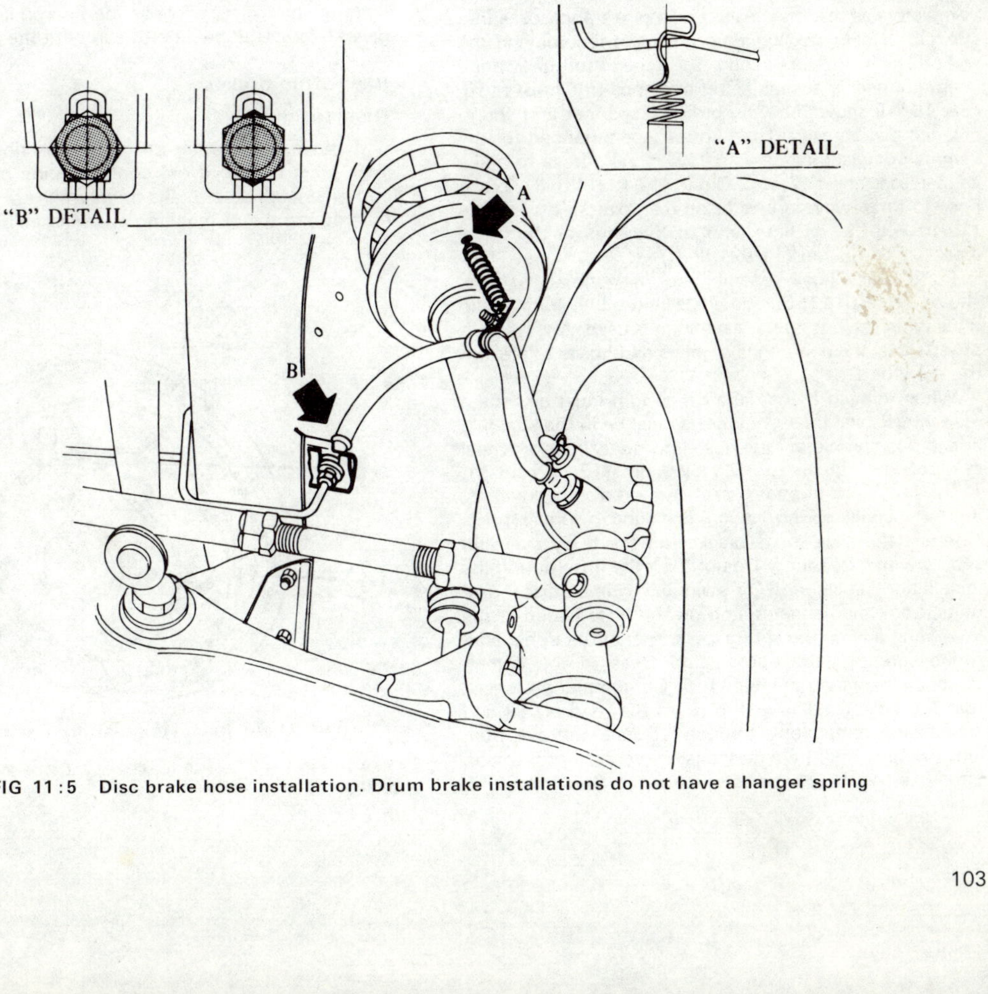

FIG 11:5 Disc brake hose installation. Drum brake installations do not have a hanger spring

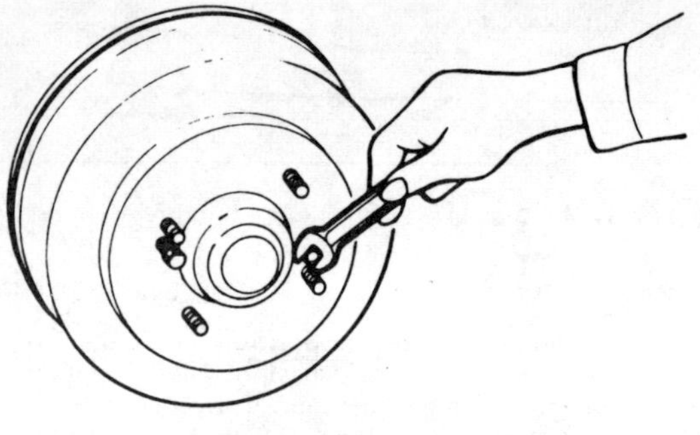

FIG 11 :6 Brake drum removal

down to a thickness of less than 2mm (0.079in) all four front brake pads must be renewed as described in **Section 11 :5**. **Do not renew pads singly or on one side only or unbalanced braking will result.** All four brake pads should also be renewed if any lining is broken or contaminated with grease or oil.

11 :3 Brake hoses

When carrying out certain servicing procedures on front brake units it will be necessary to disconnect the flexible hose which connects between the brake unit and the pipe mounting on the car bodywork. When refitting brake pipes and hoses take care not to overtighten the connectors as this may leave brake pipes and hoses in a strained or deformed condition. Datsun recommend the use of a small torque wrench. This type of torque wrench is not commonly available, but reference to **Chapter 10, FIG 10 :18** shows how an ordinary spanner and spring balance can be used. The torques recommended for the various connections are as follows: brake hose to brake caliper assembly 1.7 to 2.0kgm (12 to 14lb ft), brake hose to three-way connector on rear axle 1.7 to 2.0kgm (12 to 14lb ft), all flare units at the ends of the brake pipes 1.5 to 1.8kgm (11 to 13lb ft).

Front brake hose assembly for disc brake units is shown in **FIG 11 :5**. The installation for drum brake units is similar, but no hanger spring is used. Always plug or tape over the open ends of pipes and hoses to prevent the entry of dirt.

When refitting a hose, the car weight must be on the road wheels and the front wheels must be in the straight-ahead position. Screw the hose into the caliper or wheel cylinder and tighten to 1.7 to 2.0kgm (12 to 14lb ft). Always fit a new copper gasket and, on disc brake units, a new hanger spring, when installing a brake hose. Connect the hose to its bracket on the body side and secure with lock spring. Do not twist the hose during the installation procedure. On swinging caliper disc brake units, hook the hanger spring on the hose clamp at the lower end and on the spring lower seat at the upper end. Make sure that the hose clamp faces in the correct direction as shown in **FIG 11 :5**. On completion, check that the hose remains well clear of the road wheel and suspension components through full steering travel from left to right and fully suspension vertical movement. Finally, bleed the brakes as described in **Section 11 :7**.

Brake indicator switch:

A brake indicator switch is located in the front and rear brake lines and is operated by pressure difference between the two lines. The switch operates a warning light on the instrument panel. The light coming on indicates that there is a fault in the braking system. Locate the fault and correct it and then bleed the braking system. The switch will then automatically return to its original position.

If it is suspected that the switch is faulty do not attempt to repair it but fit a new unit.

11 :4 Drum brakes

Inspecting friction linings:

Raise the car so that the appropriate road wheel is clear of the ground and safely support on floor stands. When working on front brake units, fully apply the handbrake. When working on rear brake units, chock the front wheels against rotation and fully release the handbrake. Remove the road wheel and brake drum. If difficulty is experienced in removing the brake drum, screw in two bolts 8mm diameter, 1.25mm pitch and tighten them evenly as shown in **FIG 11 :6** to pull off the drum. Inspect the lining thickness on each brake shoe. If any lining is at or near the wear limit of 1.5mm (0.059in), broken or contaminated with grease or oil, all four brake shoes on that axle (front or rear) must be renewed. **Do not renew shoes singly or on one side only as unbalanced braking will occur.** If renewal is necessary, remove the old shoes and fit new or reconditioned units in their place. Follow the appropriate instructions given later in this section to carry out the work.

Rear drum brakes:

Dismantling:

Remove the brake drum as described previously. Take great care to avoid contamination of brake linings and inner surface of brake drum with grease, oil or brake fluid during the dismantling and reassembly procedures.

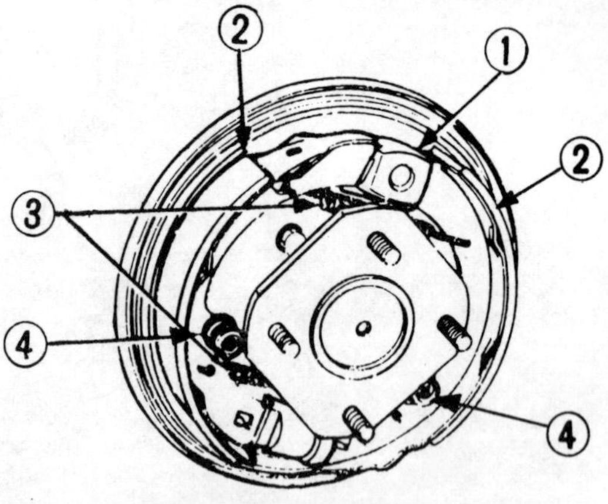

FIG 11 :7 Removing rear drum brake shoes

Key to Fig 11 :7 1 Adjuster 2 Brake shoe 3 Return spring 4 Anti-rattle pin

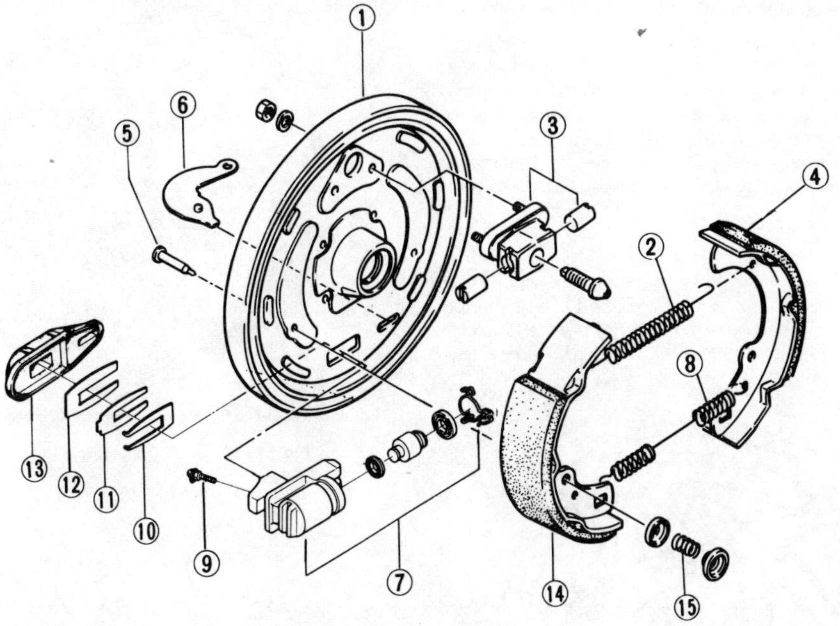

FIG 11:8 Rear drum brake components

Key to Fig 11:8 1 Backplate 2 Return spring adjuster side 3 Brake shoe adjuster 4 Brake shoe assembly fore 5 Anti-rattle pin 6 Lever 7 Wheel cylinder 8 Return spring cylinder side 9 Bleed screw 10 Lockplate A 11 Lockplate B 12 Lockplate C and D 13 Dust cover 14 Brake shoe assembly aft 15 Anti-rattle spring

Refer to **FIG 11:7**. Turn anti-rattle pins 4 through 90° and remove springs and washers. Unhook return springs 3 and detach brake shoes 2. No further dismantling is required for brake shoe renewal.

Refer to **FIG 11:8**. Remove securing nuts and washers then detach adjuster. Disconnect the brake tube from the rear of the brake backplate, plugging the end of the tube to prevent the entry of dirt. Remove the clevis pin to separate handbrake cable and lever. Remove dust cover, adjusting shims and lockplates, then detach wheel cylinder assembly. Remove nuts securing brake backplate to suspension arm on models with independent rear suspension or to rear axle casing on standard models.

Reassembly:

This is a reversal of the removal procedure, noting the following points:

To install wheel cylinder, fit handbrake lever into backplate and install wheel cylinder in position. Drive in appropriate lockplates in the alphabetical order shown in **FIG 11:9**, according to model type.

Apply a thin coat of multi-purpose grease to the shoe-to-disc sliding surfaces in six places, and to the anchorage points in the wheel cylinder and adjuster as shown by the arrows in **FIG 11:10**. Take care not to allow grease to contact the brake shoe linings.

On completion, bleed the braking system as described in **Section 11:7** and adjust the brakes as described in **Section 11:2**.

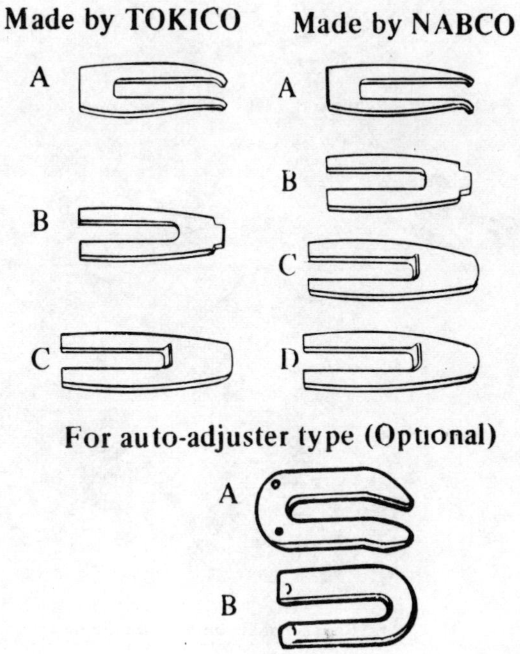

FIG 11:9 Alternative types of wheel cylinder lock plates

Servicing wheel cylinder:

The wheel cylinder can be dismantled while remaining in place on the brake backplate, so do not remove the cylinder unless renewal of the body is essential. Remove the brake shoes as described previously, then refer to **FIG 11:11**. Remove circlip, dust cover, piston and piston cup, in that order. Take care not to damage contact surfaces of cylinder and piston. Discard old piston cup.

Wash all components in commercial alcohol, methylated spirits or approved brake fluid. Use no other cleaner or solvent on the components. Inspect all components for wear, corrosion or scoring. The cylinder bore should be completely smooth. If the bore is faulty, a new wheel cylinder assembly must be fitted. Renew any faulty components.

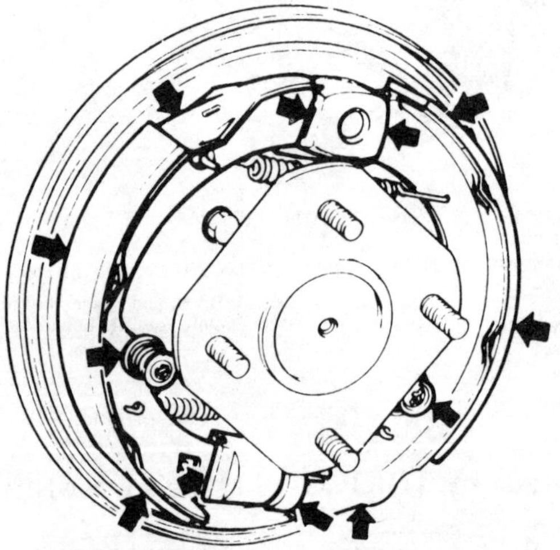

FIG 11:10 Rear drum brake unit lubrication points

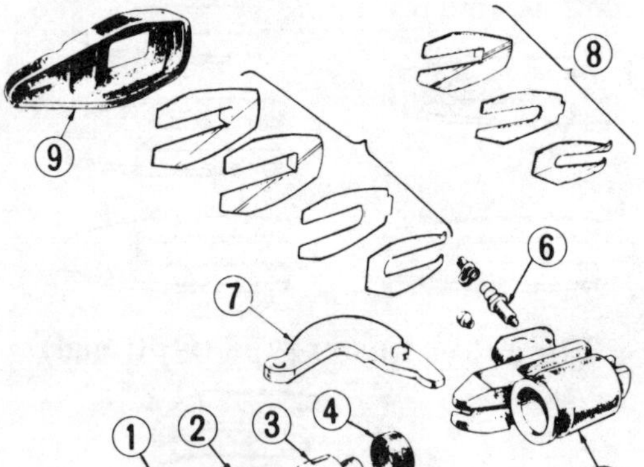

FIG 11:11 Rear wheel cylinder components

Key to Fig 11:11 1 Circlip 2 Dust cover 3 Piston 4 Piston cup 5 Cylinder 6 Bleed screw 7 Handbrake lever 8 Lockplates 9 Dust cover

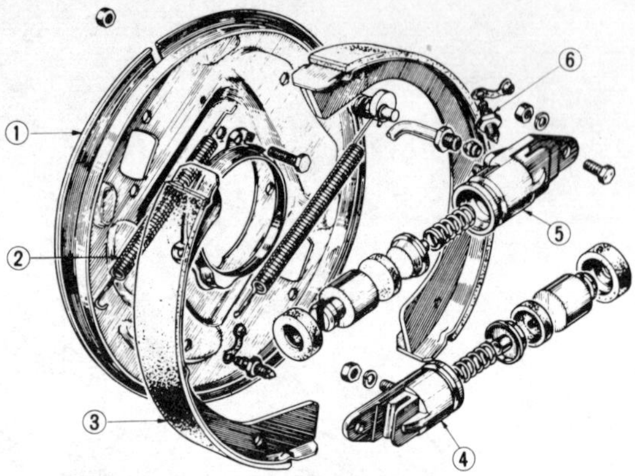

FIG 11:12 Front drum brake components

Key to Fig 11:12 1 Brake backplate 2 Return spring 3 Brake shoe assembly 4 Wheel cylinder (fore) 5 Wheel cylinder (aft) 6 Bleed screw

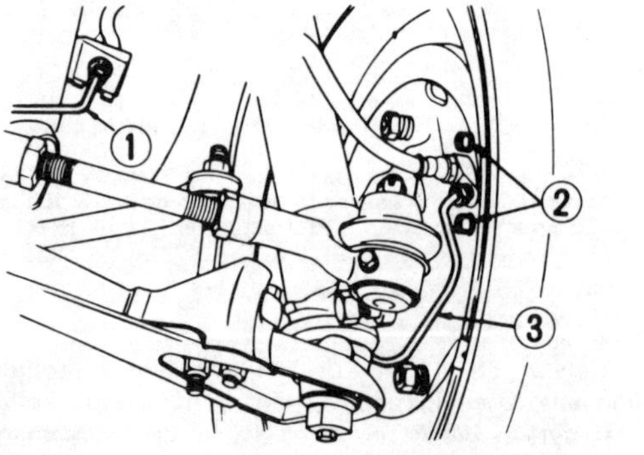

FIG 11:13 Front brake pipe and wheel cylinder attachment points

Key to Fig 11:13 1 Brake pipe 2 Wheel cylinder attaching bolts 3 Bridge pipe

Reassemble the wheel cylinder in the reverse order of dismantling. Apply approved rubber grease or new brake fluid to the internal components. Always fit a new piston cup 4.

Front drum brakes:

Dismantling:

Remove the brake drum as described previously. **FIG 11:12** shows drum brake components. Unhook return springs 2 and detach brake shoes 3. No further dismantling is needed for brake shoe renewal.

Disconnect the brake pipe and bridge pipe from the rear of the brake backplate, as shown in **FIG 11:13**. Remove wheel cylinder attaching bolts 2 and detach wheel cylinders from brake unit. Remove the four fixing bolts and detach brake backplate.

Reassembly:

This is a reversal of the dismantling procedure, noting the following points:

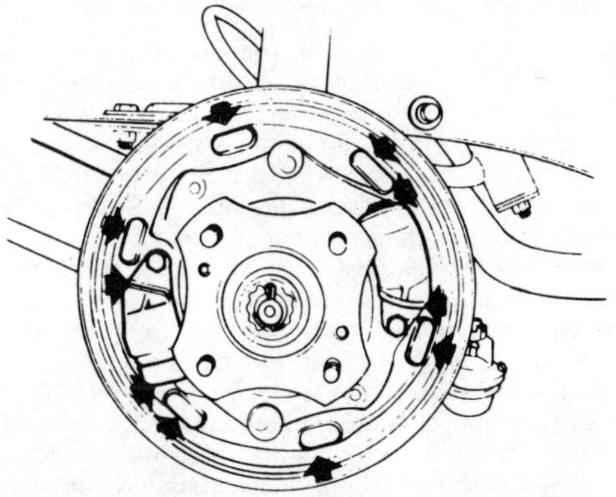

FIG 11 :14 Front drum brake lubrication points

When installing brake backplate to spindle, take care not to invert the backplate or grease shield. After tightening the backplate fixing bolts to 2.7 to 3.7kgm (20 to 27lb ft), stake the grease shield flare to lock the bolts. Correctly differentiate between the fore and aft wheel cylinders (see **FIG 11 :12**). When installing wheel cylinders and brake pipes, tighten pipe flare nut to 1.5 to 1.8kgm (11 to 13lb ft), small cylinder attaching nut to 0.5 to 0.7kgm (3.6 to 5.1lb ft) and large cylinder attaching nut to 1.4 to 1.8kgm (10 to 13lb ft).

Apply a thin smear of multi-purpose grease to brake shoes sliding surfaces arrowed in **FIG 11 :14**. Take care to keep grease from brake shoe lining surfaces.

On completion, refit the brake drum and road wheel then bleed the brakes as described in **Section 11 :7**. Carry out the brake shoe adjustment procedure as described in **Section 11 :2**.

Wheel cylinder servicing:

Remove the wheel cylinders from the brake backplate as described previously. Refer to **FIG 11 :15** and remove dust cover 1. Apply compressed air to the brake pipe hole in cylinder body to force out piston, piston cup, spring retainer and spring. Discard the old piston cup. Wash all remaining parts in commercial alcohol, methylated spirits or approved brake fluid. Use no other cleaner or solvent on the components. Inspect all components for wear, corrosion or scoring. The cylinder bore should be completely smooth. If the bore is scored or damaged, fit a new cylinder assembly complete. Renew all faulty internal components.

Reassemble the components in the reverse order of dismantling, lubricating with clean approved brake fluid when doing so. Always fit a new piston cup 3.

On completion, bleed the braking system as described in **Section 11 :7** and adjust the brake shoes as described in **Section 11 :2**.

11 :5 Disc brakes

The two sorts of disc brake assembly, the swinging caliper type and the sliding caliper type, require different servicing procedures. Refer to the appropriate parts of this section.

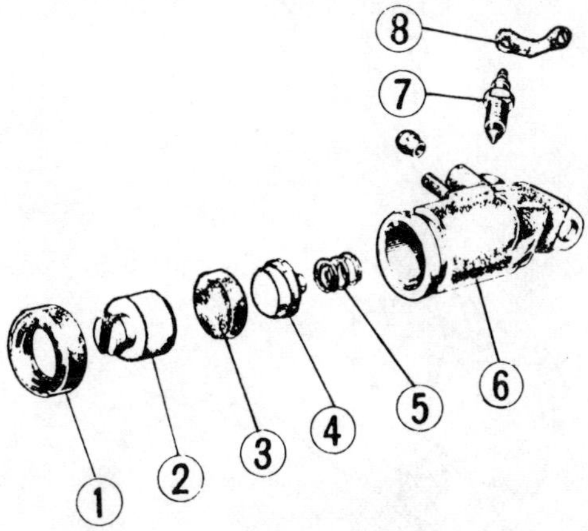

FIG 11 :15 Front wheel cylinder components

Key to Fig 11 :15 1 Dust cover 2 Piston 3 Piston cup 4 Spring retainer 5 Spring 6 Cylinder 7 Bleed screw, aft cylinder 8 Dust cap, aft cylinder

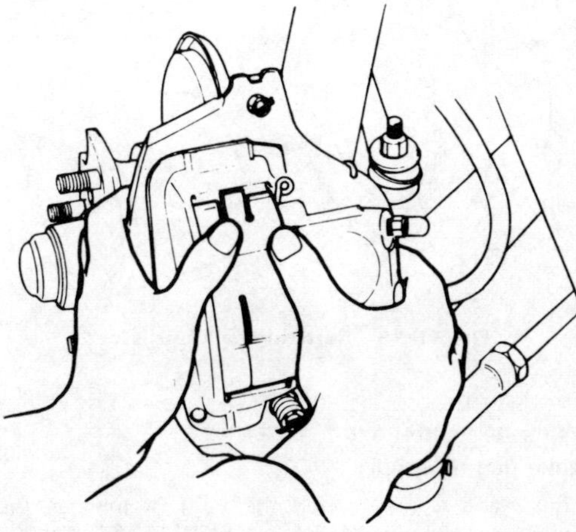

FIG 11 :16 Removing disc brake pad retaining clip

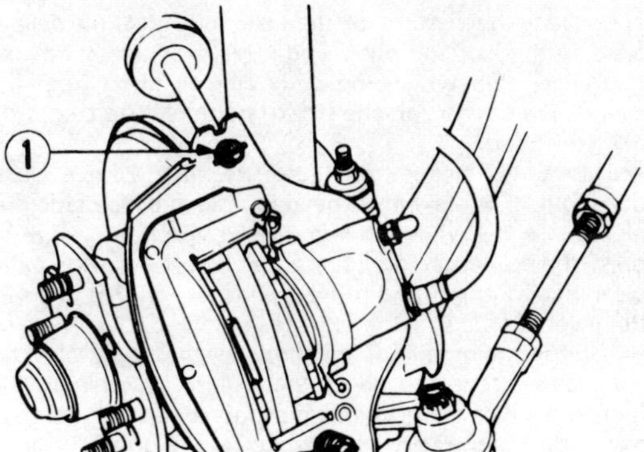

FIG 11 :17 Caliper securing pin 1 and pivot pin 2

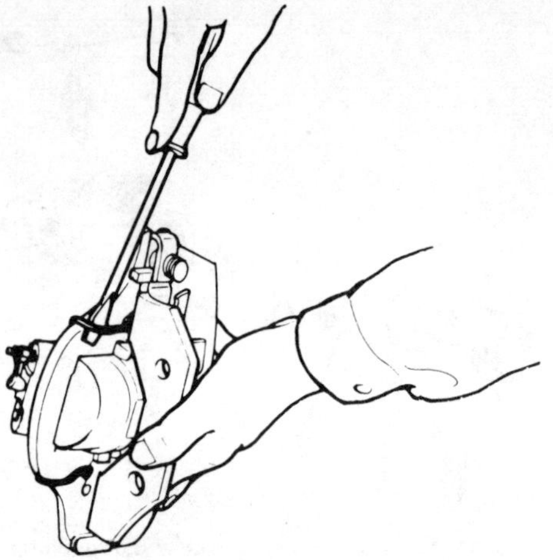

FIG 11 :18 Removing caliper torsion spring

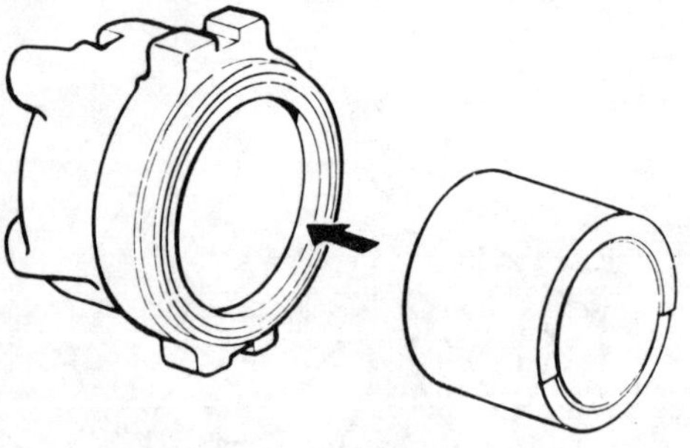

FIG 11 :19 Refitting caliper piston

Swinging caliper type:

Brake pad renewal:

Raise and safely support the front of the car, then remove the road wheels. Refer to **FIG 11 :16** and release the pad retaining clip by pushing on the upper part of the clip. Fit a suitable screwdriver behind the back of the pad opposite to the piston side, then carefully lever the caliper plate to the extreme outer end. This provides extra pad clearance, after which the pads can be lifted from the caliper. **Do not touch the brake pedal while the pads are removed.**

Thoroughly clean the caliper assembly with a clean dry cloth. If a solvent is needed, use only commercial alcohol or methylated spirits. Use a wooden wedge to press the caliper piston down in its bore to provide extra clearance for the fitting of new pads. When this is done, the level of fluid in the brake master cylinder will rise, so check this point and if overflow seems likely slacken the bleed screw and allow the excess to drain away. Remember that brake fluid is poisonous and will damage paintwork. Fit the new pads, replacing the original shims, if fitted. Refit the pad retaining clip. On completion, pump the brake pedal several times to correctly adjust the brake unit. If this is not done, the brakes may not work the first time that they are used on the road.

Piston seal renewal:

If brake fluid leaks from the piston unit are noticed or if the pads do not return properly and cause brake binding, the piston and cylinder assembly should be examined and the seal renewed in the following manner:

Remove the brake pads as described previously and disconnect the brake hose as described in **Section 11 :3**. Remove splitpins from securing pin and pivot pin, then remove fixing nuts (see **FIG 11 :17**). Disengage the caliper yoke from its mounting bracket.

Wipe away grease and road dirt from the caliper before dismantling. Remove torsion spring and detach cylinder from caliper plate as shown in **FIG 11 :18**. Hold the piston with a finger to avoid damage, then apply gentle air pressure at the fluid hose connection point to eject the piston from the cylinder. Carefully remove the seal and seal retainer. Discard the old seal and dust cover.

Wash all remaining parts in commercial alcohol, methylated spirits or approved brake fluid. Use no other cleaner or solvent on the components. Inspect all components for wear, corrosion or scoring. The cylinder bore should be completely smooth. If the bore is scored or damaged, the cylinder assembly should be renewed complete. No further attempt should be made to clean the cylinder bore or piston, as this would damage the plated surface. Renew any faulty internal components.

Wet all internal components with clean brake fluid during reassembly. Carefully fit a new piston seal into the groove in the cylinder bore. Carefully fit the piston to the cylinder bore, taking care not to damage the seal (see **FIG 11 :19**). Reassemble the remaining components in the reverse order of removal, bleeding the brake system on completion as described in **Section 11 :7**.

Caliper removal:

If the caliper assembly is being removed in order to carry out other servicing operations, do not disconnect

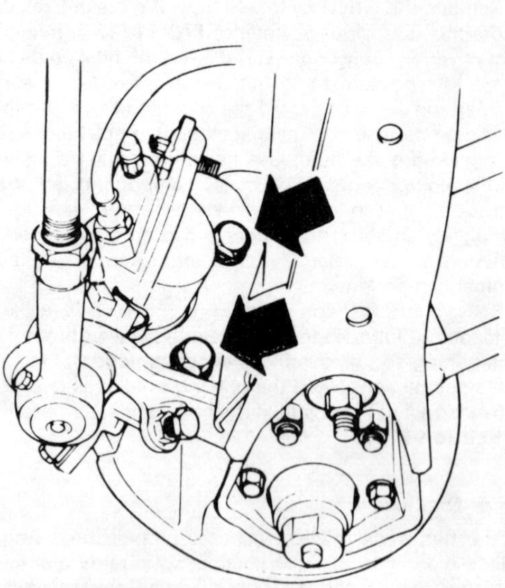

FIG 11 :20 Caliper mounting bolts

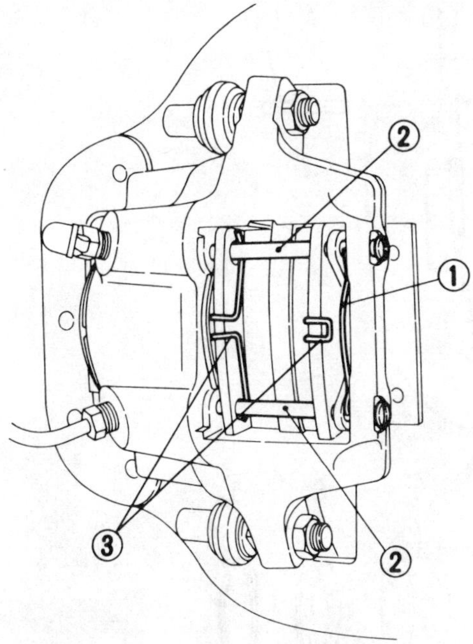

FIG 11 : 21 Removing disc brake pads

Key to Fig 11 : 21 1 Clip 2 Pad retaining pin 3 Anti-squeal spring

the brake hose from the caliper. If the caliper assembly is to be overhauled, detach the brake hose as described in **Section 11 : 3**.

Remove the brake pads as described previously, then disengage caliper assembly from steering knuckle by removing bolts arrowed in **FIG 11 : 20**.

Refit the caliper assembly in the reverse order of removal, tightening the caliper mounting bolts to 7.3 to 9.9kgm (53 to 72lb ft). Bleed the brakes as described in **Section 11 : 7** if the hose was disconnected.

Sliding caliper type:

Brake pad renewal:

Raise and safely support the front of the car, then remove the road wheels. Refer to **FIG 11 : 21**, remove the clip 1 and withdraw the pad retaining pins while holding the anti-squeal springs 3. The pads can now be withdrawn from the caliper. Do not touch the brake pedal while the pads are removed.

Thoroughly clean the caliper assembly with a clean dry cloth. If a solvent is needed, use only commercial alcohol or methylated spirits. Use a piece of wood to press the piston adjacent to the disc back into its bore until the dust seal groove of the piston coincides with the end surface of the retaining ring on the dust seal as shown in **FIG 11 : 22**. If the piston is pushed too far the groove on the piston will pass inside the piston seal. Should this occur the caliper assembly will have to be removed and dismantled so that the piston can be removed by pushing it out in the direction shown by the arrow. Install inner brake pad. Pull the yoke fully out and install outer brake pad. Note that while this is done the level of fluid in the master cylinder reservoir will rise and the excess should be drained off by slackening the caliper bleed screw. Remember that brake fluid is poisonous and will damage paintwork. Refit the pad retaining pins and clips. On completion pump the brake pedal several times to correctly adjust the brake unit. If this is not done, the brakes may not work the first time that they are used on the road.

Caliper removal:

The removal procedure for these units is similar to that for the swinging caliper unit.

Caliper dismantling:

Wipe away grease and road dirt from the caliper before dismantling. Refer to **FIG 11 : 23** and remove gripper pin nuts and separate the yoke from the body. Remove the yoke holder, retaining rings and dust seals. Push pistons out of cylinder using compressed air fed gradually in through brake hose connection. Take care not to damage seals and the smooth surfaces of cylinder and piston.

Caliper servicing:

Clean all parts in commercial alcohol, methylated spirits or approved brake fluid. Use no other cleaner or solvent on the components. Inspect all components for wear, corrosion or scoring. The cylinder bore should be completely smooth. If the bore is scored or damaged, the cylinder assembly should be renewed complete. No further attempt should be made to clean the bore or piston as this would damage the plated surface. Renew any faulty internal components.

Caliper assembly:

Wet all internal components with clean brake fluid during reassembly. Carefully fit new piston seals into the grooves in the cylinder bore. Carefully fit the pistons to

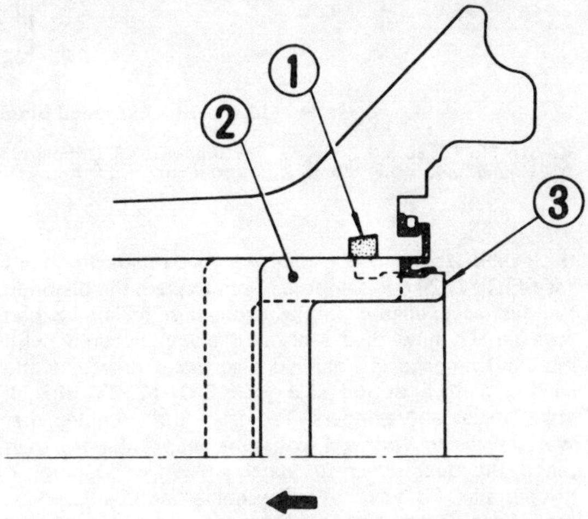

FIG 11 : 22 Correct retracted position of piston. In the position shown dotted the piston cannot return past the seal

Key to Fig 11 : 22 1 Piston seal 2 Piston 3 Correct position

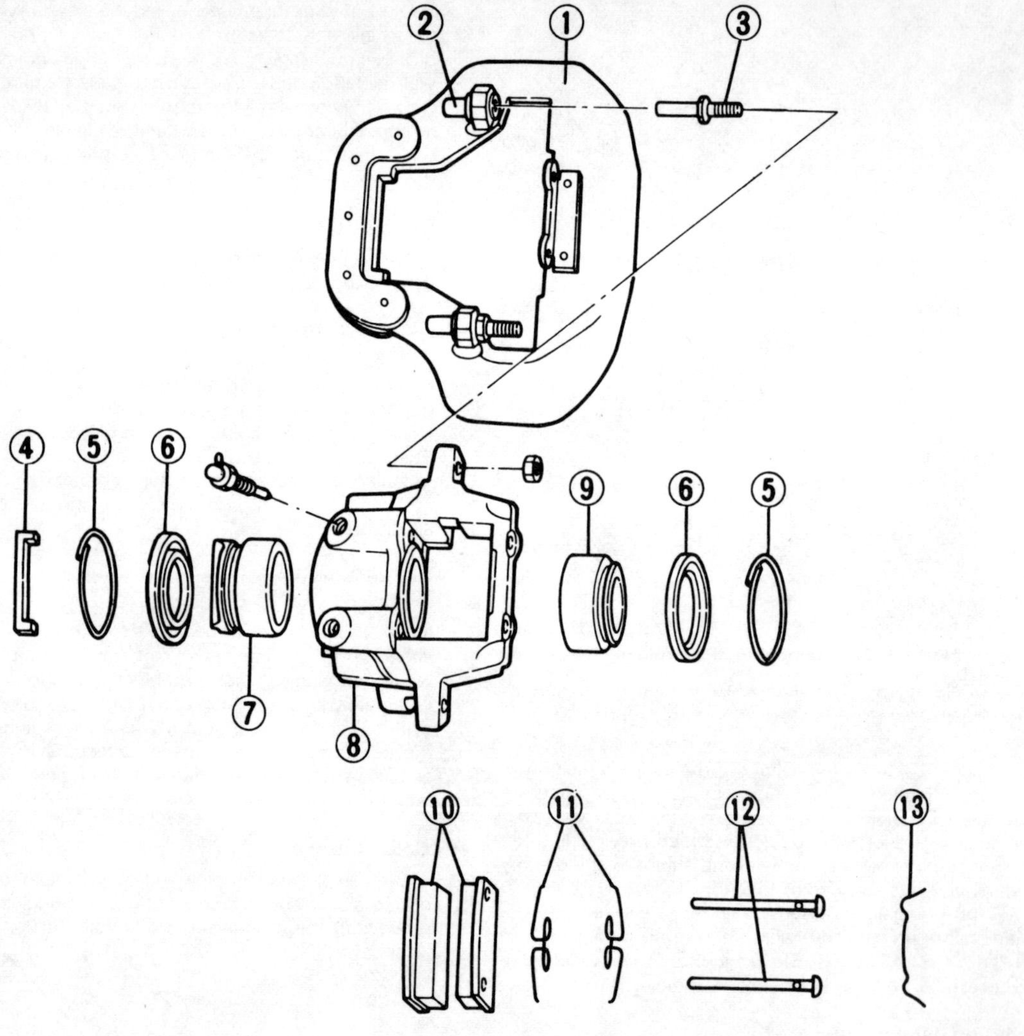

FIG 11:23 Exploded diagram of sliding caliper components

Key to Fig 11:23 1 Yoke 2 Gripper 3 Gripper pin 4 Yoke holder 5 Retainer ring 6 Dust seal 7 Piston A 8 Cylinder body 9 Piston B 10 Pad 11 Anti-squeal spring 12 Pad pin 13 Clip

the cylinder bore, taking care not to damage the seals (see **FIG 11:24**). It is important not to push the piston in too far, as explained in the procedure for brake pad renewal. Fit new dust seals and clamp securely with retaining ring, having applied disc brake grease to the sealing surface of the seal (see **FIG 11:25**). Install yoke holder and grippers. To install the grippers, first wet the inside with a 1 per cent soap solution, then pinch the dust cover to expel air while pushing in gripper pin. Fit yoke to yoke holder and, supporting the piston B on a wooden bridge piece (as shown in **FIG 11:26**), press yoke into yoke holder with a force of 20 to 30kg (44 to 66lb). Finally, tighten gripper pin nuts to 1.6 to 2.1kgm (12 to 15lb ft). Refit caliper assembly and brake pads as described previously.

Brake disc removal:

Remove front hub assembly complete with brake disc as described in **Chapter 9**. Remove the four fixing bolts to detach the brake disc from the hub.

Use a suitable solvent to clean all dirt and grease from the disc. Examine the operating surfaces for cracks or deep score marks. Light scoring is normal and needs no attention. A badly scored or damaged disc should be resurfaced at a service station, or renewed if too worn for this remedial work to be carried out satisfactorily. Check the thickness of the disc at several places around the circumference. If thickness is below 8.4mm (0.331in) at any point, a new disc should be fitted.

Refit the disc to the wheel hub and evenly tighten

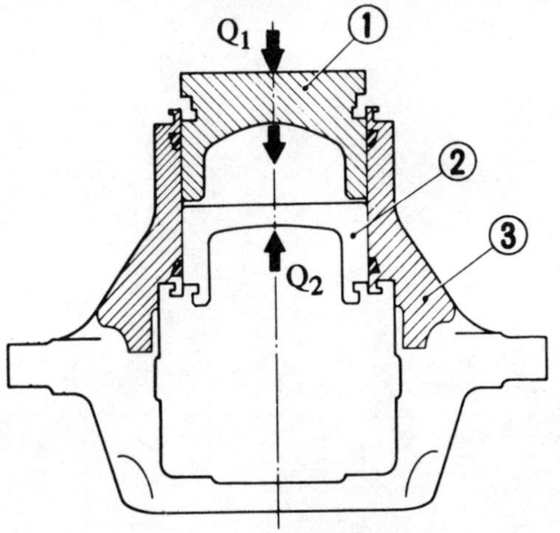

FIG 11:24 Fitting pistons

Key to Fig 11:24 1 Piston A 2 Piston B 3 Body

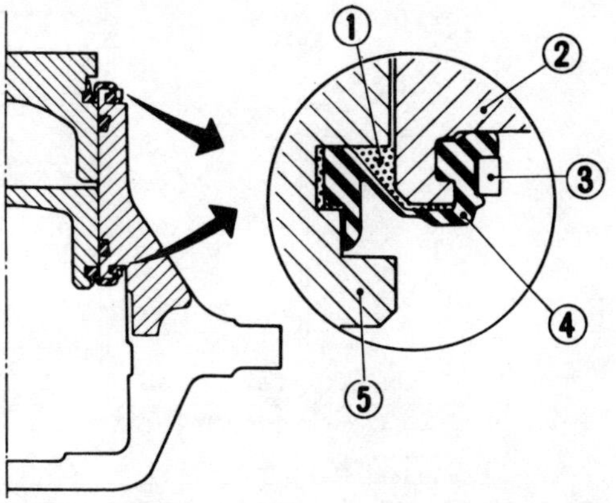

FIG 11:25 Installing dust seal

Key to Fig 11:25 1 Grease 2 Cylinder body 3 Retaining ring 4 Dust seal 5 Piston

the fixing bolts to 3.9 to 5.3kgm (28 to 38lb ft). Carry out the wheel bearing adjustment procedure described in **Chapter 9**. Use a dial gauge to check for warping of the brake disc. Arrange the dial gauge so that its operating pin contacts the side of the disc in the centre of the brake pad contact area. Rotate the disc and hub through one full turn and check maximum runout. If the figure obtained exceeds 0.12mm (0.0047in) excessive warpage is indicated. Try removing the disc from the hub and refitting it in a different position, then recheck runout. If no improvement results, a new disc must be fitted.

11:6 The master cylinder

Two alternative types of master cylinder units are fitted, one for disc brakes and the other for drum brakes (see **FIGS 11:27** and **11:28**). The two differ from each other in fluid reservoir capacity and the type of check valve fitted. The servicing instructions in this section apply to both types of master cylinder assembly, unless otherwise stated.

The master cylinder fluid reservoirs are fitted with retention caps. To remove a cap, turn the retention ring fully in the REMOVE direction, then pull out retention cap. To refit, turn the cap retention ring fully in the REMOVE direction, then align the projection in retention ring with slot in reservoir and push cap fully home. Turn retention ring fully in TIGHTEN direction to lock.

Master cylinder removal:

Disconnect front and rear brake pipes from master cylinder body. Have a container ready to catch the brake fluid which will escape as the pipes are released. Plug the ends of the pipes to prevent the entry of dirt.

On models without vacuum servo units, pull out the clevis pin and separate the brake pedal from master cylinder pushrod.

Remove the nuts securing the master cylinder to bulkhead or vacuum servo unit, then lift the assembly from the engine compartment.

Servicing:

Remove the reservoir caps as described previously, then drain the old brake fluid from the reservoirs.

Refer to **FIG 11:29**. Lever off stop ring 3 using a screwdriver. Remove stop screw 4 and remove stop 5,

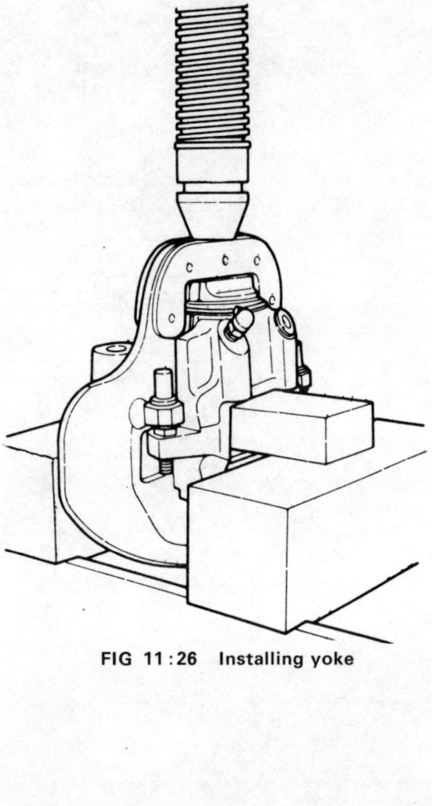

FIG 11:26 Installing yoke

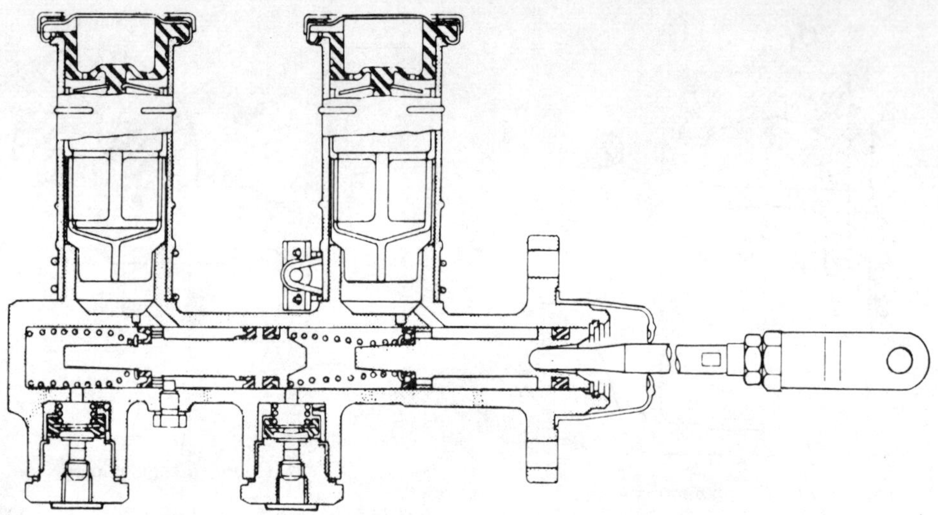

FIG 11:27 Section through master cylinder assembly used on models with all-drum brake systems

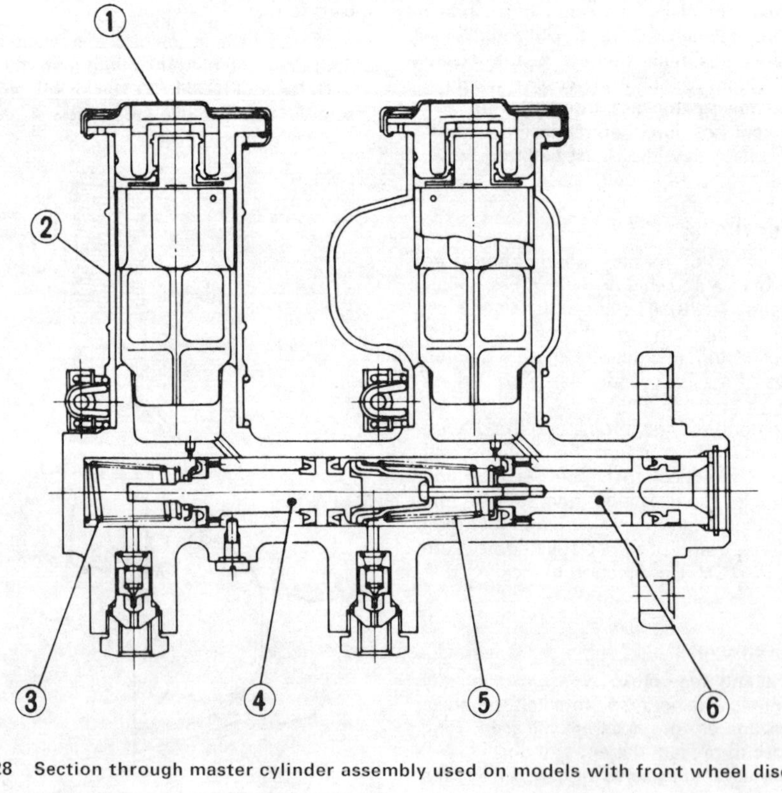

FIG 11:28 Section through master cylinder assembly used on models with front wheel disc brakes

Key to Fig 11:28 1 Reservoir cap 2 Reservoir tank 3 Secondary piston return spring 4 Secondary piston 5 Primary piston return spring 6 Primary piston

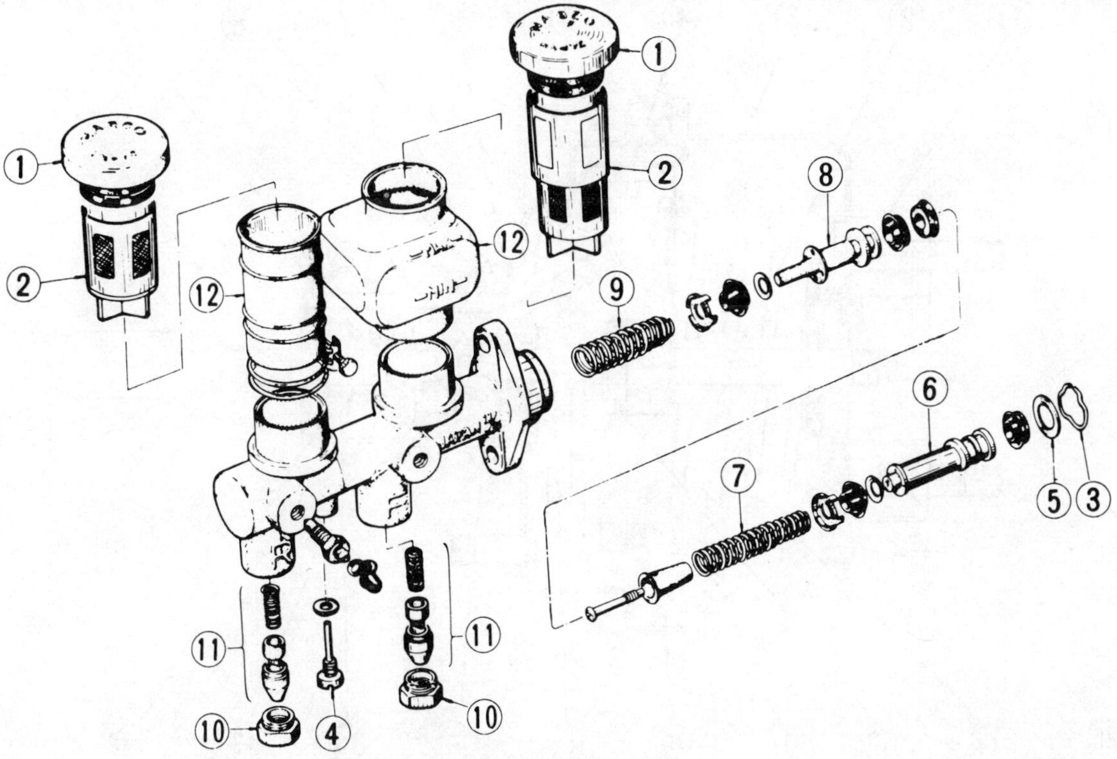

FIG 11 : 29 Master cylinder components

Key to Fig 11 : 29 1 Reservoir cap 2 Filter 3 Stop ring 4 Stop screw 5 Stop 6 Primary piston assembly 7 Primary return spring 8 Secondary piston assembly 9 Secondary return spring 10 Plug 11 Check valve 12 Reservoir

primary piston assembly 6, spring 7, secondary piston assembly 8 and spring 9. If the piston cups are in good condition, they can remain in place on the piston assemblies, but if they are removed they must be discarded and replaced by new units during reassembly.

Never detach the reservoir tanks from master cylinder body unless they are to be renewed. If the tanks are removed at any time they must be discarded and replaced by new units during reassembly.

Wash all internal parts in commercial alcohol, methylated spirits or approved brake fluid. Use no other cleaner or solvent on the components. Inspect all parts for wear, corrosion or scoring. The cylinder bore should be completely smooth. If the bore is scored or damaged, a new master cylinder assembly should be fitted. Carefully check all other components and renew any found worn or damaged. Unscrew plugs 10 so that check valves 11 can be inspected. Check springs for weakness, damage or deformation, renewing as necessary.

Reassemble the master cylinder in the reverse order of dismantling, noting the following points:

Always fit new gaskets and renew any rubber cups or seals which have been removed from their original positions. It is always safest to renew all rubber components regardless of their apparent condition. Dip all internal components in approved brake fluid and assemble them wet. Fit the secondary piston and spring assembly first and retain with stop screw 4, before fitting the primary piston and spring assembly and retaining with stop 5 and stop ring 3.

Refitting:

This is a reversal of the removal procedure. Tighten master cylinder securing nuts to 0.8 to 1.1kgm (5.8 to 8.0lb ft) and brake pipe connectors to 1.5 to 1.8kgm (11 to 13lb ft). On completion, bleed the braking system as described in **Section 11 : 7** and check brake pedal free play as described in **Section 11 : 2**.

11 : 7 Bleeding the system

This is not routine maintenance and is only necessary if air has entered the hydraulic system due to parts being dismantled, or because the level in a master cylinder reservoir has dropped too low. The need for bleeding is indicated by a spongy feeling of the brake pedal, accompanied by poor braking performance. Do not attempt to bleed the brakes with any part of the braking system dismantled.

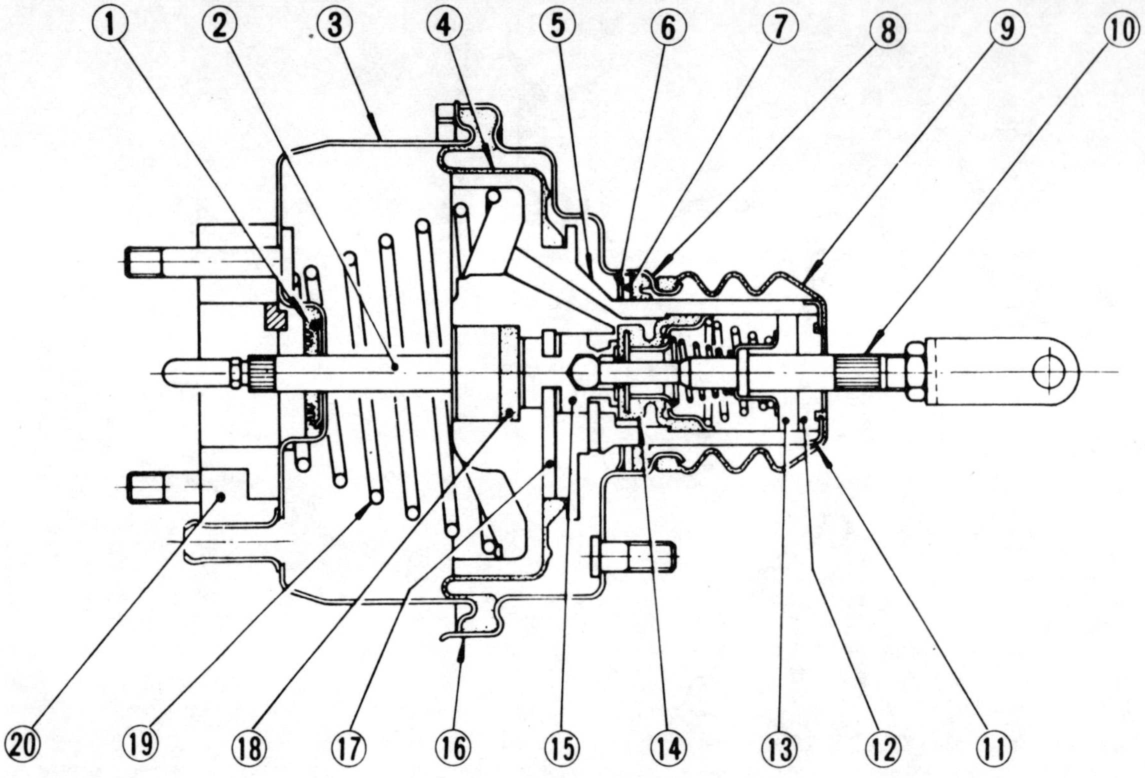

FIG 11:30 Section through the vacuum servo assembly

Key to Fig 11:30 1 Plate and seal assembly 2 Pushrod 3 Front shell 4 Diaphragm 5 Diaphragm plate and valve body 6 Retainer 7 Bearing 8 Valve body seal 9 Valve body guard 10 Valve operating rod 11 Silencer retainer 12 Silencer filter (felt) 13 Silencer (rubber) 14 Poppet assembly 15 Plunger assembly 16 Rear shell 17 Valve plunger stop key 18 Reaction disc 19 Diaphragm return spring 20 Flange

Bleed the rear brake furthest from the master cylinder first, followed by the second rear brake. Then bleed the front brake furthest from the master cylinder followed by the second front brake. Bleed screws for drum brake units are located on the wheel cylinder behind the brake backplate, bleed screws for disc brake assemblies are located on the caliper body.

Remove the caps and top up the master cylinder reservoirs to the correct level with approved brake fluid. Clean dirt from around the appropriate bleed screw and remove the dust cap. Fit a length of rubber or plastic tube to the screw and lead the free end of the tube into a clean glass jar containing a small amount of brake fluid. The end of the tube must remain immersed in the fluid during the bleeding operation.

Unscrew the bleed screw about half-a-turn and have an assistant depress the brake pedal fully and hold it to the floor. Tighten the bleed screw then have the pedal released. Wait a few seconds before repeating the operation. As the brake pedal is depressed, fluid will be pumped into the jar. Continue pumping the pedal in the manner described until no air bubbles can be seen in the fluid flowing into the jar. When no more air bubbles can be seen, hold the pedal against the floor on a downstroke while the bleed valve is tightened. **Do not overtighten.**

At frequent intervals during the operation, check the level of fluid in the master cylinder reservoirs, topping up as necessary. If the level is allowed to drop too low, air will enter the system and the operation will have to be restarted.

Remove the bleed tube, refit the dust cap and repeat the operation on the other brake units in turn.

On completion, top up the fluid in the reservoirs to the correct level. Discard all used fluid. Always store brake fluid in clean sealed containers to avoid air or moisture contamination.

11:8 Vacuum servo unit

The vacuum servo unit operates to assist the pressure applied at the brake pedal and so reduce braking effort. The vacuum cylinder in the servo is connected to the engine inlet manifold by a hose. If the vacuum servo unit is faulty or inoperative, remedial work should be carried out at a fully equipped service station. **FIG 11:30** shows a section through the vacuum servo assembly.

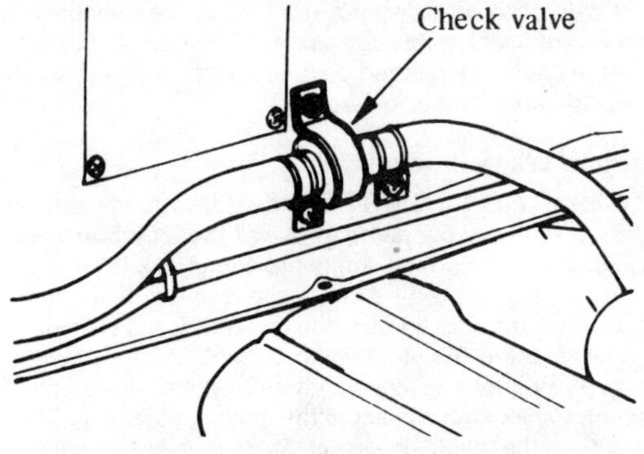

FIG 11 :31 Vacuum servo check valve installation

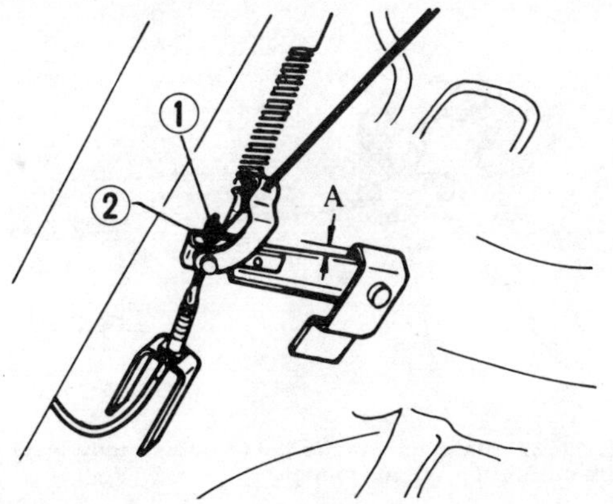

FIG 11 :32 Handbrake cable locknut 1 and adjusting nut 2 on models with rigid axle rear suspension

Testing:

To test the servo unit, switch off the engine and pump the brake pedal several times to clear all vacuum from the unit. Hold a steady light pressure on the brake pedal and start the engine. If the servo is working properly, the brake pedal will move further down without further foot pressure, due to the build-up of vacuum in the system.

With the brakes off, run the engine to medium speed and turn off the ignition, immediately closing the throttle. This builds up a vacuum in the system. Wait one to two minutes, then try the brake action with the engine still switched off. If not vacuum assisted for two or three operations, the servo check valve or vacuum hose is faulty. Check the hose for damage or faulty connections. A new check valve can be fitted by removing the retaining clip and disconnecting the hoses (see **FIG 11 :31**). Note the direction in which the valve is fitted so that the new unit can be correctly installed. The hose from the inlet manifold attaches to the shorter connection on the check valve. The hose from the servo unit connects to the longer connection on the valve, which is also of slightly smaller diameter.

More serious performance faults which indicate internal defects should be referred to a service station. Failure of the servo unit does not impair the efficiency of the brakes, but greater pedal pressure will be needed to stop the vehicle.

11 :9 The handbrake

Normally, handbrake movement is automatically corrected by the adjuster mechanism which controls the rear brake shoes, whether manual or automatic. If the handbrake mechanism is worn or if the cables have been refitted after a service operation, the linkage may need adjustment. Before carrying out any adjustments, check rear brake adjustment on models fitted with manual adjusters described in **Section 11 :2**. On models fitted with self-adjusting rear brake units, check rear brake lining thickness as described in **Section 11 :4** before adjusting handbrake cables.

Cable adjustment:

Rigid axle models:

Refer to **FIG 11 :32**. Slacken the locknut and turn the adjusting nut until the operating stroke of the handbrake

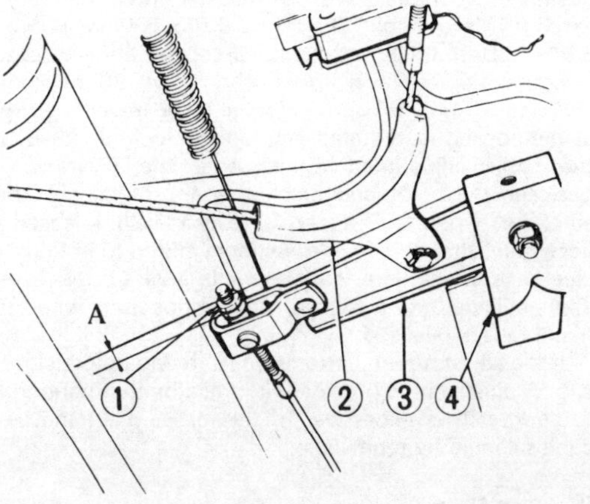

FIG 11 :33 Front handbrake cable adjustment mechanism on IRS models

Key to Fig 11 :33 1 Adjusting nut 2 Equaliser 3 Centre lever 4 Centre lever bracket

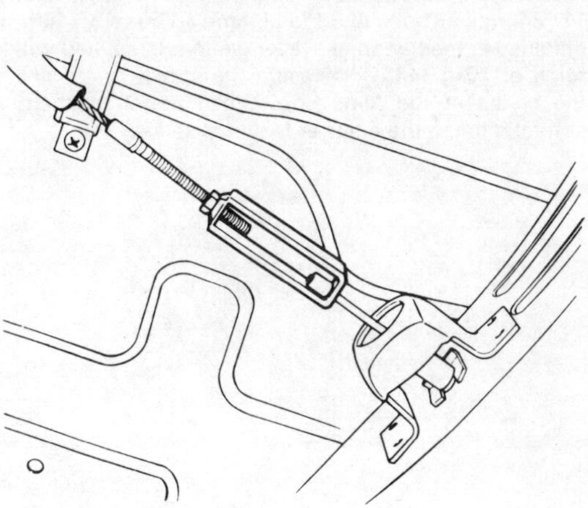

FIG 11 :34 Rear handbrake cable adjustment mechanism on IRS models

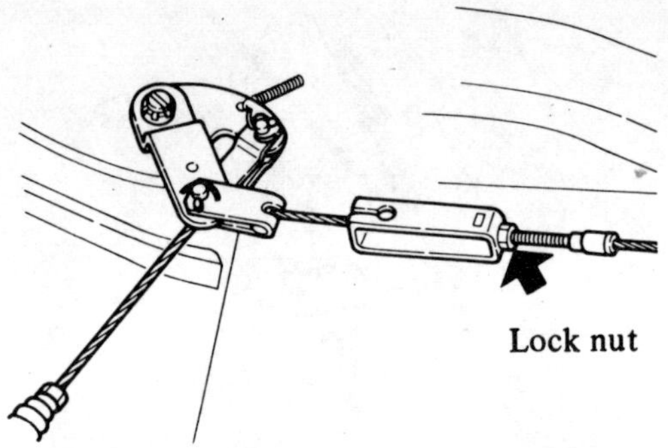

FIG 11:35 Rear handbrake cable adjustment mechanism on Station Wagon models

lever inside the car is correct. Apply the handbrake lever with a force of 20kg (44lb) and check the distance that the end of the lever has moved from the rest position. On models with a facia-mounted handbrake assembly, lever stroke should be 90 to 100mm (3.54 to 3.94in). On models fitted with a central floor-mounted handbrake lever, lever stroke should be 80 to 95mm (3.15 to 3.74in). When handbrake lever travel is correct at the applied load stated, tighten the locknut to secure the cable adjustment. Check that the clearance A between the pivot and bracket is approximately 5mm (0.197in) when the handbrake lever is fully released. If necessary, alter the cable adjustment a little to obtain this clearance. Make sure that the cable levers at each rear brake cylinder return to their original positions when the handbrake is released.

If the adjusting nut bottoms on its thread before correct cable adjustment is obtained, it indicates that handbrake cable stretch is excessive. In this case, the handbrake cables should be renewed.

IRS models:

Refer to **FIG 11:33**. Adjust the front cable adjusting nut until dimension A is approximately 5mm (0.197in) when the handbrake lever in the car is fully released. Now adjust the rear cable adjusting nut shown in **FIG 11:34** until a stroke of 80 to 95mm (3.150 to 3.740in) is obtained at the handbrake lever when it is applied with a force of 20kg (44lb). Measure the stroke at a point in the centre of the hand grip. When the adjustment is correct, tighten the adjuster locknuts securely.

If any cable adjusting nut bottoms on its threaded rod before sufficient cable tension is obtained, it indicates that the cable is stretched beyond limits. In this case, the affected cable should be renewed.

Station Wagon models:

Refer to **FIG 11:35**. Slacken the locknut and turn the adjuster until the operating stroke of the handbrake lever inside the car is correct. Apply the handbrake lever with a force of 20kg (44lb) and check the distance that the end of the lever has moved from the rest position. Lever stroke should be 80 to 95mm (3.15 to 3.74in). When the handbrake lever travel is correct at the applied load stated, tighten the locknut to secure the cable adjustment. Make sure that the cable levers at each rear brake cylinder return to their original positions when the handbrake is released.

If the adjusting nut bottoms on its thread before correct cable adjustment is obtained, it indicates that handbrake cable stretch is excessive. In this case the handbrake cables should be renewed.

11:10 Fault diagnosis

(a) Spongy pedal

1 Leak in the system
2 Worn master cylinder
3 Leaking wheel cylinders
4 Air in the fluid system

(b) Excessive pedal movement

1 Check 1 and 4 in (a)
2 Excessive lining or pad wear
3 Very low fluid level in reservoir
4 Brake adjustment incorrect

(c) Brakes grab or pull to one side

1 Distorted discs or drums
2 Wet or oily pads or linings
3 Loose backplate or caliper
4 Disc loose on hub
5 Worn suspension or steering connections
6 Mixed linings of uneven grades
7 Uneven tyre pressures
8 Broken brake shoe return springs
9 Seized handbrake linkage
10 Seized wheel cylinder piston

CHAPTER 12

THE ELECTRICAL SYSTEM

12:1 Description

All models covered by this manual have 12-volt electrical systems in which the negative battery terminal is earthed to the car bodywork.

There are wiring diagrams in **Technical Data** at the end of this manual that will enable those with electrical experience to trace and correct faults, that section also containing details and specifications for the units fitted to the models in the range.

Instructions for servicing items of electrical equipment are given in this chapter, but it must be pointed out that it may be uneconomical to try to repair units that are seriously defective, either electrically or mechanically. Such equipment should be replaced by new or reconditioned units.

12:2 The battery

To maintain the performance of the battery it is essential to carry out the following operations, particularly in winter when heavy current demands must be met.

Keep the top and surrounding parts of the battery clean and dry, as dampness can lead to current leakage. Clean off corrosion from the metal parts of the battery mountings with diluted ammonia and coat them with anti-sulphuric paint. Clean the terminal posts and smear them with petroleum jelly, remaking the connections properly and tightening the terminal clamps securely. High electrical resistance due to corrosion at the terminals can be responsible for lack of sufficient current to operate the starter motor.

Top up the electrolyte in the battery cells to the correct level at frequent intervals, using distilled water for this purpose. Test the condition of the cells, if necessary, with an hydrometer. **Never add neat acid to the battery. If it is necessary to prepare new electrolyte due to loss or spillage, add sulphuric acid to distilled water. It is highly dangerous to add water to acid.** It is safest to have the battery refilled with electrolyte, if necessary, by a service station.

The indications from the hydrometer readings of the specific gravity are as follows:

For climated below 27°C or 80°F	*Specific gravity*
Cell fully charged	1.270 to 1.290
Cell half discharged	1.190 to 1.210
Cell discharged	1.110 to 1.130
For climates above 27°C or 80°F	
Cell fully charged	1.210 to 1.230
Cell half discharged	1.130 to 1.150
Cell discharged	1.050 to 1.070

These figures assume an electrolyte temperature of 60°F or 16°C. If the temperature of the electrolyte exceeds

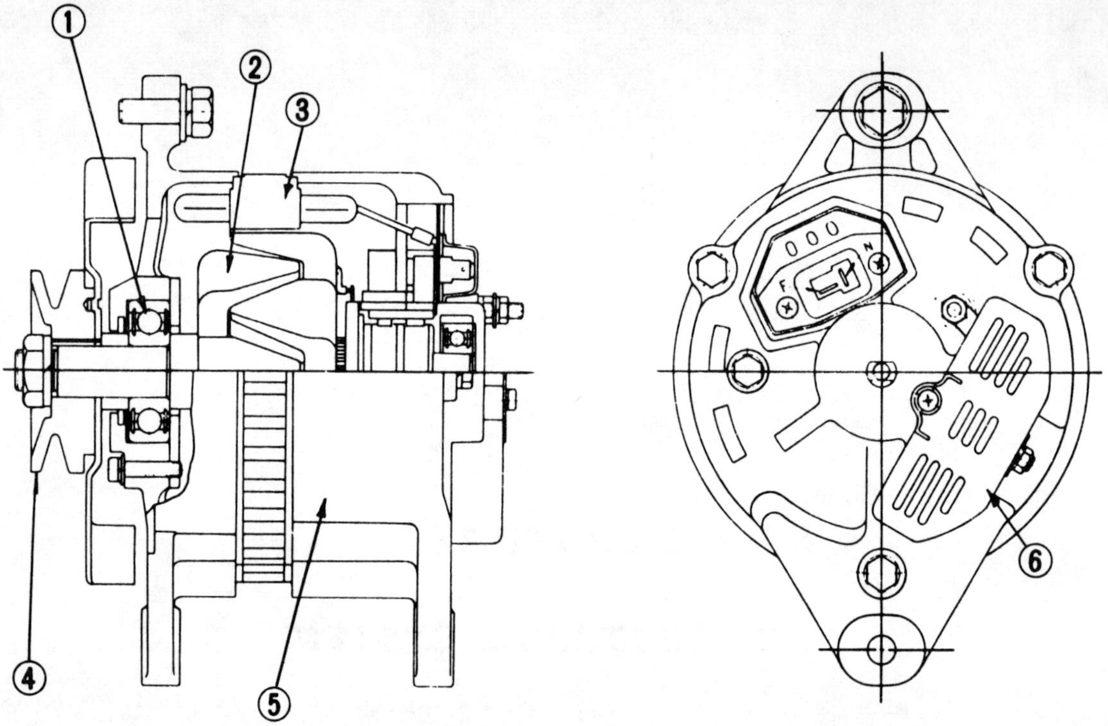

FIG 12:1 **Sections through a typical alternator unit**

Key to Fig 12:1 1 Front bearing 2 Rotor 3 Stator 4 Pulley 5 End cover 6 Encased diode rectifier

this, add 0.002 to the readings for each 5°F or 3°C rise. Subtract 0.002 for any corresponding drop below 60°F or 16°C.

All cells should read approximately the same. If one differs radically from the others it may be due to an internal fault or to spillage or leakage of the electrolyte.

If the battery is in a low state of charge, take the car for a long daylight run or put the battery on a charger at 5 amp, with the vents removed, until it gasses freely. Do not use a naked light near the battery as the gas is inflammable. If the battery is to stand unused for long periods, give a refreshing charge every month. It will be ruined if it is left uncharged.

12:3 The alternator

The alternator provides current for the various items of electrical equipment and to charge the battery, the unit operating at all engine speeds. The current produced is alternating, this being rectified to direct current supply by diodes mounted in the alternator casing. Alternator drive is by belt from the crankshaft pulley. Very little maintenance is needed, apart from the occasional check on belt tension as described in **Chapter 4, Section 4:6** and on the condition and tightness of the wiring connections.

The alternator must never be run with the battery disconnected, nor must the battery cables be reversed at any time. Test connections must be carefully made, and the battery and alternator must be completely disconnected before any electric welding is carried out on any part of the car. The battery must be disconnected when it is being boost-charged from an outside source. The engine must never be started with a battery charger still connected to the battery. These warnings must be observed, otherwise extensive damage to the alternator components, particularly the diodes, will result.

The alternator is designed and constructed to give many years of trouble-free service. If, however, a fault should develop in the unit, it should be checked and serviced by a fully equipped service station or a reconditioned unit obtained and fitted. **FIG 12:1** shows a typical alternator unit.

Alternator testing:

A simple check on alternator charging can be carried out after dark by switching on the headlamps and starting the engine. If the alternator is charging the headlamps will brighten considerably as the system voltage rises from the nominal battery voltage to the higher figure produced by the alternator. A more positive check is to connect a high resistance voltmeter, reading up to 20 volts, across the battery terminals and to note the reading when the engine is running at about 1000rev/min. The voltage should remain steady at a reading of approximately 14. A significantly higher voltage reading indicates a regulator failure, a significantly lower reading indicates a fault in the alternator itself.

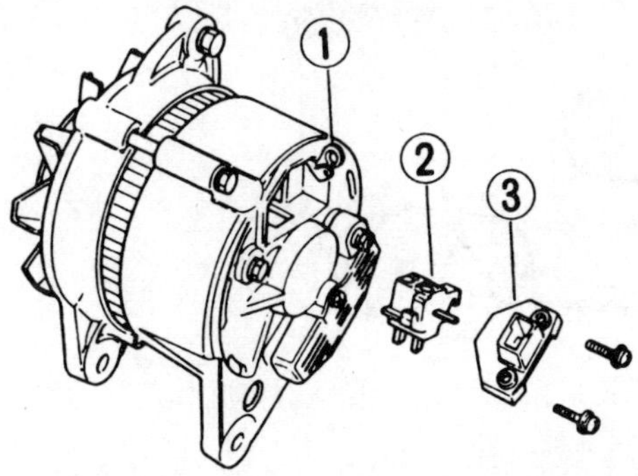

FIG 12:2 Removing alternator brushes

Key to Fig 12:2 1 N terminal of stator 2 Brush holder 3 Cover

If the alternator is not charging, check the wiring and connections in the charging circuit and inspect the brushes. If these are in order, the alternator unit is at fault and must be checked and serviced by a Datsun agent.

Alternator removal:

Disconnect the battery then disconnect the cables to the alternator. Slacken the alternator mounting bolts, swing the unit towards the engine to slacken the drive belt, then remove the belt. Unbolt and remove the alternator.

Refitting is a reversal of the removal procedure, adjusting the belt tension as described in **Chapter 4, Section 4:6**.

Inspecting brushes:

To remove the brush holder remove the fixing screws. Remove cover, brush holder and brushes. Do not disconnect 'N' terminal from stator coil (see **FIG 12:2**).

Check that the brushes move smoothly in the brush holder. If necessary clean and smooth the sides of the brush and brush holder. If the brushes are worn down near or below the specified limit (see **FIG 12:3**), replace the brush assembly.

Alternator maintenance:

Check the tension of the alternator drive belt as described in **Chapter 4, Section 4:6**. The connections should be kept tight and clean and the outside of the unit should be kept free of oil and dirt particularly around the ventilating slots in the cover.

12:4 The starter motor

The starter motor is of the pre-engaged type, equipped with an overrunning clutch and operated by a parallel solenoid which is fitted to the starter case. The armature shaft is supported in sintered metal bushes which are factory packed with lubricant and require no servicing between overhauls. **FIG 12:4** shows a section through the starter motor.

When the starter is operated from the ignition switch, the engagement lever moves the pinion into mesh with the flywheel ring gear teeth. When the pinion meshes with these teeth, the solenoid contact closes the circuit and the starter motor operates to turn the engine over. When the engine starts, the speed of the flywheel causes the pinion to overrun the clutch and armature, preventing the starter from being driven at high speed by the engine. The pinion continues in engagement until the switch is released, when it returns to the rest position under spring action.

Faults which may occur after an extended period of use include brush or commutator faults, solenoid malfunction or internal mechanical or electrical failure. The

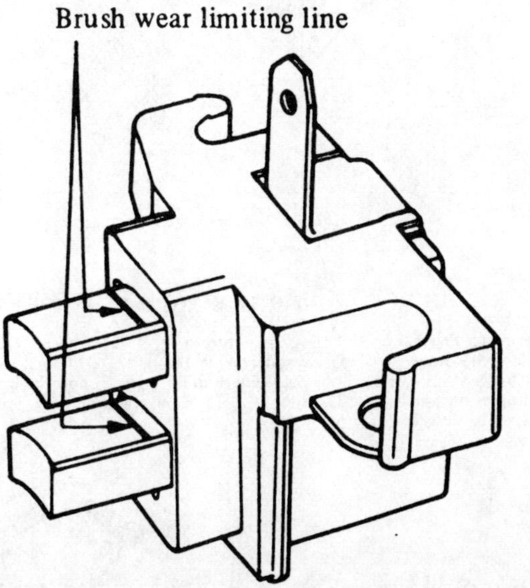

FIG 12:3 Brush wear limit

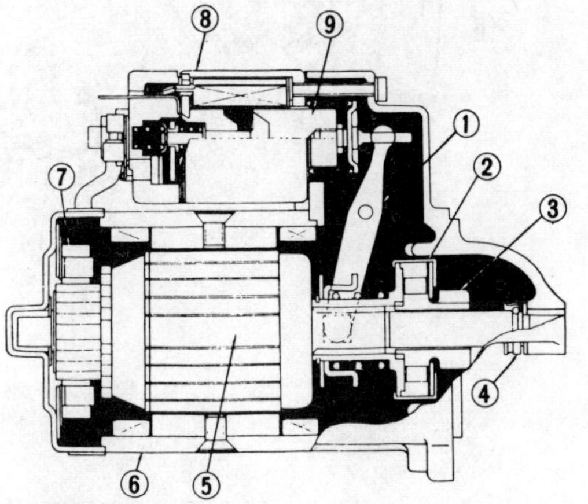

FIG 12:4 Section through the starter motor

Key to Fig 12:4 1 Engagement lever 2 Overrunning clutch 3 Pinion 4 Pinion stop 5 Armature 6 Yoke 7 Brush 8 Solenoid 9 Plunger

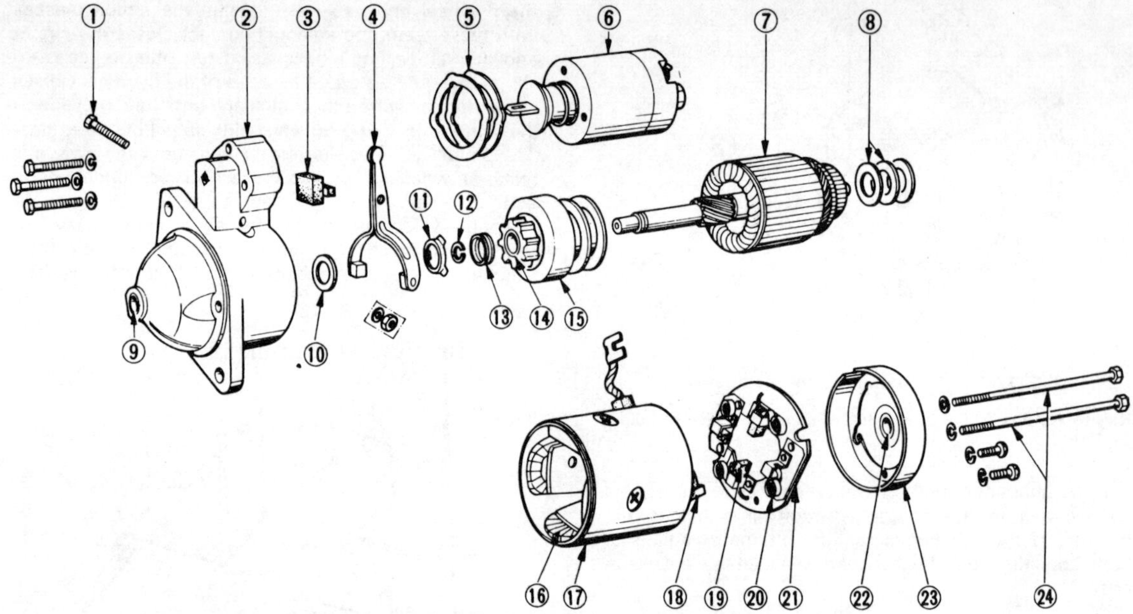

FIG 12:5 Types S114-103P and S114-126M starter motor components

Key to Fig 12:5 1 Engagement pin 2 Gear case 3 Spacer 4 Engagement lever 5 Spacer 6 Solenoid assembly 7 Armature 8 Thrust washer 9 Bush 10 Thrust washer 11 Stop washer 12 Circlip 13 Stop ring 14 Pinion 15 Overrunning clutch 16 Field coil 17 Yoke 18 Positive brush 19 Negative brush 20 Brush spring 21 Brush holder assembly 22 Bush 23 Rear cover 24 Through bolt

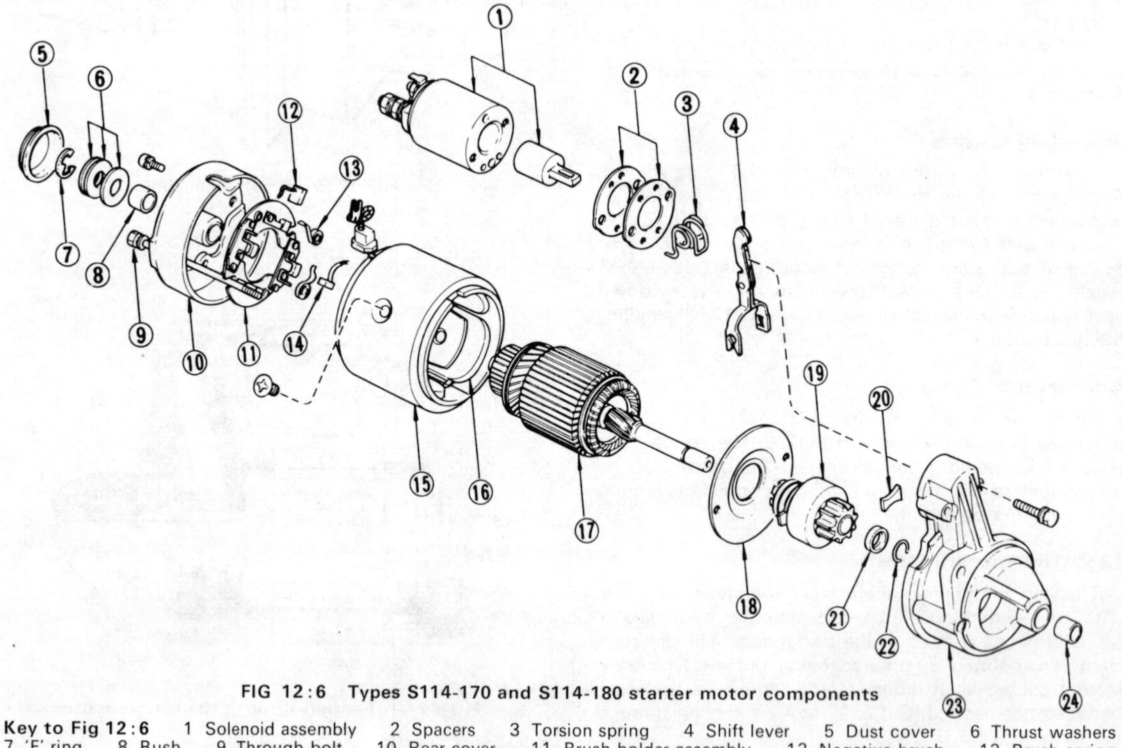

FIG 12:6 Types S114-170 and S114-180 starter motor components

Key to Fig 12:6 1 Solenoid assembly 2 Spacers 3 Torsion spring 4 Shift lever 5 Dust cover 6 Thrust washers 7 'E' ring 8 Bush 9 Through bolt 10 Rear cover 11 Brush holder assembly 12 Negative brush 13 Brush spring 14 Positive brush 15 Yoke 16 Field coil 17 Armature 18 Centre plate (type S114-180 only) 19 Pinion assembly 20 Spacer 21 Pinion stop ring 22 Clip 23 Gear case 24 Brush

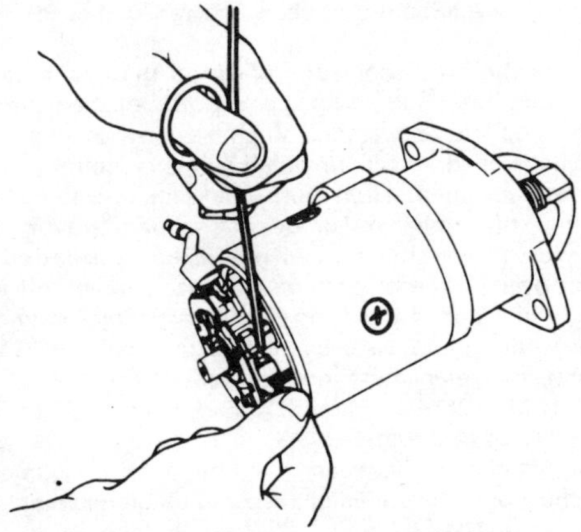

FIG 12:7 Brush removal

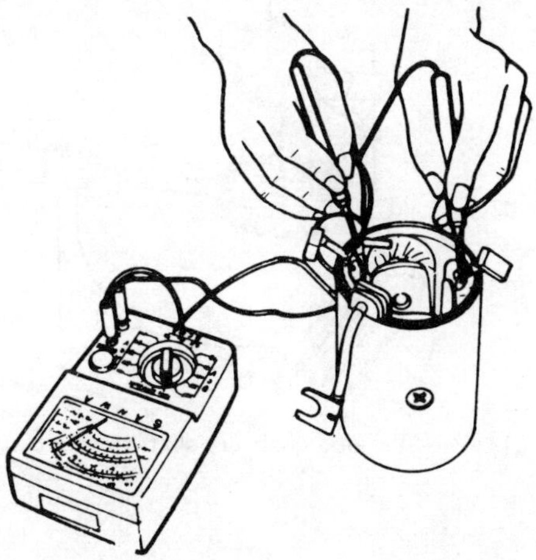

FIG 12:8 Testing field coil for continuity

starter motor can be overhauled to cure minor electrical or mechanical faults, but major faults will necessitate the fitting of a new or reconditioned unit.

Tests for an inoperative starter:

Check that the battery is in good condition and fully charged and that its connections are clean and tight. Switch on the headlamps and operate the starter switch. Current is reaching the starter if the lights go dim when the starter is operated, in which case it will be necessary to remove and service the starter as described later. If the lights do not dim significantly, switch them off and operate the starter switch while listening for a clicking sound at the starter motor which will indicate that the solenoid is operating.

If no sound can be heard at the starter when the switch is operated, check the wiring and connections between the battery and starter switch and between the switch and the solenoid.

If the solenoid can be heard operating when the starter switch is operated, check the wiring and connections between the battery and main starter motor terminals, taking care not to accidentally earth the battery to starter motor lead. If the wiring is not the cause of the trouble, the fault is internal and the starter must be removed and serviced as described later.

Starter removal:

Disconnect the earth cable from the battery terminal. Disconnect the black wire with yellow tracer and black battery cable from the starter motor solenoid. Remove the two securing bolts, then remove the starter motor assembly.

Dismantling:

FIGS 12:5 and **12:6** show the starter motor components. Remove the nut securing connecting plate to solenoid switch. Remove screws and detach solenoid assembly from starter motor body. On S114-170/180 types remove dust cover, 'E' ring and thrust washers. Remove two screws securing brush holder to rear cover. Remove through bolts and brush cover. Remove yoke

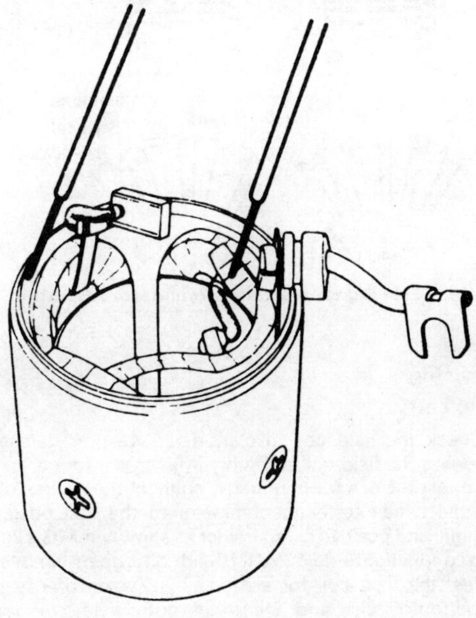

FIG 12:9 Testing field coil for earthing

assembly from case 2 by tapping gently with a wooden hammer handle. Withdraw the armature assembly complete with overrunning clutch mechanism and remove engagement lever.

Using a suitable piece of tube, drive stop ring towards the overrunning clutch, then remove circlip. Remove the pinion and overrunning clutch assembly from the armature shaft.

If the brushes are to be renewed, unsolder the brush lead connections then release brush spring pressure with a piece of wire as shown in **FIG 12:7** and remove the brushes.

Remove the brush holder from the starter yoke.

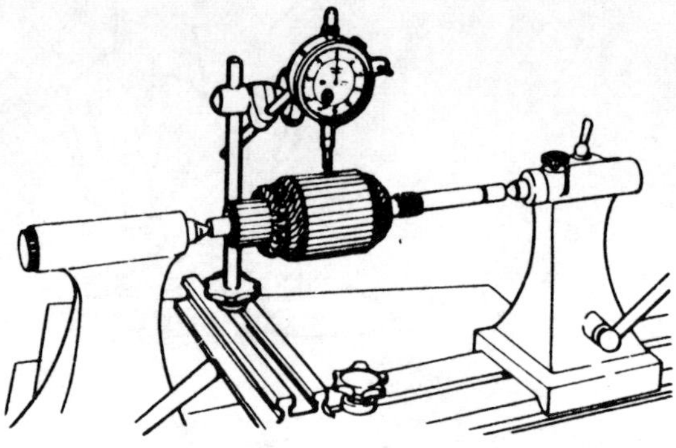

FIG 12:10 **Checking armature shaft for distortion**

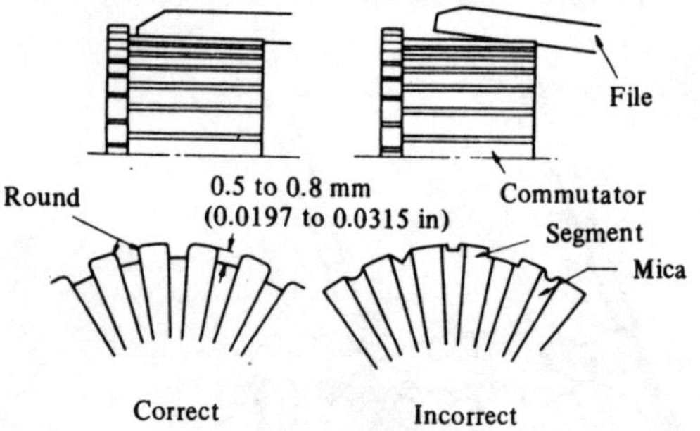

FIG 12:11 **Undercutting commutator insulation**

Servicing:

Field coil:

Check the field coil insulation for wear or damage, renewing the field coil assembly if faults are found.

To test the coil for continuity, connect the probes of a suitable circuit tester or ohmmeter to the coil positive terminal and positive brush holder as shown in **FIG 12:8**. If no conduction is indicated the field coil is open-circuited.

Test the field coil for earthing by placing one tester probe onto yoke and the other onto field coil lead (positive terminal), as shown in **FIG 12:9**. If very little resistance is indicated, the field coil is earthed.

If the tests indicate that the field coil assembly is faulty, it should be taken to a service station for repairs or renewal.

Armature:

Check the armature for charred insulation, loose segments or laminations and for scored laminations. Shortcircuited windings may be suspected if individual commutator segments are badly burned. Check the armature shaft for distortion using a dial gauge, mounting the armature between centres as shown in **FIG 12:10**. Armature shaft distortion is beyond limits if a reading of more than 0.08mm (0.0031in) is obtained in a full revolution of the armature. No repairs can be carried out to a defective armature or shaft and renewal is the only cure.

Check the brush contact surface on the commutator. The commutator should have a smooth polished surface which is dark in appearance. Wiping over with a piece of cloth moistened with methylated spirits or petrol will be sufficient cleaning. Light burn marks or scores can be polished off with fine grade glasspaper (**never use emerycloth as this leaves particles embedded in the copper**). Deeper damage may be skimmed off in a lathe, at high speed and using a very sharp tool. A diamond tipped tool should be used for a light final cut. Commutator diameter must not be reduced below: type S114-103P/126M—33mm (1.299in); type S114-170/180—31mm (1.220in).

The insulation between the commutator segments must be correctly undercut to a depth of between 0.5 and 0.8mm (0.0197 and 0.0315in), as shown in **FIG 12:11**. Clean away all dust on completion.

Brush gear:

Check the brushes for wear and renew them if they are less than: type S114-103P/126M—6mm (0.2362in); type S114-170/180—12mm (0.472in) in length or if they are contaminated. If the brushes stick in their holders, polish the sides of the brushes with a fine file and clean the brush holder with a piece of rag moistened with petrol or methylated spirits. Check brush spring tension by hooking a spring balance over the end of the spring which contacts the brush. When the spring is pulled to the top of the brush holder the reading should be at least 1.4kg (3.1lb). Renew any spring found to be weak or distorted.

Overrunning clutch:

Inspect the assembly for wear or damage. Light damage to the pinion teeth can be cleaned off with a fine file or oilstone, but deeper damage necessitates renewal of the complete drive assembly. The screw sleeve must slide freely along the armature shaft splines. If faults cannot be rectified by dressing off burrs or light damage, the

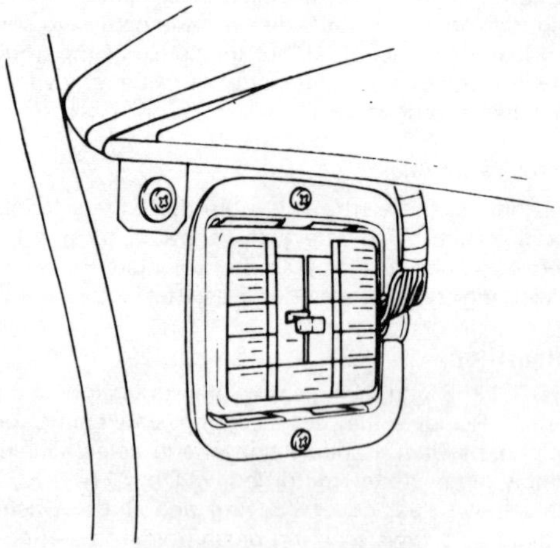

FIG 12:12 **Fuse box**

assembly must be renewed. Check that the clutch takes up drive instantaneously but slips freely in the opposite direction. Again the complete assembly must be renewed if the clutch is defective.

Bearings:

If the bushes are excessively worn, they should be renewed by a service station as press equipment, accurate mandrels and reaming tools are required to carry out the operation. Clearance between a bearing and the armature shaft must not exceed 0.2mm (0.0079in).

Reassembly and refitting:

This is a reversal of the removal and dismantling procedures. During assembly, apply grease to the bearing bushes and lightly oil the pinion mechanism.

12:5 The fuses

The fuse box is fitted with 10 separate fuses (see **FIG 12:12**).

If a fuse blows, briefly check the circuit that it protects and install a new fuse. Check each circuit in turn and if the new fuse does not blow, it is likely that the old one had weakened with age. If the fuse blows, carefully check the circuit that was live at the time and do not fit another fuse until the fault has been found and repaired. A fuse that blows intermittently will make it more difficult to correct the fault, but try shaking the wiring loom, as the fault is likely to be caused by chafed insulation allowing intermittent contact due to engine vibration or road shocks.

Never fit a fuse of higher rating than that specified. The fuse is designed to be the weak link in the circuit and if a higher rated fuse is installed the wiring may fail instead. The amperage rating is marked on each fuse.

In addition to the normal fuses just described, a fusible link is mounted on a relay bracket located at the front righthand side of the engine compartment (see **FIG 12:13**). The fusible link prevents long sections of wiring from being burned out in the event of a shortcircuit. The only section of wiring which can burn out under these conditions is the short length between the fusible link and the components it serves. When an electrical failure occurs, check the link after ensuring that the main fuses are intact, and renew if found burned out. Never wrap the fusible link wire with vinyl tape or other insulating material and make sure that the link does not contact any other part of the wiring harness or vinyl or rubber parts.

12:6 Windscreen wipers

The wiper motor is a two-speed unit controlled by a two position switch. If the wiper motor is inoperative, check the fuse, wiring and connections. If the motor runs but operation is slow, noisy or laborious, check the linkage from binding or damage.

Wiping area adjustment:

To adjust the wiping area, loosen the wiper arm set nut and adjust blade to correct installation angle to clear the lower part of the windscreen surround as shown in

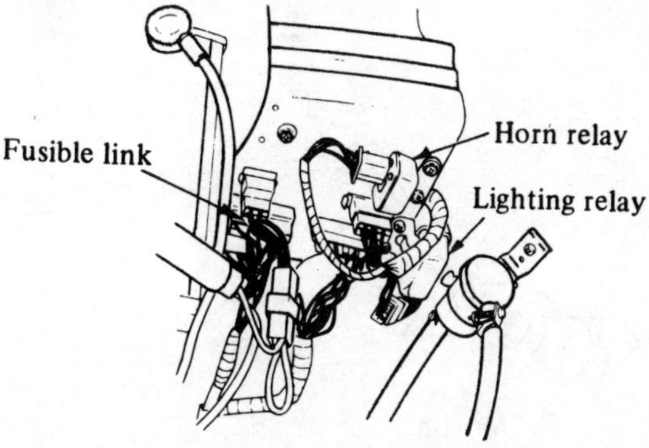

FIG 12:13 Fusible link location

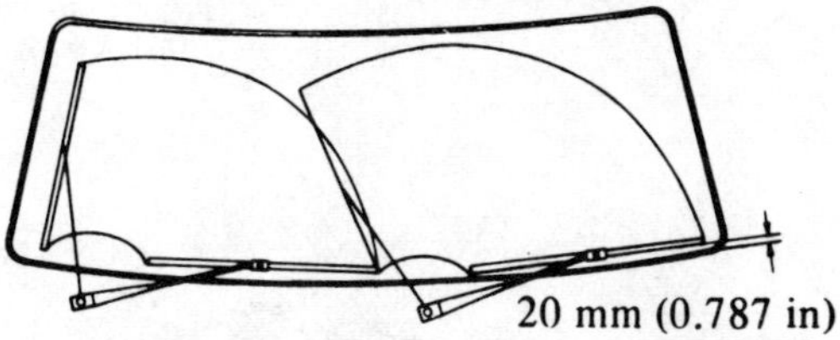

FIG 12:14 Wiper operating area adjustment

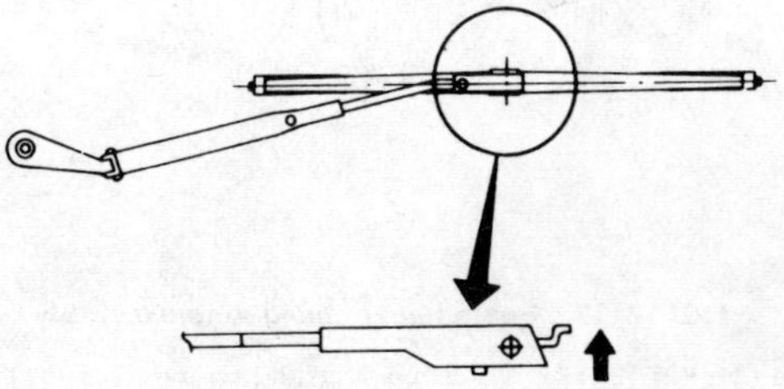

FIG 12:15 Wiper blade removal

FIG 12:14. On completion, tighten the set nut to 0.8 to 0.9kgm (5.8 to 6.5lb ft).

Wiper blade and arm removal:

To remove a wiper blade, lift the tab to release the lock and pull the blade from the end of the arm (see **FIG 12:15**).

To remove a wiper arm, raise the wiper blade from the windscreen and unscrew the arm set nut. The arm can then be pulled from the pivot. When refitting, be sure to set the arm and blade position correctly as shown in **FIG 12:14**.

Wiper motor removal:

Remove the wiper arms as described previously. Open the bonnet and disconnect the wiring from the wiper motor. Remove the retaining screws and detach the cowl top grille. Remove the three wiper motor retaining bolts,

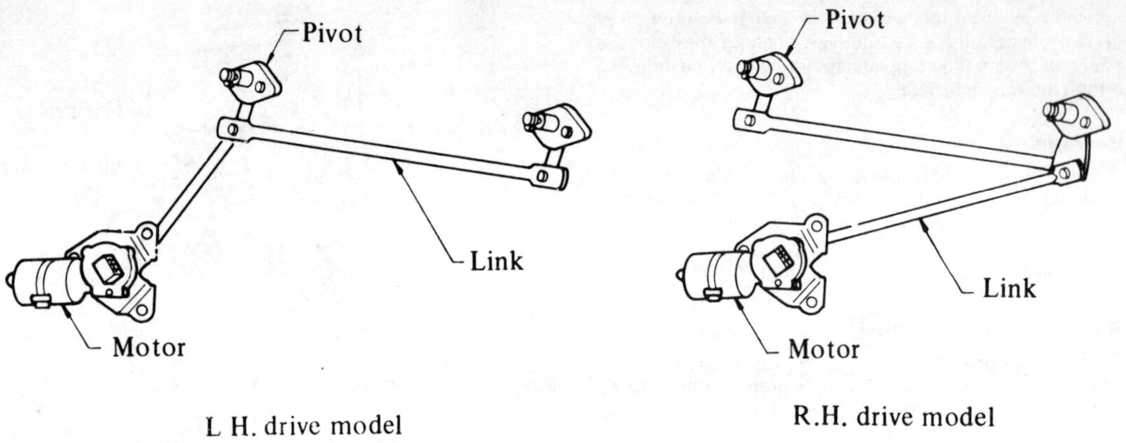

FIG 12:16 Wiper motor and linkage

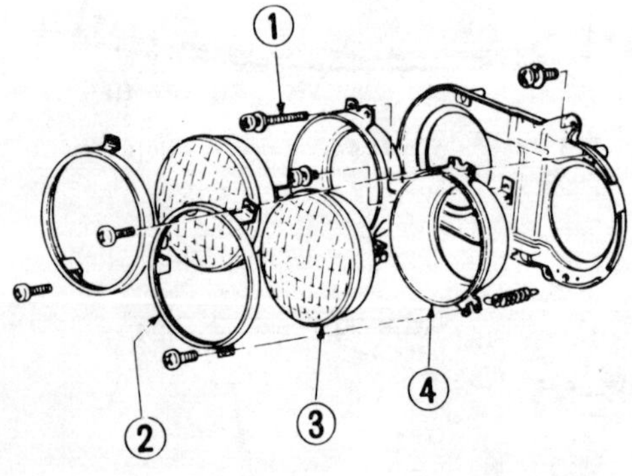

FIG 12:17 Sealed beam headlamp assembly

Key to Fig 12:17 1 Aiming adjusting screw 2 Headlamp retaining ring 3 Headlamp unit 4 Headlamp mounting ring

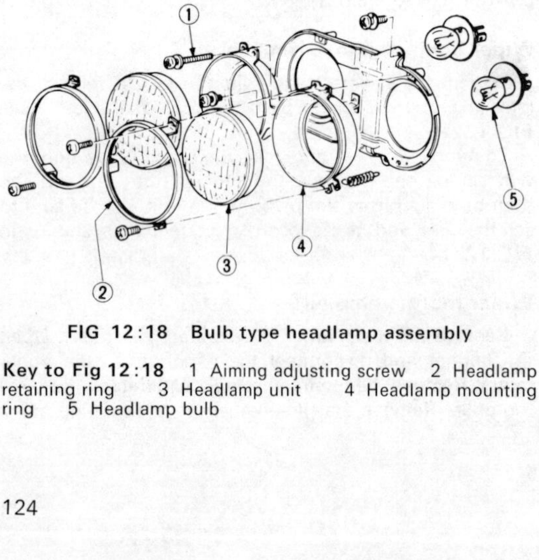

FIG 12:18 Bulb type headlamp assembly

Key to Fig 12:18 1 Aiming adjusting screw 2 Headlamp retaining ring 3 Headlamp unit 4 Headlamp mounting ring 5 Headlamp bulb

then pull the wiper motor assembly outwards a little and disconnect the motor from the linkage at the junction point. Remove two flange nuts attaching pivot to cowl top panel and detach the link assembly (see **FIG 12:16**).

Refitting is a reversal of the removal procedure.

12:7 Headlamps

The headlamp units may be of either the sealed beam type as shown in **FIG 12:17**, or of the separate bulb type as shown in **FIG 12:18**.

Sealed beam unit renewal:

Take out the retaining screws and remove the radiator grille. Loosen the three headlamp retaining ring screws. It is not necessary to remove these screws. Remove the retaining ring by rotating it clockwise. Do not disturb the headlamp aiming adjustment screws. Remove the headlamp unit from the mounting ring and disconnect wiring connector.

Fit the new headlamp unit and connect the wiring connector. Fit the headlamp in position so that the three location tabs behind the unit locate with the three hollows on the mounting ring. Make sure that the 'Top' mark on the headlamp lens is uppermost. Fit the retaining ring by rotating clockwise and tighten the retaining screws. Refit the radiator grille.

Headlamp bulb renewal:

Take out the retaining screws and remove the radiator grille. Loosen but do not remove the three headlamp retaining screws. Remove the retaining ring by rotating clockwise. Do not disturb the headlamp aiming adjustment screws. Remove the headlamp unit and disconnect the wiring connector. Remove the boot from the rear of the headlamp. Rotate the bulb socket clockwise to remove the bulb.

Fit the new bulb to the socket and fit the wiring connector. Fit the headlamp unit in place so that the three location tabs locate with the three hollows on the mounting ring. The 'Top' mark on the lens must be uppermost. Refit the retaining ring by rotating clockwise and tighten the retaining screws. Refit the radiator grille.

Headlamp beam setting:

The headlamp beam angles are adjusted by means of the appropriate adjustment screw which is shown in **FIGS 12:17** or **12:18**.

Headlamp main beams should be set so that when the car is normally loaded the main beams are parallel to each other and to the road. The dipped beams should be set so that they provide a good spread of light to the front and nearside of the car without dazzling oncoming drivers. Accurate beam-setting is best left to a service station having special optical equipment.

12:8 Lighting circuits

Lamps give insufficient light:

Refer to **Section 12:2** and check the condition of the battery, recharging it if necessary. Check the setting of the headlamps as described in **Section 12:7** and renew any lamp units or bulbs which have darkened with age.

Bulbs burn out frequently:

Have the regulator setting checked by an auto-electrical service station.

Lamps light when switched on but gradually fade:

Refer to **Section 12:2** and check the battery, as it is not capable of supplying current for any length of time.

Lamp brilliance varies with the speed of the car:

Check the condition of the battery and its connections. Make sure that the connections are clean and tight and renew any faulty cables.

12:9 Fault diagnosis

(a) Battery discharged

1 Terminal connection loose or dirty
2 Shorts in light circuits
3 Alternator not charging
4 Regulator faulty
5 Battery internally defective

(b) Insufficient charge rate

1 Check 1 and 4 in (a)
2 Drive belt slipping
3 Alternator diodes defective

(c) Battery will not hold charge

1 Low electrolyte level
2 Battery plates sulphated
3 Electrolyte leakage from cracked case
4 Battery plate separators defective

(d) Battery overcharged

1 Regulator faulty

(e) Alternator output low or nil

1 Belt broken or slipping
2 Regulator needs adjusting
3 Brushes sticking, spring weak or broken
4 Defective rotor or stator windings
5 Defective diode(s)

(f) Starter motor lacks power or will not turn

1 Battery discharged, loose cable connections
2 Starter switch or solenoid faulty
3 Brushes worn or sticking, leads detached or shorting
4 Commutator dirty or worn
5 Starter shaft bent
6 Engine abnormally stiff, perhaps due to rebore

(g) Starter runs but will not turn engine

1 Pinion engagement mechanism faulty
2 Broken teeth on pinion or flywheel gears

(h) Noisy starter when engine is running

1 Pinion return mechanism faulty

(j) Starter motor inoperative

1 Check 1 and 4 in (f)
2 Armature or field coils faulty

(k) Starter motor rough or noisy

1 Mounting bolts loose
2 Pinion engagement mechanism faulty
3 Damaged pinion or flywheel teeth

(l) Lamps inoperative or erratic

1 Battery low, bulbs burned out
2 Faulty earthing of lamps or battery
3 Lighting switch faulty, loose or broken connections

(m) Wiper motor sluggish, taking high current

1 Wiper motor defective internally
2 Lack of lubrication
3 Linkage worn or binding
4 Wiper motor fixing bolts loose

(n) Wiper motor runs but does not drive arms

1 Wiper linkage faulty
2 Wiper transmission components worn

(o) Gauges do not work

1 Check wiring for continuity
2 Check instruments and transmitters for continuity

NOTES

CHAPTER 13

THE BODYWORK

13:1 Bodywork finish

Large scale repairs to body panels are best left to expert panel beaters. Even small dents can be tricky, as too much hammering will stretch the metal and make things worse instead of better. If panel beating is to be attempted, use a dolly on the opposite side of the panel. The head of a large hammer will suffice for small dents, but for large dents a heavy block of metal will be necessary. Use light hammer blows to reshape the panel, pressing the dolly against the opposite side of the panel to absorb the blows. If this method is used to reduce the depth of dents, final smoothing with a suitable filler will be easier, although it may be better to avoid hammering minor dents and just use the filler.

Clean the area to be filled, making sure that it is free from paint, rust and grease, then roughen the area with emerycloth or a file to ensure a good bond. Use a proprietary fibreglass filler paste mixed according to the instructions and press it into the dent with a putty knife. Allow the filler to stand proud of the surrounding area to allow for rubbing down after hardening. Use a file and emerycloth or a disc sander to blend the repaired area to the surrounding bodywork, using finer grade abrasives as the work nears completion. Apply a coat of primer surfacer and, when it is dry, rub down with 'Wet-or-Dry' paper lubricated with soapy water, finishing with 400 grade. Apply more primer and repeat the operation until the surface is perfectly smooth. Take time in achieving the best finish possible at this stage as it will control the final effect.

The touching-up of paintwork can be carried out with self-spraying cans of paint, these being available in a wide range of colours. Use a piece of newspaper or board as a test panel to practise on first, so that the action of the spray will be familiar when it is used on the panel. Before spraying the panel, remove all traces of wax polish. Mask off large areas such as windows with newspaper and masking tape. Small areas such as trim strips or door handles can be wrapped with masking tape or carefully coated with grease or petroleum jelly. Apply the touching-up paint, spraying with short bursts and keeping the spray moving. Do not attempt to cover the area in one coat, applying several successive coats with a few minutes drying time between each. If too much paint is applied at one time, runs will develop. If so, do not try to remove the run by wiping, but wait until it is dry and rub down as before.

After the final coat has been applied, allow a few hours of drying time before blending the new finish to the old

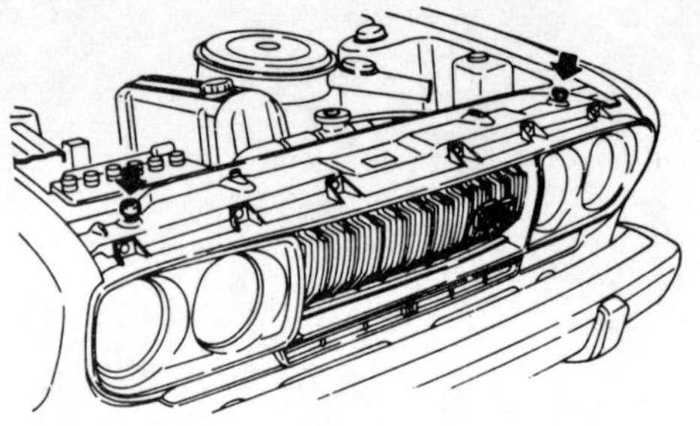

FIG 13:1 The bonnet rubber buffers

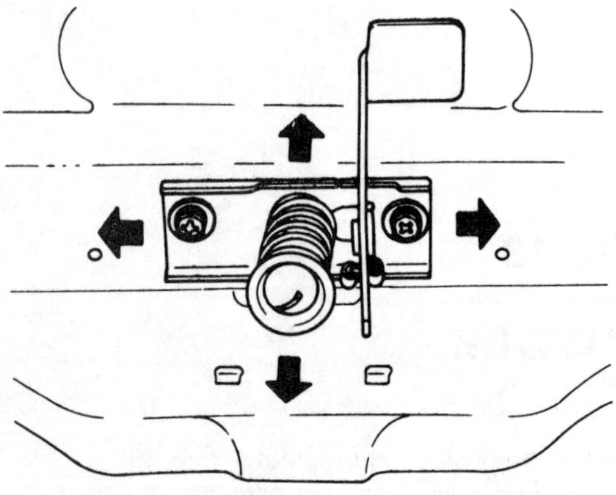

FIG 13:2 Adjusting dovetail bolt position

with fine cutting compound and a cloth, buffing with a light, circular motion. Leave the paint to harden for a period of weeks rather than days before applying wax polish.

13:2 Bonnet and luggage compartment lid

Bonnet removal:

Raise the bonnet and mark the outline of the hinge plates on the bonnet panel so that the bonnet can be refitted in its original position. Have an assistant steady the bonnet, then remove the fixing bolts and lift the bonnet away. Refit the bonnet in the reverse order of removal, aligning the hinge plate with the marks made before removal.

Bonnet adjustment:

The bonnet should be adjusted so that it is correctly centred in the aperture and its sides are flush with the surrounding bodywork. Mark the outline of the hinge plates on the panel before loosening the fixing bolts, so that the bonnet can be realigned in its original position if necessary. Slacken the fixing bolts just enough to allow the panel to be moved relative to the hinge plates. Adjust the bonnet position as necessary, then tighten the fixing bolts and check for correct bonnet alignment.

To adjust the height of the front of the bonnet in the closed position, the bonnet lock setting must be modified in the following manner. With the bonnet correctly aligned in the aperture as described previously, loosen the bonnet buffer locknuts and lower the buffers so that they are not contacted by the bonnet when it is closed (see **FIG 13:1**). Lower the bonnet slowly to check that the dovetail bolt aligns correctly with the lockplate. If not, loosen the dovetail bolt mounting plate bolts just enough to allow the plate to be moved (see **FIG 13:2**). Move the plate to correct the alignment of the dovetail bolt, then firmly tighten the securing bolts. Close the bonnet and check the alignment of the front of the bonnet with the wing panels on each side. If necessary, slacken the locknut and turn the dovetail bolt by means of the slot in its tapered end until the bonnet panel is between 1 and 3mm (0.039 and 0.118in) below the top of the front wings. Tighten the locknut to secure the adjustment. Now, raise the two bonnet buffers until the bonnet closes flush with the front wings. Check the bonnet operation several times and make certain that full engagement is obtained between the dovetail bolt and the lockplate. If not, readjust the dovetail bolt as necessary. Make sure that the safety catch lever retains the bonnet properly when the bonnet lock is disengaged.

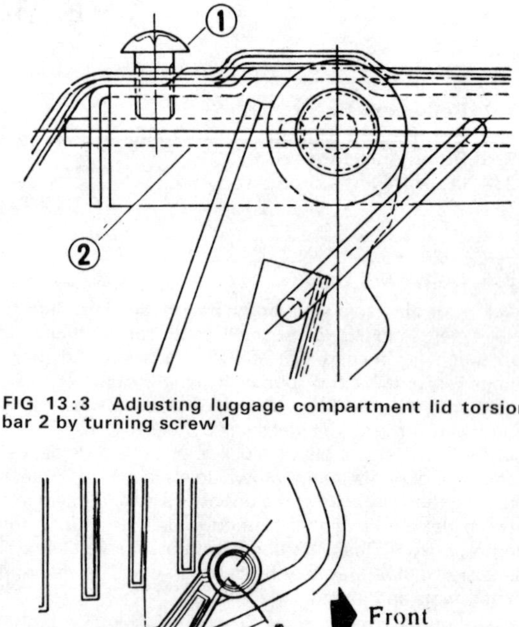

FIG 13:3 Adjusting luggage compartment lid torsion bar 2 by turning screw 1

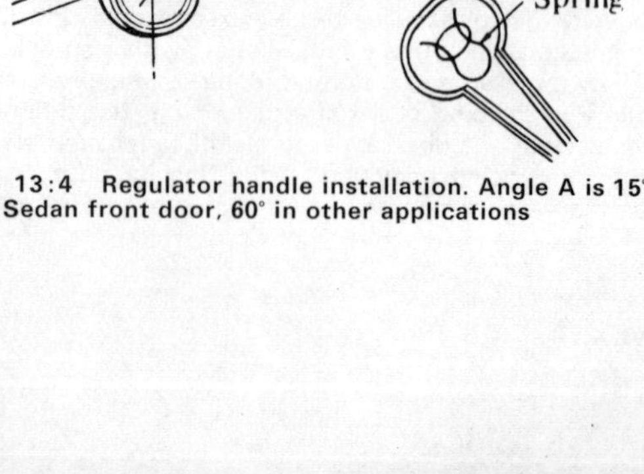

FIG 13:4 Regulator handle installation. Angle A is 15° for Sedan front door, 60° in other applications

Luggage compartment lid:

Removal and adjustment of the luggage compartment lid is carried out in a similar manner to that described previously for the bonnet panel. If the lid does not fit snugly against the weatherstrip on the body panels, loosen the fixing bolts and move the lock striker plate as necessary. Tighten the fixing bolts securely then close the lid to check for correct fit.

When the lock is operated to open the luggage compartment, the lid should spring up by a small amount. If not, the torsion bar tension can be increased by turning the adjusting screw on the hinge bracket clockwise (see **FIG 13:3**).

13:3 Removing door trim

Open the door fully. Lift lock knob and remove grommet, then turn lock knob anticlockwise. Remove lock knob and grommet on Sedan models. Remove the hand grip on Sedan models or armrest on Hardtop models. Remove the securing screw and detach the inside handle escutcheon. On rear door, remove ashtray.

Use a suitable wire hook to remove the spring clip and detach regulator handle and washer (see **FIG 13:4**). Remove the door trim pad by inserting a screwdriver blade between pad and door panel, then carefully levering away from retaining clips. If necessary, remove water seal from door panel.

Refit the trim pad in the reverse order of removal. If the water seal is damaged or shows signs of leakage it should be renewed. With the door glass raised fully, set the regulator handle at the correct angle as shown in **FIG 13:4**.

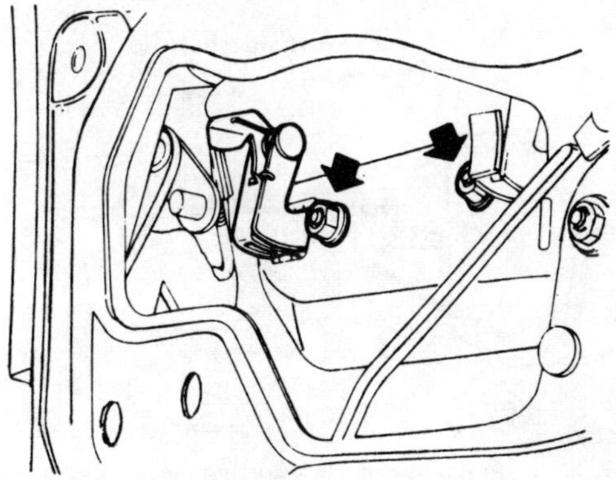

FIG 13:5 Removing outside door handle

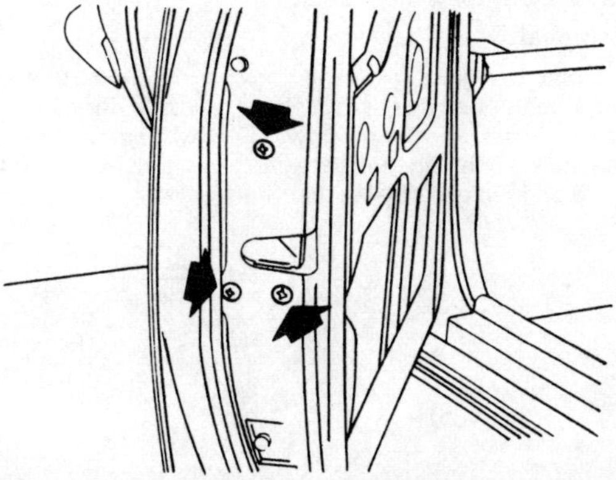

FIG 13:6 Removing door lock assembly

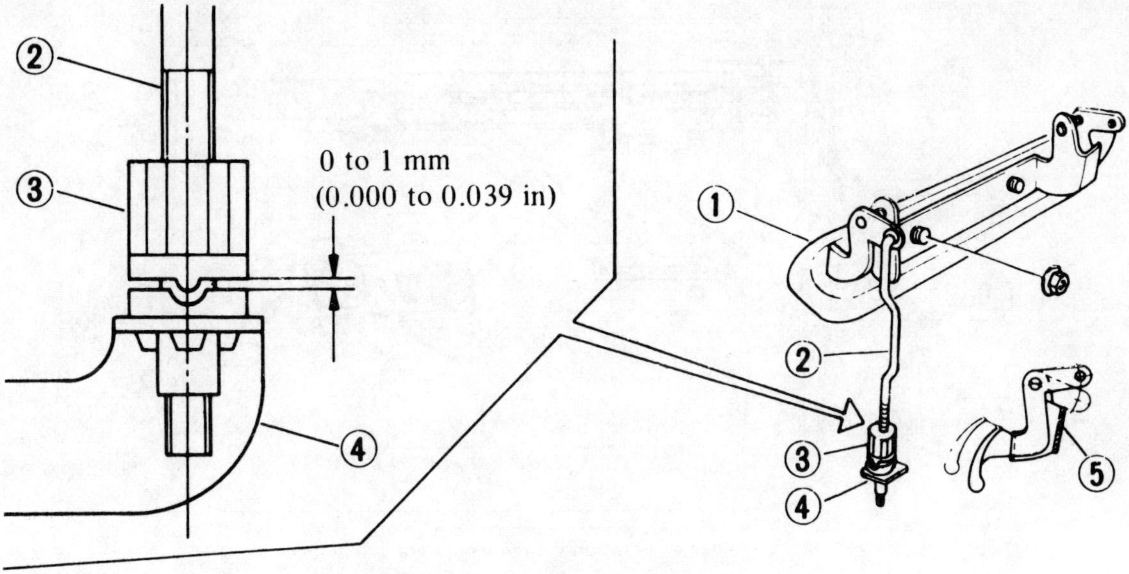

FIG 13:7 Adjusting outside door handle free play

Key to Fig 13:7 1 Outside door handle 2 Remote control rod 3 Nylon adjusting nut 4 Lock lever 5 Stopper

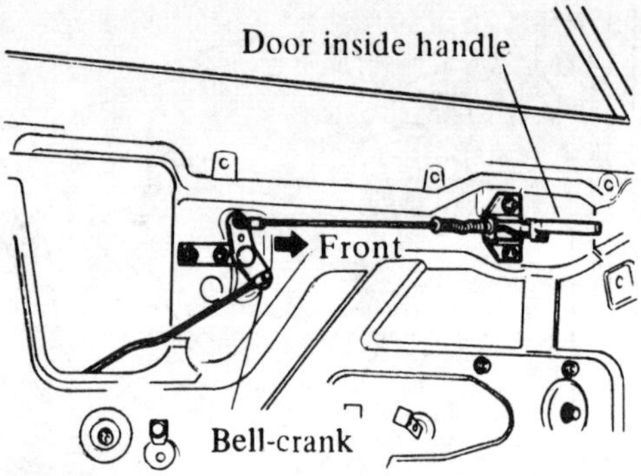

FIG 13:8 Adjusting inside door handle on Sedan and Station Wagon models

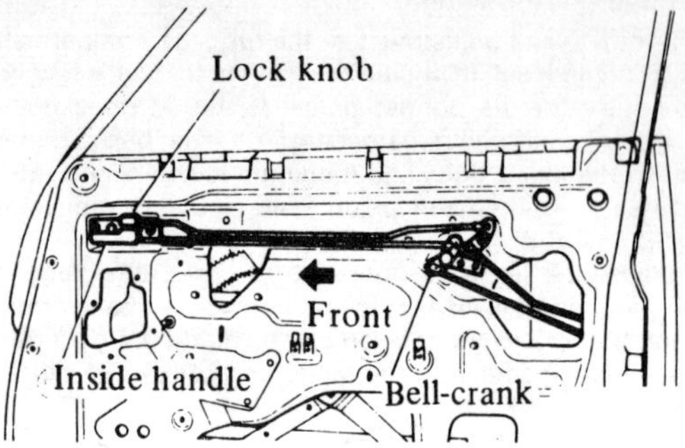

FIG 13:9 Adjusting inside door handle on Hardtop models

13:4 Door lock mechanism

Removal:

Open the door fully and remove the door trim as described in **Section 13:3**. Remove inside door handle and bellcrank attaching screws. Remove remote control and lock knob rod. Remove the nuts arrowed in **FIG 13:5** and remove outside door handle.

Remove screws arrowed in **FIG 13:6** and detach door lock assembly.

Refitting is a reversal of the removal procedure. Apply a thin smear of multi-purpose grease to all moving parts.

Adjustment:

To adjust outside door handle, refer to **FIG 13:7** and

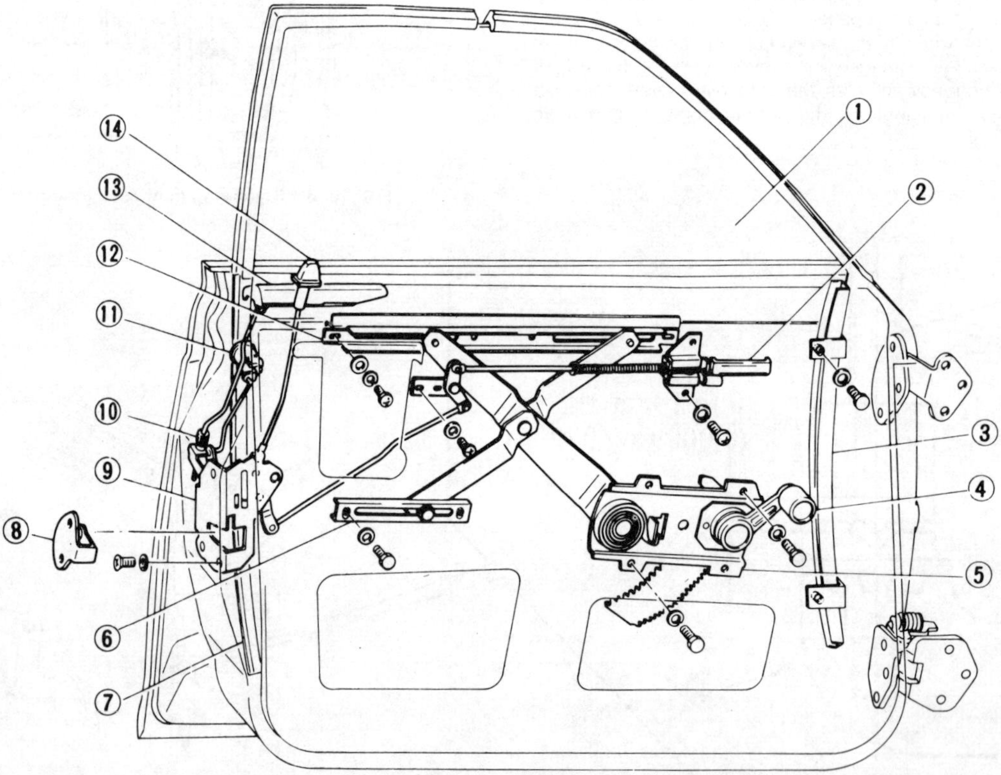

FIG 13:10 Sedan and Station Wagon front door components

Key to Fig 13:10 1 Door glass 2 Inside door handle 3 Front lower sash 4 Regulator handle 5 Regulator assembly 6 Guide channel A 7 Rear lower sash 8 Door lock striker 9 Door lock assembly 10 Adjusting nut 11 Door lock cylinder 12 Guide channel B 13 Outside door handle 14 Inside door lock knob turn nylon adjusting nut to obtain clearance of 0 to 1mm (0 to 0.039in).

To adjust inside door handle, refer to **FIG 13:8** or **13:9**. Remove the door trim as described in **Section 13:3**, then move the inside door lock knob to the locked position. Move bellcrank in elongated hole towards front of door as far as it will go. Tighten bellcrank retaining screws in this position, then check the operation of inside door handle and lock.

The door lock striker can be moved vertically and horizontally to adjust closed position of door. Slacken the screws, move the striker plate as necessary then firmly tighten the screws. Scribe around the striker plate before moving it so that it can be realigned in its original position if necessary.

13:5 Door glass and regulator removal

Sedan and Station Wagon front door:

Lower the door glass then remove the trim pad as described in **Section 13:3**. Remove outside door moulding and weatherstrip.

Refer to **FIG 13:10**. Remove fixing screws and detach front lower sash 3 from door glass. It is not necessary to

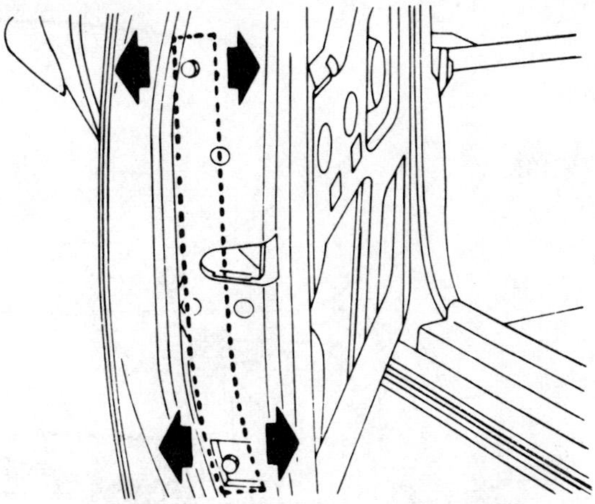

FIG 13:11 Rear lower sash adjustment

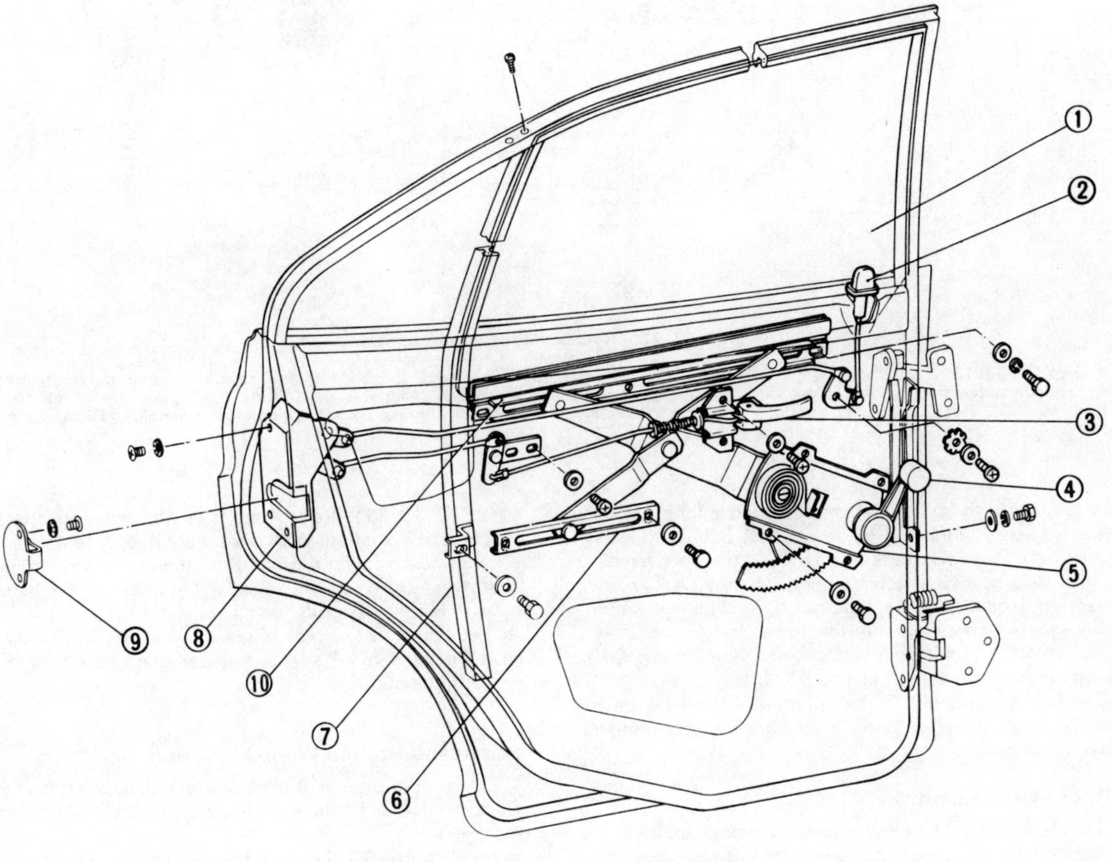

FIG 13:12 Sedan rear door components

Key to Fig 13:12 1 Door glass 2 Inside door lock knob 3 Inside door handle 4 Regulator handle 5 Regulator assembly 6 Guide channel A 7 Centre sash 8 Door lock assembly 9 Door lock striker 10 Guide channel B

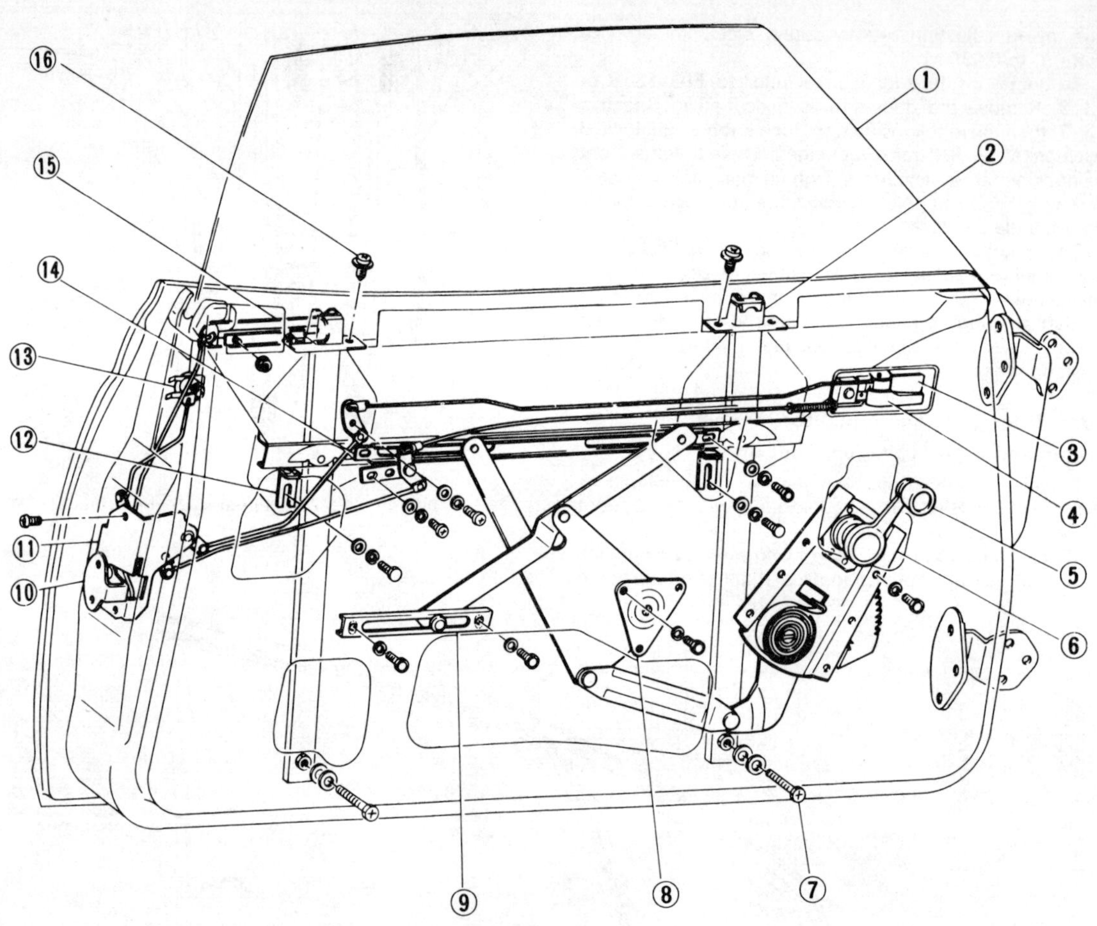

FIG 13:13 **Hardtop door components**

Key to Fig 13:13 1 Door glass 2 Guide rail 3 Inside door lock knob 4 Inside door handle 5 Regulator handle 6 Regulator assembly 7 Adjusting bolt 8 Regulator arm base 9 Guide channel A 10 Door lock striker 11 Door lock assembly 12 Door glass upper stopper 13 Door lock cylinder 14 Guide channel B 15 Outside door handle 16 Adjusting bolt

remove the sash from door panel. Support door glass and remove screws retaining guide channel B (12) to glass backplate. Raise the glass and remove from door panel.

Remove screws attaching guide channel A (6) and base of regulator 5, then remove regulator assembly through lower opening of inside door panel. If necessary, remove front and rear lower sashes. Rear lower sash fixing screws are shown in **FIG 13:11**.

Refit the regulator and door glass in the reverse order of removal, carrying out the adjustment procedures described next.

Door glass adjustment:

Correct fit of window glass in door aperture is obtained by adjusting front and rear lower sashes and guide channel A. Temporarily tighten front and rear lower sashes, then raise glass fully. Adjust rear lower sash from side to side to align with glass and front lower sash (see **FIG 13:11**). Raise and lower the glass to check for smooth operation. With glass fully raised, set the top of glass parallel with top of door frame by moving guide channel A up or down. Raise guide channel if rear of glass is low, lower guide channel if front of glass is low. Adjust sideways free play of glass by moving front lower sash fore and aft. Raise and lower glass to check for smooth operation.

Sedan and Station Wagon rear door:

Lower door glass and remove trim pad as described in **Section 13:3**. Remove door outside weatherstrip and rear sash.

Refer to **FIG 13:12**. Remove screws attaching centre sash 7 and guide channel B (10) to glass backplate and remove door glass from door. Remove screws attaching guide channel A (6) and base of regulator 5, then remove regulator assembly from lower opening of inside door panel.

Refit regulator and door glass in the reverse order of removal, carrying out the adjustment procedures described previously for front door assemblies.

Hardtop front door:

Lower door glass and remove trim pad as described in **Section 13:3**. Remove outside door moulding.

Refer to **FIG 13:13**. Raise glass until upper glass stoppers 12 on each side appear in upper opening of inside door panel. Remove upper glass stoppers. Lower glass fully, then support glass and remove screws attaching glass backplate to guide channel B (14). Lift the door glass to remove it from door panel.

Remove bolts 7 and 16 from guide rails 2 on each side, then remove guide rails from door. Remove screws attaching guide channel A (9), regulator arm base 8 and base of regulator 6, then remove regulator assembly through lower opening of inside door panel.

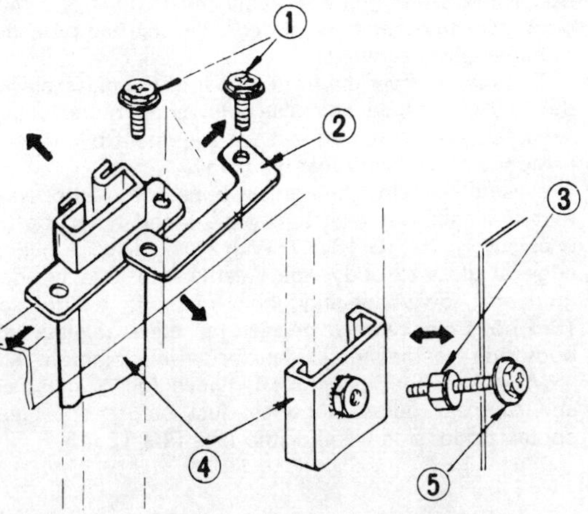

FIG 13:14 Guide rail adjustment mechanism

Key to Fig 13:14 1 Upper adjusting bolts 2 Spacer 3 Locknut 4 Guide rail 5 Lower adjusting bolt

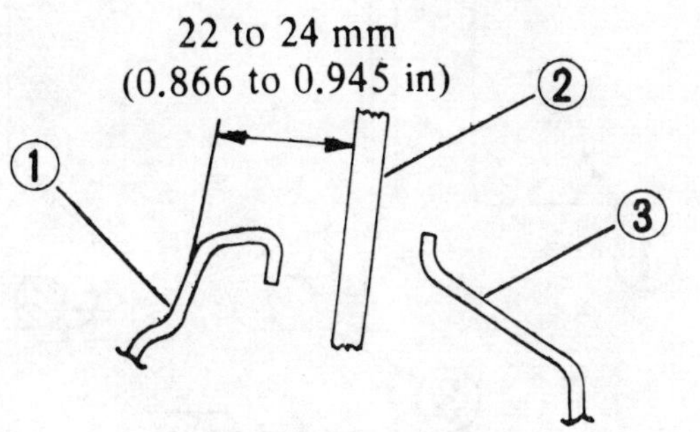

FIG 13:15 Correct clearance between glass and door panel

Key to Fig 13:15 1 Outside door panel 2 Glass 3 Inside door panel

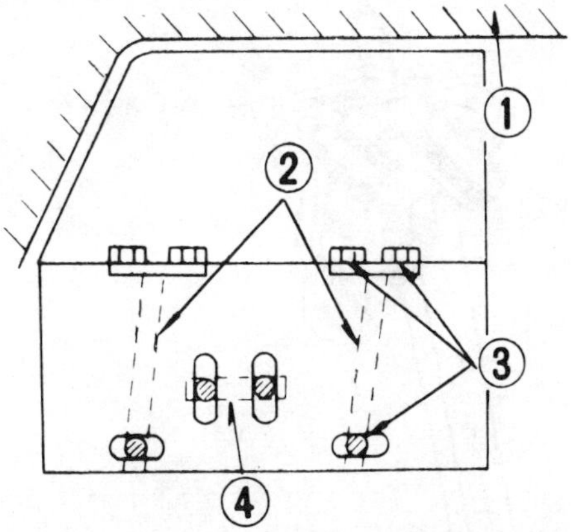

FIG 13:16 Hardtop front door glass adjustment

Key to Fig 13:16 1 Body side weatherstrip 2 Guide rail 3 Guide rail adjusting bolts 4 Guide channel A

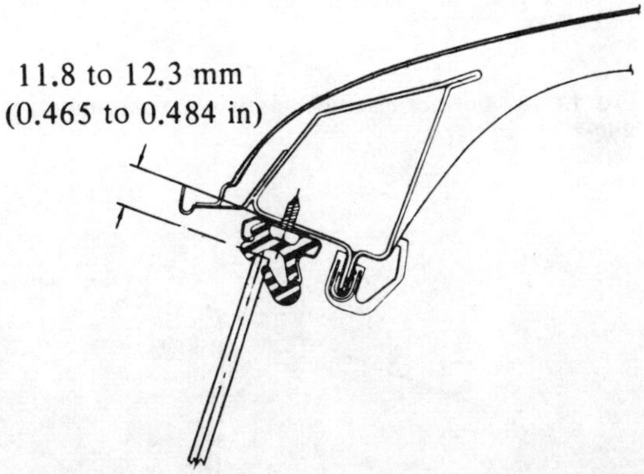

FIG 13:17 Correct clearance between glass and outer roof rail

Install regulator assembly, guide rails and door glass in the reverse order of removal, carrying out the adjustment procedures described next.

Door glass adjustment:

Refer to **FIG 13:14**. With door glass fully raised, temporarily tighten upper and lower guide rail adjustment bolts in the neutral positions. For upper bolts this is the centre of the elongated holes. The lower adjusting bolt should be tightened fully, then loosened by four complete turns and the locknut tightened to secure.

Now adjust guide rail upper adjusting bolts so that clearance between outside door panel and outside face of glass is as shown in **FIG 13:15**. Fit outside door finisher in place and make sure that outside door weatherstrip makes proper contact with door glass when glass is raised and lowered. Raise door glass fully and align with body weatherstrip to obtain an accurate fit. Adjustment is carried out at the guide rail and guide channel A as shown in **FIG 13:16**.

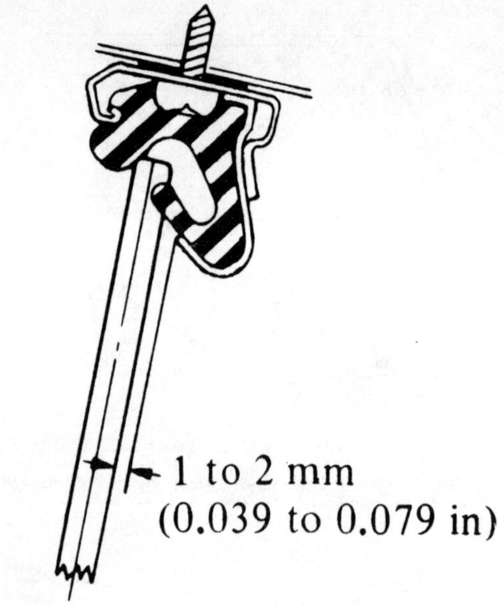

FIG 13:18 Correct clearance between glass and glass guide

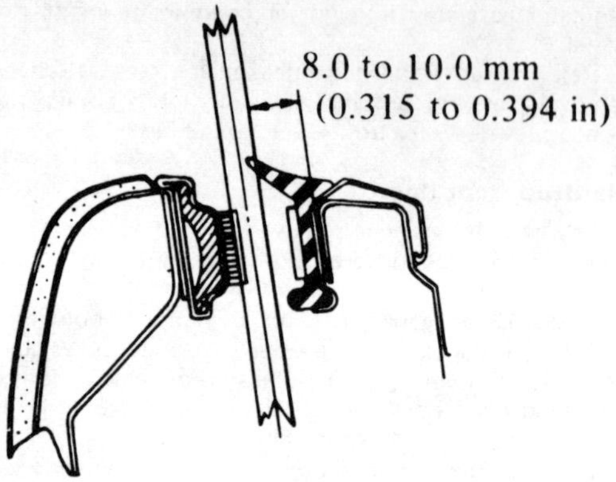

FIG 13:20 Correct clearance between glass and rear wing

To move glass forwards in aperture, slacken both upper and lower guide rail adjustment bolts and move guide rails towards front of door. Reverse the procedure to move glass rearwards.

To raise or lower the front or rear of the glass, slacken the adjustment bolts and raise or lower the guide channel A as necessary, then correct the alignment by adjusting positions of front and rear guide rails.

Raise glass fully, then adjust upper glass stoppers so that clearance between top of glass and outer roof rail is as shown in **FIG 13:17**. With glass raised, move top edge of glass to body side weatherstrip. Evenly adjust guide rail lower adjusting bolt to obtain a tight seal. Turn bolts clockwise to release top edge of glass from body side weatherstrip or anticlockwise to tighten.

Make sure that clearance between top of glass and end of glass guide is correct just before door glass contacts door side weatherstrip (see **FIG 13:18**).

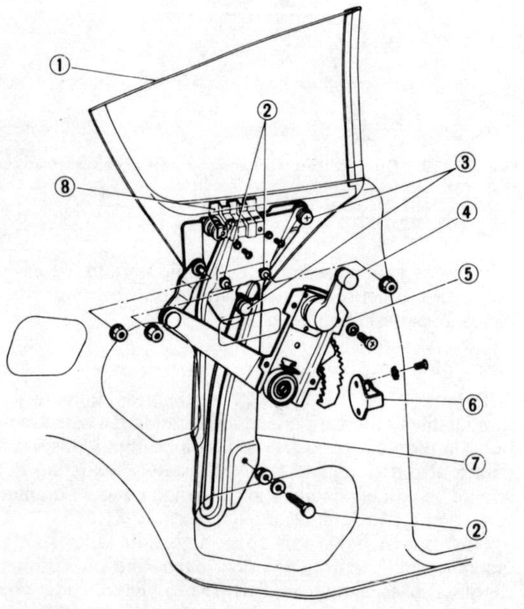

FIG 13:19 Hardtop rear side window glass and regulator components

Key to Fig 13:19 1 Door glass 2 Adjusting bolts 3 Guide roller 4 Regulator handle 5 Regulator assembly 6 Door lock striker 7 Guide plate 8 Trim fixing bracket

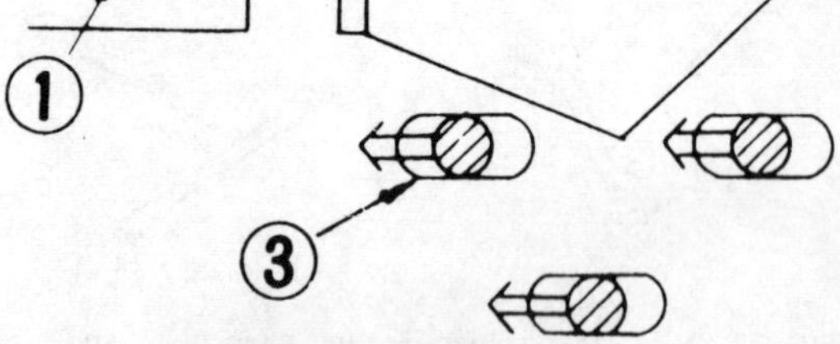

FIG 13:21 Rear side window glass adjustment

Key to Fig 13:21 1 Door glass 2 Side window glass 3 Guide plate adjusting bolt

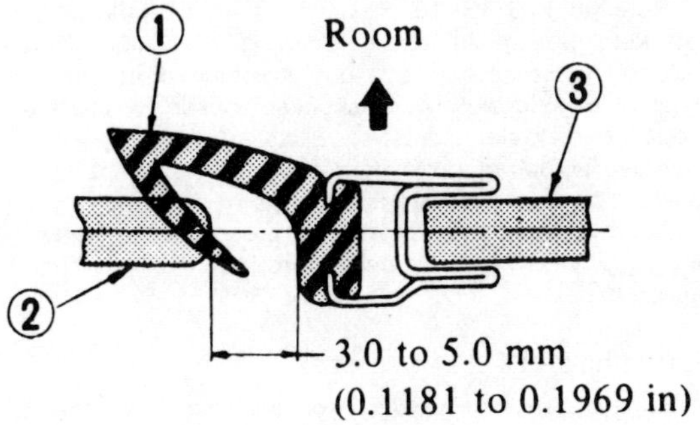

FIG 13:22 Correct side window glass to weatherstrip clearance

Key to Fig 13:22 1 Weatherstrip 2 Door glass 3 Side window glass

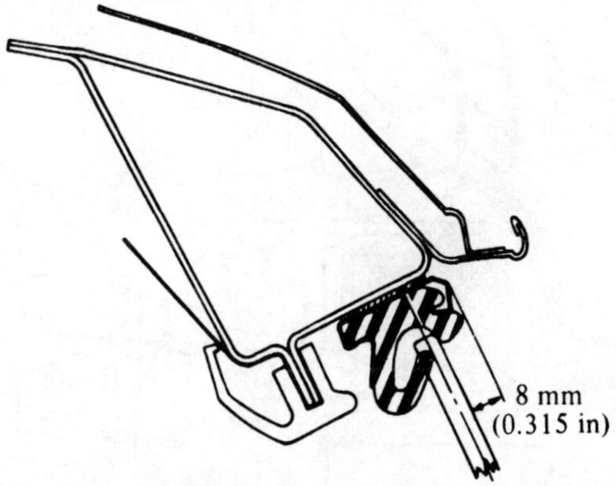

FIG 13:23 Correct glass to weatherstrip retainer clearance

Raise and lower door glass to check smoothness of operation. The force needed at the regulator handle knob to move the glass should be less than 3.5kg (7.7lb). If greater effort is needed, lubricate guide rollers, guide rails and regulator linkage, then perform outside and inside weatherstrip to door glass adjustments. Make sure that guide rails are adjusted in parallel and that upper glass stoppers are properly aligned.

Hardtop rear window and regulator:

Removal:

Remove rear seat cushion and backrest from body. Remove lap belt if fitted. Remove kicking plate. Remove rear finishers. Lower window glass fully, then remove armrest and regulator handle. Remove rear side finisher and water seal.

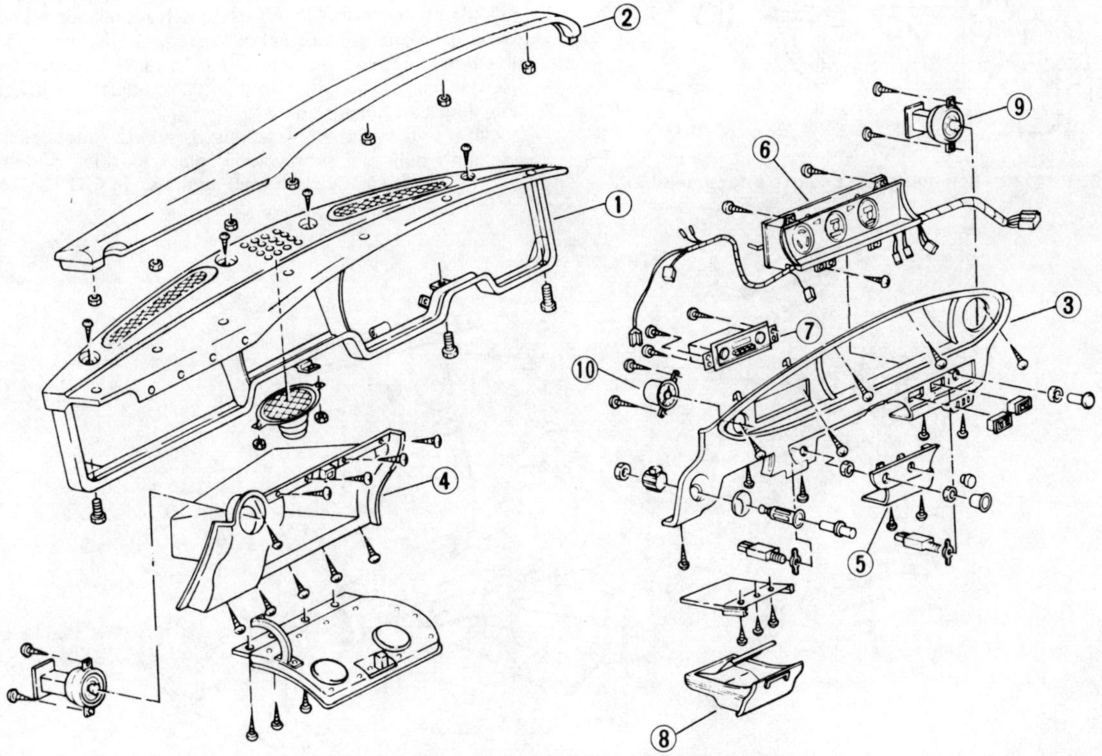

FIG 13:24 Instrument panel and facia components

Key to Fig 13:24 1 Facia assembly 2 Panel pad 3 Instrument panel 4 Glove compartment 5 Lower panel 6 Instrument housing 7 Radio (optional) 8 Ashtray 9 Ventilator grille 10 Clock

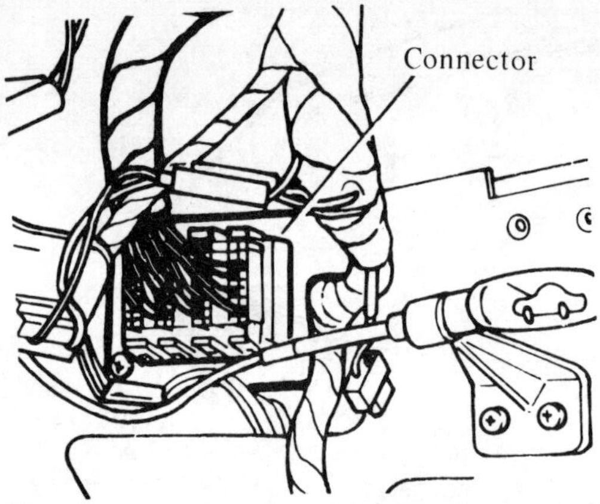

FIG 13:25 Body and instrument wiring harness connector

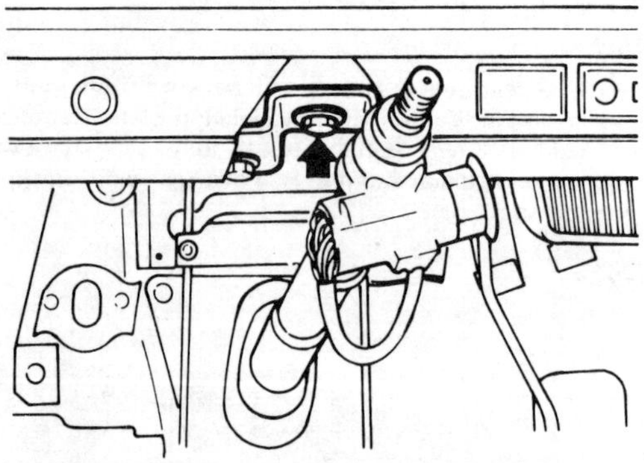

FIG 13:26 Removing facia centre attachment bolt

Refer to **FIG 13:19**. Raise glass until regulator arm bracket appears in upper opening of inside panel. Support glass and remove nut attaching regulator arm bracket to side window backplate. Loosen locknuts on upper and lower adjusting bolts of guide plate 7. Remove adjusting bolts from guide plate. Lift window glass and remove towards passenger compartment.

Remove attaching screws from base of regulator 5 then remove regulator assembly through lower opening of inside panel.

Refitting:

This is a reversal of the removal procedure, carrying out the adjustment procedures described next.

Side window glass adjustment:

With window glass lowered, temporarily tighten guide plate adjusting bolts in the neutral positions, this being in the centre of the elongated holes. Tighten these bolts all the way then loosen the two upper bolts by five complete turns and the single lower bolt by 11 complete turns. Secure the bolts in these positions. Adjust guide plate upper adjusting bolt to obtain correct clearance between window glass and rear wing as shown in **FIG 13:20**.

Close front door and raise door glass and side window glass fully. Align side window glass with door window glass and body side weatherstrip by adjusting guide plate adjusting bolts as shown in **FIG 13:21**. Adjust according to the arrows to move side glass forwards, or in the reverse direction to move glass rearwards. To raise or lower the front or rear of the side window glass, adjust the lower adjusting bolt position only.

With side window glass raised, adjust guide plate adjusting bolts so that window glass to side window weatherstrip clearance is correct as shown in **FIG 13:22**.

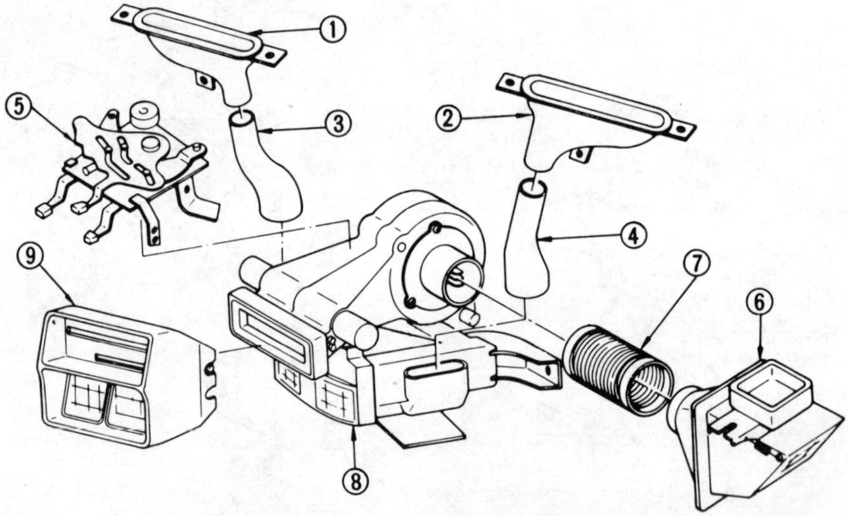

FIG 13:27 Heater unit components

Key to Fig 13:27 1 Demister nozzle, lefthand 2 Demister nozzle, righthand 3 Demister duct, lefthand 4 Demister duct, righthand 5 Heater control 6 Intake box 7 Intake duct hose 8 Heating unit grille 9 Centre ventilator

Align window glass with body side weatherstrip to obtain a tight seal by adjusting guide plate lower adjusting bolt (see **FIG 13:23**).

13:6 Instrument panel and facia

Instrument panel removal:

Disconnect the earth cable from the battery.

Refer to **Chapter 9** and remove steering wheel, column shell covers and turn signal switch. Reach behind instrument panel and disconnect speedometer cable from rear of speedometer. Refer to **FIG 13:24** and remove lower panel 5. Remove fixing screws and withdraw instrument panel 3 rearwards. Disconnect appropriate wiring harnesses from rear of instrument housing, then remove housing assembly.

Refitting is a reversal of the removal procedure.

Glove compartment removal:

Remove package tray then refer to **FIG 13:24**. With lid open, remove the fixing screws and detach glove compartment from facia. Refitting is a reversal of the removal procedure.

Facia removal:

Disconnect the earth cable from the battery, then refer to **Chapter 9** and remove steering wheel and column shell covers. Reach behind instrument panel and disconnect speedometer cable from rear of speedometer. Remove radio antenna cable if fitted. Disconnect body and instrument harness at the connector shown in **FIG 13:25**. Remove attaching screws from top of facia assembly 1, using a suitable tool (see **FIG 13:24**).

Refer to **Chapter 9** and remove bolts attaching steering column clamp to pedal bracket and bolts attaching steering tube jacket to dashboard panel, then remove bolt attaching instrument panel to pedal bracket as shown in **FIG 13:26**. Remove each lower facia mounting bolt, then remove facia assembly rearwards.

Refitting is a reversal of the removal procedure.

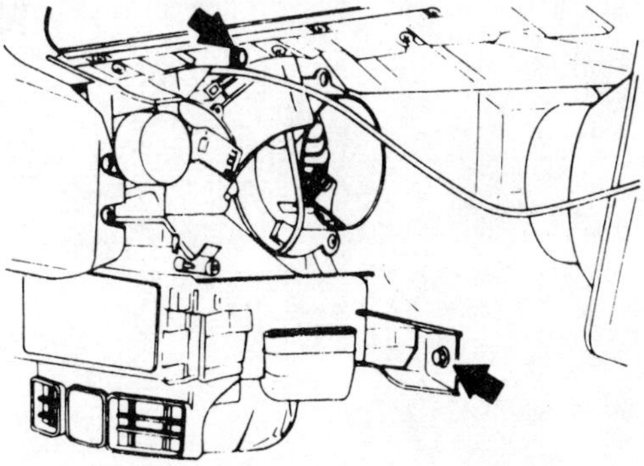

FIG 13:28 Heater unit removal

13:7 The heater

Owners of vehicles fitted with air conditioning (refrigeration) systems should not attempt to remove or dismantle any of the related components, due to the possibility of refrigerant leakage which can be very dangerous.

Heater removal:

Disconnect the earth cable from the battery. Drain the cooling system and remove the heater inlet and outlet hoses at engine compartment connections (see **Chapter 4**).

Refer to **FIG 13:27**. Remove intake duct 7 and demister ducts 3 and 4 from heater unit. Remove console box if fitted. Disconnect main wiring harness connector from heater harness. Remove cable retaining clamp and remove control cables at heater intake box. Remove two retaining bolts from each side of heater unit and one retaining bolt on top of heater unit as shown in **FIG 13:28**. Remove heater unit assembly from passenger compartment.

Installation is a reversal of the removal procedure.

NOTES

CHAPTER 14

EMISSION CONTROL EQUIPMENT

14:1 Introduction

Concern about the noxious substances contained in motor vehicle exhaust gases has led to the introduction of legislation in many countries setting mandatory emissions standards. To meet these, cars for some markets, notably North America, have had to be fitted with a range of emission control devices aimed principally at reducing the output of unburnt fuel, carbon monoxide and, more recently, nitrous oxide.

The devices fitted to models covered in this manual consist firstly of modifications to the fuel system to ensure a correct fuel/air mixture in all circumstances and to prevent fuel vapour escaping, and ignition system modifications to control timing accurately, the aim in these areas being to ensure as complete combustion as possible. Secondly, there are an air injection system, exhaust gas recirculation and a catalytic converter to deal with pollutants not controlled by the improvements in combustion. Typical layouts of these components are shown in **FIG 14:1**, but variations from year to year and from market to market make it impossible to detail every combination.

The transistorised ignition system fitted to cars destined for California from 1975 is covered in **Chapter 3**.

Many emission control devices are basically simple in construction and operation, and checks and adjustments within the scope of the amateur are described in this chapter. But specialised equipment is sometimes required and, ideally, any work should be followed by a full emissions check. **Legal restrictions may limit what can be done in some areas, a point which should be carefully checked.**

14:2 Air injection system

This system reduces emissions of unburnt or partially burnt fuel by injecting a jet of compressed air into the exhaust manifold adjacent to the exhaust valve enabling the unburnt fuel and carbon monoxide to oxidise fully to the harmless carbon dioxide. The air is supplied by a rotary belt-driven pump connected by piping to an air gallery with nozzles into the exhaust manifold. All systems have an air relief valve to prevent excess pressure and an anti-backfire valve; the Californian system is additionally equipped with an air control valve and an emergency air relief valve to prevent the catalytic converter, which is fitted to these models, from overheating.

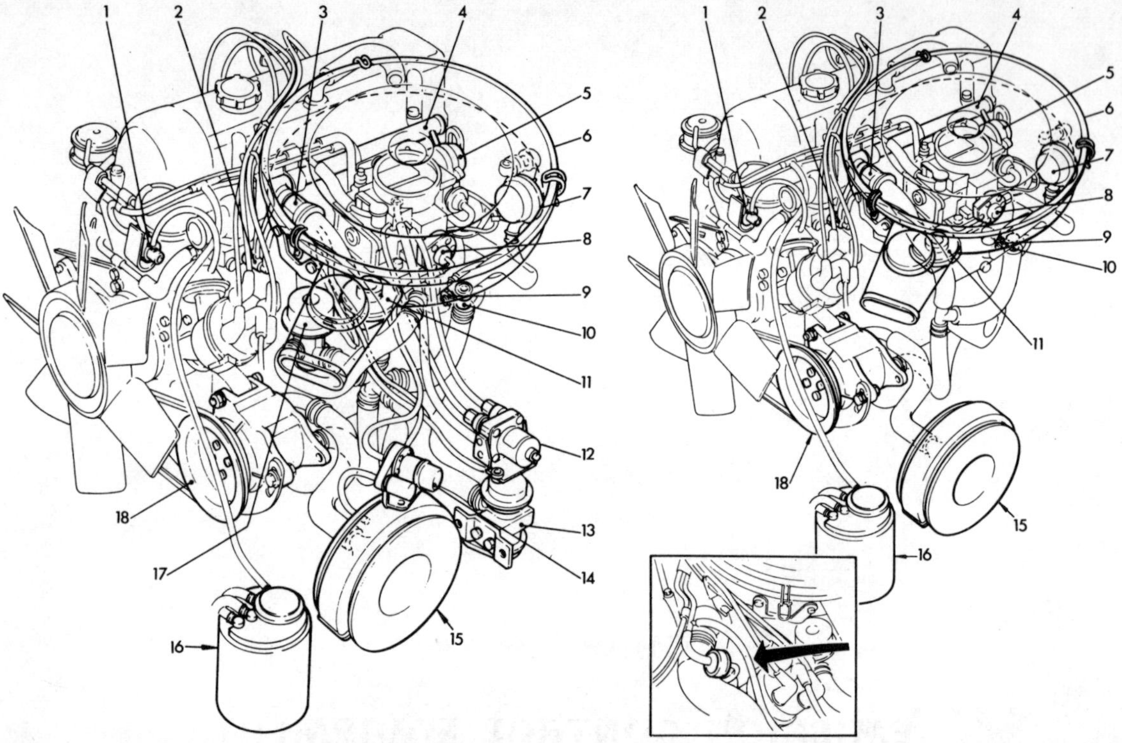

FIG 14:1 Locations of emission control components. Left, California. Right, non-California. Inset: Location of spark delay valve

Key to Fig 14:1 1 Vacuum switching valve 2 Thermal vacuum valve 3 Check valve 4 Air gallery pipe 5 Auto choke 6 Automatic temperature control air cleaner 7 Anti-backfire valve (AB valve) 8 Boost controlled deceleration device (BCDD) 9 PCV valve 10 Air relief valve 11 EGR control valve 12 Altitude compensator (optional) 13 Emergency air relief valve 14 BCDD control valve and solenoid valve 15 Air pump air cleaner 16 Carbon canister 17 Air control valve 18 Air pump

Air pump:

The air pump is either a three-vane or a two-vane type, of which the latter is more common. The pump casing is die-cast aluminium and the rotor and vanes are steel with carbon seals. The construction is shown in the exploded diagram, **FIG 14:2**.

The pump belt tension should be checked every 5000km (3000 miles) and adjusted if necessary. **FIG 14:3** shows the free movement that the belt should allow when pressed with about 10kg (22lb). The element of the air cleaner attached to the left side of the engine compartment should be replaced periodically.

The pump can be dismantled for repair if this is essential. Care is required and the inexperienced are advised to leave the job to a service station. The vanes and the bearings are subject to wear and kits are available to replace them. Refer to **FIG 14:2** and dismantle as follows:

1 Detach the air hoses from the pump, slacken the pump mountings and remove the belt, then remove the pump from the car.
2 Unscrew the four pulley bolts 1 and detach the pulley 2. Clamp the pump drive hub in a vice and unscrew the four end cover bolts 3.
3 Tap the end cover 4 around the dowel pin with a soft mallet to loosen it and lift it aft. Mark the rotor ring 6 and the rotor 7 to ensure correct reassembly, unscrew the Allen screws 5 and remove the rotor ring. **Discard the Allen screws as new ones must be used on reassembly.**
4 Remove the vanes 8 from the rotor 7. Remove the carbon seals 9 and the springs 10 from the rotor (see **FIG 14:4**), using tweezers. Note that seal A is 1mm (0.039in) wider than seal B and do not confuse them.
5 If the front bearing 14 requires replacement, remove the pump drive hub 11 with a puller, undo the four screws 12 and remove the bearing cover 13. Press out the rotor 7 with Datsun tools ST19890000 and ST19940000, taking care not to damage the pump casing 15.

Reassembly is the reverse of dismantling. The drive hub must be pressed on, the vanes lubricated on their bearings with a high-melting point grease (MIL-G-3545A, ESSO ANDOK 260 or equivalent) and fitted to the rotor with a dummy shaft (ST19900000). The seal springs 10 are installed after the seals and vanes with the convex curve to the seal (**FIG 14:5**). The rotor ring

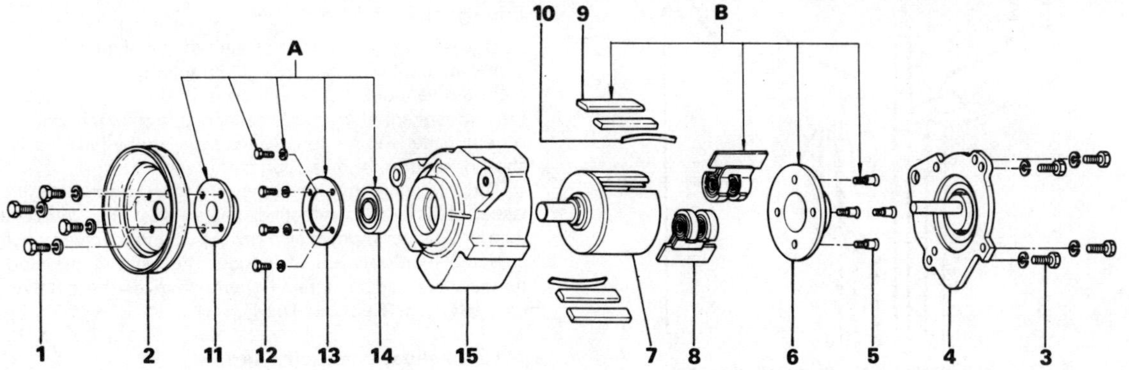

FIG 14:2 Air pump components

Key to Fig 14:2 1 Pulley bolt 2 Pulley 3 End cover bolt 4 End cover 5 Allen screw 6 Rotor ring 7 Rotor 8 Vane 9 Carbon seal 10 Seal spring 11 Drive hub 12 Screw 13 Bearing cover 14 Bearing 15 Pump casing A Bearing kit B Vane kit

screws 5 are tightened to 0.5 to 0.7kgm (3.6 to 5.1lb ft), the vane shaft and the bearings are packed with high melting point grease and the cover bolts and pulley bolts are tightened to 0.7 to 0.9kgm (5.1 to 6.5lb ft).

The car must be driven at not more than 50 mile/hr for 10 miles after refitting the pump to bed in the parts. The pump cannot be lubricated once it is completely assembled.

Exhaust manifold nozzles:

The compressed air from the pump is piped to a gallery above the exhaust manifold from which it is injected close to the exhaust valves by nozzles in each branch of the manifold. The nozzles are secured by threaded sleeves and need no sealing rings. The only maintenance required is to check the tightness of these sleeves every 20,000km (12,000 miles).

Removal of the air gallery is difficult and almost certain to result in damage; for this reason it should not be attempted unless completely essential. Care should be taken and the threaded sleeves must be well soaked in penetrating oil beforehand and lubricated with engine oil frequently as they are unscrewed.

Anti-backfire valve:

The anti-backfire valve is operated by inlet manifold vacuum to leak air into the inlet manifold during sudden deceleration. This leans the mixture which otherwise becomes too rich for complete combustion when the throttle is shut at more than moderate road speeds. An excessively rich mixture causes unburnt fuel to pass through the engine to the exhaust manifold where it ignites explosively with the air from the air injection system nozzles as well as generating high levels of exhaust emissions. The valve is located close to the air cleaner, on the top of the engine.

The connections to the valve should be examined and repaired if leaks are suspected. The valve can be tested by warming up the engine, disconnecting the hose from air cleaner and feeling at its open end with a finger for a sudden suction when the engine is run at 3000rev/min

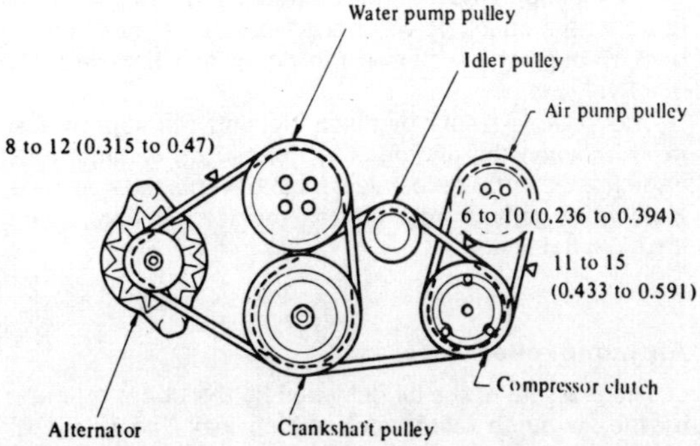

FIG 14:3 Drive belt tension. Figures indicate free movement in mm (inch) under a pressure of 10kg (22lb)

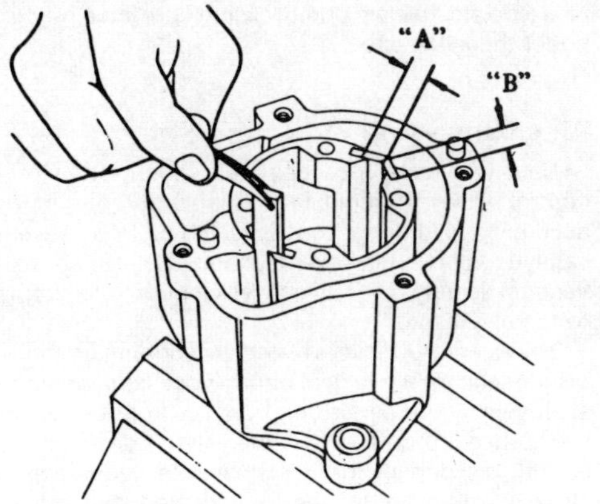

FIG 14:4 Removing rotor seals and springs. Seal A is 1mm wider than B

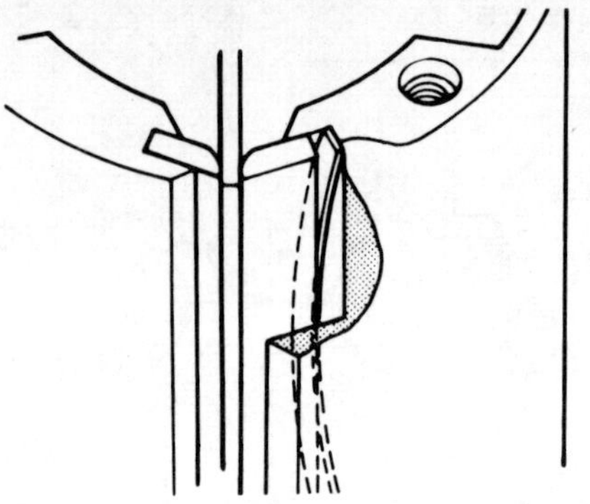

FIG 14:5 Correct installation of seal spring

unloaded and the throttle is suddenly shut. If this is not felt or other evidence of malfunction is found the valve must be replaced complete as it is a sealed unit.

Check valve:

The air supply hose from the pump to the air gallery is fitted with a check valve to prevent exhaust gas flowing back through the system if the pump belt breaks or the relief valve fails.

The valve is tested by disconnecting the supply hose from it; when the engine is run briefly no exhaust must issue from it. If it is defective it must be replaced complete. Hold the air gallery flange with a wrench when unscrewing it to avoid damage.

Air pump relief valve:

The pressure of the air delivered by the pump is limited by the air pump relief valve, which leaks air to the air cleaner if the pressure rises too high. It can be checked by detaching and blocking the air supply hose at the air gallery and on California models the air control valve and running the engine at 3000rev/min; a stream of air should issue from the outlet of the valve. If the valve is defective it must be replaced complete. Before 1975 this valve was pressed into the air pump casing, on later models it is under the air cleaner.

Air control valve:

Cars with catalytic converters are fitted with an air control valve to regulate the quantity of air injected according to the load on the engine. This prevents the catalytic converter overheating. The inlet manifold vacuum actuates the valve to leak air from the supply hose to the air cleaner.

The air control valve is tested by warming up the engine, disconnecting the valve outlet hose and feeling for a steady stream of air issuing from it when the engine is at idling speed. If no air flows the valve is defective; if air is issuing disconnect the inlet manifold vacuum pipe and close it with a finger; the air flow from the valve outlet hose should then cease.

If the valve is defective it must be replaced complete.

Emergency air relief valve:

This is a safety device to protect the catalytic converter if the air control valve fails. It is actuated by the inlet manifold vacuum and bleeds air from the supply hose to the atmosphere. It must be checked at regular intervals by running the engine at 2000rev/min unloaded; no air should issue from the outlet.

The inlet vacuum pipe is then detached and air should issue steadily. A defective valve must be replaced complete. Later models also have a solenoid valve which cuts the inlet vacuum to actuate the valve if the floor temperature sensor detects overheating of the catalytic converter (see **Section 14:4**).

14:3 Exhaust gas recirculation

The exhaust gas recirculation system (EGR) returns part of the exhaust gas to the inlet manifold, lowering the temperature at which the mixture burns in the cylinders and thus considerably reducing the quantity of nitrogen oxides in the exhaust gases. The exhaust gases are carried from the exhaust manifold by a tube to the EGR control valve which meters the quantity introduced into the inlet manifold via the EGR passage according to the inlet manifold vacuum. A thermal vacuum valve prevents the EGR system working until the engine is warmed up, to minimise adverse effects on performance. **FIG 14:6** shows the layout of these components. Early models are fitted with a solenoid valve and a temperature sensor in place of the thermal vacuum valve.

A warning system is installed to indicate when the EGR system must be inspected.

Thermal vacuum valve:

This unit is installed in the engine thermostat housing and connected into the inlet manifold vacuum pipe to the EGR control valve. It contains a bi-metal strip and a spring-loaded valve so that the EGR control valve cannot be actuated by the manifold vacuum until the engine

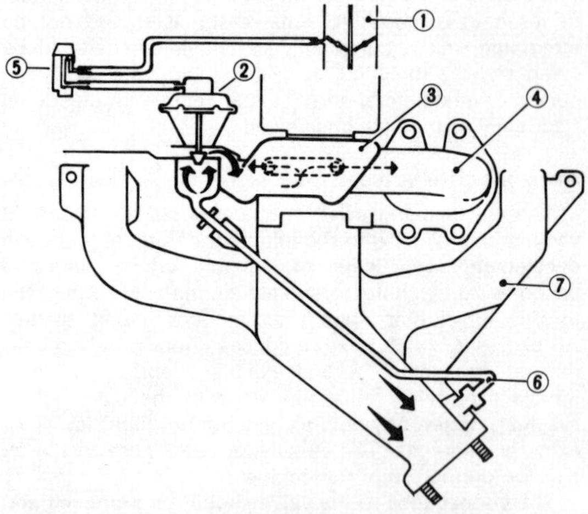

FIG 14:6 Exhaust gas recirculation (EGR) system

Key to Fig 14:6 1 Carburetter 2 EGR control valve 3 EGR passage 4 Inlet manifold 5 Thermal vacuum valve 6 EGR tube 7 Exhaust manifold

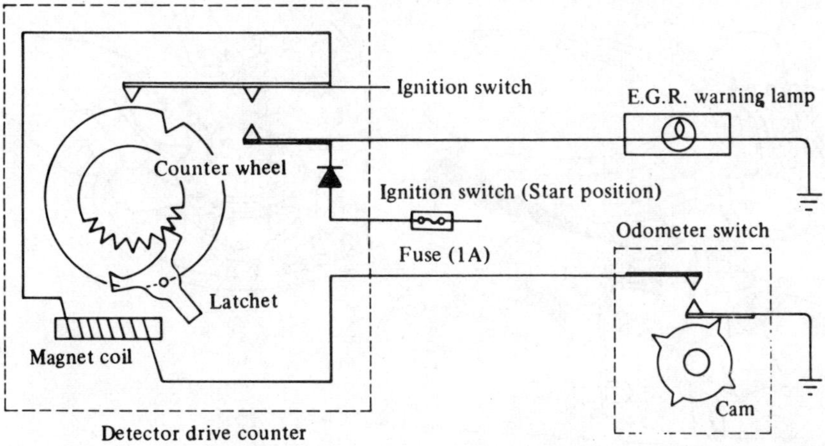

FIG 14:7 EGR warning system circuit

coolant is at 57° to 63°C (135° to 145°F), when the deflection of the bi-metal strip opens the valve.

The valve can be tested by removing it from the engine and heating it to its operating temperature in a water bath. **Water must not be allowed to enter it.**

EGR control valve:

This is a diaphragm operated valve. The inlet manifold vacuum moves the diaphragm against the spring thus lifting the valve from its seat and allowing the exhaust gas into the inlet manifold. Note that the thermal vacuum valve must be open.

The exact specification of the EGR control valve varies according to model and transmission and any replacement must have the same part number stamped on the valve top as the replaced unit. Most units open at a vacuum of about −70mm Hg (−2.76in Hg) except on engines sold in California which open at −50mm Hg (−1.97in Hg). The valve can be tested with a vacuum gauge by sucking on the connection and noting when the valve opens.

Pre-1975 EGR systems:

The EGR systems installed before 1975 are identical in function but different in detail design. An electric temperature sensor, a control box or modulator and a solenoid valve are used instead of the thermal vacuum valve. The solenoid can be tested by energising it with 12 volts to shut it. The temperature sensor should exhibit a resistance of 2300 to 3700 ohms at 15° to 25°C (59° to 77°F) and 650 to 980 ohms at 45° to 55°C (113° to 131°F). The modulator unit cannot be checked without special equipment. The EGR control valve is slightly different in design to the later unit and should open at −120 to −130mm Hg (−4.7 to −5.1in Hg).

EGR warning system:

The EGR warning system is not connected with any part of the EGR system. The purpose of it is to register the distance travelled and give a positive warning when the system must be serviced. It comprises an odometer switch, a detector drive counter and a warning light, see **FIG 14:7**. The odometer switch supplies a pulse of electricity every 0.4km (0.25 mile) travelled which energises an electromagnet to advance the detector drive counter one pitch. When the counter has registered 50,000 pulses it trips a switch to illuminate the EGR warning light on the dashboard. When this occurs the EGR system must be thoroughly checked. The detector drive counter has a window through which the number of pulses registered is visually displayed, indicating the distance to be travelled before the next check. The EGR warning light also glows when the starter is used and a check can be made of the bulb by this provision.

The detector drive counter is attached to the windscreen wiper rotor with a metal strap. The EGR warning light is beside the windscreen wiper knob. The odometer switch is fixed with two screws to the speedometer (see **FIG 14:8**); the speedometer must be removed with the printed circuit housing and then detached from it to remove this unit (see **Chapter 13**). The components are tested in a conventional fashion with a multimeter.

The counter drive counter is reset after the EGR system is serviced by removing the grommet on its side and operating the resetting knob inside the hole with a screwdriver.

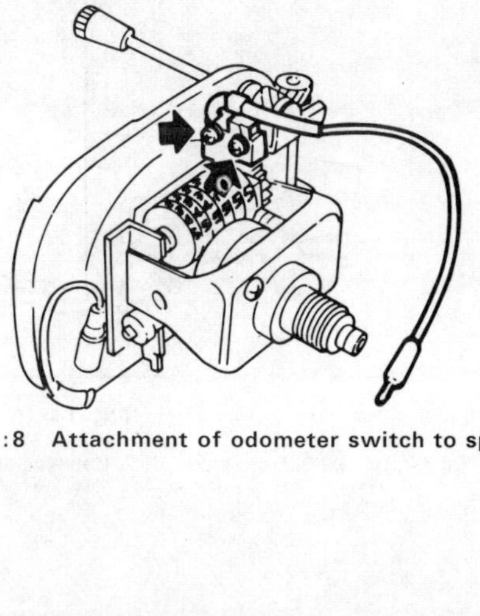

FIG 14:8 Attachment of odometer switch to speedometer

FIG 14:9 Checking EGR control valve

Servicing the EGR system:

When the EGR warning light comes on the system must be checked. Canadian and Californian models should be referred to a service station. Models in other areas can be checked by an owner with some mechanical experience providing a systematic approach is adopted. Proceed as follows:

1 Clean the engine and EGR system of dirt and oil. Thoroughly examine the system for leaks, damage or other visible faults.

2 Check the EGR warning system, ensuring that the detector drive counter has tripped at the correct mileage. Reset it, but ensure that the car is not used before the EGR system has been completely inspected.

3 Push the EGR control valve diaphragm upwards with a finger to check for jamming (see **FIG 14:9**). Start the engine, checking that the EGR warning light glows as the starter is used. Detach the vacuum pipe from the EGR control valve before the engine warms up and ensure that the thermal vacuum valve is shut and no vacuum is felt at the pipe's end, then replace it.

4 Allow the engine to warm up and check that the EGR control valve operates when the engine speed rises from 3000 to 3500rev/min by feeling the diaphragm with a finger. If it does not, detach the vacuum pipe and check that the thermal vacuum valve has opened. If either the EGR control valve or the thermal vacuum valve is suspect, the unit can be removed and tested, as described in the sections dealing with them, and replaced if necessary.

5 Remove the EGR control valve and carefully clean it of scale and deposits around the valve port with a wire brush and compressed air. Replace it and check it again.

14:4 Catalytic converter

Some pollutants are still generated despite the devices fitted to the engine. These are removed by the catalytic converter which is fitted to cars sold in areas with strict emissions laws. It is fitted into the exhaust piping as shown in **FIG 14:10**. The remaining unburnt hydrocarbons and carbon monoxide are caused to oxidise in the air from the exhaust manifold nozzles by a catalyst in a finely divided state deposited in the porous filling of the converter. The catalyst remains unchanged by this chemical

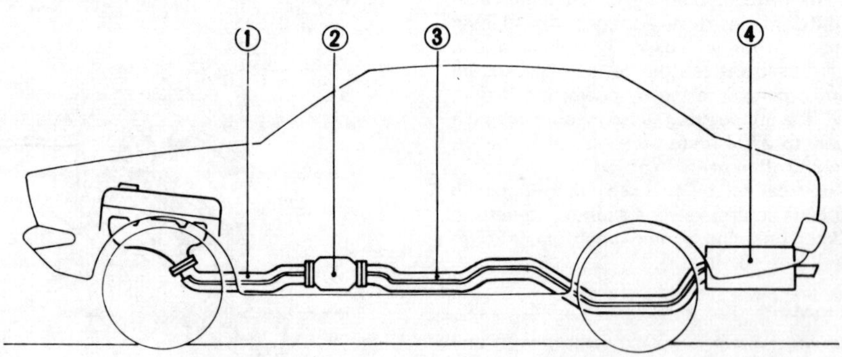

FIG 14:10 Location of catalytic converter

Key to Fig 14:10 1 Front pipe 2 Catalytic converter 3 Centre pipe 4 Main silencer reaction but the heat released causes the unit to run at a high temperature producing slow deterioration and necessitating a warning system in case it overheats.

Inspection and maintenance:

The unit has no moving parts and can only be checked for correct opertion by metering the carbon monoxide level of the exhaust. The other emission control systems must be thoroughly checked and correctly adjusted before doing this. If carbon monoxide emissions are more than 0.3 per cent with all other systems working correctly the converter must be replaced with a new unit.

The converter is removed by jacking up the car, with necessary precautions, detaching the cover plate and unbolting the exhaust pipe connections and mounting brackets. The mounting bolts are tightened to 2.6 to 3.4kgm (19 to 24lb ft) when refitting.

Floor temperature warning system:

If excessive emissions are generated due to failure of the other control systems or a continuous overload on the engine, the converter will overheat. This is prevented by a floor-mounted temperature sensitive switch, located under the rear seat directly above the exhaust pipe, which lights a warning on the dashboard and cuts the ignition with the circuit shown in **FIG 14:11**. The switch operates when the temperature exceeds 115°C (239°F). The warning is wired so that it lights when the ignition is on and the engine stopped to enable the bulb to be checked. The system relay is located behind the dashboard above the gearbox.

The warning system should be first checked by conventional means if it activates, in case of malfunction. The fuel and carburation system, the ignition system and all the associated emission control systems must then be systematically checked to find the cause of the converter overheating. Overheating because of engine overloads is uncommon; driving a heavily laden car fast down a steep hill with a low gear engaged for a long period of time is the sort of extreme situation which will cause this.

Pre-1976 models have an electronic system with a temperature sensor on the converter and a solenoid to actuate the emergency air relief valve. This system should be dealt with by a garage as specialised equipment is needed.

14:5 Fuel system controls

Emission controlled models have the same basic fuel system as other models, covered in **Chapter 2**, but with modifications and additions both to reduce emissions and to minimise the effects of other emission control systems on performance. Some of the devices in the latter category such as the temperature control air cleaner are now fitted to cars without full emission control equipment. Simpler items like the anti-dieseling valve and the dashpot which controls throttle closure are included in **Chapter 2**.

Carburetter adjustment:

The emission control systems must be in good order and operating correctly before carburetter tuning can be carried out successfully. The procedure is the same as for engines without emission controls except for the analysis of the exhaust gas to ensure conformity to local legislation and to set the idle mixture. Analysis of exhaust is best done by a reputable garage and requires special equipment.

The idle mixture must be adjusted so that the emitted carbon monoxide level is 2 ± 1 per cent with the ignition timing at 12° BTDC and the engine running at 750rev/min (manual) or 650rev/min (automatic in D). The hose between the three-way connector and the air check valve should be disconnected and plugged (see **FIG 14:12**).

Temperature control air cleaner:

This type of cleaner has two air intakes, one (cold) which admits air at engine compartment temperature and another (hot) for air drawn from around the exhaust manifold. These intakes can be selectively opened or closed by an air control valve actuated by a vacuum motor in such a manner to obtain an intake temperature of approximately 43°C (110°F).

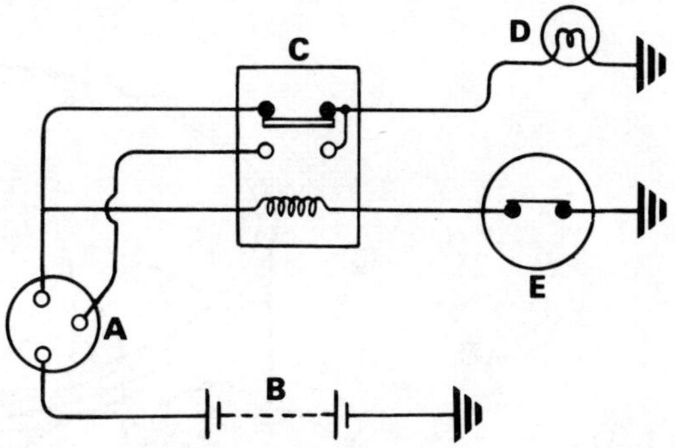

FIG 14:11 Floor temperature warning system circuit

Key to Fig 14:11 **A** Ignition switch **B** Battery **C** Relay **D** Warning lamp **E** Floor temperature sensing switch

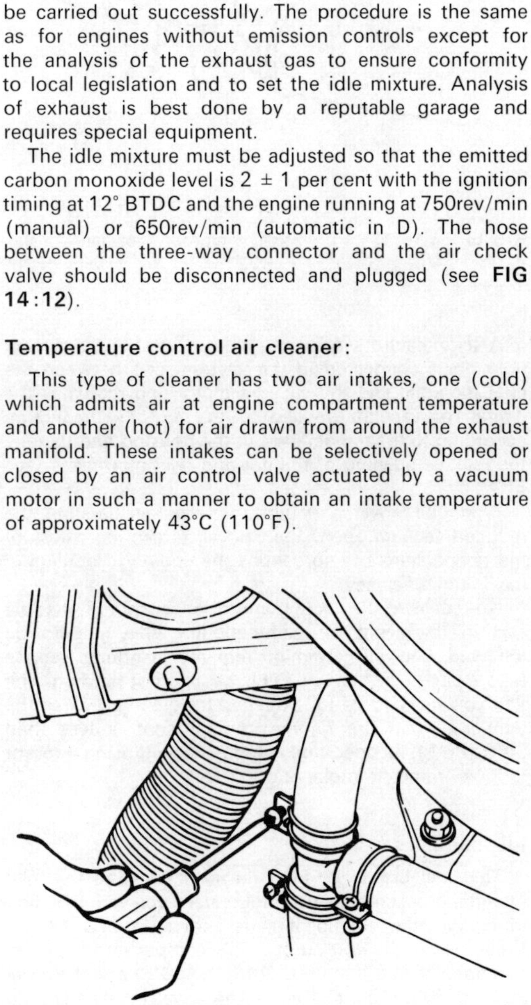

FIG 14:12 Disconnecting hose from air check valve before setting idle mixture

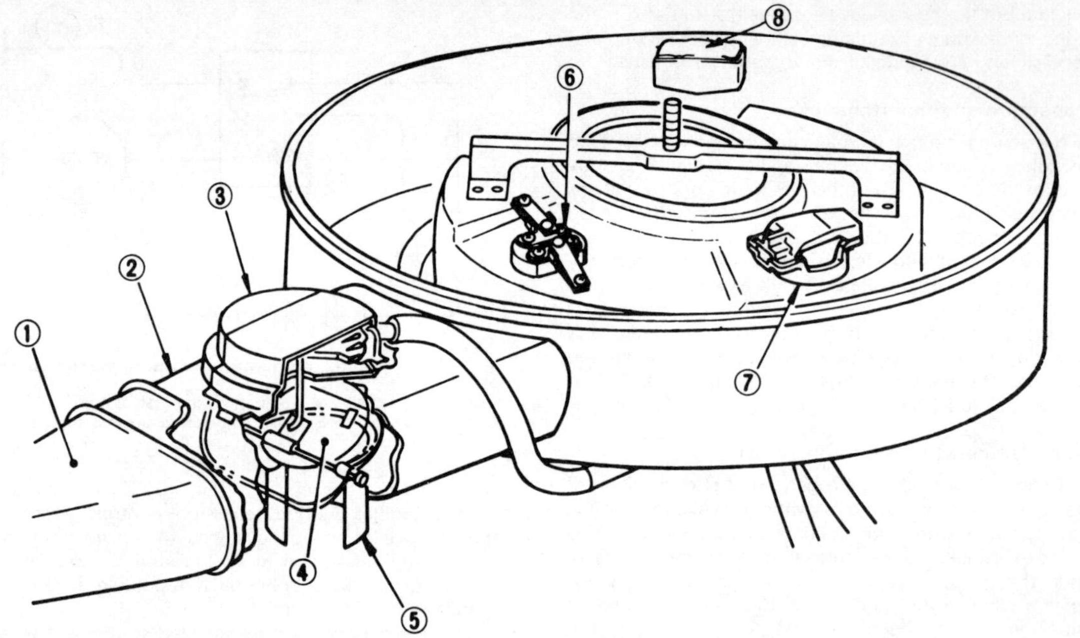

FIG 14:13 Temperature control air cleaner

Key to Fig 14:13 1 Fresh air duct (not Canadian models) 2 Air inlet pipe 3 Vacuum motor assembly 4 Air control flap 5 Hot air pipe 6 Idle compensator 7 Temperature sensor 8 Crankcase ventilation filter

A temperature sensor mounted inside the air cleaner housing is connected in the vacuum line between the inlet manifold and the vacuum motor and regulates the degree of vacuum applied to the motor's diaphragm according to the temperature in the housing and thereby the relative opening of the hot and cold air intakes (see **FIG 14:13**).

When full power is required, as when accelerating, the reduced vacuum opens the cold air intake regardless of the temperature and so permits the engine to operate at maximum efficiency.

No repairs to the vacuum motor or sensor are possible and in the event of malfunctioning they should be renewed. The only attention required in normal service is to ensure that the valve linkages are not binding. The flap valve should be fully opened for warm air when the temperature in the engine compartment is less than 30°C (86°F). Its operation can be checked using a mirror to look up the air intake duct.

Idle compensator:

This unit bleeds air from the air cleaner to the inlet manifold to compensate for greater fuel vapourisation in hot weather. Its location is shown in **FIG 14:13**. Combined in the unit are two idle compensator devices, one opening at 60° to 70°C (140° to 158°F) and the other at 70° to 90°C (158° to 194°F). The valves must be airtight and the unit can be tested by heating in a water bath to check that it operates at the correct temperature.

Thermostatic hot-spot:

The exhaust manifold is fitted with a hot-spot or 'stove' to heat the carburetter for improved fuel vapourisation. A flap is fitted in the manifold below it on a shaft rotated by a bi-metallic spring to deflect the exhaust gases onto it when the engine is cold. As the engine warms up the flap rotates to clear the exhaust. It can also swing against the spring to allow large throttle openings when the engine is cold.

The device can be checked by warming the engine up from cold and observing its movement. The shaft can be rotated manually if binding is suspected to feel its freeness. If the flap and shaft are completely seized the manifold must be replaced complete.

Altitude compensator:

The conventional carburetter tends to deliver a richer mixture at lower barometric pressures. The altitude compensator prevents this by bleeding air from the air cleaner to the carburetter emulsion tubes at altitudes above 600m (1968ft). As fitted this unit has three connecting pipes: a red one to the primary choke; a green one to the secondary choke; and a white one to the air cleaner.

The altitude compensator is usually fitted to models with the catalytic converter to prevent it overheating at altitude. The unit usually fails by operating below its set altitude producing symptoms of lean carburation; if this occurs it must be replaced.

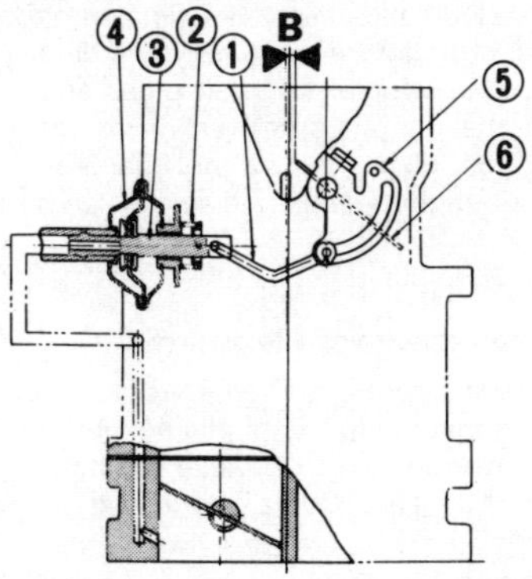

FIG 14:14 Choke vacuum system adjustment

Key to Fig 14:14 1 Choke piston rod 2 Choke spring 3 Choke piston 4 Diaphragm rod 5 Choke piston lever 6 Choke valve

Automatic choke:

The automatic chokes of some models have a bi-metal spring to open the choke butterfly which is heated by either one or two coils. The second coil is switched on at higher ambient temperatures by a bi-metallic strip to open the choke faster. Both coils are fed through a relay energised by the charging circuit so that they can only function when the engine is running.

The choke is also fitted with a fast-idle linkage, a vacuum system and a choke unloader. The fast-idle linkage is adjusted to set the idling rpm with the choke in use. The vacuum system adjusts the mixture precisely and is set as in **FIG 14:14** so that the clearance 'B' is 1.7mm (0.067in) for 1974 and earlier cars, 1.65mm (0.065in) for 1975 cars, 1.42mm (0.056in) for 1976 non-California cars, or 1.5mm (0.059in) for 1976 in California. The choke unloader opens the choke at large throttle openings and is adjusted by bending the tongue to give a choke butterfly to carburetter body clearance of 4.4mm (0.173in) on 1974 and earlier cars, or 2.45mm (0.096in) on 1975 and later cars, when the throttle is wide open and the choke operated.

The electrical system and relay are tested conventionally; the relay is situated at the front righthand side of the engine compartment.

Boost-controlled deceleration device (BCDD):

The BCDD system reduces the emission of unburnt hydrocarbons which are produced when the engine is running in gear at high rev/min with the throttle shut, as in deceleration or coasting down hills. The high manifold vacuum and resulting low air volume prevent complete combustion under these circumstances. The BCDD system prevents this by allowing extra fuel and air into the engine when the inlet manifold vacuum exceeds a set value. A solenoid is energised from either a speedometer switch or the inhibitor switch on automatic transmission which releases the actuating vacuum to allow the engine to slow to idling speed without racing or stalling. The system on cars sold in California has altitude compensation.

All checks and adjustments to the pressure setting of the BCDD system should be done by the manufacturer's agents as specialised equipment is necessary.

Evaporative emissions control:

To prevent the escape of fuel vapour to the atmosphere the fuel tank vent pipe runs to the engine compartment. On earlier cars it is linked by a flow guide valve to the crankcase breather system so that it either feeds air from the air cleaner to the tank or allows fuel vapour to be

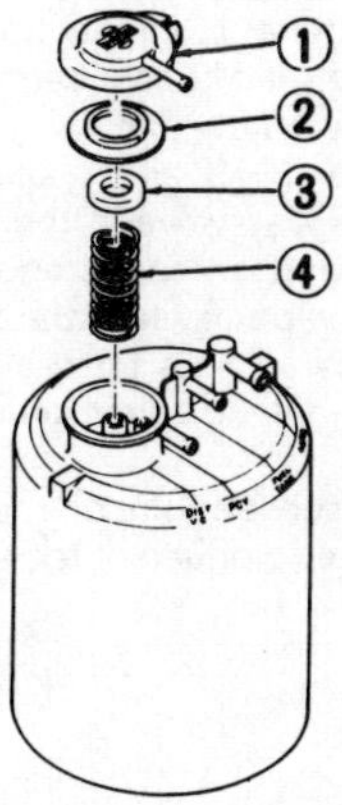

FIG 14:15 Carbon canister showing purge control valve dismantled

Key to Fig 14:15 1 Valve cover 2 Diaphragm 3 Retainer 4 Spring

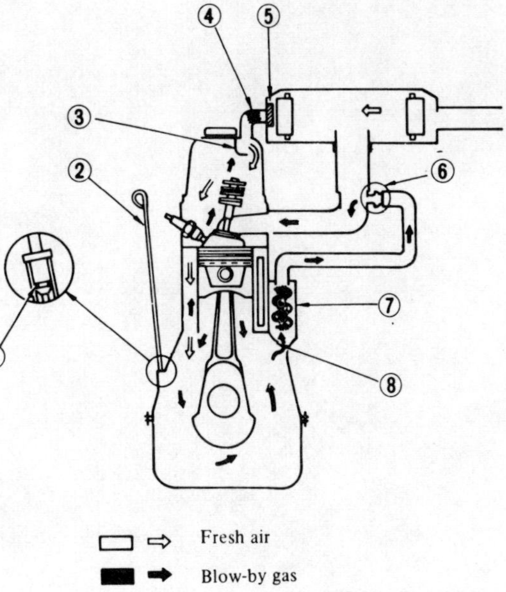

FIG 14:16 Positive crankcase ventilation (PCV) system

Key to Fig 14:16 1 'O' ring 2 Dipstick 3 Baffle plate 4 Flame arrester 5 Filter 6 PCV valve 7 Steel net 8 Baffle plate drawn into the breather system according to the prevailing balance of pressure. The flow guide valve connections are marked A (from air cleaner), F (fuel tank vent pipe) and C (to crankcase), and the operation of the valve may be checked as follows:

1 Remove the three pipes from the valve.
2 Apply low pressure air to connection F. This air should flow out of connection C.
3 Apply low pressure air to connection A. This air should flow out of connection F.
4 Apply suction to connection F. Air should flow in at connection A and be sucked out at connection F. No air should flow in at connection C.

A defective flow guide valve cannot be repaired and must be replaced by a new unit.

On models from 1975 air is allowed to enter the tank through a one-way valve in the filler cap. The vent pipe leads to a canister containing activated carbon which adsorbs the vapour when the engine is at rest or idling. As engine speed rises fresh air is drawn through the canister into the inlet manifold purging the carbon of fuel vapour.

The air filter in the bottom of the canister must be renewed if it becomes clogged. If the system is suspected of faults, check the filler cap valve, renewing the complete cap if it will not allow air to pass inwards or allow flow both ways, check for leaks in all pipes and remove the cover from the purge control valve on the canister to check that the diaphragm is not damaged (see **FIG 14:15**). Diaphragm retainer and spring can be renewed if necessary.

Positive crankcase ventilation (PCV):

On emission controlled engines the rocker cover breather is connected to the air cleaner and the crankcase breather connected to a PCV valve on the inlet manifold (see **FIG 14:16**). The PCV valve opens at high vacuum in the inlet manifold and draws a flow of air from the air cleaner through the engine. At low vacuum the fumes are drawn into the air cleaner in a conventional fashion. The dipstick is sealed with an 'O' ring.

The system must be cleaned occasionally with compressed air. The PCV valve can be tested by feeling the suction at the air cleaner connection at idling speed, a strong vacuum will be noticeable unless the PCV valve is not working or the cylinder bores and pistons are very worn and excessive 'blow-by' is occuring.

APPENDIX

Inches	Decimals	Millimetres	Inches to Millimetres: Inches	Inches to Millimetres: mm	Millimetres to Inches: mm	Millimetres to Inches: Inches
1/64	.015625	.3969	.001	.0254	.01	.00039
1/32	.03125	.7937	.002	.0508	.02	.00079
3/64	.046875	1.1906	.003	.0762	.03	.00118
1/16	.0625	1.5875	.004	.1016	.04	.00157
5/64	.078125	1.9844	.005	.1270	.05	.00197
3/32	.09375	2.3812	.006	.1524	.06	.00236
7/64	.109375	2.7781	.007	.1778	.07	.00276
1/8	.125	3.1750	.008	.2032	.08	.00315
9/64	.140625	3.5719	.009	.2286	.09	.00354
5/32	.15625	3.9687	.01	.254	.1	.00394
11/64	.171875	4.3656	.02	.508	.2	.00787
3/16	.1875	4.7625	.03	.762	.3	.01181
13/64	.203125	5·1594	.04	1.016	.4	.01575
7/32	.21875	5.5562	.05	1.270	.5	.01969
15/64	.234375	5.9531	.06	1.524	.6	.02362
1/4	.25	6.3500	.07	1.778	.7	.02756
17/64	.265625	6.7469	.08	2.032	.8	.03150
9/32	.28125	7.1437	.09	2.286	.9	.03543
19/64	.296875	7.5406	.1	2.54	1	.03937
5/16	.3125	7.9375	.2	5.08	2	.07874
21/64	.328125	8.3344	.3	7.62	3	.11811
11/32	.34375	8.7312	.4	10.16	4	.15748
23/64	.359375	9.1281	.5	12.70	5	.19685
3/8	.375	9.5250	.6	15.24	6	.23622
25/64	.390625	9.9219	.7	17.78	7	.27559
13/32	.40625	10.3187	.8	20.32	8	.31496
27/64	.421875	10.7156	.9	22.86	9	.35433
7/16	.4375	11.1125	1	25.4	10	.39370
29/64	.453125	11.5094	2	50.8	11	.43307
15/32	.46875	11.9062	3	76.2	12	.47244
31/64	.484375	12.3031	4	101.6	13	.51181
1/2	.5	12.7000	5	127.0	14	.55118
33/64	.515625	13.0969	6	152.4	15	.59055
17/32	.53125	13.4937	7	177.8	16	.62992
35/64	.546875	13.8906	8	203.2	17	.66929
9/16	.5625	14.2875	9	228.6	18	.70866
37/64	.578125	14.6844	10	254.0	19	.74803
19/32	.59375	15.0812	11	279.4	20	.78740
39/64	.609375	15.4781	12	304.8	21	.82677
5/8	.625	15.8750	13	330.2	22	.86614
41/64	.640625	16.2719	14	355.6	23	.90551
21/32	.65625	16.6687	15	381.0	24	.94488
43/64	.671875	17.0656	16	406.4	25	.98425
11/16	.6875	17.4625	17	431.8	26	1.02362
45/64	.703125	17.8594	18	457.2	27	1.06299
23/32	.71875	18.2562	19	482.6	28	1.10236
47/64	.734375	18.6531	20	508.0	29	1.14173
3/4	.75	19.0500	21	533.4	30	1.18110
49/64	.765625	19.4469	22	558.8	31	1.22047
25/32	.78125	19.8437	23	584.2	32	1.25984
51/64	.796875	20.2406	24	609.6	33	1.29921
13/16	.8125	20.6375	25	635.0	34	1.33858
53/64	.828125	21.0344	26	660.4	35	1.37795
27/32	.84375	21.4312	27	685.8	36	1.41732
55/64	.859375	21.8281	28	711.2	37	1.4567
7/8	.875	22.2250	29	736.6	38	1.4961
57/64	.890625	22.6219	30	762.0	39	1.5354
29/32	.90625	23.0187	31	787.4	40	1.5748
59/64	.921875	23.4156	32	812.8	41	1.6142
15/16	.9375	23.8125	33	838.2	42	1.6535
61/64	.953125	24.2094	34	863.6	43	1.6929
31/32	.96875	24.6062	35	889.0	44	1.7323
63/64	.984375	25.0031	36	914.4	45	1.7717

UNITS	Pints to Litres	Gallons to Litres	Litres to Pints	Litres to Gallons	Miles to Kilometres	Kilometres to Miles	Lbs. per sq. In. to Kg. per sq. Cm.	Kg. per sq. Cm. to Lbs. per sq. In.
1	.57	4.55	1.76	.22	1.61	.62	.07	14.22
2	1.14	9.09	3.52	.44	3.22	1.24	.14	28.50
3	1.70	13.64	5.28	.66	4.83	1.86	.21	42.67
4	2.27	18.18	7.04	.88	6.44	2.49	.28	56.89
5	2.84	22.73	8.80	1.10	8.05	3.11	.35	71.12
6	3.41	27.28	10.56	1.32	9.66	3.73	.42	85.34
7	3.98	31.82	12.32	1.54	11.27	4.35	.49	99.56
8	4.55	36.37	14.08	1.76	12.88	4.97	.56	113.79
9		40.91	15.84	1.98	14.48	5.59	.63	128.00
10		45.46	17.60	2.20	16.09	6.21	.70	142.23
20				4.40	32.19	12.43	1.41	284.47
30				6.60	48.28	18.64	2.11	426.70
40				8.80	64.37	24.85		
50					80.47	31.07		
60					96.56	37.28		
70					112.65	43.50		
80					128.75	49.71		
90					144.84	55.92		
100					160.93	62.14		

UNITS	Lb ft to kgm	Kgm to lb ft	UNITS	Lb ft to kgm	Kgm to lb ft
1	.138	7.233	7	.967	50.631
2	.276	14.466	8	1.106	57.864
3	.414	21.699	9	1.244	65.097
4	.553	28.932	10	1.382	72.330
5	.691	36.165	20	2.765	144.660
6	.829	43.398	30	4.147	216.990

TECHNICAL DATA

Dimensions are in millimetres (inches) unless otherwise stated

ENGINE

Type	Four cylinder in-line
Displacement:	
L14	1428cc (87.1cu in)
L16	1595cc (97.3cu in)
L18	1770cc (108.0cu in)
L20B	1952cc (119.1cu in)
Bore and stroke:	
L14	83 × 66 (3.27 × 2.60)
L16	83 × 73.7 (3.27 × 2.90)
L18	85 × 78 (3.35 × 3.07)
L20B	85 × 86 (3.35 × 3.39)
Compression ratio:	
L14	9.0:1
L16 single carburetter	8.5:1
L16 twin carburetter	9.5:1
L18 single carburetter	8.5:1
L18 twin carburetter	9.5:1
L20B	8.5:1
Firing order	1–3–4–2
Number of main bearings	5
Valve clearance (warm):	
Inlet	0.25 (0.010)
Exhaust	0.30 (0.012)
Valve clearance (cold):	
Inlet	0.20 (0.008)
Exhaust	0.25 (0.010)
Valve head diameter:	
L14 inlet	38 (1.536)
L14, L16 exhaust	33 (1.299)
L16, L18, L20B inlet	42 (1.653)
L18, L20B exhaust	35 (1.378)
Valve stem diameter:	
Inlet	7.965 to 7.980 (0.3136 to 0.3142)
Exhaust	7.945 to 7.960 (0.3128 to 0.3134)
Valve spring free length:	
L14 inlet	49.00 (1.929)
L14 exhaust outer	49.98 (1.968)
L14 exhaust inner	44.85 (1.766)
L16, L18, L20B inlet and exhaust outer	49.98 (1.968)
L16, L18, L20B inlet and exhaust inner	44.85 (1.766)
Valve guide length:	
Inlet and exhaust	59.0 (2.323)
Valve guide height from head surface	10.6 (0.417)
Valve guide inner diameter:	
Inlet and exhaust	8.000 to 8.018 (0.3150 to 0.3154)
Valve guide to stem clearance:	
Inlet	0.020 to 0.053 (0.0008 to 0.0021)
Exhaust	0.040 to 0.073 (0.0016 to 0.0029)
Valve seat width:	
L14 inlet	1.8 (0.071)
L14 exhaust	1.7 (0.067)

L16, L18 inlet	1.4 (0.055)
L16, L18 exhaust	1.3 (0.051)
L20B inlet	1.5 (0.059)
L20B exhaust	2.0 (0.079)
Valve seat angle	45°
Camshaft end play	0.08 to 0.38 (0.003 to 0.015)
Camshaft journal diameter	47.949 to 47.962 (1.8877 to 1.8883)
Camshaft bend	0.02 (0.0007)
Camshaft journal to bearing clearance	0.038 to 0.067 (0.0015 to 0.0026)
Camshaft bearing inner diameter	48.000 to 48.016 (1.8898 to 1.8904)
Connecting rod centre distance:	
L14	136.6 (5.35)
L16	133.0 (5.24)
L18	130.35 (5.132)
L20B	146.0 (5.748)
Bearing thickness (standard)	1.493 to 1.506 (0.0588 to 0.0593)
Undersize bearings available	0.06, 0.12, 0.25, 0.50, 0.75, 1.00
Big-end play	0.20 to 0.30 (0.0079 to 0.0118)
Connecting rod bearing clearance	0.025 to 0.055 (0.0010 to 0.0022)
Main bearing journal diameter:	
L14, L16, L18	54.942 to 54.955 (2.1631 to 2.1636)
L18 (USA), L20B	59.942 to 59.955 (2.3599 to 2.3600)
Journal taper and out of round	0.00 to 0.01 (0.0000 to 0.0004)
Crankshaft free end play	0.05 to 0.18 (0.0020 to 0.0071)
Wear limit of free end play	0.3 (0.0118)
Crankpin diameter	49.961 to 49.974 (1.9670 to 1.9675)
Crankpin taper and out of round	0.00 to 0.01 (0.0000 to 0.0004)
Main bearing thickness (standard)	1.822 to 1.835 (0.0717 to 0.0722)
Undersize bearings available	0.25, 0.50, 0.75, 1.00
Main bearing clearance	0.020 to 0.062 (0.0008 to 0.0024)
Wear limit of main bearing clearance	0.12 (0.0047)
Crankshaft bend	0.05 (0.0019)
Piston diameter (standard):	
L14, L16	82.985 to 83.035 (3.2671 to 3.2691)
Oversize pistons available	0.25, 0.50, 0.75, 1.00, 1.25
L18, L20B	84.965 to 85.035 (3.3491 to 3.3478)
Oversize pistons available	0.50, 1.00
Piston to bore clearance	0.025 to 0.45 (0.0010 to 0.0018)
Piston ring groove width:	
Top	2.000 to 2.050 (0.0787 to 0.0807)
Second	2.000 to 2.040 (0.0787 to 0.0803)
Piston ring height:	
Top	1.977 to 1.990 (0.0778 to 0.0783)
Second	1.970 to 1.990 (0.0776 to 0.0783)
Piston ring side clearance:	
Top:	
L14, L16	0.040 to 0.080 (0.0016 to 0.0031)
L18	0.045 to 0.080 (0.0018 to 0.0031)
L20B	0.040 to 0.073 (0.0016 to 0.0029)
Second	0.030 to 0.070 (0.0012 to 0.0028)
Piston ring gap:	
Top:	
L14	0.23 to 0.38 (0.0091 to 0.0150)
L16	0.25 to 0.40 (0.0098 to 0.0157)
L18	0.35 to 0.55 (0.0138 to 0.0217)
L20B	0.25 to 0.40 (0.0098 to 0.0157)

Second:
L14, L16 .. .. 0.15 to 0.30 (0.0059 to 0.0118)
L18, L20B .. .. 0.30 to 0.50 (0.0118 to 0.0197)
Oil .. .. 0.30 to 0.90 (0.0118 to 0.0354)

Oil pump:
Rotor side clearance (outer to inner rotor) .. 0.04 to 0.08 (0.0016 to 0.0031)
Wear limit 0.20 (0.0079)
Rotor tip clearance .. .. 0.00 to 0.12 (0.0000 to 0.0047)
Wear limit 0.20 (0.0079)
Outer rotor to body clearance .. .. .. 0.15 to 0.21 (0.0059 to 0.0083)
Wear limit 0.50 (0.0197)
Rotor to bottom cover clearance .. .. .. 0.03 to 0.13 (0.0012 to 0.0051)
Wear limit 0.20 (0.0079)
Oil pressure regulator valve spring free length .. 52.5 (2.067)
Regulator valve opening pressure .. .. 3.5 to 5.0kg/sq cm (50 to 71lb/sq in)

FUEL SYSTEM

Carburetter:
Single carburetter:
All except USA export models:
Primary outlet diameter:
L14, L16 .. .. 28 (1.1024)
L18 .. .. 30 (1.1811)
Secondary outlet diameter:
L14, L16 .. .. 32 (1.2598)
L18 .. .. 34 (1.3386)
Primary venturi diameter:
L14 .. .. 21 × 7 (0.8268 × 0.2756)
L16 .. .. 22 × 7 (0.8661 × 0.2756)
L18 .. .. 23 × 14 × 7 (0.9055 × 0.5512 × 0.2756)
Secondary venturi diameter:
L14 .. .. 28 × 10 (1.1024 × 0.3937)
L16 .. .. 29 × 10 (1.1417 × 0.3937)
L18 .. .. 30 × 10 (1.1811 × 0.3937)
Primary main jet:
L14 96
L16, L18 102
Secondary main jet:
L14, L16 165
L18 170
Main air bleed 60
Primary 1st slow air bleed 1.0 (0.0394)
Primary 2nd slow air bleed:
L14 220
L16 180
L18 210
Secondary 2nd slow air bleed 100
Slow economiser 1.6 (0.0630)
Power jet:
L14 50
L16 45
L18 55
Float level 22 (0.8661)
Fuel pressure .. .. 0.24kg/sq cm (3.414lb/sq in)

Primary main nozzle:	
L14	2.2 (0.0866)
L16, L18	2.3 (0.0906)
Secondary main nozzle:	
L14, L16	2.5 (0.0984)
L18	2.8 (0.1102)

Twin carburetters:

Bore	38 (1.4961)
Piston lift	29 (1.1417)
Jet needle	M-76
Nozzle jet diameter	2.34 (0.0921)
Suction spring	23
Float chamber needle valve inner diameter	1.5 (0.0591)
Float level	23 (0.9055)
Float venting	Inner vent type
Fuel pressure	0.24kg/sq cm (3.4140lb/sq in
Throttle clearance at full throttle	0.6 (0.0236)
Position at full throttle	6.5°

USA export models:

Primary outlet diameter	30 (1.18)
Secondary outlet diameter	34 (1.34)
Primary venturi diameter:	
L18	23 × 8 (0.906 × 0.315)
L20B	24 (0.945)
Secondary venturi diameter:	
L18	30 × 9 (1.181 × 0.354)
L20B	31 (1.220)
Primary main jet:	
L18	100
L20B (1975)	97
L20B (1975 California)	99
L20B (1976)	99
L20B (1976 California)	101
Secondary main jet:	
L18	170
L20B	160
Primary main air bleed:	
L18	60
L20B	70
Secondary main air bleed	60
Primary slow jet:	
L18	45
L20B	48
Secondary slow jet:	
L18	90
L20B	100
L20B (California)	80
Power jet:	
L18	41
L20B (1975)	48
L20B (1975 California)	43
L20B (1976)	43
L20B (1976 California)	40
Fuel level	23 (0.906)

IGNITION SYSTEM

Distributor:

All except USA export models:	
Type:	
L14	Hitachi D411-63
L16, L18 (twin carburetter)	Hitachi D409-54K
L16, L18	Hitachi D411-58K
Rotating direction	Anticlockwise
Dwell angle	49° to 55°
Contact points gap	0.45 to 0.55 (0.018 to 0.022)
Condenser capacity	0.22 to 0.44 microfarad
Ignition timing:	
L14	8° BTDC at 600rpm
L16, L18 (twin carburetter)	14° BTDC at 650rpm
L16, L18	10° BTDC at 600rpm
USA export models:	
Type:	
L18	Hitachi D4A2-01
L20B	Hitachi D4A4-04
L20B automatic	Hitachi D4A4-06
L20B (California 1975 on)	Hitachi D4F4-04 electronic
L20B automatic (California 1975 on)	Hitachi D4F4-03 electronic
Rotating direction	Anticlockwise
Dwell angle	49° to 55°
Contact points gap	0.45 to 0.55 (0.018 to 0.022)
Condenser capacity	0.20 to 0.24 microfarad
Air gap (D4F4-04, D4F4-03)	0.20 to 0.40 (0.008 to 0.016)
Ignition timing:	
L18 manual transmission	12° BTDC at 800rpm
L20B manual	12° BTDC at 750rpm
L18, L20B automatic transmission	12° BTDC at 650rpm in 'D' range

Sparking plugs:

Type:	
L14, L16, L18 (single carburetter)	NGK BP-5ES
L16, L18 (twin carburetters)	NGK BP-6ES
L18, L20B (USA export)	NGK BP-6ES, L45-PW
L20B (California)	NGK BP-6ES-11, L45-PW-11
Gap:	
All except USA export models	0.8 to 0.9 (0.031 to 0.035)
L18 (USA export)	0.7 to 0.8 (0.028 to 0.031)
L20B	0.8 to 0.9 (0.031 to 0.035)
L20B (California)	1.0 to 1.1 (0.039 to 0.043)

COOLING SYSTEM

Thermostat:

Valve opening temperature:	
Standard	82°C (180°F)
For cold areas	88°C (190°F)
For tropical areas	76.5° (170°F)
Maximum valve lift:	
Standard	Above 8mm at 95°C (0.315 in at 203°F)
For cold areas	Above 8mm at 100°C (0.315 in at 212°F)
For tropical areas	Above 8mm at 90°C (0.315 in at 194°F)

CLUTCH

Clutch cover:	
Out of flatness of pressure plate	0.1 (0.004)
Allowable refacing limit	1.0 (0.039)
Clutch disc:	
Facing thickness	3.5 (0.138)
Number of torsion springs	6
Minimum depth of rivet head from surface	0.3 (0.012)
Allowable backlash of spline	0.4 (0.016)
Clutch pedal:	
Pedal height:	
LHD models	180 (7.087)
RHD models	175 (6.890)
Play at pedal pad	1 to 5 (0.039 to 0.197)

MANUAL TRANSMISSION

Model	F4W63L
Number of speeds	4
Ratios	3.382, 2.013, 1.312, 1.000, 3.364 (R) 3.657, 2.177, 1.419, 1.000, 3.638 (R)
Model	FS5W63A
Number of speeds	5
Ratios	3.382, 2.013, 1.312, 1.000, 0.854, 3.570 (R)

AUTOMATIC TRANSMISSION

Torque converter:	
Type	Symmetrical 3-element, 1-stage, 2-phase torque converter
Stall torque ratio	2.0:1
Transmission:	
Gear ratios	2.458, 1.458, 1.000, 2.182 (R)

REAR AXLE AND SUSPENSION

Type:	
Standard	Rigid axle, horizontal leaf springs, telescopic hydraulic dampers
Super Sports	Independent, with semi-trailing control arms and telescopic hydraulic dampers

FRONT SUSPENSION AND HUBS

Type	Independent, with MacPherson struts, transverse links, tension rods and anti-roll bar
Wheel bearings:	
Rotation starting torque:	
Adjustment with old parts	4.5kg cm (63in oz)
At wheel hub bolt	0.79kg (1.7lb)
New parts	8.5kg cm (118in oz)
At wheel hub bolt	1.49kg (3.3lb)
Lower ball joint end play	0.1 (0.0039)

Toe-in (vehicle unladen):	
Rigid axle	11 to 14 (0.43 to 0.55)
Rigid axle (USA models)	8 to 11 (0.31 to 0.43)
Rigid axle (USA models from 1976 with radial tyres)	4 to 6 (0.16 to 0.24)
Rigid axle (USA models from 1976 with bias-belted tyres)	6 to 8 (0.24 to 0.31)
Independent rear suspension models:	
Standard	11 to 14 (0.43 to 0.55)
Hard suspension	9 to 12 (0.35 to 0.47)

STEERING

Steering gear	Recirculating ball type
Steering gear ratio	15:1, 16.48:1 (USA models)
Turns of steering wheel (lock to lock)	3.3
Ball stud:	
Axial play	0.1 to 0.5 (0.0039 to 0.0197)
Swing torque	0.5kgm or less (3.6lb ft or less)
Steering wheel play	35 or less (1.378 or less) at outer circumference of steering wheel
Worm bearing starting torque:	
New bearing	4.0 to 8.0kg cm (56 to 111in oz)
Readjusted bearing	2.0 to 6.0kg cm (28 to 83in oz)
Worm bearing shim:	
Standard total thickness	1.5 (0.0591)
End play between sector shaft and adjusting screw	0.01 to 0.03 (0.0004 to 0.0012)
Gear backlash at gear arm top end	0.1 or less (0.0039 or less)

BRAKES

Brake pedal:	
Pedal height	185 (7.283)
Free play at pedal pad	1 to 5 (0.039 to 0.197)
Handbrake:	
Type	Mechanically operated on rear wheels
Normal stroke	80 to 95 (3.150 to 3.740)
Front drum brake:	
Type	Twin leading shoe drum
Wheel cylinder inner diameter	22.22 (0.875)
Brake drum inner diameter	228.6 (9.0)
Repair limit of drum diameter	230.0 (9.055)
Maximum drum out-of-round	0.02 (0.0008)
Lining	40 × 4.5 × 219.5 (1.575 × 0.177 × 8.642)
Minimum thickness of lining	1.5 (0.059)
Front disc brake:	
Type (L14, L16, L18)	SC swinging caliper
Wheel cylinder inner diameter	50.80 (2.00)
Brake rotor outer diameter	232 (9.134)
Maximum rotor run-out	0.06 (0.0024)
Repair limit of rotor (thickness)	8.4 (0.331)
Pads	39.7 × 9 × 86 (1.563 × 0.354 × 3.386)
Minimum thickness	1.0 (0.039)
Type (L20B)	N32
Wheel cylinder inner diameter	51.10 (2.012)

Brake rotor outer diameter	245 (9.65)
Maximum rotor run-out	0.12 (0.0047)
Repair limit of rotor (thickness)	8.4 (0.331)
Pads	41.2 × 10 × 61.4 (1.622 × 0.394 × 2.417)
Minimum thickness	2.0 (0.079)
Rear drum brake:	
Type	Leading and trailing shoe type
Wheel cylinder inner diameter:	
Standard	22.22 (0.875)
SSS and USA export models	20.64 (0.813)
Brake drum inner diameter	228.6 (9.000)
Maximum drum out-of-round	0.02 (0.0008)
Repair limit of drum diameter	230 (9.055)
Lining	40 × 4.5 × 219.5 (1.575 × 0.177 × 8.642)
Minimum thickness of lining	1.5 (0.059)

ELECTRICAL SYSTEM

Polarity	Negative earth
Alternator:	
Nominal rating:	
LT.135-13	12-volt, 35 amps
LT.150-05	12-volt, 50 amps
LT.150-13	12-volt, 50 amps
LT.160-24	12-volt, 60 amps
LT.135-13B	12-volt, 35 amps
Output current:	
LT.135-13	28 amps
LT.150-05	37.5 amps
LT.150-13	37.5 amps
LT.160-24	45 amps
LT.135-13B	28 amps
Starter motor:	
Type	Pre-engaged

CAPACITIES

Engine, including filter	4.65 litres (8.25 Imp. pints, 9.75 US pints)
Manual transmission:	
Four-speed units	2 litres ($3\frac{1}{2}$ Imp. pints, $4\frac{1}{4}$ US pints)
Five-speed units	1.7 litres ($2\frac{7}{8}$ Imp. pints, $3\frac{5}{8}$ US pints)
Automatic transmission	5.5 litres ($8\frac{3}{4}$ Imp. pints, $11\frac{3}{4}$ US pints)
Differential case:	
Standard and De Luxe models	1.3 litres ($2\frac{1}{4}$ Imp. pints, $2\frac{3}{4}$ US pints)
Super Sports models	0.8 litre ($1\frac{3}{8}$ Imp. pints, $1\frac{3}{4}$ US pints)
Steering gear	0.27 litre ($\frac{1}{2}$ Imp. pint, $\frac{5}{8}$ US pint)
Cooling system	6.5 litres $11\frac{1}{2}$ Imp. pints, $13\frac{3}{4}$ US pints)
Fuel tank:	
Standard and De Luxe models	50 litres (11 Imp. galls, $13\frac{1}{4}$ US galls)
Super Sports models	55 litres ($12\frac{1}{8}$ Imp. galls, $14\frac{1}{2}$ US galls)
Station Wagon models	45 litres ($9\frac{7}{8}$ Imp. galls, $11\frac{7}{8}$ US galls)
Station Wagon models (California)	50 litres (11 Imp. galls, $13\frac{1}{4}$ US galls)

WIRING DIAGRAMS

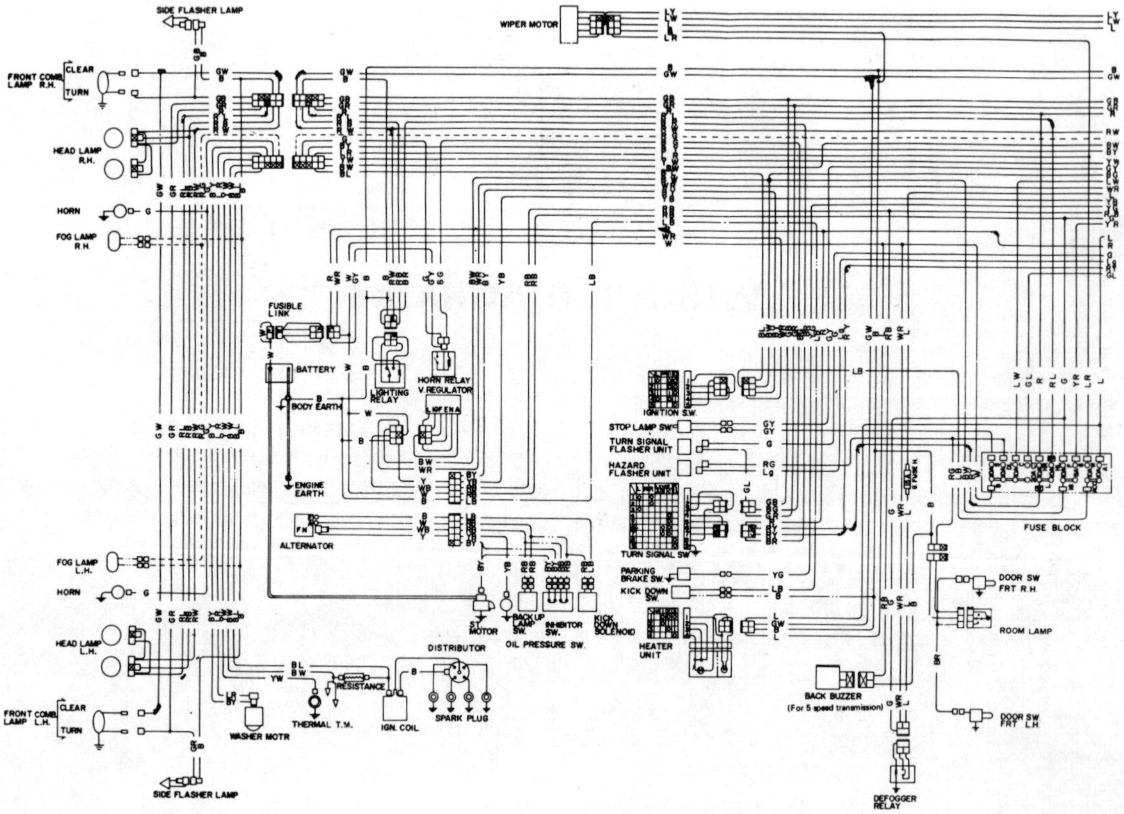

FIG 15:1 Wiring diagram, righthand drive models—part 1

Wiring colour code **B** Black **W** White **R** Red **Y** Yellow **G** Green **L** Blue **Lg** Light green **Br** Brown

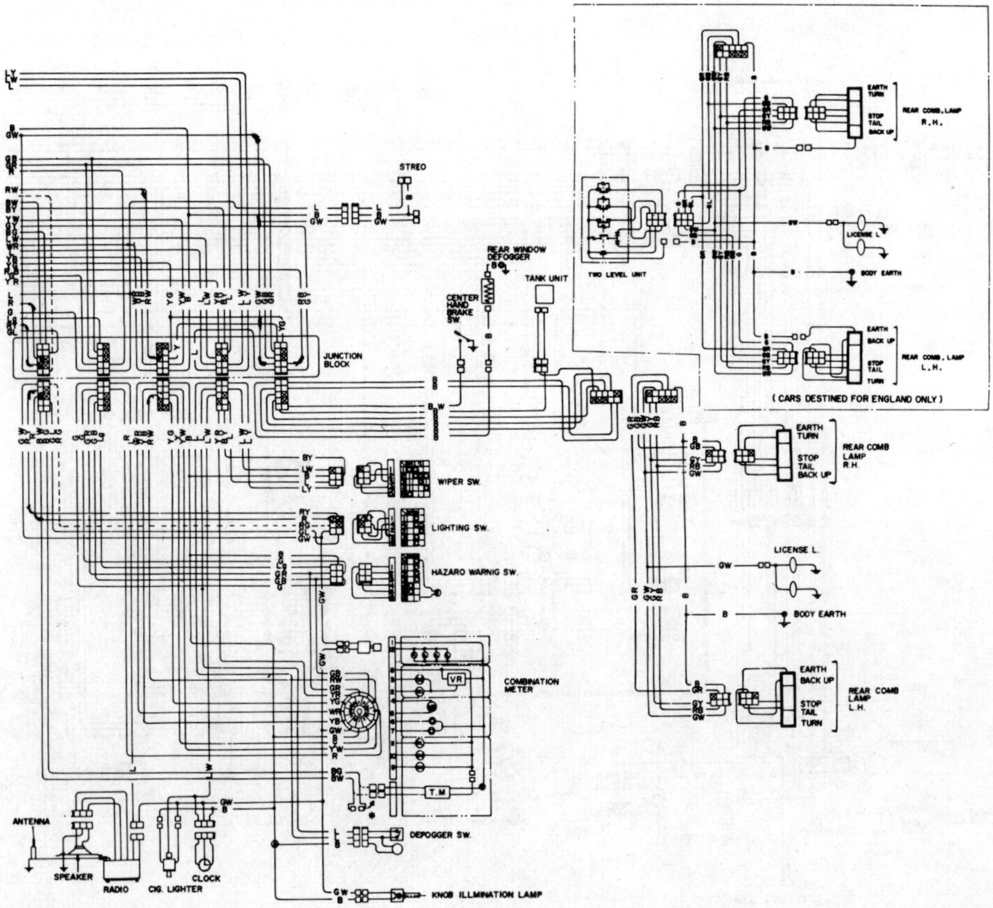

FIG 15:1 Wiring diagram, righthand drive models—part 2

*Optional tachometer connection

Wiring colour code **B** Black **W** White **R** Red **Y** Yellow **G** Green **L** Blue **Lg** Light green **Br** Brown

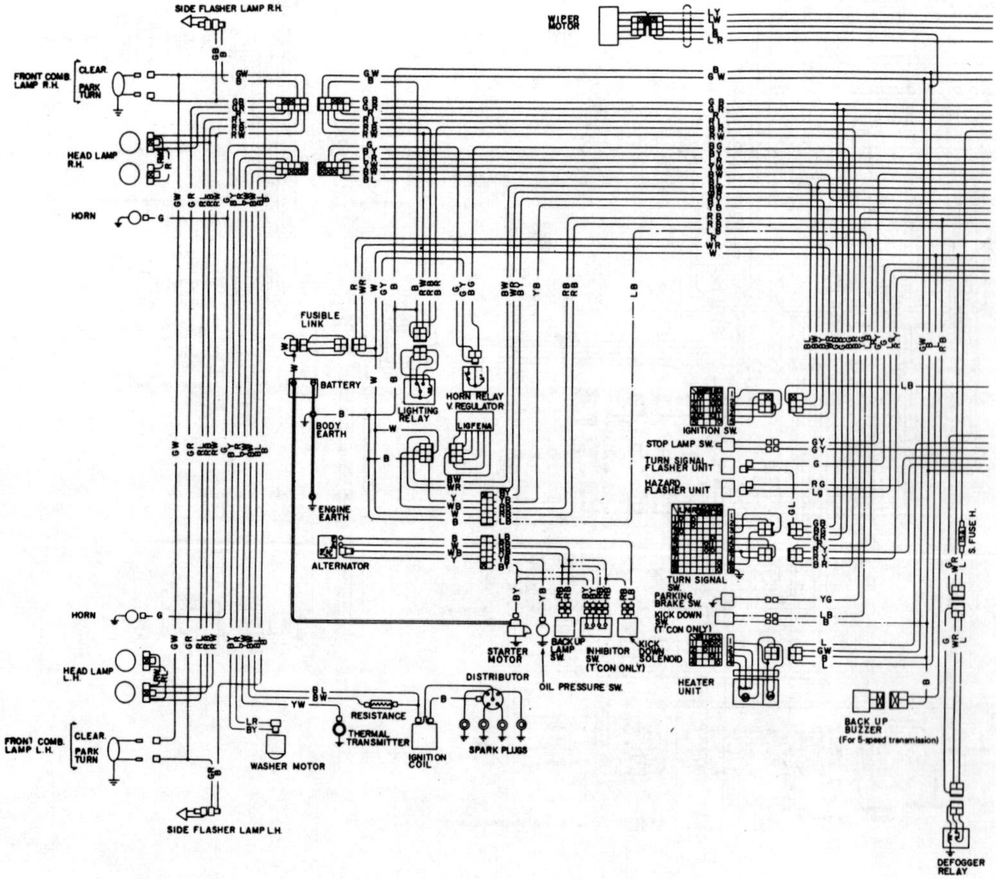

FIG 15:2 Wiring diagram, lefthand drive models (not USA)—part 1

Wiring colour code **B** Black **W** White **R** Red **Y** Yellow **G** Green **L** Blue **Lg** Light green **Br** Brown

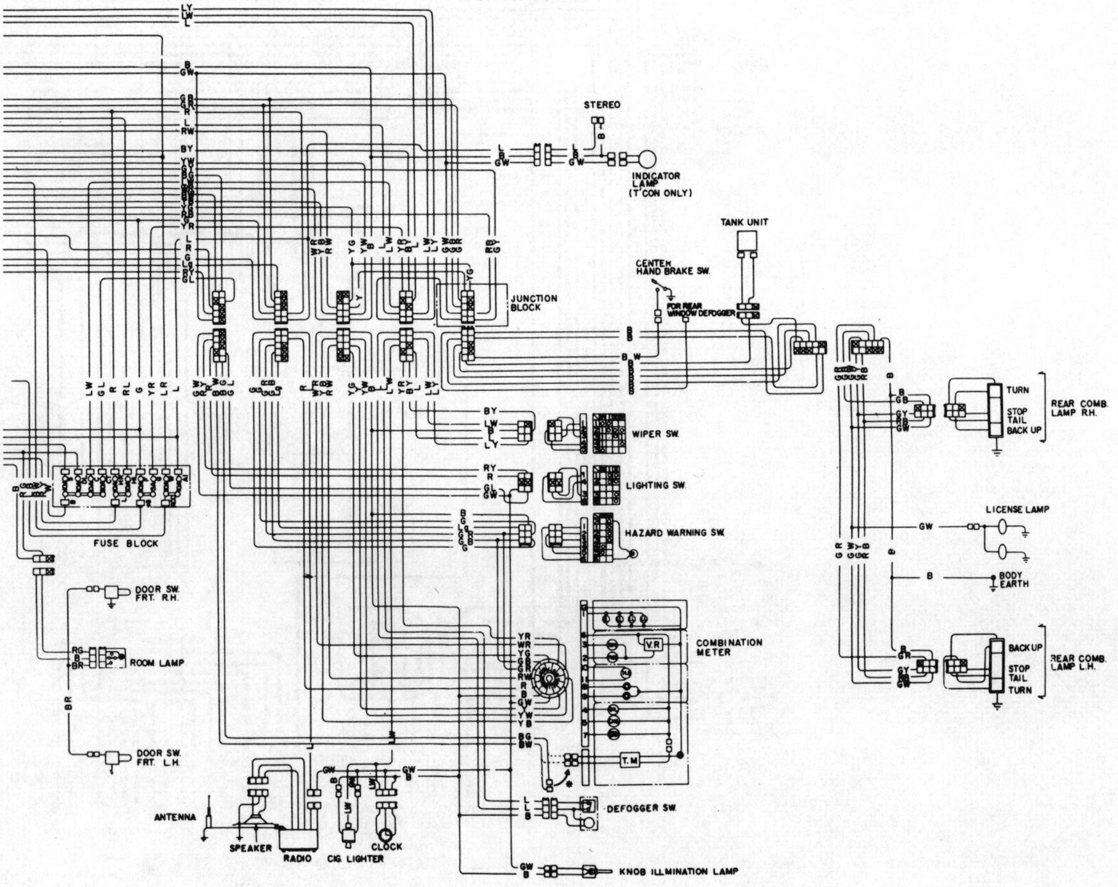

FIG 15:2 Wiring diagram, lefthand drive models (not USA)—part 2

* Optional tachometer connection

Wiring colour code **B** Black **W** White **R** Red **Y** Yellow **G** Green **L** Blue **Lg** Light green **Br** Brown

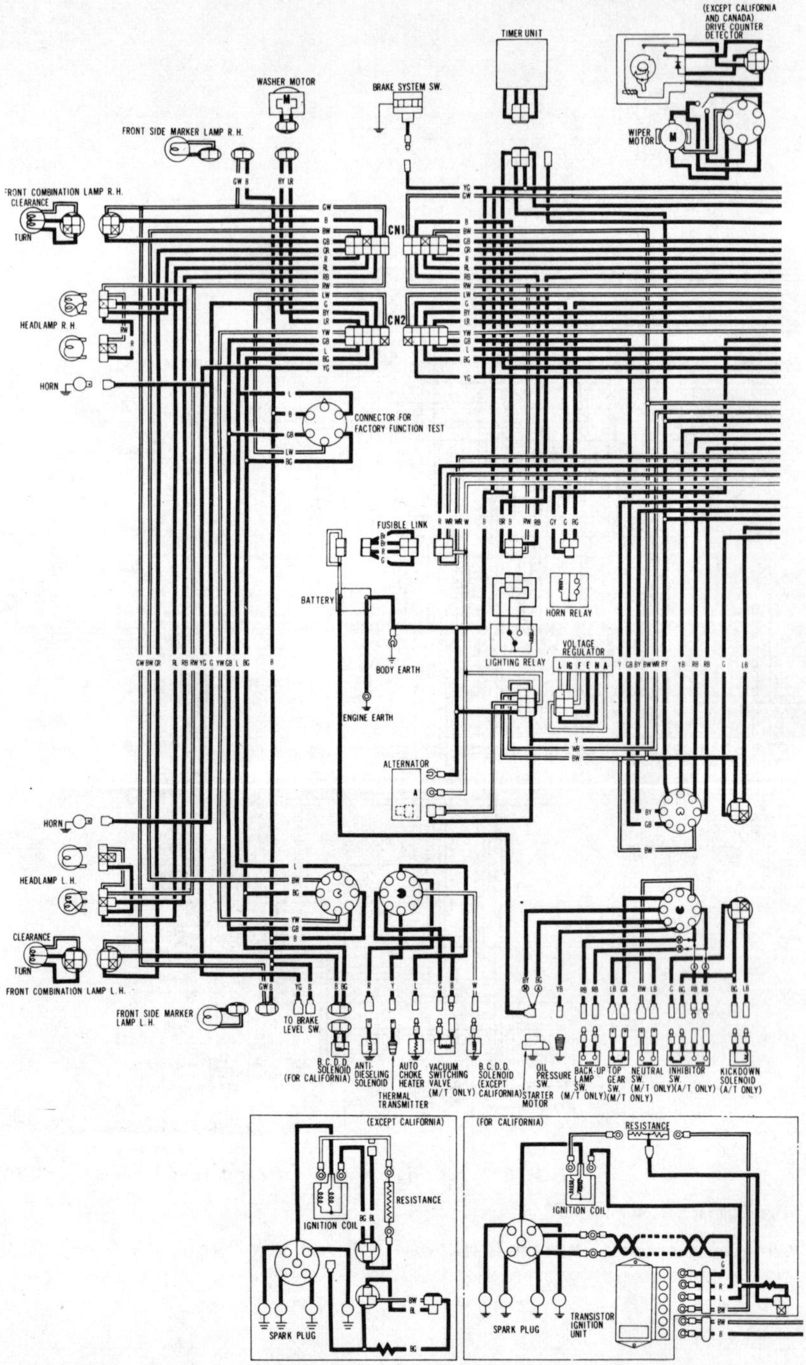

FIG 15:3 Wiring diagram, USA models—part 1

Key to Fig 15:3 A/T Automatic transmission M/T Manual transmission
Switch and relay positions 1 Ignition switch locked, key removed 2 Lighting or wiper switch off 3 Seats unoccupied 4 Doors closed 5 Transmission in neutral 6 Handbrake released

Wiring colour code **B** Black **W** White **R** Red **Y** Yellow **G** Green **L** Blue **Lg** Light green **Br** Brown

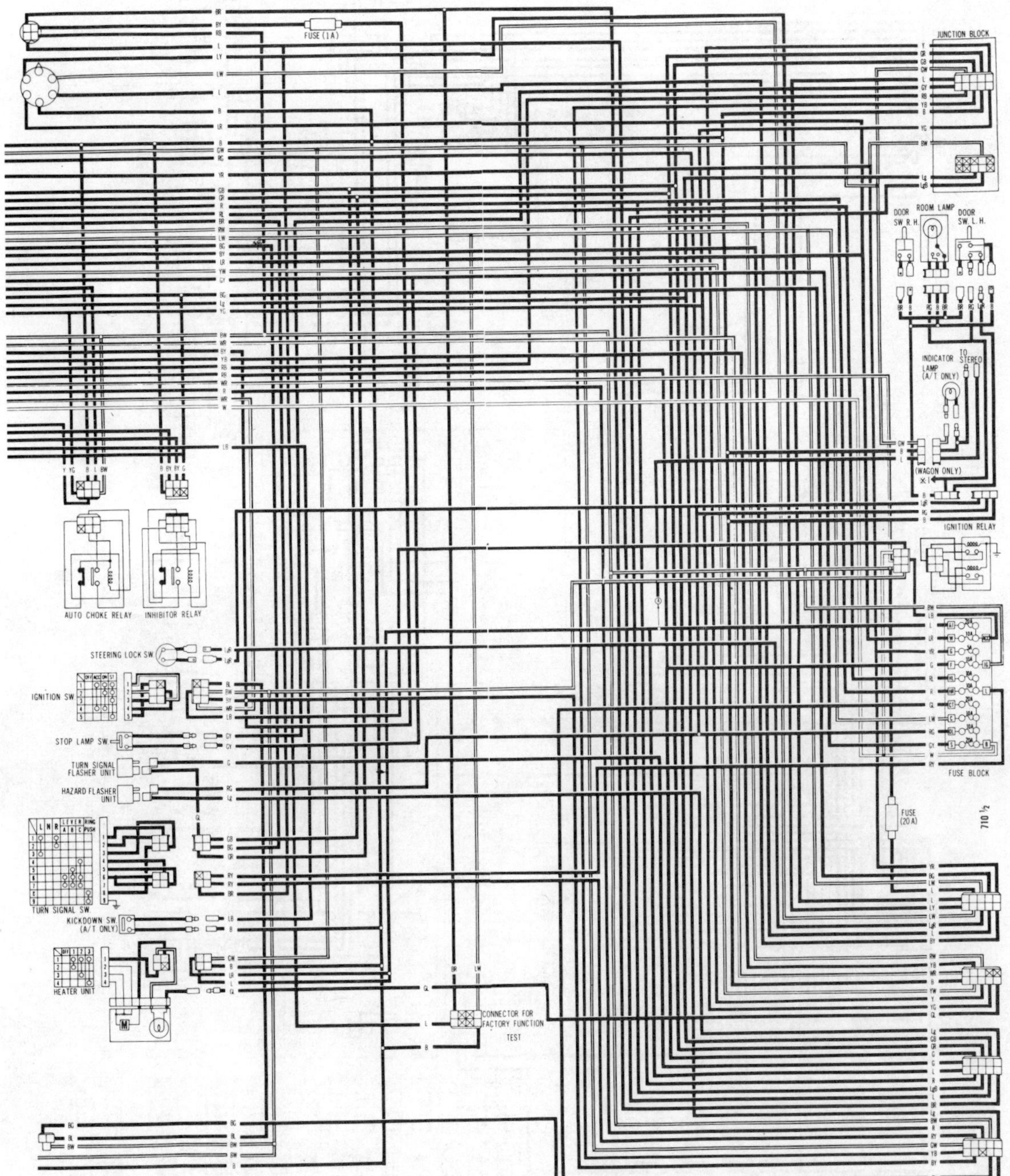

FIG 15:3 Wiring diagram, USA models—part 2

Key to Fig 15:3 A/T Automatic transmission M/T Manual transmission
Switch and relay positions 1 Ignition switch locked, key removed 2 Lighting or wiper switch off 3 Seats unoccupied 4 Doors closed 5 Transmission in neutral 6 Handbrake released

Wiring colour code **B** Black **W** White **R** Red **Y** Yellow **G** Green **L** Blue **Lg** Light green **Br** Brown

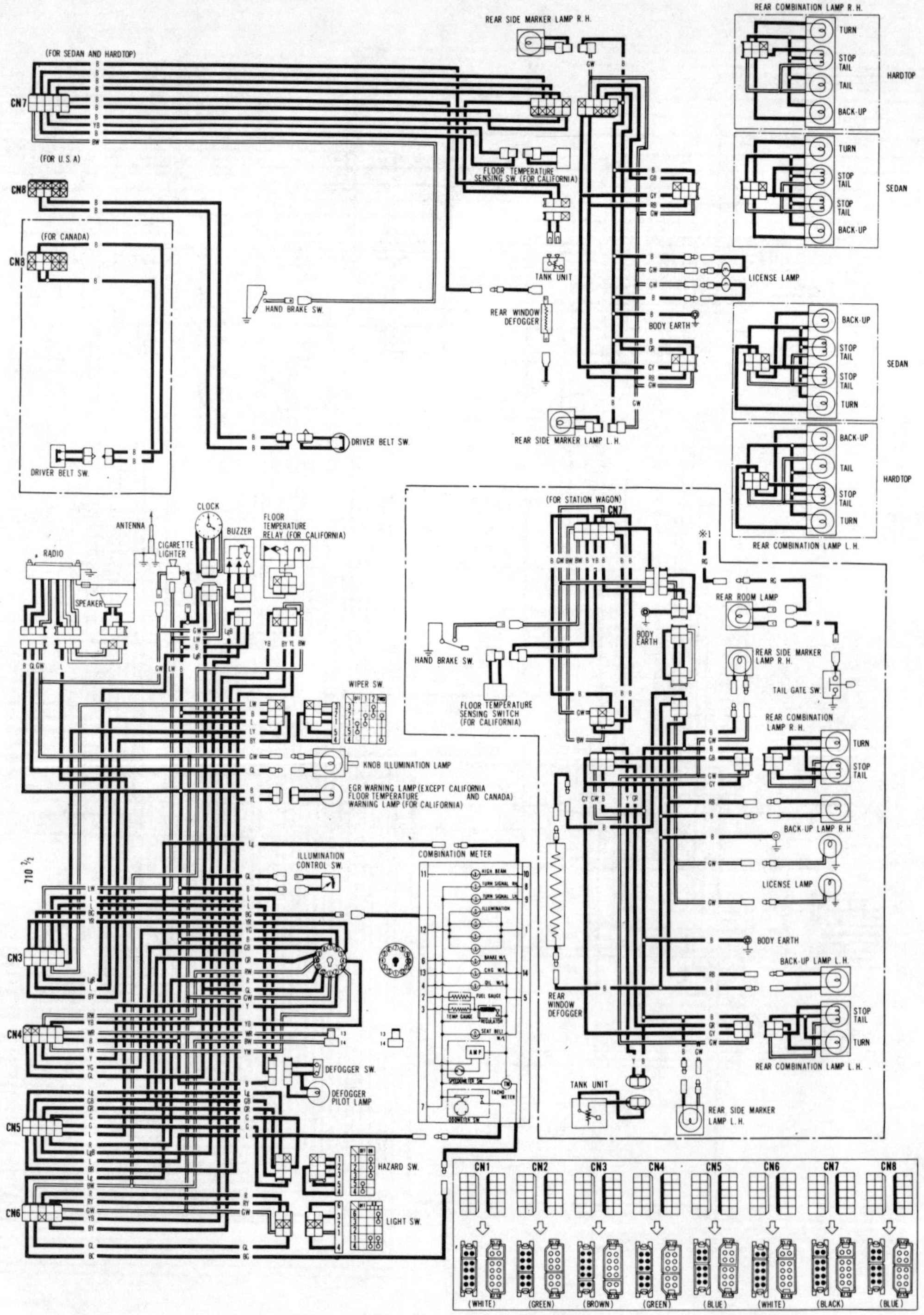

FIG 15:3 Wiring diagram, USA models—part 3

Key to Fig 15:3 A/T Automatic transmission M/T Manual transmission
Switch and relay positions 1 Ignition switch locked, key removed 2 Lighting or wiper switch off 3 Seats unoccupied 4 Doors closed 5 Transmission in neutral 6 Handbrake released

Wiring colour code **B** Black **W** White **R** Red **Y** Yellow **G** Green **L** Blue **Lg** Light green **Br** Brown

HINTS ON MAINTENANCE AND OVERHAUL

There are few things more rewarding than the restoration of a vehicle's original peak of efficiency and smooth performance.

The following notes are intended to help the owner to reach that state of perfection. Providing that he possesses the basic manual skills he should have no difficulty in performing most of the operations detailed in this manual. It must be stressed, however, that where recommended in the manual, highly-skilled operations ought to be entrusted to experts, who have the necessary equipment, to carry out the work satisfactorily.

Quality of workmanship:

The hazardous driving conditions on the roads to-day demand that vehicles should be as nearly perfect, mechanically, as possible. It is therefore most important that amateur work be carried out with care, bearing in mind the often inadequate working conditions, and also the inferior tools which may have to be used. It is easy to counsel perfection in all things, and we recognize that it may be setting an impossibly high standard. We do, however, suggest that every care should be taken to ensure that a vehicle is as safe to take on the road as it is humanly possible to make it.

Safe working conditions:

Even though a vehicle may be stationary, it is still potentially dangerous if certain sensible precautions are not taken when working on it while it is supported on jacks or blocks. It is indeed preferable not to use jacks alone, but to supplement them with carefully placed blocks, so that there will be plenty of support if the car rolls off the jacks during a strenuous manoeuvre. Axle stands are an excellent way of providing a rigid base which is not readily disturbed. Piles of bricks are a dangerous substitute. Be careful not to get under heavy loads on lifting tackle, the load could fall. It is preferable not to work alone when lifting an engine, or when working underneath a vehicle which is supported well off the ground. To be trapped, particularly under the vehicle, may have unpleasant results if help is not quickly forthcoming. Make some provision, however humble, to deal with fires. Always disconnect a battery if there is a likelihood of electrical shorts. These may start a fire if there is leaking fuel about. This applies particularly to leads which can carry a heavy current, like those in the starter circuit. While on the subject of electricity, we must also stress the danger of using equipment which is run off the mains and which has no earth or has faulty wiring or connections. So many workshops have damp floors, and electrical shocks are of such a nature that it is sometimes impossible to let go of a live lead or piece of equipment due to the muscular spasms which take place.

Work demanding special care:

This involves the servicing of braking, steering and suspension systems. On the road, failure of the braking system may be disastrous. Make quite sure that there can be no possibility of failure through the bursting of rusty brake pipes or rotten hoses, nor to a sudden loss of pressure due to defective seals or valves.

Problems:

The chief problems which may face an operator are:

1 External dirt.
2 Difficulty in undoing tight fixings.
3 Dismantling unfamiliar mechanisms.
4 Deciding in what respect parts are defective.
5 Confusion about the correct order for reassembly.
6 Adjusting running clearance.
7 Road testing.
8 Final tuning.

Practical suggestions to solve the problems:

1 Preliminary cleaning of large parts—engines, transmissions, steering, suspensions, etc.,—should be carried out before removal from the car. Where road dirt and mud alone are present, wash clean with a high-pressure water jet, brushing to remove stubborn adhesions, and allow to drain and dry. Where oil or grease is also present, wash down with a proprietary compound (Gunk, Teepol etc.,) applying with a stiff brush—an old paint brush is suitable—into all crevices. Cover the distributor and ignition coils with a polythene bag and then apply a strong water jet to clear the loosened deposits. Allow to drain and dry. The assemblies will then be sufficiently clean to remove and transfer to the bench for the next stage.

On the bench, further cleaning can be carried out, first wiping the parts as free as possible from grease with old newspaper. Avoid using rag or cotton waste which can leave clogging fibres behind. Any remaining grease can be removed with a brush dipped in paraffin. If necessary, traces of paraffin can be removed by carbon tetrachloride. Avoid using paraffin or petrol in large quantities for cleaning in enclosed areas, such as garages, on account of the high fire risk.

When all exteriors have been cleaned, and not before, dismantling can be commenced. This ensures that dirt will not enter into interiors and orifices revealed by dismantling. In the next phases, where components have to be cleaned, use carbon tetrachloride in preference to petrol and keep the containers covered except when in use. After the components have been cleaned, plug small holes with tapered hard wood plugs cut to size and blank off larger orifices with grease-proof paper and masking tape. Do not use soft wood plugs or matchsticks as they may break.

2 It is not advisable to hammer on the end of a screw thread, but if it must be done, first screw on a nut to protect the thread, and use a lead hammer. This applies particularly to the removal of tapered cotters. Nuts and bolts seem to 'grow' together, especially in exhaust systems. If penetrating oil does not work, try the judicious application of heat, but be careful of starting a fire. Asbestos sheet or cloth is useful to isolate heat.

Tight bushes or pieces of tail-pipe rusted into a silencer can be removed by splitting them with an open-ended hacksaw. Tight screws can sometimes be started by a tap from a hammer on the end of a suitable screwdriver. Many tight fittings will yield to the judicious use of a hammer, but it must be a soft-faced hammer if damage is to be avoided, use a heavy block on the opposite side to absorb shock. Any parts of the steering system which have been damaged should be renewed, as attempts to repair them may lead to cracking and subsequent failure, and steering ball joints should be disconnected using a recommended tool to prevent damage.

3 If often happens that an owner is baffled when trying to dismantle an unfamiliar piece of equipment. So many modern devices are pressed together or assembled by spinning-over flanges, that they must be sawn apart. The intention is that the whole assembly must be renewed. However, parts which appear to be in one piece to the naked eye, may reveal close-fitting joint lines when inspected with a magnifying glass, and, this may provide the necessary clue to dismantling. Left-handed screw threads are used where rotational forces would tend to unscrew a righthanded screw thread.

Be very careful when dismantling mechanisms which may come apart suddenly. Work in an enclosed space where the parts will be contained, and drape a piece of cloth over the device if springs are likely to fly in all directions. Mark everything which might be reassembled in the wrong position, scratched symbols may be used on unstressed parts, or a sequence of tiny dots from a centre punch can be useful. Stressed parts should never be scratched or centre-popped as this may lead to cracking under working conditions. Store parts which look alike in the correct order for reassembly. Never rely upon memory to assist in the assembly of complicated mechanisms, especially when they will be dismantled for a long time, but make notes, and drawings to supplement the diagrams in the manual, and put labels on detached wires. Rust stains may indicate unlubricated wear. This can sometimes be seen round the outside edge of a bearing cup in a universal joint. Look for bright rubbing marks on parts which normally should not make heavy contact. These might prove that something is bent or running out of truth. For example, there might be bright marks on one side of a piston, at the top near the ring grooves, and others at the bottom of the skirt on the other side. This could well be the clue to a bent connecting rod. Suspected cracks can be proved by heating the component in a light oil to approximately 100°C, removing, drying off, and dusting with french chalk, if a crack is present the oil retained in the crack will stain the french chalk.

4 In determining wear, and the degree, against the permissible limits set in the manual, accurate measurement can only be achieved by the use of a micrometer. In many cases, the wear is given to the fourth place of decimals; that is in ten-thousandths of an inch. This can be read by the vernier scale on the barrel of a good micrometer. Bore diameters are more difficult to determine. If, however, the matching shaft is accurately measured, the degree of play in the bore can be felt as a guide to its suitability. In other cases, the shank of a twist drill of known diameter is a handy check.

Many methods have been devised for determining the clearance between bearing surfaces. To-day the best and simplest is by the use of Plastigage, obtainable from most garages. A thin plastic thread is laid between the two surfaces and the bearing is tightened, flattening the thread. On removal, the width of the thread is compared with a scale supplied with the thread and the clearance is read off directly. Sometimes joint faces leak persistently, even after gasket renewal. The fault will then be traceable to distortion, dirt or burrs. Studs which are screwed into soft metal frequently raise burrs at the point of entry. A quick cure for this is to chamfer the edge of the hole in the part which fits over the stud.

5 **Always check a replacement part with the original one before it is fitted.**

If parts are not marked, and the order for reassembly is not known, a little detective work will help. Look for marks which are due to wear to see if they can be mated. Joint faces may not be identical due to manufacturing errors, and parts which overlap may be stained, giving a clue to the correct position. Most fixings leave identifying marks especially if they were painted over on assembly. It is then easier to decide whether a nut, for instance, has a plain, a spring, or a shakeproof washer under it. All running surfaces become 'bedded' together after long spells of work and tiny imperfections on one part will be found to have left corresponding marks on the other. This is particularly true of shafts and bearings and even a score on a cylinder wall will show on the piston.

6 Checking end float or rocker clearances by feeler gauge may not always give accurate results because of wear. For instance, the rocker tip which bears on a valve stem may be deeply pitted, in which case the feeler will simply be bridging a depression. Thrust washers may also wear depressions in opposing faces to make accurate measurement difficult. End float is then easier to check by using a dial gauge. It is common practice to adjust end play in bearing assemblies, like front hubs with taper rollers, by doing up the axle nut until the hub becomes stiff to turn and then backing it off a little. Do not use this method with ballbearing hubs as the assembly is often preloaded by tightening the axle nut to its fullest extent. If the splitpin hole will not line up, file the base of the nut a little.

Steering assemblies often wear in the straight-ahead position. If any part is adjusted, make sure that it remains free when moved from lock to lock. Do not be surprised if an assembly like a steering gearbox, which is known to be carefully adjusted outside the car, becomes stiff when it is bolted in place. This will be due to distortion of the case by the pull of the mounting bolts, particularly if the mounting points are not all touching together. This problem may be met in other equipment and is cured by careful attention to the alignment of mounting points.

When a spanner is stamped with a size and A/F it means that the dimension is the width between the jaws and has no connection with ANF, which is the designation for the American National Fine thread. Coarse threads like Whitworth are rarely used on cars to-day except for studs which screw into soft aluminium or cast iron. For this reason it might be found that the top end of a cylinder head stud has a fine thread and the lower end a coarse thread to screw into the cylinder block. If the car has mainly UNF threads then it is likely that any coarse threads will be UNC, which are not the same as Whitworth. Small sizes have the same number of threads in Whitworth and UNC, but in the $\frac{1}{2}$ inch size for example, there are twelve threads to the inch in the former and thirteen in the latter.

7 After a major overhaul, particularly if a great deal of work has been done on the braking, steering and suspension systems, it is advisable to approach the problem of testing with care. If the braking system has been overhauled, apply heavy pressure to the brake pedal and get a second operator to check every possible source of leakage. The brakes may work extremely well, but a leak could cause complete failure after a few miles.

Do not fit the hub caps until every wheel nut has been checked for tightness, and make sure the tyre pressures are correct. Check the levels of coolant, lubricants and hydraulic fluids. Being satisfied that all is well, take the car on the road and test the brakes at once. Check the steering and the action of the handbrake. Do all this at moderate speeds on quiet roads, and make sure there is no other vehicle behind you when you try a rapid stop.

Finally, remember that many parts settle down after a time, so check for tightness of all fixings after the car has been on the road for a hundred miles or so.

8 It is useless to tune an engine which has not reached its normal running temperature. In the same way, the tune of an engine which is stiff after a rebore will be different when the engine is again running free. Remember too, that rocker clearances on pushrod operated valve gear will change when the cylinder head nuts are tightened after an initial period of running with a new head gasket.

Trouble may not always be due to what seems the obvious cause. Ignition, carburation and mechanical condition are interdependent and spitting back through the carburetter, which might be attributed to a weak mixture, can be caused by a sticking inlet valve.

For one final hint on tuning, never adjust more than one thing at a time or it will be impossible to tell which adjustment produced the desired result.

NOTES

GLOSSARY OF TERMS

Allen key Cranked wrench of hexagonal section for use with socket head screws.

Alternator Electrical generator producing alternating current. Rectified to direct current for battery charging.

Ambient temperature Surrounding atmospheric temperature.

Annulus Used in engineering to indicate the outer ring gear of an epicyclic gear train.

Armature The shaft carrying the windings, which rotates in the magnetic field of a generator or starter motor. That part of a solenoid or relay which is activated by the magnetic field.

Axial In line with, or pertaining to, an axis.

Backlash Play in meshing gears.

Balance lever A bar where force applied at the centre is equally divided between connections at the ends.

Banjo axle Axle casing with large diameter housing for the crownwheel and differential.

Bendix pinion A self-engaging and self-disengaging drive on a starter motor shaft.

Bevel pinion A conical shaped gearwheel, designed to mesh with a similar gear with an axis usually at 90 deg. to its own.

bhp Brake horse power, measured on a dynamometer.

bmep Brake mean effective pressure. Average pressure on a piston during the working stroke.

Brake cylinder Cylinder with hydraulically operated piston(s) acting on brake shoes or pad(s).

Brake regulator Control valve fitted in hydraulic braking system which limits brake pressure to rear brakes during heavy braking to prevent rear wheel locking.

Camber Angle at which a wheel is tilted from the vertical.

Capacitor Modern term for an electrical condenser. Part of distributor assembly, connected across contact breaker points, acts as an interference suppressor.

Castellated Top face of a nut, slotted across the flats, to take a locking splitpin.

Castor Angle at which the kingpin or swivel pin is tilted when viewed from the side.

cc Cubic centimetres. Engine capacity is arrived at by multiplying the area of the bore in sq cm by the stroke in cm by the number of cylinders.

Clevis U-shaped forked connector used with a clevis pin, usually at handbrake connections.

Collet A type of collar, usually split and located in a groove in a shaft, and held in place by a retainer. The arrangement used to retain the spring(s) on a valve stem in most cases.

Commutator Rotating segmented current distributor between armature windings and brushes in generator or motor.

Compression ratio The ratio, or quantitative relation, of the total volume (piston at bottom of stroke) to the unswept volume (piston at top of stroke) in an engine cylinder.

Condenser See capacitor.

Core plug Plug for blanking off a manufacturing hole in a casting.

Crownwheel Large bevel gear in rear axle, driven by a bevel pinion attached to the propeller shaft. Sometimes called a 'ring gear'.

'C'-spanner Like a 'C' with a handle. For use on screwed collars without flats, but with slots or holes.

Damper Modern term for shock-absorber, used in vehicle suspension systems to damp out spring oscillations.

Depression The lowering of atmospheric pressure as in the inlet manifold and carburetter.

Dowel Close tolerance pin, peg, tube, or bolt, which accurately locates mating parts.

Drag link Rod connecting steering box drop arm (pitman arm) to nearest front wheel steering arm in certain types of steering systems.

Dry liner Thinwall tube pressed into cylinder bore

Dry sump Lubrication system where all oil is scavenged from the sump, and returned to a separate tank.

Dynamo See Generator.

Electrode Terminal, part of an electrical component, such as the points or 'Electrodes' of a sparking plug.

Electrolyte In lead-acid car batteries a solution of sulphuric acid and distilled water.

End float The axial movement between associated parts, end play.

EP Extreme pressure. In lubricants, special grades for heavily loaded bearing surfaces, such as gear teeth in a gearbox, or crownwheel and pinion in a rear axle.

Fade	Of brakes. Reduced efficiency due to overheating.
Field coils	Windings on the polepieces of motors and generators.
Fillets	Narrow finishing strips usually applied to interior bodywork.
First motion shaft	Input shaft from clutch to gearbox.
Fullflow filter	Filters in which all the oil is pumped to the engine. If the element becomes clogged, a bypass valve operates to pass unfiltered oil to the engine.
FWD	Front wheel drive.
Gear pump	Two meshing gears in a close fitting casing. Oil is carried from the inlet round the outside of both gears in the spaces between the gear teeth and casing to the outlet, the meshing gear teeth prevent oil passing back to the inlet, and the oil is forced through the outlet port.
Generator	Modern term for 'Dynamo'. When rotated produces electrical current.
Grommet	A ring of protective or sealing material. Can be used to protect pipes or leads passing through bulkheads.
Grubscrew	Fully threaded headless screw with screwdriver slot. Used for locking, or alignment purposes.
Gudgeon pin	Shaft which connects a piston to its connecting rod. Sometimes called 'wrist pin', or 'piston pin'.
Halfshaft	One of a pair transmitting drive from the differential.
Helical	In spiral form. The teeth of helical gears are cut at a spiral angle to the side faces of the gearwheel.
Hot spot	Hot area that assists vapourisation of fuel on its way to cylinders. Often provided by close contact between inlet and exhaust manifolds.
HT	High Tension. Applied to electrical current produced by the ignition coil for the sparking plugs.
Hydrometer	A device for checking specific gravity of liquids. Used to check specific gravity of electrolyte.
Hypoid bevel gears	A form of bevel gear used in the rear axle drive gears. The bevel pinion meshes below the centre line of the crownwheel, giving a lower propeller shaft line.
Idler	A device for passing on movement. A free running gear between driving and driven gears. A lever transmitting track rod movement to a side rod in steering gear.
Impeller	A centrifugal pumping element. Used in water pumps to stimulate flow.
Journals	Those parts of a shaft that are in contact with the bearings.
Kingpin	The main vertical pin which carries the front wheel spindle, and permits steering movement. May be called 'steering pin' or 'swivel pin'.
Layshaft	The shaft which carries the laygear in the gearbox. The laygear is driven by the first motion shaft and drives the third motion shaft according to the gear selected. Sometimes called the 'countershaft' or 'second motion shaft.'
lb ft	A measure of twist or torque. A pull of 10 lb at a radius of 1 ft is a torque of 10 lb ft.
lb/sq in	Pounds per square inch.
Little-end	The small, or piston end of a connecting rod. Sometimes called the 'small-end'.
LT	Low Tension. The current output from the battery.
Mandrel	Accurately manufactured bar or rod used for test or centring purposes.
Manifold	A pipe, duct, or chamber, with several branches.
Needle rollers	Bearing rollers with a length many times their diameter.
Oil bath	Reservoir which lubricates parts by immersion. In air filters, a separate oil supply for wetting a wire mesh element to hold the dust.
Oil wetted	In air filters, a wire mesh element lightly oiled to trap and hold airborne dust.
Overlap	Period during which inlet and exhaust valves are open together.
Panhard rod	Bar connected between fixed point on chassis and another on axle to control sideways movement.
Pawl	Pivoted catch which engages in the teeth of a ratchet to permit movement in one direction only.
Peg spanner	Tool with pegs, or pins, to engage in holes or slots in the part to be turned.
Pendant pedals	Pedals with levers that are pivoted at the top end.
Phillips screwdriver	A cross-point screwdriver for use with the cross-slotted heads of Phillips screws.
Pinion	A small gear, usually in relation to another gear.
Piston-type damper	Shock absorber in which damping is controlled by a piston working in a closed oil-filled cylinder.
Preloading	Preset static pressure on ball or roller bearings not due to working loads.
Radial	Radiating from a centre, like the spokes of a wheel.

Radius rod	Pivoted arm confining movement of a part to an arc of fixed radius.
Ratchet	Toothed wheel or rack which can move in one direction only, movement in the other being prevented by a pawl.
Ring gear	A gear tooth ring attached to outer periphery of flywheel. Starter pinion engages with it during starting.
Runout	Amount by which rotating part is out of true.
Semi-floating axle	Outer end of rear axle halfshaft is carried on bearing inside axle casing. Wheel hub is secured to end of shaft.
Servo	A hydraulic or pneumatic system for assisting, or, augmenting a physical effort. See 'Vacuum Servo'.
Setscrew	One which is threaded for the full length of the shank.
Shackle	A coupling link, used in the form of two parallel pins connected by side plates to secure the end of the master suspension spring and absorb the effects of deflection.
Shell bearing	Thinwalled steel shell lined with antifriction metal. Usually semi-circular and used in pairs for main and big-end bearings.
Shock absorber	See 'Damper'.
Silentbloc	Rubber bush bonded to inner and outer metal sleeves.
Socket-head screw	Screw with hexagonal socket for an Allen key.
Solenoid	A coil of wire creating a magnetic field when electric current passes through it. Used with a soft iron core to operate contacts or a mechanical device.
Spur gear	A gear with teeth cut axially across the periphery.
Stub axle	Short axle fixed at one end only.
Tachometer	An instrument for accurate measurement of rotating speed. Usually indicates in revolutions per minute.
TDC	Top Dead Centre. The highest point reached by a piston in a cylinder, with the crank and connecting rod in line.
Thermostat	Automatic device for regulating temperature. Used in vehicle coolant systems to open a valve which restricts circulation at low temperature.
Third motion shaft	Output shaft of gearbox.
Threequarter floating axle	Outer end of rear axle halfshaft flanged and bolted to wheel hub, which runs on bearing mounted on outside of axle casing. Vehicle weight is not carried by the axle shaft.
Thrust bearing or washer	Used to reduce friction in rotating parts subject to axial loads.
Torque	Turning or twisting effort. See 'lb ft'.
Track rod	The bar(s) across the vehicle which connect the steering arms and maintain the front wheels in their correct alignment.
UJ	Universal joint. A coupling between shafts which permits angular movement.
UNF	Unified National Fine screw thread.
Vacuum servo	Device used in brake system, using difference between atmospheric pressure and inlet manifold depression to operate a piston which acts to augment brake pressure as required. See 'Servo'.
Venturi	A restriction or 'choke' in a tube, as in a carburetter, used to increase velocity to obtain a reduction in pressure.
Vernier	A sliding scale for obtaining fractional readings of the graduations of an adjacent scale.
Welch plug	A domed thin metal disc which is partially flattened to lock in a recess. Used to plug core holes in castings.
Wet liner	Removable cylinder barrel, sealed against coolant leakage, where the coolant is in direct contact with the outer surface.
Wet sump	A reservoir attached to the crankcase to hold the lubricating oil.

NOTES

INDEX